DATE DUE

DEMCO 38-296

COMPETITIVE GLOBAL MANAGEMENT

Principles and Strategies

Abbass F. Alkhafaji, Ph.D.
Department of Management and Marketing
Slippery Rock University
Slippery Rock, Pennsylvania

S^t_L

St. Lucie Press

Printed and bound in the U.S.A. Printed on acid-free paper.
10 9 8 7 6 5 4 3 2 1

Library of Congress Cataloging-in-Publication Data

Alkhafaji, Abbass F.
    Competitive global management : principles & strategies / Abbass
F. Alkhafaji.
        p.   cm.
    Includes bibliographical references and index.
    ISBN 1-884015-36-0 (alk. paper)
    1. International business enterprises—Management.
    2. Competition, International.   I. Title.
    HD62.4.A4   1995
    658'.049—dc20   94-17214
                                                                   CIP

Phone: (407) 274-9906
Fax: (407) 274-9927

S^t_L

Published by
St. Lucie Press
100 E. Linton Blvd., Suite 403B
Delray Beach, FL 33483

DEDICATION

To

Alliah, Sheamah, and Ahmed,

whom I love very much
and who make my life more enjoyable

CONTENTS

SECTION III
INTERNATIONAL HUMAN RESOURCE MANAGEMENT AND TECHNOLOGY TRANSFER

SECTION IV
COMPARATIVE MANAGEMENT

SECTION V
TECHNOLOGY TRANSFER

PREFACE

This book is designed for current and future executives, managers, and other individuals who are pursuing or might pursue trade in international business. International management, more so than domestic management, is affected by the environment. The multinational corporation has become a major factor in the growth of global trade and investment. The greater the number of countries in which a corporation operates, the more "multinational" it is. Uncontrollable influences such as economic conditions, sociocultural considerations, technology, competition, and legal restrictions vary tremendously from country to country. An international management strategy cannot be formulated without a full grasp of these variables.

This book is an important educational tool for both undergraduate and graduate students majoring in business. It provides investigations into and evaluations of the mechanics of doing business abroad and thoroughly explores the challenges that management faces today within an international environment. More specifically, such issues as human resource management in the international environment and managerial and technology transfer are emphasized.

Readers are introduced to the exciting and rewarding field of global management and are provided with a good understanding of the fundamental concepts of management. The importance of cultural, economic, political, and environmental aspects when doing business overseas is covered extensively, and how these aspects affect U.S. businesses operating abroad is integrated throughout the book. It is important to fully comprehend the increasing significance of international management, international business, and multinational corporations. Each area involves activities that transcend national boundaries. Special consideration is given to the culture of the Middle East.

More specifically, this book:

- Provides managerial applications and deals with issues confronting managers in a competitive international market

- Provides real-world examples that add relevance to the analysis presented

- Includes a section on international human resource management to help management cope with the difficulties of overseas assignment

- Includes case studies to reinforce the discussion of related materials

Strategic management and human resource management provide the unifying theme of the book. Management research and major functional areas are analyzed and integrated. The strategies of multinational corporations are outlined, and international human resources, international marketing, and the issue of technology transfer are examined in detail.

The book is divided into seven sections, each of which is designed to carefully lead into the next section in a way that covers the subject from various angles. The seven sections are as follows:

I.   Introduction

II.   Multinational Companies

III.   International Human Resource Management and Technology Transfer

IV.   Comparative Management

V.   Technology Transfer

VI.   Business Ethics and Corporate Social Responsibility

VII.   Strategic Issues in International Management

This book is a practical tool for every member of a multinational corporation. It is designed to help businesses and future managers become better prepared for future assignments in the international arena. Researchers will also find this book valuable in their future reference and research activities.

ACKNOWLEDGMENTS

No book is a product of one or two individuals, and this one is no exception. Many people have contributed to revising and improving this text, and I take this opportunity to express my thanks to all of them.

I extend my thanks to my colleagues and students (especially in my international management and management seminars) for reviewing this book and to friends at Slippery Rock University for providing a good academic environment for teaching and research. Special thanks to Sharon Furman for her assistance in finalizing the format of the book.

My appreciation is extended to my wife, who deserves no end of credit for her understanding and support in finishing this project, and baby Ahmed, as well as to my father, mother, and two lovely daughters, Alliah and Sheamah, whom I love and miss very much.

My thanks to Sandy Pearlman for her efforts in editing the entire book.

I am grateful to the following students in my international management classes who reviewed most of the chapters and provided valuable input: Michael Bauer, Melissa Bixler, Kristin Blair, James Bouril, Cynthia Broz, Jay Cincinnati, Natalie Cowan, Tibor Cseszneki, Christopher Cummings, Linda Davis, David Dively, Terry Dreihaup, Robert Eannarino, Imran Farooq, Trisha Felsing, Virgil Fleming, Frank Girardi, Thomas Goodrich, Viruna Gunawardane, Galina Haralambova, Sheila Hnida, Imtiaz Hussain, Annette Jamiel, Saadat Khan, Elias Latouf, Sarah Melvin, Friedo Meyer, Paula Miller, James Navarre, Diana Peterson, Jane Rigby, Kathy Rihel, Jim Rothenberger, Shelley Scott, Morris Sibatene, Karen Stauffer, Karen Strohm, Brian Taylor, Franklin Walsh, and Gi Il Yoon.

I am indebted to the following friends, without whose help and support it would not have been possible to complete the final version of this book on time: Abbas Ali, Manton Gibbs, Cecil Howard, Gihan Neangoda, William Martin, Mary S. Thibodeaux, Khalil Al-Shamma', Masouad Kavoosi, Ron Sardessai, Abdalla Hayajneh, Gabriel Bassiry, Dilnawaz Siddiqui, Shahid Siddiqi, Amer El-Ahraf, Parameswar Krishnakumar, Jafor Chowdary, Rauf Khan, C. Jayachandran, Sirinimal Withane, Richard Ramsey, Vinay Kothari, and Rogene Buchholz.

THE AUTHOR

Dr. Abbass F. Alkhafaji is Professor of Management at Slippery Rock University. His teaching responsibilities include an array of management courses, with special emphasis on business policy and international management. Originally from Baghdad, Iraq, Dr. Alkhafaji holds a Ph.D. in Management from the University of Texas at Dallas, an M.B.A. from Bowling Green State University (Ohio), an M.S. in Accounting and an M.S. in Economics from Northern Texas State University, and a B.A. in Business from the University of Baghdad.

Dr. Alkhafaji is the founder of the International Academy of Business Disciplines and serves as executive vice president. His professional experience has been broad and includes such diverse activities as research and consulting in the area of business strategy. He has conducted many seminars on current issues in management (i.e., total quality management and management diversity) for business executives and academicians.

Dr. Alkhafaji is the author of a number of books and numerous articles on corporate governance and international management. He received the Presidential Award for Outstanding Publication at Slippery Rock University in 1989 and 1992 and the Dean's Research Award in 1990 and 1994.

SECTION I

INTRODUCTION

Two chapters are presented in this section. Chapter 1 provides an overview of the nature and importance of international management. It highlights the difficulty of conducting business on a global basis. Emphasis is on how the emergence of a global economy and a globe trade market has transformed the world into one massive business division. The remainder of Chapter 1 provides a preview of the rest of the chapters in this book.

Chapter 2 deals with the diverse work force in a global context and, in particular, how the diversity of the work force will represent a major challenge to future managers. The main characteristics of the nature of business today are also briefly discussed.

1

THE IMPORTANCE OF INTERNATIONAL MANAGEMENT

ABSTRACT

In our rapidly changing world, the demand on countries to produce, expand, develop, and advance has become overwhelming. International competition for goods and services has gone far beyond national boundaries. The impact of the changing world on American businesses is the focus of this chapter. What will it take for American businesses and industries to be able to compete successfully in the international market? A discussion of management's role in such a dynamic environment is also presented in this chapter. Finally, a preview of the remaining chapters in this book is provided.

INTRODUCTION

The international dimensions of business have not always been a significant part of American managerial thought. The demand for American goods and services all over the world in the past was not the result of U.S. managers being highly dedicated to international business or trade. The demand for U.S. products was due to the fact that the label "Made in the USA" stood for excellence in quality and durability. American business and industry by and large has had no real interest or need to compete in international markets. The United States was rich in natural resources, and this abundance provided an unparalleled degree of independence and self-sufficiency. The country also had the world's largest consumer market and led the world in technology and management.

Such a combination enabled the United States to become one of the most productive of all industrialized nations. Increasing productivity led to a high standard of living, and the U.S. economy became one of the most developed in the history of nations. It is not surprising, therefore, that American managers were not concerned with the rest of the business world. Business was concentrated at home and was not well developed abroad. However, the world has advanced dramatically in all areas of life. In such areas as communication and travel, the of time it takes to visit and communicate with other nations has been shortened considerably. In no time at all, we can converse with someone on the other side of the world via telephone, fax, or modem. In just hours, we can be sitting on that person's doorstep via an airplane. With these innovations in communication and travel, the world has become a smaller place in which to live. In turn, conducting business with other nations is not uncommon, as it was centuries ago. No longer do we have to sail for months across water in order to trade goods with the rest of the world. No longer do we use horse-drawn carriages to transport products. A phone call or fax now produces a link of trucks, planes, and ships ready to carry goods to other parts of the world. Anything can go anywhere in days. The world has become one large business community.

GOING INTERNATIONAL

Conducting business on a global scale is far more complex than operating in a domestic setting. The study of international business has become increasingly important in recent years, so important that since 1974 the American Assembly of the Collegiate Schools of Business (AACSB) has called for the "internationalization" of business curricula. All of the schools that are accredited by the AACSB must require students to complete at least one course in international business. The AACSB suggests that a portion of the curriculum should include an international dimension. Since 1977, the AACSB has launched programs to encourage faculty to internationalize their curricula. However, according to a recent survey by Porter and McKibbin,[1] most business school curricula still do not offer these important international business courses.

By the beginning of the 1990s, about 40 seminars/workshops had been conducted in various parts of the country, and about 1500 faculty members and deans of business schools participated in these seminars. In addition to the efforts of the AACSB, the internationalization process has received extensive publicity in most business periodicals and journals. Despite these efforts, Cohen[2] indicated that as of 1989 only about 33% of the AACSB schools in the southern part of the United States had developed the required courses in international business. A similar percentage of schools in other areas had developed an elective course in international business/management. If this process is to succeed, universities must support their interested faculty members. The support and sponsorship of business schools around the country for professional international organizations is a contributing factor in the internationalization of business curricula. Conferences, proceedings, articles, and books published recently on managing in a global environment have contributed to the advancement and the importance of the internationalization process. The future of business is obviously international, a fact that today's business students cannot afford to ignore.

With the growth of international trade and investment and the emergence of multinational corporations, the utilization of resources has become more efficient. This has led to economic progress and increasing prosperity for many nations. These developments, however, have caused some profound problems for multinational corporations. Cultural differences, trade policies, and the division of the economic benefits of trade have led to fervent debates among nations. As the economies of nations become more tightly intertwined and interdependent, the economic health of those same nations becomes more dependent on external forces.

The emergence of the international arena has created many challenges for business managers. Unfamiliar economic, political, and cultural conditions, along with the various national laws and attitudes toward business, must be dealt with by multinational companies in a way that will allow them to retain their competitive advantages in the international market.

The emergence of a global economy and a global trade market has transformed the world into one massive business community. American corporations must prepare for the global markets or America may well decline as a major industrial power. In recent years, the American competitive advantage in this new global economy has been damaged severely, largely as a consequence of loss of market share to such Asian competitors as Japan, South Korea, and Taiwan, as well as a unified Europe.

CHALLENGES TO THE U.S. ECONOMY

Adapting to the globalization of the world economy and to the related shift from domestic to global business requires adopting a new strategy as well as new managerial skills. If America is to succeed, the business leaders of tomorrow will have to be able to operate effectively and comfortably in a global, multicultural, multilingual, and geocentric environment. However, as of 1992, only a few colleges and universities in the United States offered courses, much less majors, in international business. Americans are falling behind in the business world in which they live and can no longer be so naive as to believe that they will always be self-sufficient. According to a University of Montana study,[3] administrators at many U.S. educational institutions think that it is important to teach an international business curriculum, but few actually do so. A driving catalyst is needed to make this concept a reality. An international business major must be established in every undergraduate and graduate educational institution in America. This would partially help to ensure the U.S. position as a leader in the global market.

Furthermore, schools should be required to teach a minimum of five years in some foreign language, starting as early as the fifth grade. This would serve to bring Americans closer to the rest of the world. Americans have not recognized the importance of learning to speak other languages, as have the people of Europe. For example, Italy, Germany, Austria, and France are all located within a few hundred miles of each other and rely on each other for trade. For the most part, the people who do business in these countries have some working knowledge of the others' languages. As a result, a European economic community has been formed among all nations in Europe. It is treated as one market in which every country has become more affluent by way of the open border policy.

HOPEFUL SIGNS

In order to be able to compete and rise to leadership positions, the United States must develop global training programs for its business school students. According to a November 1979 study by the President's Commission on Foreign Language and International Studies, U.S. businesses must develop a better understanding of geography and learn foreign languages. The commission emphasized increased knowledge in these two areas as a prerequisite for success in international business. Realizing that the future of the U.S. global economy will rest on an international basis, many scholars are suggesting the improvement and implementation of international business programs.[1] These improved programs will better prepare students for the emerging global economy.

Clearly, the United States has begun to fight back in an attempt to regain lost market share and its reputation as a quality producer. There is ample evidence that the United States is making real progress in improving the quality of its products and services. The U.S. educational system is beginning a reform movement that should eventually make the U.S. work force much more competitive with other countries. If these trends continue, the United States should regain its position of leadership in the world marketplace. However, technology is too widespread and there are too many highly motivated players in a very competitive game for any one producer to dominate. U.S. companies are beginning to show real signs of strength in the world economy. Some of this surge in imports is due to the recent drop in the value of the U.S. dollar, but most believe that there are many other reasons for America's surge in exports and that the trend will continue. If Americans work hard in the future to reform education and if management makes a sincere effort to develop a cooperative attitude with labor that is based on a team marketplace, the United States will have every opportunity to regain its market share in many industries.

At least three main issues need to be addressed in order to cope with the global market. The first issue is understanding the changes in the international market and their effect on the U.S. market now and in the future. The second issue is the global challenges that businesses face and how to prepare to meet these challenges. The third issue is how to prepare qualified individuals who can understand as well as deal with the changes taking place in the global market.

Business schools should provide guidance and appropriate programs that help to address the above-mentioned issues. The internationalization process requires a sincere commitment from all those involved in the process. Resources must be allocated, experienced faculty with international perspectives must be hired or trained, and different levels of education in the various academic programs must be implemented.

Exposure to global topics will expand the horizons of students, who are the end product of the internationalization of business education. This will also prevent them from further developing any ethnocentric perspectives they might possess. International understanding will provide the knowledge needed to deal with a global market and will help develop the confidence needed to adequately deal with problems.

America can benefit from the world market by learning more about it. Knowledge is power, and power, if used correctly, brings prosperity. The United States is a nation of strength, but prosperity has to come from within. America can no longer rely solely on itself and must become more involved in world trade. This will ensure our children's future.

If efforts are concentrated on treating the world as a single economy, we will all be better off. Of course, new trade laws would probably have to be written to safeguard against unfair trade practices, but that is not the biggest problem. The main problem is changing people's minds to accept that fair free trade among nations is good for all. All will prosper in a world of free trade. Teaching international business is definitely a major step in the right direction.

PREVIEW

The remainder of this chapter provides a brief overview of rest of this book.

Chapter 2
A Diverse Work Force in a Global Context: Facing the Challenge

Chapter 2 takes a close look at the challenges U.S. businesses face as a result of the changing world economy. The global economy is now a reality. The nature of business today and nine features that characterize it are described. The results of studies conducted on multicultural work groups, which demonstrate that cultural diversity has both positive and negative impacts on groups, are discussed. The challenge of the future for the United States, other economic powers, and the work force is to develop the skills necessary to effectively deal with a broad spectrum of people and cultures.

Chapter 3
Multinational Corporations:
Problems and Prospects in an International Environment

As communication and transportation systems are improved throughout the world, the power and influence of multinational corporations will increase. The future power, influence, and scope of multinational corporations have yet to be decided. However, the role these corporations play in a global society will have a significant impact.

Chapter 4
The Effects of Culture on International Management

Chapter 4 emphasizes the effects of different cultures in international management as a concern that every multinational enterprise must consider. Four major points are presented: (1) an American manager in a foreign country should understand and appreciate the host country's culture, (2) orientations and values of managers recruited for international business should reflect those of the host country, (3) indigenous personnel should be recruited with the utmost care and consideration, and (4) it is always advantageous to hire qualified persons from the host country who know the country and its culture. Also, understanding the concept of codetermination, which is standard in other countries, will greatly benefit American firms.

Chapter 5
International Human Resources

Human resource management (HRM) is the basis for the success of any organization. In today's world, people understand more about the importance of the human resource professional and the need for knowledge in this field. An analysis of international human resources aimed at exploring issues that are important to present and future managers, businesses, and the academic community at large is presented. This chapter deals with the changing environment of today's big business society and domestic versus international human resource management. In making the transition from domestic to international positions, human resource professionals must recognize the importance of cultural as well as cross-cultural training, know the recruitment philosophies and selection criteria used by multinational corporations in identifying managers to represent them, and be able to deal with the problems that managers' families will encounter.

Chapter 6
Diversity of the Work Force:
Variables Affecting Managers and Employees

Managers are facing global changes. In order to meet these challenges, managers will have to perform effectively using their personal knowledge. Shaping a company to reach the global medium is difficult for many reasons, including cultural values, motivation through incentives, and the different levels of expectation that employees have of their managers. The diversity of the work force in the United States and in other countries and governments dramatically increases the complexity of the workplace. Managers will be called on to perceive problems with a broader and deeper understanding.

Sending managers overseas to run a subsidiary company is not always the right decision. Managers have a difficult time adjusting to and understanding the different cultures. Employees in the United States, Europe, Australia, the Arab countries, and Japan all expect something different from their managers. Adjusting to the different values is not always as smooth as managers might expect. In order for a company to become successful overseas, it must set up a multination human resource management strategy that provides managers with direction and guidance.

Chapter 7
Managerial Skills and the Flow of Technology

International technology transfer is addressed in this chapter. Certain characteristics are necessary for a successful transfer of technology. With expanding global markets, practitioners of international management have observed that technological innovations that led to increased productivity in particular organizations in some countries have failed in other places. The seemingly erratic reactions of organizations to new technologies have prompted some researchers to speculate on this topic.

Chapter 8
Japan's Economic Competitiveness: A Critical Appraisal

During the past half century, Japanese industries have acquired an economic strength and influence over the world economy. The literature is full of examples about the unique Japanese management system and attempts to analyze how Japan achieved such remarkable economic success in recent years. Those aspects of Japanese management that do not generally receive much attention are examined in this chapter, which also includes a discussion of why America seems to have difficulty keeping its position as a world-class competitor. Finally, suggestions are offered as to how the United States can meet the economic challenge of the mid-1990s and beyond.

Chapter 9
Corporate Governance in Developed Countries:
A Comparative Study

Corporate governance has been ignored for a long time, but over the past few years it has received attention from and become increasingly important to both critics and friends of business. The ideological differences among corporate governance systems in the United States, Germany, Japan, and Sweden are presented in this chapter.

Chapter 10
Culture in the Middle East

Many Americans are not familiar with Middle Eastern culture. The differences in language, religion, logic, and notions of truth and freedom, honor, trust, family, friendship, and hospitality account for the misunderstandings that persist between Arabs and the West. The two main periods in the Middle Eastern economy are identified as before and after World War II. The importance of the region, human resource developments, the dominant religion in the area, and the economic and political environment are examined in this chapter.

Chapter 11
Multinational Companies and
Less Developed Countries/Commodity-Driven Societies

The relatively new concept of the multinational corporation includes three requirements that must be met in order for a firm to be considered multinational. The first is that the operation is a direct investment in a foreign land, which ultimately has control over decision making. The second element is a collective transfer of resources, which includes such inputs as knowledge of entrepreneurship and investment of capital. The third requirement is that the income-generating assets acquired by this process must be located in a number of countries. Many have argued that these large corporations have become too powerful and cause more harm than good to host countries.

Chapter 12
Academic Training to Prepare Managers for a Global Economy

Because American businesses are competing in a global marketplace, there is a vital need to better prepare managers for the twenty-first century. Universities usually accept this challenge of preparing future managers by providing the educational leadership needed in such an environment. The university must serve as the conduit to change the international perceptions in our society.

Chapter 13
International Technology Transfer

The rate of technological innovation and development of technology has recently come to be considered a major factor in determining economic growth. The various theories of technology transfer and the debate surrounding them are presented in this chapter. It can be concluded from the discussion that this issue will be an important factor in decision making at the top level of management. The complications and the importance of transferring modern technology are addressed. A framework to assist management in less developed countries to acquire and adopt technology is introduced.

Chapter 14
Joint Ventures

This chapter covers the process and the form by which technology in one country is transferred to another. Internationalization of the various forms of technology is discussed in some detail, including foreign trade, licensing, franchising, and joint ventures. The process and importance of joint ventures are discussed more thoroughly. The factors that need to be considered when selecting a partner in a joint venture are also analyzed.

Chapter 15
Social Responsibility: A Requisite for Corporate Survival

This chapter addresses the issue of corporate social responsibility and how it has become an important part of corporate decision making. The culture that surrounds management plays an important role in the productivity of an organization. No longer can an organization function just to maximize profits; it must also consider the environment in which it operates and its occupants.

The concept of social responsibility has broadened and changed over time as the values and norms of society have changed. Large corporations not only perform the traditional economic functions, but are also called upon to support social and environmental concerns. Society demands that organizations assist in solving societal problems that were created by business. In addition to pursuing traditional economic goals, corporations are protecting and improving the welfare of the community, and thus becoming socially responsible. The arguments for and against being socially responsible are presented in this chapter. Recent examples about what some companies have done to become socially responsible are also included.

Chapter 16
Business Ethics

No longer is maximizing profit the only justification for doing business domestically or internationally. Society at large today is more concerned with the behavior of business than at any other time. Multinational companies have been criticized for paying bribes, kickbacks, and other unethical or illegal contributions when doing business overseas. These ethical and many other related issues are addressed in this chapter. The importance of understanding the values and traditions of the country in which a business operates is emphasized. The purpose is to help managers evaluate a particular practice in an organization and how to apply it in a different cultural setting. Developing a code of conduct for all organizations is proposed, along with certain measures that must be taken when unethical practices are used. This code of conduct must be well communicated by top management to all members of the organization, along with their commitment to adhere to it. It is important that expatriates are trained to be aware of the consequences of their actions for their companies as well as society in general. Theories of business ethics are briefly presented, focusing on the Foreign Corrupt Practices Act of 1977 and amendments made to it. Finally, a discussion of negotiation in various cultures is provided, along with examples.

Chapter 17
International Strategic Management

In working in a foreign country, knowledge and consideration of the foreign environment are necessary in order to create a good strategic plan. How an international company can design its future strategies is addressed in this chapter. The difference between domestic and international strategic management is discussed. The elements of strategic management are presented, and how to assess a different environment is analyzed.

Chapter 18
Multinational Companies: An Integrated Strategy

In recent years, it has become necessary for many corporations to expand their business activities beyond their domestic borders to achieve their desired growth. The importance of integrating strategies and logistics, international cultures, international marketing, international law, and the environment is covered in this chapter. These terms are related to specific corporations where appropriate. Expansion in the international market can be divided into three main arenas: the OPEC countries, Third World countries, and Fourth World countries.

Chapter 19
The Structure of Global Organizations

Structural design in a complex environment is discussed in this chapter. Firms operating in international business today are faced with greater environmental complexity and uncertainty than ever before. Empirical research on structure has consistently failed to identify successful formal structures for global companies. Of the traditionally defined formal organizational structure, the matrix structure provides a well-defined basis for decisions on a broad range of influences. This structure is often suggested for firms operating in a complex environment.

REFERENCES

1. L.W. Porter and L.E. McKibbin, *Management Education and Development* (New York: McGraw-Hill), 1988.
2. E.T. Cohen, "An Empirical Investigation of Attitudinal and Environmental Factors Affecting Coverage of International Topics," presented at American Accounting Association National Meeting, Toronto, 1990.
3. Maureen J. Fleming, Nader H. Shooshtari, and Susan S. Wallwork, "Teaching International Business Courses: A Survey of Faculty Selection, Evaluation, and Reward," *Journal of Global Business,* pp. 10–16, Fall 1992.

BIBLIOGRAPHY

Aggrawal, R., "Strategies for Internationalizing the Business Schools: Educating for the Global Economy," *Journal of Marketing Education,* pp. 59–64, Fall 1989.

Alkhafaji, Abbass F., *International Management Challenge* (Acton, Mass.: Copley), 1990.

Bennet, Amanda, "The Chief Executives in Year 2000 Will Be Experienced Abroad," *Wall Street Journal,* pp. A1, 7, February 1989.

Dymsza, W.A., "The Education and Development of Managers for Future Decades," *Journal of International Business Studies,* pp. 9–18, Winter 1982.

Joyal, D.L., *Trends and Developments in Business Administration Programs* (New York: Praeger), 1982.

Nehrt, L.C., *Business and International Education* (Washington, D.C.: American Council on Education), 1977.

Nehrt, L.C., "The Internationalization of the Curriculum," *Journal of International Business Studies,* 18:83–90, 1987.

Serey, T., W. Lindsay, and M. Myers, "Internationalizing Colleges of Business: Applying a Strategic Planning Framework," *Journal of Teaching in International Business,* 2:5–25, 1989.

2 A DIVERSE WORK FORCE IN A GLOBAL CONTEXT: FACING THE CHALLENGE

ABSTRACT

Businesses in the United States are faced with several challenges as a result of the changing world economy. The purpose of this investigation is to shed light on management responses to the global challenges that businesses must face in the 1990s and beyond. In addition, this chapter focuses on some of the problems that the United States must address in the coming decade regarding the complexity of its work force.

CHAPTER OBJECTIVES

1   To understand cultural diversity

2   To discuss the global challenges that businesses will face in the 1990s and beyond, i.e., the unification of the European Community, passage of the North American Free Trade Agreement (NAFTA), the nature of global competition, etc.

3   To understand the effectiveness and efficiency of culturally diverse work groups

4   To understand how to train or oversee a highly diverse work force

5   To explore the strategies needed to properly respond to these challenges

CASE STUDY
Levi Strauss & Co.

Levi's CEO Robert B. Haas finds it funny when he shows off an old 1908 Levi Strauss & Co. brochure, because it lists blouses and pants at laughably low prices. But the brochure also shows an uglier side of Levi Strauss. In Levi's factory, the copy proclaims, "none but white women and girls are employed." Robert Haas is laughing not because he's proud of it, but because of how far Levi's has come. Today, Levi Strauss & Co. is recognized as among the most ethnically and culturally diverse companies in the U.S., if not the world. At the end of 1991, 56% of its 23,000 U.S. employees belonged to minority groups. Since the mid-1980s Haas has been working to eliminate a "glass ceiling" that he believes has prevented some qualified minorities and women from reaching the company's top management levels.

Education is the cornerstone in Haas's efforts. Levi's spends $5 million a year on its "Valuing Diversity" educational programs. This also includes a three-day workshop for senior managers. When it comes to job opportunities, Levi's "strongly encourages" minorities to apply. Levi's also supports in-house networking groups. Part of managers' bonuses is even tied in its "Aspiration Statement," which demands that employees aspire to appreciate diversity.

Top executives at Levi's all agree that the payoff is more than an accumulation of credit in heaven. As the U.S. labor force becomes increasingly diverse, companies that want to hire the best people must be open to that diversity. Levi Strauss & Co. gives people a feeling that there is opportunity there when they interview with them. Loraine Binion says this is so because there is diversity at senior management levels.

Promoting diversity in the work force makes good marketing sense for Levi's. "It's tough to design and develop merchandise for markets you don't understand," says Dan Chew, manager of corporate marketing. There is also a flip side to this situation, because when you value employees' ideas, some good ideas for products make their way back to headquarters. This is how the Dockers line of casual pants was developed. An Argentine employee thought up the idea, and Levi's broadened it. The line now is worth $1 billion a year.

The bottom line comes down to the realization that diversity in the workplace is here to stay. With a growing population, not only in the U.S., companies are going to have to incorporate diversity with design. Levi Strauss is one of the best examples of how a company has incorporated diversity within its organization.

Source: Michael Janofsky, "Levi Strauss: American Symbol with a Cause," *New York Times,* p. C4, January 3, 1994; Christopher Palmeri, "Joe Three Fights Back," *Forbes,* 152:46–47, November 22, 1993.

INTRODUCTION

There is plenty of evidence to demonstrate that parts of the American industrial sector are in a period of decline and change. The national debt is estimated to be $4.5 trillion dollars, which consists of several years of about $250-billion budget deficits. Another problem facing the United States today is the **recession**. Recession is defined by most economists as a downturn in economic activity characterized by declining *real* GNP [the estimated total dollar value of all final goods and services produced in the economy during a year] and rising unemployment. Recession is an economic problem that periodically recurs in the business cycle. All countries go through periods of normal product change, which may be due to such factors as technological innovations that displace the need for the product or reduce the manpower intensity requirement. Market penetration by competitors, as a result of competitive pricing or marketable quality improvements, has much to do with reduced success in an industry. Some declines have to do with aging industrial plants, machinery, and tools that can no longer produce as effectively as newer plants located in the next state or the next country. At the same time, recession intensifies the sense of slippage. All too often, foreign economies are selected as the target for blame.

THE NATURE OF BUSINESS TODAY

The nature of business today is characterized by at least nine features, as summarized in the following paragraphs.

1. Business is intensely competitive.   It demands optimum quality, while at the same time exerting extreme pressure on pricing. Many companies have adopted the total quality management approach to achieve a competitive advantage. Total quality management involves everyone in the organization—from the chairman to the employees. Companies like Xerox and Motorola have implemented aggressive education programs to ensure that their employees understand total quality and statistical process control. The Malcolm Baldrige Award was created to encourage the transformation process and a commitment to quality.

2. The nature of competition is global.   Products that were once considered proprietary in nature, because of either the high level of capital expenditure or the technology they require, are now produced in many sectors of the international marketplace.

3. The unification of the European Community and the movement of the Third World and Eastern European nations toward the free market economy represents another challenge to the United States.   American managers should actively participate in the integration process taking place in Europe, through franchising, strategic alliances, and joint ventures. Western and Eastern Europe as well as the Middle East represent potential unexplored markets for the United States.

4. Americans are becoming increasingly worried about jobs leaving the country and going to nations with lower wage scales. Americans and some of their political representatives are calling for trade protectionism. Workers, their families and neighbors, merchants, and some factory owners are clamoring for barriers to free trade and for their fellow citizens to buy only American-made products. The passage of the North American Free Trade Agreement (NAFTA), which went into effect on January 1, 1994, has generated even more concern. This agreement was designed to eliminate trade barriers between the United States, Canada, and Mexico. Opponents of the agreement argue that many American companies will be moving their business to Mexico, where the labor laws are not as strict and the minimum wage is much less than in the United States. This means a possible loss of American jobs to Mexico. Proponents of the agreement suggest that the market in Mexico will be opened for American products. It has been estimated (in a debate on NAFTA between Ross Perot and Vice-President Al Gore in November 1993) that American companies will sell about one million cars a year to Mexico. Those in favor of NAFTA also disagree with the idea that many jobs will be lost to Mexico. Actually, American business that make high-quality and high-priced goods will not be able to afford the trip south. The costs of relocating, training unskilled workers, and new tooling would make the venture unprofitable.

While it is true in the short run that American jobs may be lost and some factories closed, in the long run jobs and market share will increase. NAFTA is expected to expand the ability of the United States to do business abroad. In the long run it might also promote efficiency through specialization and lead to economies of scale. Such integration may boost the transfer of technology, which could serve to intensify competition and innovation in addition to reallocation of resources in order to maximize their use and value. In addition, the United States may have no alternative but to meet the challenges resulting from the full unification of Europe and the emerging market economies in former Communist countries.

This restructuring of positions and attitudes puts tremendous pressure on the existing patterns of trade. The future will witness increased economic integration, especially among neighboring countries. There is an urgent need to prepare American workers to meet these imminent challenges. This can be achieved by providing them with the training necessary to upgrade their skills and their ability to perform a variety of tasks, which is especially important for those who have lost or may lose their jobs in the future. Businesses and government should invest now in the education and training of the future work force, an investment that will definitely pay off in the future.

5. America is a melting pot. The majority of the world's immigrants choose the United States over other countries. It has been estimated that approximately 600,000 people a year immigrate to the United States, in addition to a large number of illegal immigrants. Immigrants bring a broad range of racial, ethnic, and cultural backgrounds, which businesses must learn how to integrate into tomorrow's work force and manage effectively. This diversification of the future work force affects employers in various ways, from cultural differences to the education and training that will be needed in the future job market. Employers also need to be aware of the growing number of older workers and utilize their years of experience, reliability, and loyalty. The fastest growing sector of the work force in the United States since 1970 is part-time workers. In addition, America is moving toward "nontraditional" households, which includes those headed by a single parent and those in which both partners work full time. Businesses must recognize this change and begin to provide child-care services and flexibility in the workplace to accommodate these employees.

Immigrants from developing areas also represent a factor that employers need to recognize. Large numbers of immigrants from areas such as Southeast Asia and Latin America have settled in the United States. They bring to the workplace their attitudes, values, and beliefs. As they begin to adopt the English language and American customs, they learn new skills and adapt old skills to their jobs. Perhaps the single most serious challenge that employers will face in the future is the estimated lack of people in the next five to ten years to fill the jobs that the U.S. economy is expected to generate. About 20 million new jobs will be created during the 1990s. The number of people between the ages of 18 to 24 who will be available to work will be 500,000 less than in 1980. Also, foreign companies are employing more and more U.S. employees. The number of U.S. workers employed by foreign companies rose to 4.6 million in 1991.

To overcome this challenge, management needs to motivate and increase the skill levels of present workers so that productivity can be increased or at least maintained. New technological advances must be implemented so that organizations can become more competitive. Educators need to reinforce communication skills, both written and verbal. Learning a foreign language and understanding the culture of the immigrant work force are extremely important. The need for improved teaching of mathematical and computer skills cannot be overemphasized. Obviously, the ability to meet future challenges starts in the classroom.

6. Capital is an important element of development. Since 1975, the United States has become a debtor nation, largely financed by borrowed foreign dollars. Foreign capital is both buying and financing America. Europeans and Japanese are buying American companies and real estate. American capital, along with American executives, is flowing out to be invested in the international market.

7. The number of people working in America is increasing faster than the population growth. While the population increased 38% between 1965 and 1984, the number of jobs increased 45%, more than half of which occurred since 1973. The number of jobs in Japan, on the other hand, grew only 10% during this period, and in Western Europe the number declined.[1]

8. American corporations face large economic losses when they neglect the proper selection and training of global leaders.   More than 75% of 80 American businesses reported that 10 to 40% of foreign transfers were recalled or dismissed because of poor performance. Most of these managers were previously ranked as being excellent domestic performers. A businesses invests between $150,000 to $250,000 per annum to maintain a U.S. family overseas.[2] Therefore, when a global manager fails, the company suffers a major economic loss. When returning to the United States, the failed repatriate may choose to leave the company, which will then need to recruit, train, and support a new global leader.[3]

9. Americans are not aware of their own cultural biases.   Many American managers believe that they understand foreign countries because they have seen videos, attended training sessions, or vacationed abroad. U.S companies continue to send poorly prepared managers overseas to work on short-term or long-term projects. They arrive in a foreign country, unable to speak the language and with no understanding of the culture, and try to conduct business in the manner to which they are accustomed in the United States. This way of doing business is no longer acceptable in foreign countries. It is viewed as a lack of respect for the land and its language. To make matters worse, Europeans and Japanese working in these same countries have been trained and prepared for their international mission. This puts the American manager at a tremendous disadvantage. However, it is a disadvantage that can be remedied with a more serious approach to going global.

This more serious approach should start with intensive language instruction prior to the manager's departure. Language, as discussed in Chapter 4, is the key to proper adaptation to a foreign culture. When a manager, as well as his or her family, arrives at their destination able to communicate in the native language, the manager will be better received by the business community and the whole family will be better received socially. In conjunction with language instruction, the whole family should be given an acculturation program (to be discussed further in future chapters). The manager should be prepared for differences in lifestyle as well as ways of doing business. For example, in South America and the Middle East, at least a two-hour lunch is the norm, when little if any business is discussed. In Brazil, it is more important to like and to trust a manager than to discuss figures and deadlines. Any attempt to challenge these customs is viewed as being pushy, showing disregard for the country, or hiding one's true intentions.

In addition to the pre-mission training, it is important to have on-site help for everything from where to shop to schools for the children. The more comfortable and at ease the whole family is made to feel, the more productive the manager will be. A similar program when the manager returns home is also of vital importance to avoid the feeling of being a foreigner in one's native land. This should be coupled with a well-thought-out program for his or her employment upon return.

Perhaps one of the most important considerations is the selection of the manager who will work overseas. He or she must, of course, be capable and dynamic as a manger, but must also be open-minded and able to adapt well to change. Many a good manager has floundered overseas due to an inability to adapt to a foreign culture and foreign ways. Let's explore some examples. Americans become frustrated when the British procrastinate in a business meeting, which is the British manager's way of saying no. In addition, the British use humor to indicate when they are serious. Conversely, the Germans and Swiss rarely mix humor with business. Italians are shocked when Americans attend a business meeting wearing casual attire when they are impeccably dressed.[4] Career, cultural, language, psychological, organizational, and leadership challenges await global managers.

The preceding factors pose serious challenges to America's ability to compete successfully in a more technological world. In such a world, the United States will no longer be the dominant economic, or perhaps even military, power.

LITERATURE REVIEW

Studies of multicultural work groups have demonstrated that cultural diversity has both positive and negative impacts on groups. These studies showed that while cultural diversity could eventually lead to greater efficiency and higher productivity, multicultural work groups must first overcome the difficulties that diversity adds to the group process.[5] Steiner indicated that multicultural work groups tend to suffer from "process losses" due to the inability to communicate clearly, frequent disagreements on expectations, and attitudinal problems such as dislike, mistrust, and lack of cohesion. Such a loss often negates the potential value of diversity to multicultural groups.[6] The effectiveness and efficiency of culturally diverse work groups, therefore, appear to be directly related to the extent to which these groups are able to overcome these "process problems." While the differences in the interactions of culturally diverse and culturally homogeneous groups are somewhat understood, research on the effect of these problems on decision making and the performance of culturally diverse groups is still meager. Comparison of the group interaction behaviors of culturally diverse and culturally homogeneous groups has revealed that the two groups differ significantly in three dimensions: expectation and integration, cohesiveness, and fight or flight.[7]

Unless these challenges are understood and the strategies needed to respond properly are prepared, the risk of economic decline will continue. The growth and power of international trading regions has begun to supersede national interests, as demonstrated by the European Community and Third World and Eastern European blocs. People in business and education will encounter more and more problems that are linked to this growing diversity. This includes diversity of the work force as well as investments in the United States and around the world. It is important to recognize these emerging problems on all levels and begin to respond to them before they become a permanent risk that threatens the economic stability of the United States.

The new global economy is not located in one city or one country. It consists of a network of relationships bound together by sophisticated electronic communication between computers, phones, fax machines, electronic mail, satellites, TV, and people. Automotive parts are made in several countries and shipped to central assembly plants. American-brand VCRs are made overseas. American products are also being exported for manufacture under foreign nameplates. In the end, what all this means is diversity—of ownership, of production, of consumers, of capital, and of the work force. The major challenge that business and education leaders face is managing this diversity in a global economic environment.

THE DIVERSE WORK FORCE OF THE FUTURE

The United States and other economic powers face the challenge of developing the skills necessary to interface with a broad spectrum of people and cultures. This means that people in business and education must ensure that these skills can be acquired. Americans must learn how to deal with people of other cultures throughout the world and how to manage a multiracial, multiethnic, multilingual work force at home.

It has been estimated that by the year 2005, the U.S economy will create more than 26 million jobs. At the same time, according to the Bureau of Labor Statistics census,[8] population growth is projected to be slow from 1990 to 2005, with the total population growing only 1% from 1990 to 1995 and 0.9% from 1995 to 2005. This will create a shortage in the labor force. For example, in 1970 there were 18 million people age 16 to 24 in the labor force, and the number rose to 25 million by 1985–90; however, the number will be 24 million by 2005 due to a decrease in the birth rate.

The American labor force now includes more women and older persons, and this trend is expected to continue until 2005. A large increase in the number of immigrant workers from Asia and Latin America is also projected. From 1990 to 2005, entrants into the work force will consist of 33% female white non-Hispanic, 32% male white non-Hispanic, 7% female black, 6% male black, 9% male Hispanic, 7% female Hispanic, 3% male Asian, and 3% female Asian, as shown in Table 2.1.

The work force of the future will be much more diverse, which will complicate the jobs of American managers. Organizations will have to develop a comprehensive strategy to deal with such a complex and diverse work force. In the future, only those organizations that develop an open culture in which all kinds of workers are welcome—without discrimination

TABLE 2.1 Civilian Labor Force, 1990 and Projected to 2005, and Projected Entrants 1990–2005

Group	Labor force 1990	Entrants 1990–2005	Labor force 2005
	%		
Share			
Total	100.0	100.0	100.0
Male	54.7	50.5	52.6
Female	45.3	49.5	47.4
White non-Hispanic	78.5	65.3	73.0
Male	43.1	32.2	38.2
Female	35.4	33.1	34.8
Black	10.7	13.0	11.6
Male	5.3	6.2	5.7
Female	5.4	6.8	5.9
Hispanic	7.7	15.7	11.1
Male	4.6	9.1	6.6
Female	3.1	6.6	4.6
Asian and other	3.1	6.0	4.3
Male	1.7	3.0	2.2
Female	1.4	3.0	2.1

Source: "Outlook 1990–2005," Bureau of Labor Statistics, U.S. Department of Labor, May 1992.

based on age, creed, religion, ethnic background, or gender—will succeed. Future organizations will have a larger proportion of minority workers in their work force and will need to understand the cultures of their employees. As the proportion of minorities in the work force increases, organization will have to hire more minority managers, who are more likely to be sensitive to the needs of other minorities.

The employee of the future will require much more education and training. The more educated personnel will assume jobs as executives, managers, professional workers, and technicians. The number of jobs that require less education (such as administrative and clerical workers, support personnel, operators, fabricators, and other lower skill positions) will grow slowly or even decline, as shown in Table 2.2. Consequently, American jobs in the future will require a higher level of skill, more education, and greater technical expertise. This means that people will require education and training. It also means they will have to be able to demonstrate enterpreuership, adaptability, and personal initiative.

In addition, more minorities and disabled individuals will enter the work force. It has been estimated that the white male segment will fill only

TABLE 2.2   Occupations with Largest Growth and Decline, 1990–2005 (numbers in thousands)

Occupation	Employment		Numerical change	Percent change
	1990	2005		
General managers and top executives	3086	3684	598	19.4
System analysts and computer scientists	463	829	366	78.9
Accountants and auditors	985	1325	340	56.1
Lawyers	587	793	206	35.1
Computer programmers	1362	1675	317	23.0
Clerical supervisors and managers	1218	1481	263	21.6
Home health aides	287	550	263	91.7
Farmers	1074	850	−224	−20.9
Electrical and electronic assemblers	232	128	−105	−45.1
Machine-forming operators and tenders	174	131	−43	−28.6
Meter readers, utilities	50	37	−12	−24.8

Source: "Outlook 1990–2005," Bureau of Labor Statistics, U.S. Department of Labor, May 1992.

15% of new jobs. This loss will be offset by women and minorities. By 1995, women will represent about 50% of the work force. Most will be in their childbearing years and will require flexible work schedules and child-care programs.[1] In 25 years, one in every three Americans will be a member of a so-called "minority," whether female, immigrant, or ethnic. This group will provide 85% of the new workers by the turn of the century.

Managerial talent will have to be able to cross national boundaries freely. This includes Americans managing U.S. investments overseas, non-Americans managing foreign investments in the United States, and trainees living in the United States and preparing for careers of revolving overseas assignments. Everyone in the world will have to learn to live and work with everyone else.

COMPOSITION OF THE FUTURE WORK FORCE

The composition of the future American work force will present serious challenges. Because of population shortages, the people who will be needed to fill the jobs of tomorrow are the disadvantaged and the inexperienced of today. These are the very people who traditionally drop out of high school or who do not generally go to college or enter a training program.

The educational system as it is presently constructed is not equipped to teach these people the skills they must have to be able to function in the technological world ahead. The requisite skill levels are continually increasing as global competition intensifies. It is alarming—indeed, tragic— that not nearly enough is being done for them or by them. They are being left behind, just at the time they are becoming most needed. It has been estimated that about 13% of all 17-year-olds in the United States today cannot read, write, or do basic arithmetic. They will soon be faced with jobs that demand a high level of those skills.

DISCUSSION AND CONCLUSION

Today, with the standard of the U.S. educational system declining, businesses can help train students effectively by offering financial support for students to attend conferences that will better equip them for the "real world" and encourage better communication, critical thinking, and partici-pation in extra-curricular activities. In the long run, this will save the larger corporations millions of dollars and the smaller ones thousands of dollars. American industry is now spending about $30 billion a year for worker training. Some of it is used to teach the basic skills that should have been learned in grammar school. For example, the American Banking Associa-tion estimates that one in three banks now offers basic reading, writing, and arithmetic training to employees, at a total cost of $32 million a year.

The fact is that existing management is not prepared to train or oversee the highly diverse work force. Therefore, educators and business people are faced with a most daunting challenge: to see that the quality of education in high schools and colleges is continually improved. Equally important, education and business must unite to create practical opportu-nities to learn. This should include co-op, intern, and mentor programs, as well as summer employment opportunities. In addition, it should include training and development for business supervisors and managers so that they will be able to lead the more diverse and more educated work force of the emerging global economy.

Tax dollars, corporate funding, and personal contributions should be wisely used to provide the changing work force with the new skills needed to function successfully in tomorrow's economic environment. It is also important to ensure that teachers and managers are equipped with the required skills to hire, train, educate, and supervise a very "nontraditional" work force. Managers must learn how to function effectively in a culturally diverse workplace. The corporate culture should be built around serving its stakeholders while satisfying the needs of its customers. There is also a need for improved labor–management relationships, in which employees are treated with respect and granted the autonomy to get the job done with confidence and in which excellent performance is both supported and rewarded.

This needs to be accomplished on timely basis. It is imperative that the forces of business and education combine to upgrade the basic educational level of the emerging work force. Fundamental skills such as reading, writing, mathematics, and computers, as well as communication and interpersonal skills, are needed by every member of the work force in order to function successfully in more demanding jobs. People should heighten their understanding and tolerance of other cultures, languages, viewpoints, and traditions. All people share common hopes and the dream for a better future.

Cooperation between business and academia is very important to both and to the future of all countries. Leaders and their businesses must become directly involved. They need to demand excellence in education, insist on new and innovative programs in high schools and colleges, and form alliances between their organizations and educational institutions.

For academics to concur with the business world, children will need a broad background in order to make the United States a thriving society. Students will need strong written and verbal communication skills, a strong background in the social and physical sciences, the ability to work higher level equations and use them in the "real world," in-depth knowledge of a foreign culture and its language, computer skills, an appreciation of the fine arts, a thorough understanding of the U.S. government and economy, and the ability to use all their knowledge and abilities to solve an array of problems.

A manager must be able to convey ideas in a manner that can be fully understood by an employee. A broad knowledge of all subjects allows a person to fully interpret a situation and pursue the best possible outcome.

If local businesses offer a hands-on approach, students will be better able to conceptualize a particular job and what it involves. This will help students to make more educated decisions in choosing a career. Today, too many people attend institutions of higher education for a number of years only to find out, after thousands of dollars have been invested, that they are preparing for occupations that they do not really want to do for the rest of their lives.

Finally, the world has become global, multiethnic, multiracial, multilingual, and diverse and will remain that way. We must recognize this fact if we are to succeed. There is no other choice. The companies that will have the best chance for success in the future are those that are best able to meet these demands. They will have to learn the new skills needed to manage many different human beings in a changing world, provide meaningful jobs and a challenging environment, and offer the flexibility to accommodate the needs of their employees.

What we do, or fail to do, will determine the future competitiveness of the United States. Our vision for the future must encompass such factors as the innovative spirit, quality control, appropriate training and planning for domestic and international assignments, job security for expatriates upon return, an understanding of how the work force is motivated, application of an effective reward system, and an understanding of people's expectations, values, ethics, and political systems.

REFERENCES

1. W.E. Watson, K. Kumar, R. Subramanian, and S.A. Nonis, "Differences in Decision Making Regarding Risk Between Culturally Diverse and Culturally Homogeneous Groups," *IAMM Proceeding,* 1:130–132, April 1990.
2. F. Murray and Ann Murray, "SRM Forum: Global Managers for Global Businesses," in *Selected Readings in Business,* Myra Schulman (Ed.) (Ann Arbor: The University of Michigan Press), 1991, pp. 247–252.
3. Gilbert Fuchsberg, "As Costs of Overseas Assignment Climb, Firms Select Expatiates More Carefully," *Wall Street Journal,* p. B1, B4, January 9, 1992.
4. Peter G. Keen, "Sorry Wrong Number," in *Selected Readings in Business,* Myra Schulman (Ed.) (Ann Arbor: The University of Michigan Press), 1991, pp. 266–269.
5. L.R. Anderson, "Management of the Mixed-Cultural Work Group," *Organizational Behavior and Human Performance,* 31:303–330, 1983.
6. I.D. Steiner, *Group Process and Productivity* (New York: Academic Press), 1972.
7. N.J. Adler, R. Doktor, and G.S. Redding, "From the Atlantic to the Pacific Century: Cross Cultural Management Reviewed," *Journal of Management,* 12:295–318, 1986.
8. "Outlook 1990–2005," Bureau of Labor Statistics, U.S. Department of Labor, May 1992.

BIBLIOGRAPHY

Adler, N.J., *International Dimensions of Organizational Behavior* (Boston: PWS-Kent), 1991.

Anderson, L.R., "Small Group Behavior," in *Management of Urban Crisis,* S.E. Seashore and R.J. McNeill (Eds.) (New York: Free Press), pp. 69–112, 1971.

Bettenhausen, K.L., "Five Years of Group Research: What Have We Learned and What Needs to be Addressed," *Journal of Management,* 17:345–381, 1991.

Cox, T., S.A. Lobel, and P.L. McLeod, "Effects of Ethnic Group Cultural Differences on Cooperative and Competitive Behavior on a Group Task," *Academy of Management Journal,* 4:827–847, 1991.

Peak, Martha H., "Developing an International Style of Management," *Management Review,* 80:32–35, February 1991.

Watson, Warren E., Kamalesh Kumar, and Larry K. Michaelsen, "Cultural Diversity's Impact on Interaction Process and Performance: Comparing Homogeneous and Diverse Task Groups," *Academy of Management Journal,* 36:590–602, 1993.

Wittenbert-Cox, Avivah, "Delivering Global Leaders," *International Management,* 46:52–55, February 1991.

SECTION II

MULTINATIONAL COMPANIES

This section deals with how multinational corporations have become an important element of today's society. Chapter 3 covers why corporations go abroad and the significance of large corporations in the international market. The arguments for and against the role of multinational corporations in the international market and the changing profile of the global business environment are discussed

Chapter 4 deals with the effects of culture on international management. Emphasis is on the importance of understanding the host country's culture when doing business overseas. The important elements of culture are discussed, and the cultural implications that managers need to know before going abroad are also addressed.

3

MULTINATIONAL CORPORATIONS: PROBLEMS AND PROSPECTS IN AN INTERNATIONAL ENVIRONMENT

ABSTRACT

Today's business organizations face a rapidly changing business environment. These changes have occurred due to increased global competition, significant advances in international business, and changes in political and economical systems around the globe. Increased internationalization in the business arena has had a major impact on business organizations. The purpose of this chapter is to define the multinational corporation and study its impact on the global economy.

The world is split politically and geographically into some 200 separate countries, each with its own laws, courts, and boundary regulations. Our purpose here is to analyze how multinational corporations adapt to these differentials and work toward improving the economy and living standards of the society. In this century, multinational corporations have had a major impact on the economies of their host countries. Problems and prospects created by multinational corporations in host countries are issues of major concern and are analyzed in this chapter.

The theme repeated throughout this chapter is that the multinational firm has a strong economic and business rationale. From an economic perspective, host countries welcome multinational firms because they are viewed as agents of technology transfer and economic development. From a business perspective, multinational firms are eager for opportunities to invest in geographic locations where they can earn a rate of return high enough to compensate them for the perceived level of risk. Managing this perceived level of risk presents a major challenge to multinational corporations from a management point of view. Managing a multinational corporation at the strategic and operational levels is discussed.

CHAPTER OBJECTIVES

1 Why multinational corporations have increased their business transactions in foreign countries

2 The aggressive and defensive reasons why multinational corporations go abroad

3 The benefits gained by home and host countries as the result of multinational corporations doing business there

4 The impact and the responsibilities of multinational corporations when dealing with host countries

5 Restrictions imposed on multinational corporations by host and home countries

6 Degree of influence that multinational corporations have on host countries

7 The major factors that influence international business

8 The managerial mentality and attitudes of multinational corporations

9 Important future paths to multinationalism

INTRODUCTION

The term **multinational corporation** is being used more widely today due to the increasing number of business transactions conducted abroad. The term **multinational** is used to describe an organization that produces in, markets in, and obtains the components of production from one or multiple countries for the purpose of increasing benefits to the overall enterprise.[1] The more countries in which a company operates, the more multinational it is. There are many different types of multinational companies, and they do not necessarily work together. A multinational corporation (MNC) differs from a global corporation in that a global corporation sells similar goods in all areas. Both of these types of companies must work together in order to survive.[2]

Because MNCs have become such an important facet of today's society, they encounter many dimensions and factors with which domestic corporations do not have to contend. One is the relationship that the MNC must develop with its home country as well as its host country. These two different relationships must be examined and understood. In its relationship with its home country, a MNC is affected by nationalism, national interests, and government restrictions. Conflicts often arise between the two in the areas of labor, taxation, and transfer pricing. In its relationship with its host country, once it goes abroad a MNC must be able to adapt to the nationalism and national interests of the host country as well as the conflicts that often arise as a result of the emergence of the MNC.

CASE STUDY
AT&T Details Global Game Plan

AT&T plans to build a more efficient and dependable global communication system by consolidating with Singapore Telecom and KDD of Japan in WorldPartners. AT&T will own 50% of WorldPartners, and KDD and Singapore Telecom will hold the remaining 30 and 20%, respectively. Other corporations such as the Australian long-distance carrier Telstra, Korea Telecom, and Unitel (the Canadian subsidiary of AT&T) will be added as associate members in the future. The headquarters will be set up in New York and the CEO will be Simon Krieger, the current managing director of AT&T communication services in Japan. The project is estimated to cost AT&T and its partners $100 million. The focus of the venture is to deliver a one-stop global voice and data network design and services to multinational corporations in the Asia/Pacific region and North America.

AT&T is also pursuing other European carriers, such as Deutsche Telekom and France Telecom, to join WorldPartner, but is unwilling to wait for their decision because multinationals are demanding third-party network support and better global services. Moreover, AT&T is planning to expend more than $350 million and employ another 650 people to accommodate construction of new switching facilities to serve seven European countries and to add on to remaining real estate in the United Kingdom and the Netherlands. AT&T will also try to lease lines from other companies to adjust to their needs. Furthermore, WorldPartners plans to make the service available in Europe by 1994.

Source: Gautam Naik, "AT&T Bid to Acquire McCaw Cellular May Require Waiver by Federal Court," *Wall Street Journal,* p. B6, January 6, 1994; Paul Pinella, "American Telegraph and Telephone Co.," *Datamation,* 39:29–30, June 15, 1993.

Foreign investment is constantly causing shifts in the international economy. "Through the spread of technology and know-how, the industrial leader, over a period of time, loses more and more of its initial comparative advantages relative to its rising competitors. As a result, a gradual shift takes place in the locus of industrial and other economic activities from the core to the periphery of the international economy."[3] In his book entitled *US Power and the Multinational Corporation,* Robert Gilpin makes this strong statement to tell of the intricate binding of world economies. Because of these rapidly changing economies, firms must learn the means by which to stay competitive; some remain domestic, while others branch out to become multinational. One decisive factor in the reasoning to become a multinational firm lies in the doctrine of comparative advantage. This doctrine includes the classical theory of international trade, according to which a nation should specialize in the goods that it can produce and export with the highest relative efficiency and at the same time import other products from other nations that are doing the same thing. With this reasoning in mind, firms that become multinational are faced with many risks as well as benefits. The risks include tariff and nontariff barriers, the possibility of boycotts for political reasons, patriotism that leads to protectionism, and the currency exchange rate. The benefits include increased market share, increased competitiveness (through access to land, labor, and raw materials, which may in the long run decrease costs so that the price of the product can be lowered), the ability to keep on top of market developments through immediate feedback (which would not have been available if the firm were just exporting to that market), the ability to increase exports, and technology gains.

The decision to become a multinational firm is not an easy one. The problems often equal the benefits. The decision requires much planning and foresight. Once in operation, constant attention must be given to all activities as well as the changing business environment.

THE INTERNATIONAL PHENOMENON

The phenomenon of international business is not new. Even before the coming of the Industrial Revolution, international financial institutions flourished during the fourteenth and fifteenth century in such cities as Venice, Barcelona, and Genoa. This was followed by the Dutch East India Company, the Compagnie d'Occident, and the Hudson Bay Trading Company. However, only since the end of World War II has the MNC begun to emerge as a pervasive force in international relations. With the rising dominance of MNCs in the post-World War II era, the call for public social control of industry has taken on an international dimension. Technological advances in communication, transport, and trade have stimulated the growth of MNCs to the point where they are currently responsible for over 25% of world production of goods and services.[4] The growth and power of MNCs is best illustrated by the fact that 48 of the world's 100 largest economic entities are MNCs and not, as might be expected, states. Companies such as General Motors, Standard Oil (New Jersey), and Ford Motor have larger annual products than states such as Austria, Israel, Saudi Arabia, or Norway.[5]

WHY GO INTERNATIONAL?

Several reasons make the decision to go international feasible (Table 3.1). Aggressive reasons for going international include, first, "to open up new markets. Management and organizations always want growth, and if they have slow growth in their country they search for new markets outside the home country."[1] Second, companies can obtain greater profits by going oversees. There is an ever-pressing need to get ahead of the competition. Where there is less competition, a company may be able to get a better price for its goods and services. For example, General Tire had only three competitors in Spain, whereas dozens of brands are available in the United

TABLE 3.1   Why Go Abroad?

Aggressive reasons	Defensive reasons
1. Open up new markets	1. Protect domestic markets
2. Obtain greater profit	2. Protect foreign markets
3. Acquire products for the home market	3. Guarantee supply of raw materials
4. Satisfy management's desire for expansion	4. Acquire technology and management know-how
	5. Political stability

States. A company can also obtain a lower cost of goods sold, because producing in other countries can be less expensive in terms of the cost of energy, raw materials, and labor. For example, labor is inexpensive in underdeveloped nations, which enables a company to pay less for the same job. Other aggressive reasons for going abroad are the rapid expansion of the company and a greater consumer need for the product being produced.[1] A home-based company may be expanding rapidly, but not rapidly enough to keep up with market demand. A company may satisfy this demand overseas.[6]

There are also some defensive motives that make a company decide to go international. First, a company can protect its domestic market by going abroad. By moving its facilities to a country where its competition is located, a company can enjoy the same advantages in terms of the cost of labor, raw materials, and energy. A company can protect its foreign markets by going abroad. It can take advantage of any foreign exchange difficulties from the central bank of the host country's government. In times of foreign exchange scarcity, governments invariably give priority to importing raw materials and capital goods for a guest company. Manufacturers in industrialized countries are being forced to invest in other countries in order to ensure a continuous supply of raw materials. By going abroad, a company can guarantee its supply of raw materials. From a management point of view, a company can acquire technology and management know-how by going abroad. Finally, going abroad can promote political stability and mutual relationships between countries. MNCs all over the world have a significant impact on the global economy and politics.

SIGNIFICANCE OF THE MULTINATIONAL CORPORATION

Multinational corporations are unquestionably advantageous in a number of ways (Table 3.2). The most immediate benefit of the MNC is the reduction in unemployment in the countries of operation. The label "Made in Hong Kong" has become so familiar because cheap labor attracted foreign companies to set up production there. As long as conditions allow, millions of Hong Kong residents will be employed by multinational enterprises. Myriad service industries are related to the direct increase in

TABLE 3.2   Benefits of MNCs

Home country	Host country
1. Reduce unemployment	1. Employment opportunity
2. Increase tax revenues	2. Improve standard of living
3. Encourage extensive capital investment	3. Acquire technological skills
4. Increase market share	4. Increase skill level of the population
5. Increase competition	5. Increase revenue for the government
6. Increase exports	
7. Technology gains	

employment that accompanies the MNC; these business, which are created to provide for the needs of the MNC, indirectly increase the number of persons employed.

Multinationals also increase tax revenues for governments. By importing materials, employing workers, and exporting finished products, the MNC exposes itself to taxation at a number of levels. Although it has been argued that these companies often try to avoid tax burdens, it should be recognized that a great deal of revenue accrues to the host government as a result of the activities of multinationals. Among other things, this revenue allows many governments to initiate social programs and to develop physical infrastructures (roads, schools, hospitals, etc.) which would not otherwise be possible.

The capital investments made by multinational enterprises have beneficial effects as well. These investments, often in the form of plant and equipment, allow production to take place and, in some cases, encourage more extensive capital investment. In extremely underdeveloped areas, the lack of factories, plants, or other production facilities prohibits almost all but agricultural exports. By injecting capital into underdeveloped economies, the MNC creates employment, increases the skill level of the population, and allows further development to take place in the form of technology transfer and more favorable business conditions. A study of MNC investments in Britain, published by the U.K. Department of Trade and Industry, found the balance of payment effects of inward direct investments quite favorable, foreign-owned subsidiaries to be less strike-prone than their domestic counterparts, and the overall regional impact of direct investment potentially massive and favorable.[7]

Although there are many risks, and much strategy involved to offset these risks, a firm should examine some of the major reasons for becoming multinational. These benefits, as noted earlier, are increased market share, improved competitiveness, better awareness of market developments, favorable currency exchange rate, increased exports, and technology gains.

Increasing market share is a prized position for any firm. It gives a multinational firm a more competitive edge. Market share ties into efforts to retain customer loyalty and stability due to its very nature, which is closely related to increased competitiveness and market development. One aspect of this increased competitiveness is access to land, labor, and raw materials. It also increases competition between firms; because the favored firm has a greater market share, it is better able to competently compete against its contenders for market share, if it keeps abreast of market development. This takes into account local tastes and conditions, as well as the ability to provide after-sales service. Once market development enters the picture, a greater commitment by the multinational firm is perceived by the local community, as well as an increased assurance of supply stability. This in turn promotes loyalty to a specific firm, which could result in a further increase in market share, and this is potentially a cyclical process.

CRITICISMS OF THE MULTINATIONAL CORPORATION

Perhaps the most salient criticism of the MNC, and undoubtedly the oldest and most emotional, is that it exploits the raw materials and unskilled labor of developing countries without any offsetting development of a modern economic infrastructure. In social policy, governments are committed to reducing unemployment to a minimum, increasing the general educational level and technical skills of the population, and raising the real standard of living, particularly in lower income groups. The mandate of the MNC is, quite simply, to maximize profit, and this goal rarely coincides with the objectives of governmental social policy.

Another important criticism aimed at multinational enterprises concerns their vast power. A small, relatively weak government is often unable to compete with the economic power of the MNCs in its territory. Loss of sovereignty and independence and an inability to control social and economic policies without reference to the MNCs has created a genuine fear and distrust on the part of many government officials. The vast financial strength and investment or divestment capabilities of the MNCs puts them in control of certain national economies to some degree. Host governments often have little influence when it comes to product or marketing decisions, choice of technology, or even the fundamental question of continued operations.

Related to this lack of control is a fear of blackmail by the MNC. The threat of reduced or discontinued operations can have a serious destabilizing influence for a weak government, and this fear breeds resentment. Situations such as the United Fruit Company's problems in the Dominican Republic or ITT's involvement in the overthrow of the Allende regime in Chile only add fuel to such fears.*

---

* In both instances, the U.S. government took action on behalf of the American MNCs. In the Dominican Republic, proposed land reforms threatened the holdings of United Fruit, and subsequently the Marines were sent in. The Allende regime was overthrown by covert CIA actions after ITT-Chile was nationalized.

Also related to this lack of control over MNCs is a fear of becoming dependent and losing even more control over internal policies. The strength of the MNC is often the weakness of the host government, which creates a dependency that places the government at the mercy of the corporation rather than the corporation being controlled by the government. Developing countries, and even developed states, often require the capital and technological know-how of MNCs. The needs of these states often make them dependent on the goodwill of multinational enterprises. Jack Behrman has described these fears quite cogently in his study entitled *National Interests and the Multinational Enterprise.* He suggests that major sources of tension are fear of disturbance to economic plans and indifference to national order, as well as fear of industrial dominance and technological dependence.[8]

Another more substantive concern of many governments is the control that MNCs enjoy over the local capital markets of host countries. Their credit standing and borrowing capacity outweigh that of weaker indigenous firms. This dominance tends to discourage investment initiatives by local businesses and creates a virtual monopoly for the MNC. In most cases, domestic firms lack the capital and expertise to provide effective challenges to the multinationals, and local capital investment decreases accordingly.

The ability of the MNC to manipulate foreign exchange rates has become increasingly important to many states. The multinational's financial goals can inherently be in opposition to the domestic objectives of specific countries. Corporate treasurers attempt to move funds to those countries where the danger of depreciation of the currency is lowest or interest rates are highest. Protecting assets and strengthening the long-term or short-term position in each currency usually requires exactly those financial operations that each local treasury, or central bank, is trying to block. Thus, an immense strain on both foreign exchange markets and capital markets tends to occur.

MNCs have also been criticized for their attempts to reduce their tax burdens. MNCs operating in many countries try to set a tax-minimizing strategy, which can mean shifting income to lower tax areas where possible or, more often, general tax-avoidance practices. The end result is that individual government revenues can be reduced. Obviously, several goals of the MNC, within its sphere of maximizing profit, come into direct opposition to the policies of host governments.

RESPONSIBILITIES OF THE MULTINATIONAL CORPORATION

The growth of the MNC, and the increase in its power and influence, have created a host of problems for both developing and developed countries. Although a great deal has been written concerning the effects of MNCs on society, much of the literature has been in reaction to isolated incidents and often fails to consider the beneficial aspects of multinational enterprises. The role of the MNC in society, as well as its relationship to government, must be objectively considered in order to effectively evaluate its past, present, and future.

Each business has a responsibility to its host community. Consideration for the native population must take top priority when a large company moves into a small, underdeveloped community. Social responsibility is one of the keys to success. An important objective for a company should be to become a respected addition to the community. A community often welcomes big business, but sometimes a company affects a community and its people negatively.

The new firm is usually a source of funds for the native population, who can improve their standard of living. The company can help replace the old lifestyle with a more comfortable one. A new firm can provide people with the skills, training, and confidence with which to work toward a higher standard of living. Large corporations, however, may create urban areas that may be unwelcome in small communities. Although the advantages to the community are numerous, managers must be careful not to take advantage of the unskilled people trapped by a low standard of living.[6]

In addition to these traditional concerns, several nontraditional concerns face the multinational firm, including social responsibility, ethics, product liability, and jurisdictional disputes relating to violations of the host country's regulations. These particular concerns overlap to some extent.

It is often speculated that MNCs do not actually try to help these poor communities, but instead just try to make a huge profit. Do these companies go abroad just to benefit from the low cost of labor and to use the valuable resources available? The idea of profit must be considered when a major move is anticipated.

Multinational firms should be socially responsible and ethically active. They have a duty to ensure that their products are safe to use and will not harm the users. Also, if a firm is actually producing a product in a host country, every precaution should be taken so that the workers and residents of the host country do not face any unnecessary risks. The multinational firm also has an obligation to its shareholders. This issue relates directly to the firm's liability for its products. The firm must realize that it is responsible for any reasonable side effects that the product or even its production may cause. A firm must take responsibility for its product not only after an accident, but also in the design and marketing of the product.

Once a multinational firm has accepted its responsibilities, problems may arise concerning jurisdiction. Questions involving whose laws have been broken, what type of settlement is suitable, and where the litigation concerning the case shall take place all need to be answered. These questions are very difficult to answer. Conflicting interests will occur. Individual countries have their own rules and regulations concerning multinational firms. Some organizations, such as the World Bank, are setting up guidelines for firms to follow. The guidelines not only help protect the investment, but also help protect the people and the environment in the area in which a firm operates.

Experts have made several suggestions for solving these problem areas. The underlying theme appears to be the harmonization of laws and regulations concerning international firms. Having one set of rules would help eliminate many of the conflicting interests, but this is much easier said than done. However, with standards, such as the World Bank guidelines, perhaps things will move in the right direction.

RISKS TO CONSIDER

Whether or not it is a good idea to become a multinational firm depends on the individual corporation. Is its product in demand? Is it financially sound? Would it be better to lease than to own? Has there been enough research to make a sound judgment? All of these questions must be answered by a firm as part of its decision to become multinational.

In deciding whether or not to become a multinational firm, the risks must be taken into consideration, not only for the present but for future planning as well. Ways to offset these risks must be found in order to ensure the success of the firm as a competitive, profitable company. Some of the risks that must be taken into account include tariff and nontariff barriers, protectionism, politics, and exchange rates.

Tariff and nontariff barriers are a very real risk for the multinational firm, as cited by David Gerstenhaber in his article entitled "Japan's Markets Are Ripe for US Exports." He states that high tariff and strict nontariff barriers "exclude foreign firms from some of the largest segments of the Japanese food market."[9] Tariffs that are exclusionary because they are so extreme can effectively hamper a firm's ability to be competitive in a market. If the tariff were penetrable at all, the price that a firm would have to charge to offset it would render the firm noncompetitive. Nontariff barriers to international operations may be exemplified by discriminatory treatment of like firms, one foreign and the other domestic. This leads to protectionism, another of the risks associated with a firm trying to produce abroad. Protectionism is partly due to patriotism, or devotion to one's country, and shows up as a desire to support domestic firms to the fullest extent. Protectionism shows up by using politics in the form of tariff and nontariff barriers as well as other tactics. Some countries have found that this type of barrier to foreigners hurts both the foreign and the domestic markets. In an article entitled "A Free-Trade Milestone: The U.S.–Canada Pact Is on a Scale with the EC," Terry et al.[10] cite the efforts of the United States and Canada to prevent protectionism by means of open talk on the subject of future trade legislation and the possible removal of all tariffs over a period of ten years. The United States and Canada are not the only countries attempting to prevent protectionism; the 12-nation European Community is another example.

Political risks can be and often are very strong barriers to entry into international operations. In addition to tariff and nontariff barriers or protectionism, another political risk is the possibility of boycotts. The force of a boycott was felt by many U.S. companies in the Arab and Persian Gulf States. Some were able to overcome this barrier because their goods were in such high demand. In "U.S. Companies Are Back in Force in the Gulf," Slavin et al.[11] state that Xerox and Ford were officially removed from the boycott list and Coca-Cola, Union Carbide, and Colgate-Palmolive are also back because local businesses are ignoring the ban. These companies have managed to obtain a market share with consumers who consider their goods to be indispensable.

A final large risk that bares mentioning is the exchange rate. All currency values are determined by other currencies, and the associated risk is the depreciation or appreciation of one currency in terms of another currency. The cost associated with returning a foreign currency in exchange for the home currency could end up being very large.

Once these risks have been taken into consideration, a firm must find the means to protect against these situations. The practice of exchange risk management, which include forecasting exchange rate changes, measuring accounting and economic exposure, managing transaction and translation exposure, and managing long-term operating exposure, is one way an international operation can protect itself against market risks.

A MNC must look at long-term risks and develop strategies for the long term. After it makes its initial market selection, a MNC should plan future promotions, the product it presents, and how it could accommodate changes in the market. These are important inputs to the long-term strategy of a company.

HOST COUNTRY'S RESPONSE

Because each country is different, every seemingly trivial matter must be investigated before a final decision can be made. Several questions should be answered concerning the type of business and where and how it will be run. A company should find out which country best suits its needs and whether there is a potential market for its product in that country. It should also examine the investment climate; the laws and regulations concerning taxes, permits, and licenses; the country's business structure; and other strengths and weaknesses that do not fall into any of these categories.[7] More importantly than before, a company has to take into account long-term planning, because foreign investment is very risky. Many countries are much less stable than the United States. A company should look at how an overseas country views foreign business, because not all countries view it in a positive light. Most important is a company's ability to adapt to the changing environment, because developing nations present a wide variety of new challenges.[12]

As an example, MNC activity in Canada has always been extensive. Some Canadian industries were under foreign control as early as 1926. This figure grew to 59% by 1960, 44% of which was controlled by U.S. residents. Nearly three-quarters of Canada's petroleum and natural gas industry and two-thirds of its mining and smelting industries were under foreign control at this time. Of Canada's 100 largest firms in 1966, 39 were controlled by foreign companies, 26 of which were U.S.-based.[12]

Considerations ranging from heightened nationalism to strained relations with the United States inspired changes in the Canadian government's relationship with multinationals operating in its territory. A number of policies were implemented in order to control the activities of the MNCs and to curb their growth, including limits on foreign ownership in Canada, attempts to improve corporate subsidiary performance, published guidelines for good corporate behavior (the Winter's Guidelines), and incentives for Canadian investment in MNCs. Nigeria's approach to multinational enterprises has been much more militant. Considered the "gold rush country of Africa," Nigeria's oil-inspired boom created enormous wealth but also massive chaos as the nation's ports, roads, and communications systems become overwhelmed. These difficulties were complemented by an inflation rate that spiraled above 50% or more a year.[13] In response, the Nigerian government instituted "indigenization" policies, which enforce local equity participation in foreign-owned companies, and "Nigerianization" policies, which require greater Nigerian participation in the management and on the boards of directors of foreign-owned companies. Although Nigeria's response was much more militant than Canada's, both examples clearly illustrate the changing nature of the relationship between MNCs and host governments.

The relationship of the multinational enterprise to individual governments is important, but international organizations also play a significant role in the control of MNCs. The most notable areas in which international control mechanisms have been established include the United Nations, the Organization for Economic Cooperation and Development (OECD), the European Community (EC), and the Andean Common Market (ANCOM). These organizations work to establish control in different areas. One focuses on policy coordination, which is the approach of developed industrial nations and usually favors multinationals. Another seeks alteration of bargaining power, which is the approach of developing nations and labor organizations that perceive themselves as disadvantaged in their relations with multinational firms. Other efforts on the international level have concentrated creating codes of conduct or guidelines for MNCs. Although such codes are not binding, many individual companies voluntarily pledge to conform to them. The guidelines have, among other things, become benchmarks against which the behavior of MNCs can be evaluated.

THE CASE OF SOUTH AFRICA

General Motors (GM) was forced to pull its operations out of South Africa on October 20, 1986 because of continuing losses. GM had operated in South Africa for 60 years under the Sullivan Principles, which state that

U.S. companies operating in South Africa must give non-whites the same opportunity for employment as whites. For GM, this resulted in 60% of its work force being non-white. The company eventually had to pull out because of the lack of progress in South Africa in putting an end to apartheid.[14]

Several other companies have also pulled out of South Africa. Honeywell, Warner Communications, Coca-Cola, Eaton, Bell & Howell, and GE all worked toward the advancement of black South Africans. In particular, IBM, which was a leader in developing programs for black advancement, had to pull out because of lack of support from the South African government toward anti-apartheid.[15]

When South Africa was not making any progress toward ending apartheid, each decided to sell its operations there, hoping to pressure the South African government to negotiate an end to apartheid.[16] Most of the companies, however, continued to sell goods to independent units in South Africa.[17] The American government pressured these companies to completely cut their ties with South Africa, in an effort to put more pressure on the government. Some critics felt that open American support would encourage black violence and that American companies could end apartheid more peacefully.[18]

In general, the institutional framework of the international system has not been well-equipped to contend with the problems of excessive marketing power, distribution of benefits, and the threat to national sovereignty posed by MNCs. Therefore, effective control measures and coordination at both the national and international levels are needed, in addition to restraint on the part of both public policymakers and MNCs.

DIFFERING ATTITUDES IN HOST COUNTRIES

MNCs have grown considerably over the past 20 years. In the United States alone, the percentage of the Gross National Product contributed by MNCs has risen dramatically, from 12% in 1960 to 34% in 1984. MNCs now have considerable influence on the world's production of goods and the advancement of technology, and they have grown so large that they affect all aspects of society.

The MNC in its home environment is often influenced and affected by the nation's culture, ideologies, and political system. The culture of a country is made up of the general attitudes of its people, their ideals, and their pride in the country in which they live. People tend to be defensive as far as their national identity is concerned, and in times of trouble they will support their country. Concerning their national way of life, all people are similar in full vigorous support of their nation as a self-governing entity.

A MNC is affected greatly by the ideology of work attitudes of its home environment. This is especially noticeable in the difference between the American and European work ethic. Americans believe in the Protestant work ethic and commitment to the job. American management upholds the idea of promotion based on ability rather than social status; the success of the business is dependent upon every employee, coordinating the actions of top management, and consistent behavior.[19] This differs greatly from the way that Europeans view work. Europeans look to the past rather than the future; promotions are often based on social status more than the ability of the individual. Europeans have a hard time accepting success, and as a result the promotion process is slow. Top management usually makes all of the decisions, and work is not seen as quite as important as it is in the United States.[20]

In the past, home countries have viewed MNCs as extensions of their domestic systems. Today, however, MNCs have gained such great control over host country societies that home governments are beginning to place restrictions on the MNCs. Conflicts are also arising in the areas of organized labor, transfer pricing, and taxation policies.

HOST COUNTRY CONTROLS AND REGULATIONS

Regulations that governments have imposed on MNCs have been dependent to a large extent on the individual country and its own objectives at the time. In 1970, the United Kingdom imposed a great number of restrictions on MNCs because "it was concerned about the adverse effect upon its balance of payments position of capital outflow."[20] However, some countries have been concerned about foreigners dominating local business and have initiated reverse regulations; these countries impose restrictions based on the speed of goods flowing in and out of the country at a particular time. Each country regulates MNCs with a completely different style and attitude. The United States has been explicit, voluble, and nonselective among different enterprises. Similarly, The United Kingdom, France, and Japan have totally individual attitudes and styles in terms of regulation.[21]

Conflicts that have recently begun to arise between MNCs and their home countries have been due to differences in objectives, ideals, and goals in the general areas of organized labor, transfer pricing, and taxation. Organized labor has caused a great deal of trouble for the MNC. MNCs are able to obtain the technology, raw materials, and capital that are needed for production from any nation they choose. Therefore, they do not have to contend or argue with any faction of any nation. This is where the conflict arises. Labor unions are not international. While MNCs have continued to grow, labor unions have become almost dormant in their growth and influence.[21]

Because labor unions have become ineffective against MNCs, they generally view a MNC as detrimental to the domestic economy of the nation. Unions have recently begun to take legal action against MNCs by charging them with depression of investment, technology drain, export displacement, low wage imports, tax evasion, and unbalanced payments. Labor unions have also questioned the ethics of MNCs in moving from countries with high wages (in particular, America) to countries with low wages, the result of which is that the number of Americans who are out of work seems to have increased. Some MNCs have retaliated by claiming that they would have had to closed down production altogether if this movement had not taken place. There is a great need for organized labor to persuade governments to pass legislation to prevent this technology drain.

Another area that has caused a great deal of controversy is transfer pricing. Being profit oriented, MNCs adopt transfer prices that would be most beneficial to them, even if they are not in the best interest of the host government. Governments require pricing information from the MNCs, but often are not satisfied with the information that is given and impose regulations on the MNCs. The transfer price has to be within arms length of the conditions established. If the transfer price does not meet the conditions set, the MNC has to contact all its affiliated companies and make them aware of the problem. These companies may already have been taxed by their home countries, which causes additional work and problems for their respective tax offices. Host governments regard home country reallocation of affiliates' taxes as external interference in their fiscal policy and company application to that effect as illegal.

The last, and possibly the most difficult, area of controversy between a MNC and its home country is taxation. Because a MNC receives its revenue from many different sources, appropriate taxes are difficult to assign. As a result of this, the U.S. government passed a regulation called Subpart-F, which requires MNCs to include all foreign earnings in their tax reports. Neither the host country nor the MNC appreciates this, and both view it as interference in their affairs. The host country perceives it as an illegal action by the U.S. government. The MNC views its relationship with both host and home country is equally important. It should be stressed, however, that the relationships differ in terms of support, national ideology, and decision making.

The support of the host country usually is not as concrete as that of the home country. The host country has its own objectives; if they do not correspond with those of the MNC, the MNC will be forced to change or support will be withdrawn. The home country tends to support the MNC.[22] Decisions often come from headquarters located in the home country; therefore, some decisions do not reflect the true needs of the host country and therefore require adjustment.

When a MNC enters a new country, it is often faced with differences from its home country. The MNC has new ideologies and national interests, and new conflicts develop as a result of this expansion. The host country often has a very strong nationalistic attitude and is afraid of losing its sovereignty to the MNC. The host country perceives the MNC as a complex organization which can affect all aspects of its society. The changes are often abrupt, and the host country sometimes feels that the MNC is not concerned with its best interests. Therefore, the MNC must learn to adjust its activities to the needs and socio-cultural attitudes of its hosts.[23]

Another area of national interest in which a MNC must be extremely cautious is establishing objectives and introducing innovations. The host country often does not agree with the objectives of the MNC and may not want new technology imposed upon it at such a rapid pace. The MNC must introduce the technology at a slower pace, in order to avoid the perception of imperialism. The distinctive contribution of the company to the host society lies in the level of innovation it is able to contribute.

Even though a MNC has to adapt much of its structure in order to adjust to the host country, it still exerts a strong influence on the host government. This causes conflicts such as the following:

1. **Growth:** A MNC is mainly concerned with profitability. Many decisions are often made in the home country and do not take into consideration the feelings and attitudes of the host country.

2. **Control:** Host countries are afraid of losing control over local businesses due to new technology that is coming into the country.

3. **Profit:** Due to its global position, a MNC is able to reinvest its profits anywhere in the world. Host countries want MNCs to reinvest the profits back into the host country.

4. **Exporting–importing:** Host countries want MNCs to export to affiliates of the host country. A MNC usually exports to affiliates of its home country. The same is true for imports.

5. **Pricing:** MNCs usually already have established pricing policies. Transfer pricing often causes problems between governments.

6. **Research and development:** Location of facilities and ownership of findings is not always what the host country needs or wants.

7. **Human resource policies:** MNCs often attempt to impose their own work cultures, such as hiring procedures and recruitment practices, which do not always work in the host country.

A MNC interacts with both its host and home countries, and conflicts often arise as a result of this interaction. A MNC is greatly influenced by the ideologies and national interests of its host and home countries. When a MNC goes abroad, it often has to adapt its objectives to that of the host country. Sometimes these objectives may be totally different from that of its home country. A MNC is also affected by restrictions from both the host and home governments. The comparative advantage between MNCs and host countries is illustrated in Table 3.3. Conflicts arise in both the host and home countries as a result of the MNC, but the issues differ.

Home country conflicts usually take the form of tax regulations, restrictions, and government intervention to prevent a MNC from gaining too much power within the country. The host country realizes that the MNC most likely has a larger GNP than the country itself and simply wants some of the benefits. The host country wants to improve itself and learn something from the MNC, with the final result of achieving independence.

TABLE 3.3 Comparative Advantage Between MNCs and Host Countries

Host country	Multinational corporation		
	High	**Medium**	**Low**
High	Revenue R&D Standard of living	Employment	Labor Tariff barriers Raw materials Taxation Transfer pricing
Medium	Political stability Competition	Exchange rate Political risk	
Low	Technology Capital Control	Protect foreign market Increase exports	Location Government regulation

Even though MNCs are forced to interact and contend with two environments and conflicts often arise due to this interaction, this is a natural process. The conflicts and problems that a growing industry experiences ultimately strengthen it. In the future, MNCs will become a more integral part of our lives, helping to bridge the gap between industrialized nations and less developed nations.

MANAGING THE MULTINATIONAL CORPORATION

Bateman and Zeithaml point out two levels of concern in the management of MNCs. The first is the strategic level, where the basic direction of the global enterprise is established. The second level is the operations level, where strategy is implemented.

Strategy involves goal setting and the planning necessary to achieve those goals. Strategy is concerned with two factors: **synergy** and **balance**. Synergy pertains to benefits that can be shared among the different operations within a MNC's network. For example, in their book about the Honda experience, Bateman and Zeithaml discuss the synergies between the plant in Ohio and the plant in Japan. Equipment is designed only once for both plants, which saves design costs. Installation and operating techniques used in Japan are used in Ohio. Workers at the Ohio plant went to Japan to gain technical skills. Because of these synergies, the Ohio plant had lower equipment costs and higher operating efficiency during its first year.[24]

Operations in one country may encounter a different economic cycle in another country. Bateman and Zeithaml refer to this as "risk spreading," which means that when the economy is down in one country, it may be up in another. This may affect MNCs in terms of earnings. To illustrate balance, Bateman and Zeithaml describe Pan American World Airways, Inc. (Pan Am) in the mid-1980s:

> Pan Am sold its Pacific routes to United Airlines to generate cash. Events, however, hurt Pan Am's financial and competitive position in other routes. In 1986, terrorism in Europe and the U.S. military response against Libya hurt summer tourism to southern Europe. In addition, a nuclear disaster at a Russian power plant affected tourism in northern Europe. Pan Am, which relies on profitable summers to offset operating losses in other seasons, lost a lot of tourism business that summer.[24]

In this way, Pan Am was affected by the balance effect. From a MNC management point of view, the issue of balance should be considered when implementing operational strategy.

THE CHANGING PROFILE OF THE GLOBAL BUSINESS ENVIRONMENT

The increased volume of international business has heightened the importance of international management in this century. Major factors that influence international business are as follows:

1. **The tendency of most countries is to strive for free world trade and the removal of trade barriers, which is indicated by the expansion of world trade.** From 1970 to 1990, world trade expanded more than ten times. In fact, global output of goods and services increased from \$15.5 trillion in 1980 to about \$20 trillion in 1990.[25]

   Some believe that free trade is vital to economic prosperity. Others, however, believe that free access to their domestic markets should not be allowed. The imposition of trade and nontrade restrictions has created friction among the European countries, Japan, and the United States. However, there is an inexorable movement toward the removal of most trade restrictions and barriers. For example, Europe is preparing for full economic integration, which would produce a market larger than the United States. The United States, Canada, and Mexico have approved the North America Free Trade Agreement (NAFTA), which removes most trade restrictions in order to create the world's largest free trade bloc.

2. **The attitudes of many developing countries toward MNCs and foreign direct investment (FDI) have changed.** Compared to 1976, there has been a dramatic decline in the number of expropriations. Expropriation (the forced divestment of foreign assets) was frequently used as a policy choice by many developing countries in their disputes

with MNCs. Prior to 1976, many developing countries had a lack of administrative capability, a low level of economic development, and an inability to service foreign debts due to their large number of expropriations. Now developing countries can achieve their objectives through taxation and performance requirements rather than direct control. Competition to attract FDI should escalate, and governments may outbid each other with packages of investment incentives and inducements. This may result in increased international trade and may open up previously inaccessible markets.

3. **Many developing countries are adopting an export-oriented strategy for economic growth.**   The strategies of Japan, Korea, and other Asian nations have changed. During the period that these countries engaged in export-oriented strategy, the U.S. market absorbed the bulk of their exports. Consequently, because of its substantial trade deficit during this period, the United States became the largest debtor nation. Export-oriented strategy, in part, involves the participation of MNCs.

4. **Regional trade agreements and pacts are reducing trade restriction among their members and increasing intra-region trade.**   Membership in regional trade agreements is on the rise. The most notable trade agreements are the European Community (EC), the Association of South East Asian Nations (ASEAN), and the Andean Pact. Members of the EC are the 12 Western European countries: Belgium, Denmark, France, West Germany, Greece, Luxembourg, Ireland, Italy, Netherlands, Portugal, Spain, and the United Kingdom. The ASEAN countries are Brunei, Indonesia, Malaysia, the Philippines, Singapore, and Thailand. Bolivia, Colombia, Ecuador, Peru, and Venezuela are the members of the Andean Pact. The North America Free Trade Agreement, if successfully formed, will create another bloc rivaling the EC and ASEAN.

Some speculate that the EC, ASEAN, and America will be the three blocs that dominate world trade. The third bloc, America, also includes Argentina, Brazil, Canada, Chile, Mexico, and Venezuela. With expanded membership, the second bloc, ASEAN, could include Australia, India, and Japan. There will be relatively free or open trade within these blocs and few trade restriction between them. A strategic response to such a scenario is for a firm to have a foothold within each bloc or to form a strategic alliance with firms that are already operating within the blocs. Either case would result in expanding the role and scope of international management.

5. **Recent technological developments, particularly in manufacturing, have altered the nature of international business.**   Robotics, computer-aided design (CAD), computer-aided manufacturing (CAM), and flexible manufacturing have reduced production costs and labor components. As a result, countries that have traditionally had low labor

costs are losing their competitive position. Therefore, it is expected that these countries will try to tap into MNCs for technology transfer.

6. **Competition for capital will increase as the demand for it rises.** There are indications that the increased demand for capital from the newly liberated Eastern European countries, as well as the Commonwealth of Independent States (various republics of the former Soviet Union), will intensify competition in the capital market. More countries are viewing the equity capital from MNCs as a viable alternative to the sovereign debt crisis of the 1980s, when private sources of capital became scarce and costly.

7. **Slowly, but steadily, national borders are losing their effectiveness in dealing with MNCs.** There is evidence that a new global pattern is evolving that defies traditional description. For example, in June 1992 a U.S. citizen, Raffi Ovanesian, became foreign minister of Armenia. One month later another U.S. citizen, Milan Panic, was elected premier by the Yugoslav parliament. The top executives of some well-known firms are also foreign citizens.

    For many years, Europeans firms have been preparing for a borderless market, in which the nationality of a manager has no bearing on his or her selection and cross-national career advancement is the norm. The head of Michellin-Okmoto (a Japanese subsidiary of Michellin of France) is German. The manager of the Hyatt Hotel in Jakarta, Indonesia, was Danish, and Electrolux (a Swedish firm) had a French director.

8. **International linkage among countries is creating a higher degree of interdependency, characterized by an increasing volume of FDI.** Between 1965 to 1990, the FDI rose tremendously. While the U.S. FDI has been increasing, investment in the United States by other countries has also been on the rise. From 1965 to 1990, the U.S. FDI increased nearly ten times. In contrast, FDI in the United States expanded more than 40 times. By 1990, FDI in the United States was almost equal to the U.S. investment abroad.

    International linkage has been growing since World War II. It began with successive reduction of international trade restrictions, which increased world trade. The interdependency through trade was followed by financial integration, which was aided by recycling the Organization of Petroleum Exporting Countries (OPEC) surplus during the 1970s. Now we are in the third phase of international linkage, often referred to as **globalization**. Characteristic of this phase is FDI made by MNCs and the technological alliance among them. A significant and growing portion of world trade involves intra-firm trade.

It is becoming very difficult, if not impossible, to identify the national origin of many products. Today, products are originated in one area and developed further in another. This is a sign of the changing times and is due to the globalization of business. Managing in such a complex and diverse environment creates challenges for MNCs. In this context, the

TABLE 3.4 Comparison of Four Types of Management Behavior

Mentality	Characteristics
Ethnocentric	Home country mentality Views foreign market as extension of global market Products are produced for home market Subsidiaries are identified by the nationality of the home country Key managerial positions are reserved for home country executives
Polycentric	Host country mentality Production within subsidiary markets Headquarters control is exercised through financial reports Decentralized decisions usually made by autonomous subsidiaries Local managers cannot aspire to a high-level executive position at headquarters
Centocentric	Classical global mentality Views the world as one market Products are designed at home for the world market Headquarters maintains central control with global responsibilities Important decisions are made for the subsidiaries at headquarters
Geocentric	Views company as global with no geographic center Thinks globally and acts locally Integrates an independent network of worldwide decentralized and specialized companies Participative decision making based on total company performance

different types of management behavior is an issue of main concern. In this evolutionary process, a MNC may exhibit four major types of management behavior: ethnocentric (or home country mentality), polycentric (or host country mentality), centocentric (or classical global mentality), and geocentric (or supranational mentality). The type of behavior represents the managerial mentality and attitude of a MNC. These behaviors are summarized in Table 3.4.

Ethnocentric Mentality

The ethnocentric firm views foreign markets as an extension of the domestic market. It ascribes superiority to everything from its home country and inferiority to everything foreign. Products are produced for the home market and are exported only as an additional source of revenue. The headquarters and affiliates of the firm are identified by the nationality of the home country. Key managerial positions, both at headquarters and the subsidiaries, are reserved for home country executives. A foreign assignment is not considered a very desirable appointment and does not advance the professional career of a manager. In short, an ethnocentric firm views itself as a domestic firm with foreign extensions.

Polycentric Mentality

In a polycentric firm, the prevailing attitude is that foreigners are different and difficult to understand. The assumption, therefore, is that the management of foreign affiliates should be left to local people. Products are produced for local consumption in facilities that are operated by host country personnel. Headquarters exercises control through financial reports. The firm could best be characterized as a confederation of loosely connected, semi-autonomous affiliates. Although on the surface it may appear that a polycentric firm, operating in multiple markets and acting as a local company in every market, is a highly internationalized enterprise, this is far from the truth. In a polycentric firm, local managers cannot aspire to a high-level executive position at the headquarters. Consequently, local managers are pulled into a virulent ethnocentric mentality. The local responsiveness of polycentric firms results in inefficient operations. Attention to local markets, and the demands of local government, creates an infrastructure within each subsidiary that ignores internal market opportunities. Manufacturing facilities are often underutilized, and the full benefits of economies of scale are not realized.

Centocentric Mentality

A centocentric firm assumes that nations are more similar in tastes and preferences than they are different. The assumption is that the differences could be made inconsequential by providing better quality products at lower prices compared with domestic products. Therefore, uniform products could be produced at centers for distribution to all. A centocentric firm require mores central control. Headquarters maintains control by assigning products or a business manager with global responsibilities. The firm is still identified with the home country, and business managers are home country nationals, as are other key executives. The home country culture and the culture of headquarters permeate the firm and all its subsidiaries. Only local managers who identify with the dominant culture of the headquarters are promoted to key positions. Important strategic decisions are made at the headquarters, and subsidiaries are expected to implement them. Decreasing trade barriers and improvements in telecommunications technologies and transportation allow the use of the classical global strategy, which views the world as one market. With the centocentric attitude, treating the world as one market enables the firm to take advantage of economies of scale in design, manufacturing, and marketing of products and research and development. Products are often designed and manufactured at home for the world market.

Geocentric Mentality

The success of a centocentric MNC, and the power it exerts on local markets, cause resentment and apprehension. Central control over subsidiaries, which dictates major decisions from the home office and identification with the home country, produces additional concerns. To offset the perceived power and control of global firms over local markets, host governments restrict their operations. They also pressure MNCs for more local investment and technology transfer by enacting local content laws. Some governments demand changes in personnel policies to allow for local representation in the managerial ranks. Moreover, the global market has proved to be more heterogeneous than centocentric MNCs had assumed. The volatility of the global economic and political environment is an additional impetus for global firms to become locally responsive. Add to this the improvements in manufacturing technologies that enable more efficient and flexible manufacturing and smaller batch production, and the stage is set for localized strategies.

There are two simultaneous demands on a global firm. On the one hand, it is expected to be locally responsive. On the other hand, maintaining worldwide competitiveness requires a higher degree of efficiency, which is possible only with a globally integrated operation. This gives rise to the emerging geocentric firm. A geocentric firm views itself as a global company with no geographic center, in which no nationality dominates the firm. Viewing the world as its home, a geocentric firm strives for flexibility and efficiency globally. A successful geocentric firm thinks globally and acts locally. It integrates an interdependent network of decentralized and specialized companies worldwide. Perhaps the best way to describe a geocentric firm is to look at the operation of one.

A good example of a geocentric firm is Asea Brown Bovery (ABB), a global electrical systems equipment company. ABB started as a Swedish firm. It later merged with a Swiss company and made Zurich its headquarters. ABB's annual revenues exceed $25 billion, and it employs 240,000 people around the world. It generates $7 billion in annual revenues from North America with 40,000 employees. It has 10,000 employees in India and 10,000 in South America. Therefore, Percy Barnevik, president and chief executive officer, describes ABB as company with no geographic center and with a geocentric mentality.

FUTURE PATHS TO MULTINATIONALISM

The internationalization of goods and services is increasing rapidly. Each MNC is trying to gain its share of the competitive global market. Today, multinational firms are applying their own methods to reach worldwide markets. The future of the MNC looks promising due to increased global communication, political stability, and technological advancement in the global economy. Hopefully, MNCs will continue to improve their strategy and planning to penetrate the global market and adapt to the international environment using the strategies discussed in this chapter. The outlook is promising for the MNC, and the hope is for a future in which the world is one community, without racial or political boundaries.

REFERENCES

1. Donald A. Ball and Wendell H. McCulloch, Jr., *International Business: Introduction and Essentials,* 4th edition (Homewood, Ill.: Irwin), 1990, p. 18.
2. Arthur G. Bedeian, *Management* (New York: Dryden), 1986, pp. 639–643.
3. Robert Gilpin, *US Power and the Multinational Corporation* (New York: Basic Books), 1975, p. 44.
4. Lee L. Morgan, in *The Case for the Multinational Corporation,* Carl H. Madden (Ed.) (New York: Praeger), 1977, p. IX.
5. Donald A. Ball and Wendell H. McCulloch, Jr., *International Business: Introduction and Essentials,* 4th edition (Homewood, Ill.: Irwin), 1990, p. 10.
6. Karl E. Ettinger (Ed.), *International Handbook of Management* (New York: McGraw-Hill), 1965.
7. Department of Trade and Industry, *The Impact of Foreign Direct Investment on the United Kingdom* (London: HMSO), 1973.
8. Jack N. Behrman, *National Interests and the Multinational Enterprise* (Englewood Cliffs, N.J.: Prentice-Hall), 1970.
9. David Gerstenhaber, "Japan's Markets Are Ripe for US Exports," *Wall Street Journal,* p. 19, September 14, 1987.
10. Edith Terry, Bill Javentski, Stephen Dryden, and John Pearson, "A Free-Trade Milestone: The U.S.–Canada Pact Is on a Scale with the EC," *Business Week,* pp. 52–53, October 19, 1987.
11. Barbara Slavin, James B. Treece, and Michael Berger, "U.S. Companies Are Back in Force in the Gulf," *Business Week,* p. 79, October 19, 1987.
12. Robert Black, Multinationals in Contention: Responses at Governmental and International Levels, talk given at the Conference Board on Multinational Corporate Responsibility Project, New York, 1982.
13. Roger Thurow, "U.S. Exodus Touches Many South Africans," *Wall Street Journal,* p. 36, November 6, 1986.
14. Doron P. Levin and Roger Thurow, "GM to Leave South Africa and Sell Operations," *Wall Street Journal,* p. 3, October 21, 1986.
15. "Honeywell, Warner Communications Plan to Sell South African Operations," *Wall Street Journal,* p. 5, October 23, 1986.
16. Dennis Kneale, "IBM to Pull out of South Africa; Other U.S. Firms Weighing Move," *Wall Street Journal,* p. 3, October 22, 1986.
17. Lee Smith, "South Africa: Time to Stay—or Go?" *Fortune,* p. 46, August 4, 1986.
18. Dennis Kneale, "GM, IBM and Others Departing South Africa Are Faulted for Plans to Continue Sales There," *Wall Street Journal,* p. 2, October 24, 1986.
19. John Fayerweather, *International Business Strategy and Administration,* 2nd edition (Cambridge, Mass.: Ballinger), 1982, p. 122.
20. Michael Z. Brooke and H. Lee Remmers (Eds.), *The Multinational Company in Europe: Some Key Problems* (Ann Arbor: University of Michigan), 1972, p. 82.
21. Raymond Vernon and Louis T. Wells, Jr., *Manager in the International Economy* (Englewood Cliffs, N.J.: Prentice-Hall), 1981, p. 121.
22. Endel-Jakob Kolde, *Environment of International Business* (Boston: Kent), 1981, p. 370.
23. Stefan Robock and Kenneth Simmonds, *International Business and Multinational Enterprises* (Homewood, Ill.: Irwin), 1983, p. 255.
24. Bateman Thomas and Carol Zeithaml, *Management: Function and Strategy.* (Homewood, Ill.: Irwin), 1990, pp. 294–295.
25. Lester R. Brown, *State of the World* (New York: W.W. Norton), 1991, p. 7.

BIBLIOGRAPHY

Batstone, Roger and Wil Lepkowski, "World Bank Plan to Prevent Chemical Disaster," *Technology Review,* pp. 65–66, April 1986.

Bedeian, Arthur G., Michael Z. Brooke, and H. Lee Remmers (Eds.), *Multinational Company in Europe: Some Key Problems* (New York: Praeger), 1979.

Buchholz, Rogene A., *Business Environment and Public Policy* (Englewood Cliffs, N.J.: Prentice-Hall), 1986.

Fayerweather, John, *International Business Strategy and Administration,* 2nd edition (Cambridge, Mass.: Ballinger), 1982.

Gerstenhabcr, David, "Japan's Markets Are Ripe for US Exports," *Wall Street Journal,* p. 19, September 14, 1987.

Gilpin, Robert, *US Power and the Multinational Corporation* (New York: Basic Books), 1975.

Hymer, Stephen Herbert, *The International Operations of National Firms* (Cambridge, Mass.: MIT Press), 1976.

Ingram, James C., *International Economics* (New York: John Wiley), 1983.

Morgan, Lee L., *The Case for the Multinational Corporation* (New York: Praeger), 1977.

Negandi, Anant R. and B. Rajaram Baliga, *Guest for Survival and Growth: A Comparative Study of American, European and Japanese Multinationals* (New York: Praeger), 1979.

Robock, Stefan H. and Kenneth Simmonds, *International Business and Multinational Enterprises* (Homewood, Ill.: Irwin), 1983.

Rolf, Sidney E., *The International Corporation* (Istanbul: International Chamber of Commerce), 1969.

Rutenberg, David P., *Multinational Management* (Boston: Little, Brown), 1982.

Said, Abdul A. and Luiz R. Simmons, "The Politics of Transition," in *The New Sovereigns: Multinational Corporations as World Powers,* Abdul A. Said and Luiz R. Simmons (Eds.) (Englewood Cliffs, N.J.: Prentice-Hall), 1975.

Vernon, Raymond, "Economic Sovereignty at Bay," *Foreign Affairs,* 47:114, 1968.

THE EFFECTS OF CULTURE ON INTERNATIONAL MANAGEMENT

ABSTRACT

Management must recognize that there is no right or wrong or good or bad cultures—they are only different. Most people around the world feel strongly about their culture. Most feel that their culture is the best. Tools to aid managers in developing sensitivity to host countries are presented in this chapter. Firms that want to attract and retain good staff with appropriate skills must focus on continuous professional and managerial development through training and job rotation. Managers must be very professional, highly qualified, flexible, deployable, multiskilled, multidisciplinary, and cross-cultural. Firms will need to move managers around the organization to transfer technology and culture and enhance cohesion. Employees must be loyal to the firm as a whole and transfer its technology, methods, and culture to every dimension and unit.[1]

CHAPTER OBJECTIVES

1   To define culture and its implications

2   To understand cultural differences and the difficulties managers face in an international market

3   To become aware of the different elements that make up culture and possible ways of dealing with them

4   To identify different styles of management leadership and different business cultures across the world

5   To understand the importance of Hofstede's study

CASE STUDY
To Be Successful at International Business, You Need Planning Patience

Dick Thorton of Coca Cola, who trains executives and teaches cultural awareness, also suggests keeping a positive attitude. Spend an overseas flight preparing for business, not worrying about jet lag.

Once there, "politeness is very important," Thornton says. "We're a very aggressive culture." Recognize that deals may take longer to finish, and get-acquainted time is often expected before business talk begins.

Patience pays. It took Mary Thomas and her colleagues three years to win an account from a French customer. "We were persistent," says Thomas, a chemist at Dow North America in Midland, Michigan.

Craig Schroll, a safety consultant from East Earl, Pennsylvania, says business abroad takes more time and planning. "Before my first trip to Australia, I cultivated contacts for close to a year."

Other Tips for Success

1. Keep a journal and reread it before returning to a country. Note things that might be forgotten, such as names of a client's children and any gifts given, plus travel tips.

2. Learn basic words and phrases in the native language, such as please, thank you, yes, no, and where is…, suggests Chuck Blethen, a consultant with St. Paul-based Quality Institute International. "Those things in any language are worth their weight in gold." Blethen speaks French, Spanish, and German fairly well and has studied Arabic and Russian.

3. Abide by the practices of the country you are in. Daniel Rickett of Atlanta, a human resources consultant, says, "when you really respect people, that will come through."

4. David Sundvall of El Paso suggests keeping an open mind and being willing to adapt. "That's the fun part," says Sundvall, who is in charge of Latin American sales for Komax, which makes water-processing systems. "You never know what's going to happen."

Source: Chris Swingle, "Patience, Grace Avert Culture Clash," *USA Today,* p. 5E, September 14, 1993.

INTRODUCTION

In the 1990s and beyond, conducting business internationally will be the way that American businesses reposition themselves as leaders in the global market. To succeed in the international arena, American managers must have a firm grasp of the intricacies of the culture of a host country. Understanding cultural norms and customs is of paramount importance to conducting fruitful international business.

An international organization involves operations in more than one country. The greater the number of countries with which a company deals, the more international it is. Another aspect of international business is that it opens up new markets for existing firms. Once a firm has done all it can to establish itself in one country, it should consider moving into a new country and a new market.

Yet another aspect of international business is that it gives the people in a firm the opportunity to learn the way of life in a different country. The culture of that particular country can have either a positive or a negative effect on the firm, depending on how well briefed the transition is from home country to host country. If the management of a company, or even the workers, do not have a clear understanding of a country and its customs, the operation of the company can be negatively affected. On the other hand, a good understanding of a country's culture can save a company possible embarrassment and may even help it in some ways. The purpose of this chapter is to show how understanding culture can help companies doing business overseas.

DEFINITION OF CULTURE

Culture in the organizational context can be defined as "the sum of a group or nation's way of thinking, believing, feeling, and acting. It is the way of life for a group of people."[2] Culture may also be defined as intellectual production and the climate of opinion in which it takes place.[3] In 1986, Barney defined organizational culture as "a complex set of values, beliefs, assumptions, and symbols that define the way in which a firm conducts its business."[4] As Barney noted, the existence of multiple possible contradictory cultures within the same organization makes the management of culture all the more difficult.

All of the preceding definitions of culture have certain elements in common. Culture is defined here as the patterns of behavior that are attributed to the members of any given society, learned and passed on from generation to generation. It includes the language, religion, and customs of a group of people, along with their feelings and attitudes. It can be passed on by parents, the government, schools, and society in general. Culture is conservative in that it resists serious change and promotes continuity. Because culture is shared and passed on, it should be noted that each culture has a history, and everything that happens becomes a part of the cumulative history of a culture.

Georg Simmel, an early German philosopher, divided culture into two major categories: objective culture and subjective culture.[3] Objective culture is the realm of seemingly endless cultural products. It exists only to be reinforced by people, who use it for personal growth and enrichment. To become cultivated, a person must internalize the objective culture. This internalization is called subjective culture.

POSSIBLE CULTURAL DIFFICULTIES FOR MANAGERS OF MULTINATIONAL CORPORATIONS

The sociocultural differences that managers of multinational corporations (MNCs) face present a difficult challenge. This is due to several facts. The first is that culture in itself is extremely difficult to both define and describe. It is also very difficult to methodically deal with a phenomenon of such substance in real situations. The second fact, which is crucial, is that culture is intimately linked to **personality** and the way people think, act, react, etc. It is important to understand that culture affects almost everything that a person does in his or her daily life. This is because culture is learned as opposed to inherited. Culture influences personality development in terms of how people interact with one another, social patterns, and morals and beliefs. In fact, it affects a person's entire view of the world, starting with childhood experiences. It encompasses all of the influencing factors, both central and peripheral, in a person's environment, passive (e.g., one's home) as well as active (e.g., mass media). Because culture is so incorporated in the way people perceive themselves, problems of unbelievable proportion result when we try to understand persons from another culture.

As an example, consider two people from two different cultures, each trying to understand, at least on the surface, the other's culture and each seeking some sort of gain from the encounter (e.g., economic profit, social status, political achievement, etc.). This is a situation where two totally different perceptions of being and life itself meet. One person can study the other culture, and maybe even visit it for a time, and eventually come to believe that he or she understands the other person. In reality, however, that person will never truly understand the underlying foundation of the other's way of life. He or she might be able to react in an appropriate way (i.e., respond in a way that creates the desired response from the other person) on an isolated occasion or in an individual interaction, but will never be able to more deeply understand and live in the other culture. The power of a person's experiences, starting in childhood, is too strong, because these experiences are the essence of each individual's entire being.

To elaborate further, an international student who comes to the United States usually suffers from adjusting to life in a different culture. It is a stressful and troublesome situation. After living and studying in a foreign culture for some time, similar discomfort occurs upon returning home. American students in other countries share similar problems.

Time is one of the most dominant factors in many Western countries, even though it may not be thought of in that way. In fact, time describes how people live during an ordinary day. Time is merely a way of dividing the events or periods in one's life. In concrete terms, time does not exist in reality; it is an abstract phenomenon that takes on a concrete form when applied to daily life. It is only through the process of assigning numbers to periods of our life that we choose to call a period of time a "day." Time totally rules what people do, and life in Western culture cannot exist without it. To say that somewhere a culture exists that does not use time is probably an overstatement. Time is a concept that is probably created early in the development of a culture as it becomes more complex and structured. It is an example of a phenomenon that has become an integral part of every culture.

This does not imply that managers of MNCs should not attempt to understand and adapt to other cultures, or there obviously would be no international trade. It does, however, indicate the tremendous difficulties herein. A reasonable course of action would be to use a contingency approach in the truest sense, which means that nothing can be taken for granted. Every aspect must be subject to assessment and analysis in searching for ways to deal with a situation. For example, when operating in a foreign country, it should be assumed that the employees will differ from the more familiar domestic workers in all aspects of their day-to-day jobs. Employee relations, however, are relatively easier to overlook and control than, for example, factors in the remote environment, such as government restrictions and procedures.

Managers of MNCs can benefit by seeking help from colleagues with expertise in a foreign country, who have lived there and studied the culture. Such assistance may prevent obvious mistakes in establishing business procedures (e.g., not refusing a cup of coffee, not marketing a product under an inappropriate name, etc.). Perhaps the most valuable asset for managers of MNCs is the ability to recognize that they do not know enough about the culture in which they are working.

ELEMENTS OF CULTURE

Some of the major elements of culture are briefly discussed in this section.

Language Is a Key to a Culture*

Americans have a tendency not to realize how difficult a language is, and to have expectations that are too high for the amount of time they have allotted to it.

---

* *Source:* "Language Is the Key to Culture," *USA Today,* September 14, 1993.

This statement by John Ratcliffe, president of Diplomatic Services in Arlington, Virginia, illustrates that learning a foreign language is vital, and books, tapes, and schools do not offer fluency. Learning even key phrases is often quite a task, especially in a short period, and trying to master a language in a matter of weeks is virtually impossible. Despite the difficulties, learning a foreign language is becoming a necessity, because the future of management is truly global. Jeanie Watts, a program manager for the Monetary Institute for International Studies, states, "Non-verbal communication is important in every culture." Although a manager may be unable to master the language, learning gestures and other forms of communication is just as important.

Two Different Views on Learning a Language

Language Training. Many companies encourage, but do not require, studying the language study before an employee goes abroad. AT&T accommodates its people (including spouses) with private tutoring or Berlitz classes. Some companies arrange for continuing language instruction once a family arrives in a new country.

New Emphasis on Language. Although most companies do not offer language training that goes much beyond "total immersion" speed-learning techniques, more are making stronger efforts to recruit people who are bi- or multilingual. According to Larry Kroh, director of human resources at Coca Cola, when his department searches its database to identify people to fill overseas posts, the first choice is often those who speak more than one language.

A popular joke in the international business community attests to a rather serious problem:

What is a person called who speaks three languages?
A person who speaks three languages is trilingual.

What is a person called who speaks two languages?
A person who speaks two languages is bilingual.

What is a person called who speaks one language?
A person who speaks one language is called an American.

This indicates the severity of the language problem that many American MNCs face. Until recently, Americans have been content to believe that English is the universal language, which everyone is obliged to learn. To a certain extent, this is true, in that many foreigners learn English as a second or third language. This gives them an advantage over Americans, however, who often are less willing to recognize the need for a second language.

Many Americans feel self-sufficient and believe that they do not need another language. For example, American students generally do not make an effort to get to know international students or faculty and learn about their cultures. The inability to speak a foreign language and the lack of interest in learning a second language could have far-reaching implications for Americans who travel to other countries. The spoken language of a particular society is the key to its culture.

In every country of the world, a different culture has evolved and is still evolving because of the changing habits and desires of different generations. The key to unlocking the secrets of these ever-changing cultures is language. Language can be broken down into verbal and nonverbal communication. A manager who has mastered a foreign language can use this skill to gather information and to communicate on both a corporate and a social level without a translator.

Body language is also very important. It can include anything from a handshake to the way a person stands. Language reflects not only the nature and mental processes of a culture, but its intrinsic values as well.[5] Exploring a culture requires learning its language first in order to fully understand its people. MNCs that attempt to diversify their interests in the international market sometimes make a grave mistake by not selecting managers who have spent time learning the language and therefore the culture of the host country. If Chevrolet had such a manager in its Mexican organization, he or she might have changed the name of the Nova model; it was a dismal failure, because in Spanish "nova" means "no go."

As international business prospects expand throughout the world, along with improvements in information systems and transportation, language capability will be required to keep up with these improvements in the business world. Language can be defined not only as a communication tool, but also as a part of culture. Language encompasses two means of communication: verbal or nonverbal. Nonverbal communication differs in each country due to cultural differences. It includes gestures (such as forms of greeting), body language, and eye contact. In international business, language capability serves at least four functions:

1. It is important in collecting information and evaluating effort. It allows a manager to observe and hear what is happening on his or her premises.

2. It provides access to the local society. The ability to speak the local language facilitates communication in all interactions, even though English is widely spoken in other nations.

3. It is important in company communication. It can eliminate the added complication of communicating with employees or business associates through an interpreter.

4. It extends basic communication skills to include interpretation of context.

Without language capability, international business will undoubtedly encounter problems in foreign countries. Company documents and other materials must be translated into the local language or an interpreter must be used. Using an interpreter seems to be a simple answer but presents several disadvantages:

1. An interpreter could slow down negotiations or bring his or her own point of view into the discussion.
2. An interpreter costs $200 to $300 a day.
3. Using an interpreter can offend a foreign business executive who may think his or her English is good.
4. An interpreter poses a risk when discussing confidential information.

These disadvantages might be fatal to business negotiations. Therefore, foreign languages are taught as a second language to international business majors. Many Japanese firms currently teach English to new employees during their training period.

This investment in employees has not always proved successful, however. For example, Pokka Company introduced a soft drink in Japan called Pokali (sweat in Japanese), which was geared toward athletes. The product had the word "sweat" on the bottle. In the American market, people would be offended by the name. This is just one example of misuse of words by nonnative speakers.

Another well-documented case of miscommunication is the Jotter pen marketed worldwide by the Parker Pen Company. In many Latin American countries, "jotter" refers to a jockstrap, which is embarrassing to say the least. These are prime examples of the inability of major corporations to appropriately market their products, and the result was that sales suffered due to ignorance.[6]

Ignorance is used here because little if any time or money was spent on researching the culture. If these companies had even one corporate representative at their outlying operations who spoke the host country's language, both of these unfortunate incidents could have been avoided. The French and Germans, for example are very proud of their languages. Speaking English in Germany or France seldom elicits a response. However, this pride does not extend to intransigence in the French and German business communities. French, German, and Japanese businessmen have an edge over their American counterparts in international trade dealings. Why are the Japanese, Germans, and others doing so well in the international trade market? Perhaps the answer is because they not only learn another language, but also learn the customs, cultural elements, and geography of the various countries with which they do business, which gives them an advantage over their American counterparts. This may be one reason why German businesspeople often do better than Americans in the Japanese market. The combination of not being able to converse in the native language and unfamiliarity with the local traditions and customs can lead to serious misunderstandings.

If institutions, colleges, and universities do not encourage learning about other areas of the world, these problems will continue and may intensify in the future. Therefore, it is up to the academic community, including students, to do something about it. Without such a commitment, Americans will continue to be at a disadvantage in the world market.

In order for any company to be able to compete in the international arena, whether German, English, Japanese, French, or any other, it must spend adequate time exploring the culture of the host country. Arguably, the first and most important step in doing so is to learn the language. Without knowing the language, it is impossible to totally explore the cultural realm and therefore to prevent potential problems before they arise.

In conclusion, language capability is more than just vocabulary. It is the ability to communicate effectively, which includes cultural aspects. In order to overcome differences in language, an international manager must deal with both fact and interpretation of culture. Fact can be learned, whereas interpretation can be gained only through experience.

Traditional and Attitudinal Variations

There is no general agreement on the definition of culture, as discussed earlier. Every culture has its own set of attitudes and values, which influence its members. The customs and traditions of a society also establish norms for social conduct. Many managers often find conflicts between their own values and those of people from different cultural backgrounds. Some of these differences are discussed in the following paragraphs.

Values are shared beliefs that have been internalized by individuals; **attitudes** are the behaviors based on those values. Values and attitudes in the workplace, as seen by managers around the world, vary considerably and directly represent the business position of a country in the global market. In Australia, for example, managers have a strong human approach. They place a high value on honor, loyalty, tolerance, and compassion. This makes for strong ties between business partners, but limits expansion and innovation of new products worldwide. Japan, on the other hand, is always on the leading edge. The Japanese are trained to work hard to achieve their goals and become the best. Creativity flourishes through ambition passed down from generation to generation.

Americans place a higher value on the individual than the organization. Americans are more concerned with individual ability, skill, ambition, capability, and drive in getting the job done. This leads to competition within the workplace rather than with other organizations, which is one of the main reasons why American business is slipping internationally.

Customs and traditions can be important factors in business around the globe and may cause friction for managers who deal across international borders. Many managers in the United States incorrectly assume that customs and traditions are common around the world. They base decisions on their own knowledge instead of the host country's customs. Different words have different meanings in other cultures, and it is important to adapt products accordingly. Research in this area is very important, because it can uncover subtle differences in language and culture.

One problem U.S. managers encounter when dealing with companies in Spain or the Middle East in the workday. In America, the workday is from nine to five, five days a week. In Spain, however, the workday starts early in the morning and goes to midday. What Americans would call a lunch break, the Spanish call a siesta, which lasts for a couple of hours. During the siesta, managers as well as employees go home for their main meal and a nap. Afterward, they return to work until approximately eight or nine at night. In the Middle East, the workday is usually from eight in the morning until two in the afternoon, six days a week, and Friday is the day off. This simple cultural difference can cause problems in business organizations, and transactions can be delayed because of communication problems between organizations. This is but one simple example of a perceptual problem for American managers.

Other countries have different values and attitudes, as well as different customs and traditions. American managers and employees must be adequately educated and trained about the international market if they want to keep up with world competition.

Religion

Since most cultures use their religion as a reason for being, religion must be included as an element of culture. Most major holidays are tied to religion, and managers needs to understand how a country celebrates its religious holidays. The success of a MNC is, to some extent, influenced by the host culture's dominant religion. Managers must recognize that religious motivation affects results. For example, scheduling production during the Jewish, Muslim, or Hindu religious festivals is equal to scheduling production during the Christmas holiday in Christian countries. Top management must also be aware of the different roles of women in business in other countries.

As mentioned earlier, in most cultures religion is a reason for being. Therefore, it is important for international managers to be aware of the major religions of the world and their implications. Each religion has its own view about the creation of being, the form in which God is represented, and the purpose of existence. The main religions of the world—Christianity, Judaism, Islam, Hinduism, Buddhism, Animism, Confucianism, and Shintoism—each of which can have a major effect on international business, are discussed in the following sections.

Judaism

Although now practiced by only about 0.4% of the world's population, Judaism is the basis for Christianity and Islam. The main teaching of this religion is that the love for a single God complements the love for fellow human beings. Life should be lived according to the Ten Commandments, which Jews believe were given to the prophet Moses on Mt. Sinai. These commandments represent the laws of life. Jewish people focus on a future time, which they refer to as the "Kingdom of God," when all human activities, individual and collective, will reflect God. It is thought that Jews have been persecuted because their lifestyle is so different from and alien to people of other religions.

One implication for international managers is to be aware of dietary restrictions, so that inappropriate foods are not served. Managers should also know that Jews may find it unacceptable to work on Saturday, because it is their sabbath.

Christianity

Christianity is practiced by about 31% of the world's population and is predominant in such areas as North America and the United Kingdom. This religion has the most followers in the world. It was originally an offshoot of Judaism that developed about 2000 years ago. Christians worship a single God and believe that God sent his son to earth to die in order to redeem the sins of mankind.

Christianity can be divided into two main sects: Roman Catholic and Protestant. There are, however, other less dominant denominations. Protestants emphasize hard work and see it as their duty to accumulate wealth and be highly productive. From the international manager's point of view, these people should be relatively easy to motivate, as productivity and income are seen as blessings from God. Roman Catholics, on the other hand, view material gain as socially and morally unacceptable and emphasize modesty in all things.

Islam

Islam is the second largest religion in the world, and its followers see themselves as an extension of Christianity and Judaism. People who practice Islam are called Muslims. They worship one God, called "Allah." Muslim means "submitter" and Allah means "the only God"; Islam means "submitter to God's will." Muslims believe that by submitting to the will of God, they will find peace and fulfillment. They believe that God (Allah) communicated his will to the prophet Mohammed through the Qura'n (Book of Revelations). The Qura'n gives instructions for all aspects of life. In order to be a good Muslim, an individual must follow the Qura'n, which requires tremendous self-discipline.

In Islamic society, religious law extends to the economy and political and social systems. A major factor relating to business in this religion, which is extremely important for international managers to be aware of, is that charging interest on borrowed money is not permitted. Another aspect of Islam is that its followers are required to pray at five specific times throughout the day: before sunrise, early afternoon, mid-afternoon, after sunset, and nightfall. These set times for prayer are the chief religious discipline, and they are seen as the major route to spiritual purification. In areas where this religion predominates, a call to prayer will be heard at these times. Friday is the sabbath in Muslim countries.

Fasting is expected during the month of Ramadan, which can occur at any time of the year (because Islam follows the lunar calendar, which is 10 to 11 days shorter than the solar year). Fasting is abstinence from eating, drinking, smoking, or sexual activity between dawn and sunset. If Ramadan falls during the summer, fasting can be particularly difficult. It is thought to purify the body, test self-control, and evoke sympathy for the poor.

Another factor in Islam is that women play a significant role in society, although this role is restricted in some Muslim countries (i.e., Saudi Arabia and the Gulf states, to some degree).

The majority of Muslims are Sunnis or "traditionalists," and only 12 to 13% are Shiites. The Shiites are, however, a majority in Iran, Iraq, and Lebanon and are a strong political force in the Middle East. Shiites reject Western ideology and practices. A number of factors could affect the performance of a MNC in Muslim countries, and these will be discussed in greater detail in Chapter 10.

Hinduism

Hinduism is the primary religion of India and is 3000 years old. It is practiced by 13.39% of the world's population. Hindus' main belief is that the creation of the world is a continuing process shared by man. The stages of creation are carried out by three gods. At the end of each stage, Shiva (destroyer god) destroys the old world, and Brahma (god of creation) creates a new world. During each stage, Vishnu (savior) appears in human or some other form with special powers to help the human race with unsolvable problems. This cycle of stages is the basis for the Hindu belief in reincarnation. Because of this cyclical concept, time is considered infinite, and time schedules are not followed in predominantly Hindu areas.

Hindus believe that everyone is born with certain abilities at a certain stage. This stage and its respective abilities are determined by actions in past lives, which is the basis for what Hindus call the **caste** system. This system is the basis for the social divisions of labor and includes five classes:

1. **Brahmins:**   Intellectuals and priests, the most prestigious division (for example, professors, doctors, and clergy)

2. **Warriors:**   Landlords and politicians

3. **Merchants:**   Business merchants

4. **Peasants:**   Farmers and shepherds

5. **Outcastes:**   Unskilled manual laborers (for example, people who cremate the dead and other unskilled laborers)

In this religion, the transition into a different caste can only be made in a subsequent life. If bad deeds are committed in one's lifetime and punishment is required, the person is reincarnated into a lower caste. An international manager must realize that in this system it would be inappropriate to promote someone of a lower caste to a supervisory position over someone of a higher caste.

Another important aspect of this religion is **baradari**, which has to do with the delegation of authority within a family. The older generation has authority over the younger generation, and it is expected that any excess income should be shared with one's family. The closeness of Hindu families can lead to nepotism, where one family member seeks employment within his or her organization for another family member. This can lead to greater company loyalty, but can also cause serious problems if a family member is reprimanded or fired.

Buddhism

Buddhism is the religion of "those seeking to be awakened." Unlike Hinduism, there is no social segregation. Buddhism originated from a reformation of Hinduism in about 650 B.C. This philosophy is practiced in Southeast and Eastern Asia, India, and Japan by about 6.29% of the world's population. The basis for Buddhism is tolerance and spiritual equality. It started with the philosophies of Prince Siddartha, who became the Buddha, which means "awakened one." He revealed that there were three paths a person could take in life: self-indulgence, the middle path, or the path of self-mortification. Guatama showed that the middle path was the path to true happiness, because neither of the other two paths relieves suffering or brings wisdom or happiness, and according to Buddhists, relief from suffering is the true goal of life.

The ultimate goal of Buddhists is to achieve **nirvana**, which has two meanings:

1. Extinction of all craving, resentment, and covetousness, which will result in happiness
2. Release from all other reincarnations, which is the ultimate goal of both Hindus and Buddhists

One implication of this religion, therefore, is that Buddhists may be more difficult to influence because of their lack of interest in material possessions.

Confucianism

Confucianism is not exactly a religion, but more of a widely held philosophy which has shaped Chinese society for thousands of years. It is based on the teachings of Confucius, who taught that all people possess unselfish love for others. People who believe in this see the cultivation of this love as a reward in itself. Believers in Confucianism emphasize love, gentleness, and mutual respect, which is where bowing and politeness originate in these cultures. This philosophy glorifies hard work and thrift.

Shintoism

Shintoism is the religion of the majority of Japanese and, as far as is known, has no founder or book of principles. Shintoism, therefore, is based on legend that traces the foundation of Japan back to a cosmic act and gives the Emperor divine status. Even though there is no theology or organized worship, Shinto shrines are visited by thousands of people each day.

Animism

Animism is the oldest religion on earth and is practiced by African and Latin American societies. It involves the worship of both animate and inanimate phenomena and the belief that the world can be controlled by ritual and substances that have magical properties. For example, followers believe that an image of a person can be used to control that person and also believe that anything unusual can be accredited to magic, even to the extent of giving magic credit for advances in technology or product defects. It would be extremely difficult for a person from a more developed area to relate to these concepts, and management would face a very difficult challenge.

Material Culture

Material culture is the result of technology and is related to how a society organizes its economic activity. It is based on the different infra-structures in a country. Material culture, or lack of it, has an impact on business decisions, especially the level of technological development in a country.

Aesthetics

Aesthetics, as it applies to culture, refers to expression of the arts, especially the symbolism of form, music, and color. Choosing the wrong color or packaging may prove disastrous. Education is important to the international manager in terms of local employment and marketing, in particular because many companies that move abroad use local employees. The level of education will indicate how much training is needed. It is important to determine whether you are selling to an educated or an uneducated market, because this will indicate the type of marketing strategy that should be used.[7]

CASE STUDY
Cultural Training

The fast pace of change in today's global operating environment demands continuous training by MNCs throughout the careers of their executives. As a result, companies have greatly expanded their instructional offerings in recent years. Traditional pre-departure preparation for overseas assignments and a dollop of cross-cultural training are no longer viewed as sufficient by many MNCs, and they are adding substance to their programs.

IBM has three types of executive training programs. The first is a two- to three-week advanced management program designed for newly appointed executives. The program is conducted in the United States and Brussels and off-site in Tokyo and Sydney. Ideally, approximately 20 executives from multiple regions are invited to attend. "Part of the value of this training is to have people from different parts of the world spend time with each other," says Don Laidlaw, IBM director of Executive Resources and Development. The second program is a one-week executive seminar offered at the same locations for experienced executives who have not attended an executive development session for three to five years. Both programs combine sessions on management topics with discussions of international economics and politics. The third program, the International Executive Program, is considered one of the most prestigious at IBM. It is run once a year at company headquarters. Country general managers and functional heads from around the world are personally selected by IBM CEO [at the time] John Akers to spend ten days in seminar discussions sponsored by the chairman's office.

Source: "How MNC's Hone the Skills of Their Global Managers," *Business International,* p. 306.

GUIDANCE FOR INTERNATIONAL MANAGERS*

1. Always assume that a person prefers to be called by his or her surname, which is sometimes difficult to ascertain. For example, in China, the last name is written first. In Latin America, someone named Angelo Lomez Jardina would be addressed as "Mr. Lopez." It is therefore of utmost importance to be able to recognize the correct name to use when addressing someone. The answer may be to memorize or write down the surname of the person(s) you are about to meet.

2. Dress in an attire appropriate to the culture. American women may find that pants are unacceptable and wearing a skirt is more appropriate. If

---

Source: "How to Act Like a Native," *USA Today,* September 14, 1993.

women in the local culture wear saris, a visitor should consider wearing a loose fitting silky dress rather than a suit. Remember that shoes are not worn in certain places, such as a mosque.

3. Determine whether you will be conducting business in a high-context culture or a low-context culture. Americans work in M-time, which means time is of the essence and they stick to schedules. Asians tend to work in P-time, which means that they will take as long as is required to close a business deal. Make note of religious and national holidays, and do not schedule a visit during holiday periods, such as the Chinese New Year. Be aware of the differences.

4. In some countries, direct eye contact is considered to be impolite, which is the case in Japan. In England, on the other hand, not making eye contact is considered rude. In Asian or Arab countries, crossing your legs is seen as impolite, as is showing the sole of your shoe.

5. Many people exchange gifts when conducting business. In some cultures, such as the United States, this is consider a bribe, while in others, such as China, it is expected. When giving a gift, make sure that it is not offensive. For example, in Japan, giving anything that is a multiple of four is considered an offensive, because four signifies death.

6. In England, holding up two fingers in the opposite direction of the peace sign is considered the same as holding up the middle finger in the United States. In Australia, the thumbs-up sign is considered to be rude. Nodding your head in Greece means no, whereas in India it means yes. Beckoning someone with your index finger is insulting to most Middle Easterners. Crossing your fingers is considered wishing good luck in the United States and Europe, but is offensive in Paraguay. Folding your arms across your chest is a sign of arrogance and pride in Finland and is disrespectful in Fiji.

7. In the majority of Middle Eastern countries, any food not eaten at a meal indicates to the host that it was not to your liking, and thus it is advisable to take only what you can finish. In China, on the other hand, it is a positive gesture to leave some food, because it indicates to the host that he or she was generous in the amount given, since it was impossible to finish. Do not eat with your left hand when dining with clients from Malaysia or India.

HOFSTEDE'S STUDY AND ITS IMPLICATIONS FOR AMERICAN MANAGERS

In 1980, Gerte Hofstede empirically proposed four dimensions of national cultures.[8] These four dimensions can be used to analyze cultures and the differences between them in order to function more effectively in a foreign environment.

The first dimension is **power distance**, or the extent to which the people in a society generally accept a hierarchical or unequal distribution of power among individuals and institutions. There are vast differences between countries that accept high degrees of power distance and those that do not. The United States does not have a high degree of power distance in business or society. Foreign businesspeople would be well advised to treat American businesspeople as equals and not show undue humility or present themselves with an air of superiority. In an Asian country, where the degree of power distance is higher, it would be appropriate for Americans to treat their hosts with more humility and formality than they do their American colleagues.

The second cultural dimension is **uncertainty avoidance**, or the degree to which a person feels threatened by ambiguous and risky situations and tries to minimize or avoid them. The United States is apparently a nation of risk takers, because the uncertainty avoidance degree is quite low. Korean managers, on the other hand, show a high degree of this trait. An American businessperson would do well to keep this in mind when trying to strike a deal in Korea; the less risky, the better.

The third dimension identified by Hofstede is **individualism–collectivism**. This is defined as the extent to which a society expects individuals to take care of themselves and their immediate families. It includes the extent to which a society accepts individualism rather than conformity. In most countries other than the United States, individuals take care of themselves along with their extended families. This is particularly true in the Middle East, India, and most Latin American countries. In the United States, it is not unusual for an individual to only take care of himself or herself and disregard family. Family seems to be more important in other countries, compared to America. In fact, many countries place a greater importance on interpersonal relationships than America does. For example, in Guatemala, business must not be discussed until personal and family matters are completed. In Greece, business may be conducted into the evening at a local tavern and may well include spouses. On the other hand, some of these countries do not place as high a degree of importance on individualism as America does. Individualism is encouraged in the United States, but is seen as a sign of immaturity in Japan.

The final dimension proposed by Hofstede is **masculinity/femininity**. This is the degree to which a society emphasizes assertiveness, acquisition of money, material possessions, and insensitivity to feelings as dominant values. This trait is high in America, higher even than in Korea, where authoritarianism is advocated in a patriarchal, male-dominated society. Americans seems to like material returns more than most other cultures, but they do not participate in the practice of exchanging gifts at business meetings, as is customary in Japan.[8]

Certainly these dimensions are not the only factors that come into play when doing business abroad. Many other societal aspects and customs must be considered, such as the use and misuse of gestures and how to address a foreign host. Above all, if businesspeople can show their hosts that they have studied and gained an understanding of the local culture, they will present themselves as thoughtful and respectful. This will help any American to succeed in the international business arena.

CULTURAL SENSITIVITY

The focus of this section is the importance of cultural sensitivity and empathy in dealing with different nations throughout the world.

Culture is a deep-rooted social phenomenon that continues to differentiate nations. Cultural sensitivity may mean the difference between success and failure in an international business venture. Managers must recognize the value of assuming a geocentric attitude in managing people from dissimilar nations. By understanding the managerial implications of differing cultural circumstances, one can begin to develop a managerial style that is appropriate for the society with which he or she must cope. The effectiveness of a particular managerial style or action is dependent upon the cultural circumstances a manager faces.

As discussed in the preceding section, Hofstede attempted to define a set of general dimensions on which cultures tend to differ, which could be used to both describe a given national culture and to compare two or more national cultures. He proposed four dimensions:

1. **Individualism–collectivism:** The degree to which a society's members demonstrate concern for themselves and their immediate families (high individualism) versus concern for a much larger societal group, such as a tribe or village (high collectivism)

2. **Power distance:** The degree to which imbalances in power, status, and wealth are tolerated within a society

3. **Uncertainty avoidance:** The extent to which societal members act to avoid uncertainty

4. **Masculinity/femininity:** The extent to which societies distinguish between male and female social roles

Culture shapes one's perception of the world. It is difficult at best, if not impossible, to explain or predict the behavior of a group of people, particularly when dealing with people from other cultures. Realistic cultural empathy better enables a person to see the world from someone else's perspective. This holds true for people of all cultures.

In the United States, words communicate intent. In many other countries, words communicate feeling. The different use of words in different cultures is a major cause of conflict between countries.

People from different cultures not only behave differently but also think differently. Cultural empathy is important in order to appreciate the impact of culture on thought patterns.

LIMITATION OF THE HOFSTEDE STUDY

Did Hofstede meant to suggest that individuals within a given society exhibit identical values and attitudes? The answer to this question is no. All people in a given culture do not think and act the same. People tend to differ from their own culture or group in terms of certain issues. The Hofstede study, however, was based on significant similarities within a group and significant dissimilarities within a group, and not a mixture of the two.

Hofstede's work was not designed to prescribe motivational techniques, leadership styles, and organizational structures for every organization in a given society. Instead, it is a format or base that can be used to understand various cultures and to implement or learn managerial techniques that will work in different cultures.

National cultural differences are relevant to the practicing manager. A multinational manager must use different managerial techniques within different cultures and adjust to the structure of the society. There may be hundreds of adjustments to be made, but in the long run a better understanding of the different culture will be gained.

In summary, one of the most difficult aspects of management is understanding cultural differences. As discussed, it is also difficult to understand different groups within a nation. Four areas were addressed in this chapter in order to understand culture and cultural differences: (1) values and attitudes, (2) customs and traditions, (3) language and communication, and (4) religion and other social institutions.

The convergence theory of management was popular in the 1950s and 1960s. It was developed because managers assumed that increased interaction and communication would produce a managerial standard throughout the world. Going one step further, Hofstede tried to form the basis for this theory by identifying four dimensions of culture: (1) individualism–collectivism, (2) power distance, (3) uncertainty avoidance, and (4) masculinity/femininity. These dimensions are valuable when dealing with motivation, leadership, and organizational design. Although Hofstede's research still raises questions and doubts, it is a foundation for what could become a universal management system that would allow the world to work in unison.

CULTURAL IMPLICATIONS A MANAGER NEEDS TO KNOW

In addition to recognizing the cultural dimensions that differentiate societies, an international manager, according to Hofstede, must decide on the proper managerial style and the appropriate behavior to accommodate these cultural conditions. A manager must address motivation, leadership, and organizational structure.

Motivating subordinates to achieve company objectives is one of the most important responsibilities of a manager. Although individuals from different countries value different things, some generalizations can be made. For example, people in the United States are more individualistic and are motivated by monetary rewards. The extent to which a country promotes individualism or collectivism is relevant when considering motivational techniques. In contrast to the individualism in the United States, Japan is a highly collective society, and its people are committed to group accomplishment. Individuals strive to receive recognition from their work group rather than monetary rewards.

Uncertainty avoidance and masculinity/femininity also influence motivational technique. Societies with weak uncertainty avoidance and highly masculine characteristics tend to take more risks and are motivated by trying to fulfill their need for achievement. In these societies, a manager should provide challenging tasks and relatively high-level goals.

In contrast, societies with strong uncertainty avoidance and feminine characteristics find an environment that is structured, well-defined, and secure to be highly rewarding. A manager who reduces ambiguity and uncertainty in working conditions may be highly regarded in this type of society. For example, worker self-management will not work well in this type of cultural condition, as in Yugoslavia, for example.

DIFFERENCES IN LEADERSHIP STYLES ACROSS THE WORLD

Leadership can be defined as the ability of a person to inspire others to do task-related activities. However, the responsibilities of a manager and a leader are not always the same. Motivation is only one component of leadership. In addition to being a motivator, the responsibilities of a leader also include providing direction and inspiration for subordinates.

Research on leadership indicates that there is no one "best way" to lead. Many factors come into play, including the values of subordinates. Two of Hofstede's dimensions of culture, individualism–collectivism, and power distance, are relevant to leadership.

People in countries that measure high in terms of individualism like work that rewards individual effort. This does not mean, however, that they do not want some structure. Individuals from these countries prefer management programs that establish objectives and provide guidelines for reaching those objectives. On the other hand, individuals from collective societies prefer to be rewarded for group performance. Management should promote group cohesiveness and set group norms for high productivity.

People in countries that score high in power distance, such as China, prefer a more autocratic management style over one that is participatory.

Subordinates believe that a superior cannot do his or her job if the subordinates are included in the decision-making process.

COMMUNICATION AND ITS SIGNIFICANCE IN INTERNATIONAL BUSINESS

There are many aspects to be covered when studying culture in international business. One significant aspect of culture is communication. Language is the primary means of communication, and it penetrates all dimensions of a culture. It reflects the nature, mental processes, and values, as well as human behavior, of the culture from which it originates. Language is defined as the aspect of human behavior that involves the use of vocal sounds in meaningful patterns and, when they exist, corresponding written symbols to form, express, and communicate thoughts and feeling. Language training is an important part of cultural training for executives of MNCs on overseas assignments. As a part of this, it is essential to acquire the mental processes necessary to communicate well in a foreign cultural setting. Attempts have been made to develop an international language, but no standard has resulted, due in large part to insufficient interest.

When studying communication, it is important to cover low- and high-context cultures, nonverbal communication, and barriers to communication. In high-context cultures, feelings are not explicitly expressed. It is assumed that the other party understands the sentiment without discussion. In a low-context culture, communication is in the form of explicit codes and messages. Spoken words with explicit meanings are more dominant in these cultures. People in low-context cultures are usually more outspoken and expressive than people in high-context cultures. Nonverbal communication involves posture, eye contact, and many other silent forms of communication. Facial expression and body movement add meaning to the spoken message. For example, standing too far away in one culture might signify aloofness or lack of trust, whereas standing too close in another culture might indicate aggressiveness or hostility. It is advisable not to gesture with one's hands in many cultures. It is important to ensure that these differences in language do not become barriers to communication that result in incorrect translation of the message. Improper or ineffective communication, either sent or received, can cause problems and even failures for MNCs.

ORGANIZATIONAL DESIGN AND STRUCTURE

Two main topics are discussed in this section: organizational design, and power distance and uncertainty avoidance.

Organizational design is one of the most important tools for dealing with the complexity and diversity of any organization. The design of a company will determine its capacity for processing information as well as the flow of information and work throughout the company. Organizational design can be understood in terms of three components: (1) hierarchical relationships, (2) centralization or decentralization of decision making, and (3) formalization of the work process. Each of these components should be consistent with the culture in which a company operates.

Power distance and uncertainty avoidance are the two most relevant dimensions when talking about the development of an organizational design. As a general rule, societies with large power distance prefer a highly structured organizational design with very centralized decision making, whereas low power distance societies prefer a much less structured hierarchy with a decentralized decision-making process.

Uncertainty avoidance is seen to affect the structure of general work processes and thereby influences the level of formalization of the system. Weak uncertainty avoidance implies low formalization, whereas high uncertainty avoidance implies high formalization.

The type of organizational structure is implied when the power distance and uncertainty avoidance dimensions are combined. For example, a hierarchy structure is implied when large power distance and high uncertainty avoidance are combined. This type of organization would have a distinct chain of command in which decisions are made by top-level managers and employees follow a detailed set of rules and procedures. The second type of structure combines small power distance with high uncertainty avoidance. It could be called as a "well-oiled machine." This structure implies a less rigid chain of command than the hierarchy structure, but uses the same detailed set of rules for the work process. The third type is labeled a "family" organizational structure because it combines weak uncertainty avoidance and strong power distance. This structure provides for a strong leader who defines the work processes and organizational relationships as he or she sees fit. The final type of structure can be characterized as a "village market" design because it combines weak uncertainty avoidance and low power distance. It implies a structure in which very few rules govern the work process and with a very loose chain of command.

INDIVIDUAL ATTITUDES TOWARD THE GULF WAR

A brief overview of some of the cultural aspects of Iraq is provided in this section as a foundation for understanding how culture can be used as a weapon, as it was in the war between the United States and Iraq.

Iraq, formerly called Mesopotamia ("the land between two rivers"), is believed to be the site of the earliest human civilization. In fact, in the third millennium B.C. people known as Sumarians gathered into city-states and developed laws, writing, and arithmetic. Iraq's ancient history is replete with cultural advances as well as warfare. To understand the gestalt of Iraqi and other Middle Eastern cultures, it is necessary to understand the foundation on which they are built—the Islamic religion. Islam is the principal religion of the Middle East and dates back as far as 622 A.D. It has spread rapidly since that time, mainly because of its simplicity and the absence of racial discrimination (Islam promotes equality).

Islam means "submission of one's will to the will of God," and anyone who submits is referred to as a Muslim. Muslims believe that God is one, eternal, just, and merciful. The one unforgivable sin according to Islamic scripture is idolatry. Only through prophets, the book of revelations, and angels can God's will be spoken. One prophet who exemplifies "submission" is Abraham, who attempted to sacrifice his son (Ismeal) by submitting to God's will. Other prophets include Isaac, Jacob, Moses, Jesus, and Mohammed, the final prophet.

Muslims adhere to five pillars, which are referred to as forms of worshipping God:

1. Recital of the creed by which Muslims testify sincerely that "there is no god but God and Mohammed is the Prophet of God"

2. Prayer five times a day according to a set pattern of words and body postures, with purification beforehand

3. Alms (charity) for the benefit of Muslims in need and for general strengthening of the community

4. Daytime fasting during the holy month of Ramadan, which consists of no eating, drinking, smoking, or sexual activity from dawn to sunset

5. Pilgrimage to Mecca, once in a lifetime if financially feasible

Islam as a religion also influences the economic, political, and social system through the holy book (Koran) and through Islamic law (Sharia). The Koran is the basis for Islamic theology. The Sharia is the law of Islam and involves every detail of human life. As quoted by one Muslim scholar, "Islam is both belief and legislation which organizes all the relationships of man." In contrast to nations that separate church and state, Muslim countries are established as religious states.

From this discussion, it is clear that the Islamic religion plays a significant role in the development of cultural aspects of Mideast countries. The religious beliefs held by Muslims can and do affect war in the Middle East. Muslims are taught that those who die in battle for God will ascend immediately to paradise. Saddam Hussein, who has not been known as a particularly active Muslim, has used this Islamic belief to his advantage. He has called for jihad during the Gulf conflict. According to Dr. Jane McAuliff, jihad has two meanings. It can be referred to as the "greater jihad," which is a spiritual struggle, and can also be referred to as the "lesser jihad," which involves warfare to defend Islam. Dr. McAuliff states that "the Muslim notion of heaven and hell is close to that of the Christian view and Muslims believe that one who dies fighting for God's cause, the notion of jihad, is regarded as a martyr and is granted immediate entrance into heaven. That idea has been used to stir the sentiment of the soldiers."

Iraqi culture was one of the main victims of the Gulf War. Iraq suffered a tremendous loss of its cultural institutions (Iraq museum, the museum of Arab Antiquities), particularly those located in Baghdad, which house much of the historic relics of ancient Iraq. The ruins at Babylon and Nineveh, another cultural center of Iraq, were demolished during the war.

COMPARISON OF AMERICAN AND WEST GERMAN BUSINESS CULTURES

The cultural differences between the United States and West Germany are examined in this section. First, it should be noted that the history of German culture can be traced back to the Germanic tribes that attacked the Roman Empire. Therefore, Germany's culture is much more complex than that of the United States.

Both countries have social classes; West Germany is said to have seven levels and the United States five. The German social classes can be divided into elite, service, middle, working elite, false middle, working, and lower. The American social classes are basically upper, upper middle, middle, lower middle, and lower.

Although German history dates back to the Romans, big business in Germany does not. Only since the end of World War II, after Germany was divided into two separate nations, has West Germany really become noted for its international business. Today it is one of the world's leading industrial nations.

The German education system is complex and by far surpasses that of the United States. Therefore, an American firm that goes to Germany generally finds that training local employees is much easier than in most countries. A German firm that comes to the United States finds that training is not as simple. Germany has produced more than its fair share of artists and musicians, particularly compared to the United States. Germans tend to be very proud of this accomplishment, and Americans would do well to remember this when negotiating or marketing a product.

West Germany is extremely poor in natural resources, but has a large population with highly skilled workers. It depends on technology transfer to secure international competitiveness and promote world economic growth. West Germany, which ranks second in world trade, is a leading nation in the transfer of technology. In order to survive in this rapidly changing world, both Germany and the United States need the transfer of technology they receive from each other. Both countries are leaders in world trade, have direct investments in the other country, and belong to world organizations that promote the transfer of technology.

In the United States, corporate decisions are usually made by top management with little or no worker input. The main concern in American firms is to maximize the wealth of the shareholders. In West Germany, all employees have a voice in a firm's decision making at two levels: on the shop floor and at the supervisory level. The Works Constitution Act of 1972 allows for a works council elected by employees to represent their interest in company decisions that may affect them. Most Germans strongly believe in codetermination, which means that an employer cannot make a decision on an operational matter without the approval of the works council. Codetermination is used by both the works council and the supervisory board. The supervisory board usually appoints the management board and monitors its decisions. American trade unions emphasize collective bargaining, which is a private contract between a corporation and a union. West German unions, on the other hand, emphasize codetermination of working conditions and legislative recourse, which involves industry-wide agreements between employers and unions rather than individual companies.

Recently, West German managers have become opposed to codetermination because they feel that it infringes on basic ownership rights. The labor unions are beginning to feel this tension and have begun to move toward the American system of collective bargaining. The United States has been moving slowly toward a form of codetermination by allowing a labor representative on the board of directors of a company. Many are opposed to this trend and feel that if there must be a labor representative, it should be at a lower management level. Both management and labor, however, do not see the West German model of codetermination as becoming predominant in the United States in the near future.

CONCLUSION

A firm must consider at least four major factors when doing business in another country. First, an American manager in a foreign country should be at ease with and receptive to the particular culture. This requires flexibility and an appreciation of the host country's culture. Second, companies need to be careful when recruiting and selecting international managers. The orientation and values of a company's managers should be consistent with those of the foreign country. The third factor deals with human resource planning in the international arena. For many years, MNCs have tended to rely on expatriate managers for overseas assignments. Unfortunately, experience indicates that this policy is often costly and inappropriate. A long-term perspective in recruiting and developing indigenous personnel to assume managerial responsibility is critical and should not be left to chance. Finally, it would be to a firm's advantage to hire a qualified local manager who knows the host country and its culture.

Other factors to keep in mind when developing an appropriate management approach for a MNC are based on common sense and informed conjecture. A successful international manager should possess the following qualities, among others:

1. A basic knowledge of history, particularly in countries with ancient and homogeneous cultures

2. An understanding of the basic economic and sociological concepts of various countries

3. An interest in the host country and a willingness to learn and use its language

4. A respect for differing philosophical and ethical approaches to living

Basically, individuals transferred overseas should have a desire to function as well as possible in the host country's environment.

A firm that is aware of these factors improves its chance for success in another country. Another important point is the concept of codetermination, which is practiced in many Western European countries. Even though codetermination is not practiced in the United States, managers should be aware its existence when dealing with countries that do. This awareness would benefit U.S. companies by providing a better cultural understanding of host countries.

WHAT CAN WE LEARN ABOUT CULTURE?

1. The task of cultural adjustment is perhaps the most challenging and important job confronting international managers.

2. Flexibility and an appreciation of another country's culture are critical. The following exercise could prove useful:
   a. Define a business problem/goal in terms of the home country's cultural traits.
   b. Define the business problem/goal in terms of the host country's traits/norms.
   c. Isolate an influence (one of the norms) on the problem and determine how it complicates the problem.
   d. Redefine the problem without the influence and solve it.

3. Human resource management is important in establishing a long-term perspective for the recruitment and development of indigenous personnel to assume managerial responsibility. It should not simply be left to chance.

REFERENCES

1. "Long Term Human Resource Development in Multinational Operations," *Sloan Management Review,* Fall 1992.
2. Abbass F. Alkhafaji, *International Management Challenge* (Acton, Mass.: Copley), 1990, p. 74.

3. David B. King, "Culture and Society in Modern Germany: A Summary View," in *Essays on Culture and Society in Modern Germany,* Gary D. Stark and Bede Karl Lackner (Eds.) (College Station: Texas A&M University Press), 1982, p. 16.
4. J. Barney, "Organizational Culture: Can It Be a Source of Sustained Competitive Advantage," *Academy of Management Journal,* 11:656–664, 1986.
5. Ashegian Parviz and Bahman Ebrahimi, *International Business* (Philadelphia: Harper Collins), 1990, p. 262.
6. M. Katharine Glover, "Do's and Taboos; Cultural Aspects of International Business," *Business America,* pp. 2–6, August 13, 1990.
7. Michael R. Czinkota et al., *International Business* (Chicago: Dryden Press), 1989.
8. G. Hofstede, *Culture's Consequences: International Differences in Work-Related Values* (Beverly Hills, Calif.: Sage Publications), 1980.

BIBLIOGRAPHY

Alkhafaji, Abbass F., *A Stakeholder Approach to Corporate Governance* (New York: Quorum Books), 1989.

Asch, S.E., *Social Psychology* (New York: Prentice-Hall), 1952.

Bandura, A., "Self-Efficacy Mechanisms in Human Agency," *American Psychologist,* 37:122–147, 1982.

Bendavid, D. and A. Rosenbloom (Eds.), *The Handbook of International Mergers & Acquisitions* (Englewood Cliffs, N.J.: Prentice-Hall), 1990.

Buono, A. and J. Bowditch, *The Human Side of Mergers and Acquisitions* (San Francisco: Jossey-Bass), 1989.

Burke, W. and P. Jackson, "Making the Smith Kline Beecham Merger Work," *Human Resource Management,* 30:69–87, Spring 1991.

Dahrendorf, Ralf, *Society and Democracy in Germany* (New York: Doubleday), 1967.

Davis, C., First Letter to United Distillers Employees, September 1992.

Deal, T.E. and A.A. Kennedy, *Corporate Cultures* (Reading, Mass.: Addison-Wesley), 1982.

Drucker, P., "The New Productivity Challenge," *Harvard Business Review,* pp. 69–79, November–December 1991.

Goldstein, L. and W. Burke "Creating Successful Organizational Change," *Organizational Dynamics,* 19:5–7, 1991.

Hackman, J.R., "Group Influences on Individuals," in *Handbook of Industrial and Organizational Psychology,* M.D. Dunnette (Ed.) (Chicago: Rand McNally), 1976, pp. 1455–1525.

Jackson, J., "A Conceptual and Measurement Model for Norms and Roles," *Pacific Sociological Review,* 9:35–47, 1966.

Kunin, T., "The Construction of a New Type of Attitude Measure," *Personnel Psychology,* 8:65–78, 1955.

Marks, M. and P. Mirvis, "The Merger Syndrome," *Psychology Today,* 20:36–42, 1986.

Peters, T. and R. Waterman, *In Search of Excellence: Lessons from America's Best-Run Corporations* (New York: Harper & Row), 1982, chap. 1.

Phillips, N., *Managing International Teams* (London: Pitman Publishing), 1992.

SECTION III

INTERNATIONAL HUMAN RESOURCE MANAGEMENT AND TECHNOLOGY TRANSFER

The emergence of a global economy and a global trade market has transformed the world into one massive business community. If American corporations do not prepare for the global market, America may decline as a major industrial power. In recent years, the American competitive advantage in this new global economy has been damaged severely as a consequence of the loss of market share to Asian competitors, such as Japan, South Korea, and Taiwan, and a unified Europe. Adapting to the globalization of world economies and the related shift from domestic to global business requires adopting a new strategy as well as new managerial skills. If America is to succeed, the business leaders of tomorrow must be able to operate effectively and comfortably in a global, multicultural, multilingual, and geocentric environment.

The challenges that management faces today within an international environment are thoroughly investigated in this section. Such issues as human resource management in the international environment and technology transfer are the specific focus.

5 INTERNATIONAL HUMAN RESOURCES

ABSTRACT

The human resource issues that are important to present and future managers, businesses, and the academic community at large are explored in this chapter. The related literature on the challenges facing international managers as well as the skills they need to be effective is evaluated. This chapter is also designed to benefit businesses by increasing their ability to acquire and maintain overseas business and reducing their expenses when recruiting and selecting global leaders.

CHAPTER OBJECTIVES

1 To understand the challenges that international managers face in today's global economy

2 To examine the differences between domestic and international human resource management, including the transition made when managing internationally

3 To recognize the importance of cultural training

4 To explain the recruitment philosophies and selection criteria used by international human resource departments

5 To discuss the three different compensation scales for international managers

6 To formulate a strategic international human resource management plan that identifies the skills needed to succeed

7 To learn about employee development, labor relations in the international realm of business, and measuring the performance of management

CASE STUDY
The Single Market: Sustaining American Competitiveness in the European Community

John Young, who recently retired as CEO of Hewlett-Packard Company, stated that polycentric hiring policies have been vital in the success of H-P at their European facilities. He states that, "in our case it has always been a goal of having all local management at the earliest possible moment—(it) is a very important characteristic of being successful and competing." The point made here is that with the proper human resources, American firms may successfully compete in the single market of the European Community, which is rapidly emerging as an economic entity.

To succeed in an international marketplace, a company must have a global attitude, because that is how other markets (from which resources come) are opened up. For example, the market that is served is often the market that offers the human resource base needed to deliver a product or a service. Mr. Young goes on to say that, "(H)aving this kind of a presence and people in place...and enough depth to understand the market in detail is really critical to being successful. Local competitors will just kill you if you don't have that kind of capability." A critical issue that arises from market research is how well (or poorly) a company understands its markets. What is the key to gaining this knowledge?

An argument can be made for the utilization of people who are indigenous to the city, region, etc. that an American firm wants to serve. The European market as a whole has 325 million people. Add to this the many different cultures and languages, and even the most well-established firms face a formidable challenge. A company that is striving to be truly international cannot ignore the advantages that home country nationals offer in the realm of market perspective and understanding.

Europe, as has been stated, is many countries but one market. Having said this, it becomes necessary to examine the submarkets that exist within the primary market. Products, especially commodities, must be localized in order to breed familiarity among consumers. Competent personnel from the target market (country) would be able to achieve this.

Being close to the consumer is a key ingredient in the marketing mix. Some would argue that there is no better way to achieve this than hiring the very customers that a company intends to serve.

Source: John Young, "An American Business Perspective of the Single Market," *Europe,* pp. 27–29, February 1993.

INTRODUCTION

Human resource management (HRM) is the basis of any organization's success. Referred to in the past as a "soft" function, HRM has little effect on an organization's ability to serve its customers or on its profitability. The role of HRM, however, has become fairly complicated over time. In today's world, people have a better understanding of the importance of the human resource professional and the need to know more about this field.

Over a period of time, professionals in HRM have come to possess a variety of skills that can be utilized by a company. Establishing a link between a company's mission and its human resource program is one of the main objectives of the human resource professional. HRM is one of the key tools that a business uses to ensure its future survival. HRM involves the decisions that enhance employee effectiveness and that help to achieve organizational goals. Human resource managers are trained to write organizational policies that will allow for efficiency, cost containment, and equity within the organizational structure. These policies must also communicate the company's position to those outside the organization. The majority of organizations in the United States have training programs for employees in order to enhance production. Companies in the United States deal with a more diverse work force than other nations because of the large number of nationalities that are part of the American population.

Human resource managers need to be aware of the changes taking place in the domestic and international environments. They must be prepared for and open to new training tools and new technologies. Managers must be aware of real life problems and be able to offer assistance or support when needed. These issues must be addressed if America is to be competitive.

When entering foreign markets, it is important to prepare the new management teams properly. A manager who will head an expansion effort must be aware of cultural differences, government influences, and a host of other internal and external variables unique to the new country. It is also important that a manager preparing to enter a foreign market understands how to adjust fully, as well as what to expect if he or she should later leave the foreign country and return home. A thorough understanding of the global market ensures greater success.

In order to enhance production, a majority of organizations in the United States have implemented training programs for their employees. These companies deal with greater diversity in the work force than do companies in other nations. This diversity is due to the "melting pot" nature of the American work force. This point must be emphasized if American managers are to compete effectively in the global market.

The issues that are important to present and future managers, businesses, and the academic community at large are explored in this chapter. The related literature about the challenges facing international managers, as well as the skills they need to be effective, is discussed. These challenges include understanding the global economy and its development, HRM, preparing managers for overseas assignments, reinstating expatriates, managerial development in less developed countries, the role of universities in preparing global managers, and ways to effectively transfer technology. This chapter is also designed to benefit businesses by increasing their ability to acquire and maintain overseas business and reducing their expenses when recruiting and selecting global leaders.

THE CHANGING ENVIRONMENT

Today's big business environment is constantly changing, and the ability to adapt to this changing environment is critical to the future success of large companies. As companies adapt, they will have to expand into international markets. As firms move from domestic to international markets, management philosophy must change to better suit the cultural diversity of the personnel of a multinational corporation (MNC). The way management handles the move to a foreign market can increase the probability of success in the foreign arena. With proper recruitment and selection criteria, the appropriate staff can be chosen to help run foreign subsidiaries.

DOMESTIC VERSUS INTERNATIONAL HUMAN RESOURCE MANAGEMENT

Competitive advantage in international business has changed the world's manufacturing environment considerably. While there are many reasons for this change, technical advances seem to be the most significant. There is scant literature to guide an examination of the similarities and differences between international and domestic HRM. Given that the rapid growth of international business enterprises is a relatively recent event, this lack of research material on either international HRM or the differences between international and domestic HRM is not surprising. As Leap and Oliva[1] point out, an examination of the history of HRM shows that changes in organizational practice typically occur well in advance of academic interest in these issues.

Acuff[2] states that distinctions between domestic and international HRM can be divided into four broad categories. International HRM is characterized by more heterogeneous functions, greater involvement in an employee's personal life, different emphasis on management training, and more external influences. International HRM practitioners must be particularly diligent because there is generally greater dissatisfaction in an international environment than in a domestic environment.

An international human resource department must engage in a number of activities that differentiate domestic and international HRM. Acuff[2] states that a domestic human resource department at corporate headquarters or field locations typically divides its time among eight activities: employment and resources planning, wage and salary administration, employee benefits, training and management development, labor relations, safety, personnel systems and policy, and equal employment opportunities. At the corporate headquarters level, the two major activities that differentiate domestic and international HRM are taxation and relocation/orientation.

THE TRANSITION FROM A DOMESTIC TO AN INTERNATIONAL POSITION

A firm generally begins with a domestic operation, which concentrates on the home market. As the home market becomes saturated, usually due to competition, a domestic firm begins to rely more heavily on exports. By exporting products to foreign markets, a company can make up lost earnings in the home market. In addition, the need for cheap labor, additional resources, and new technology can lead to expansion into a new market in the international arena.

As a firm begins to export and eventually branch out, establishing production facilities and offices abroad, it must also find ways to better service its new market. A MNC must recognize the new environment in which it is operating and make changes to fit the different needs of the individuals in this market. A firm must understand many different criteria in order to be successful in a foreign market. Managers of MNCs must familiarize themselves with the differences in culture, social beliefs, language, philosophy, religious beliefs, work habits, and overall customs of the market in which they will function. Adapting to these differences is a key element in the ongoing success of a company competing in the international marketplace. As a firm grows, understanding these differences becomes essential. In other words, cultural and political differences do not necessarily restrict business opportunities.

After a corporation has dealt with the external environment, it must then begin to look at the internal environment. One important area is developing a corporate culture and establishing HRM policies.

BUREAUCRATIC CULTURE

A company that operates in a **bureaucratic** culture exhibits an impersonal style, relies completely on standards, and follows rigid procedures. This type of culture is supported by a centralized hierarchy with little internal competition. It is common in developing countries and in companies that operate in stable, protected markets. A **managerial** culture is commonly found in companies that operate in highly competitive and innovative industries. It is characterized by a performance-oriented culture with a true managerial style. The organization is flexible and very adaptive. Typically, a **technical** culture is common in countries with a history of technical expertise and companies operating in traditional industries. It is characterized by a paternalistic style and relies on technical expertise. The organization is highly functional, which sometimes leads to fierce interdepartmental competition.[3]

The type of culture influences company policy in terms of employee selection, training, evaluation, rewards and compensation, and termination. Management–employee relations is also strongly influenced by a firm's culture. A MNC must adopt a multicultural perspective in both its operations and the way it deals with employees. Managers from different cultures have different ideas about the proper way to manage. Employees from different cultures have different opinions about job-related behavior and the role of management, which could lead to conflict if not handled appropriately. Because a MNC operates in a culturally diverse environment, it should adapt its management style to better fit the home country and its culture.

IMPORTANCE OF CULTURAL TRAINING

One of the most critical factors in economic progress is understanding the host culture. Although a country may have natural and manpower resources, it still can be relatively poor in terms of properly trained managers. Properly trained individuals are able to efficiently manage corporate resources in the production and distribution of useful goods and services. It is important to understand that management functions (planning, organizing, leading, control, and evaluation) are the same all over the world. However, the application of these functions differs across cultures. Management performance in a host country depends largely on the adaptability of the culture of the parent organization to that of the host country.

These cultural variations among countries tend to result in variation in business cultures. For example, French financial managers are concerned about solvency, but their American counterparts worry about return on investment. The Japanese executive is more likely to be interested in the company's long-term profits than today's figures. The tendency to act in unison, a strong consciousness of the "spirit of gathering together," is a noticeable feature of daily life in Japan. The Japanese consider harmony a virtue and, as a rule, avoid dispute. Unlike Americans, who see the individual as important, the Japanese see the needs and goals of the group as more important. Their priority is the accomplishment of tasks by groups. The Japanese stress teamwork and group harmony, as opposed to competition. Japan is a nation where the individual fits in and where people stress relations, not rights.

In contrast, American managers compete for power and position and may not cooperate when working on related tasks. Individual accomplishment is a priority. Decision making in Japanese companies is the result of the collective participation of people at many different levels of management. Decision making in the United States is individual oriented, with a relative top-down emphasis, while in Japan decisions are made by consensus, with a group orientation and a bottom-up emphasis. Employment in the United States tends to be short term, unstable, and insecure, while in Japan it is long term, relatively secure, and stable. Americans get upset when the British procrastinate in a business dealing, which is the British manager's way of saying no, but Americans tend to pause before replying to a question. The Japanese distrust fluency in speech and like periods of silence, whereas Americans find silence awkward. The British use humor to indicate when they are serious. Germans and Swiss, on the other hand, rarely mix humor with business. Italians are offended when Americans attend a business meeting wearing casual clothes when the Italians are dressed for business.[4] American managers should not assume that they understand a foreign country just because they have seen videos, attended training sessions, or vacationed abroad. Rather, they must have a thorough knowledge of each country's culture because each is unique. This is particularly important when an international manager not only functions in the workplace but also lives in the community of a foreign country.

CROSS-CULTURAL TRAINING

Cross-cultural training improves awareness of cultural differences and how people differ throughout the world. The Society for Inter-Cultural Education, Training and Research actively promotes professional development through conferences, workshops, and various publications. Human resource and development efforts in cross-cultural training have special meaning in terms of global management. Training in Japan begins at least one year prior to an expatriate's departure. Managers are thoroughly prepared to work in a foreign culture. Japanese companies take management training very seriously. Japanese managers learn intercultural and stress management skills, and each is assigned a mentor. Employees and their families are also prepared for the return to Japan.[5] In contrast, American companies tend to provide short courses about a foreign country. They neglect the social, psychological, and cultural aspects of adjustment. Approximately 68% of American companies provide no formal training.[5]

Companies such as Dow, Exxon, and Procter and Gamble send their managers to training courses provided by consulting agencies such as Global Leadership Programme Consortium. This outward-bound school teaches teamwork and cultural awareness for a fee of $30,000 per person.[6] Over 40 years ago, the American Graduate School of International Management began to stress human factors such as flexibility, diversity, and challenge.[7] FAM Associates takes a problem-centered approach which concentrates on acquiring both practical skills and information. Trainers customize such activities as role-playing, case studies, and discussion to a particular foreign country.[5]

Cross-cultural training is vital for today's international organizations.

CASE STUDY
West Meets East: Succeeding with Japanese Audiences

It is a well-known fact that American and Japanese employees differ. It is therefore assumed that their training should also differ. Many American managers forget this when they go to Japan to train employees.

A major difference between Americans and Japanese is apparent at the start of a presentation. An American presenter exudes knowledge to show his or her expertise in a particular subject. Japanese audience members seem bewildered by this behavior. The American presenter, therefore, might want to start by either apologizing for his or her lack of knowledge of the Japanese language or by using a Japanese phrase. A Japanese presenter begins with an apology, such as telling the audience that they know more about the subject or that he or she is not well prepared. The presenter wants to show humility at the beginning and prove to the audience by the end of the presentation that he or she is knowledgeable about the subject.

A major problem that Western trainers face after an initial presentation is assuming a position of authority, especially if the participants are around the same age as the trainer. In Japan, it is assumed that younger trainers are not as well informed as older trainers. A more comfortable approach might be for the trainer to state his or her rank and position within the company so that the participants know exactly where they are in relation to the trainer. One way of doing this would be for the trainer to give a copy of his or her resume to each participant. Rather than giving the impression that the trainer is being boastful about his or her accomplishments, this lets the Japanese participants know where they stand in relation to their trainer.

A trainer should provide instructional materials before the training pro-

Training in foreign cultures also eases the assimilation process when relocating abroad. Cross-cultural training programs are designed to prepare individuals for life in another culture and to help them deal more effectively with various cultures. They encourage sensitivity, foster greater understanding, improve customer and employee relationships, promote awareness of the underlying values of a culture, increase job performance, and build rapport, trust, confidence, and overall profitability. The emergence of a global economy and trade market has transformed the world into one community. If American management cannot compete on a global scale, the position of the United States as a major industrial power will decline.

Cross-cultural training helps to avoid cultural faux pas and promotes participation in international organizations and meetings. Training in foreign cultures also eases the assimilation process when relocating abroad. This type of training is beneficial in terms of client relations, productivity, profitability, and foreign relations.

cess begins. The Japanese are used to studying until late at night, and this helps them learn the material. The Japanese also discuss the information that they are learning throughout the training lesson with the other participants, which helps them understand the information more clearly. A trainer should not be offended by this behavior, because this is a part of the Japanese learning process.

Even though the Japanese spend much time studying and working in groups, they tend to distrust group decisions. They will work on an assignment for long periods of time, and it is not unusual for a Japanese group to turn a ten-minute exercise into a ninety-minute job. It is the quest of the Japanese to find the one true answer.

After the training is over, the entire group goes out to celebrate, and the trainer is also expected to attend. Each person in the group gets up and sings a song to the entire group. Either at this time or before the class has officially ended, the trainer is expected to give a small gift to those participants who helped him or her. The Japanese are offended if the gift is inexpensive. Gifts should be practical. Women are usually given silk scarves and men are given blue ties. These items can be purchased in the United States before going overseas.

The differences between Japanese and Americans are abundant. American managers should keep these differences in mind when working with the Japanese. Previous problems should be used as a guide to prevent their recurrence. If American managers are willing to change their behavior, the Japanese market can be theirs.

Source: Linda Dillon, "West Meets East: Succeeding with Japanese Audiences," *Training and Development*, pp. 40–43, March 1993.

In summary, cross-cultural training serves to:

- Encourage sensitivity
- Foster greater understanding
- Improve managerial effectiveness
- Improve customer and employee relationships
- Increase the cross-cultural skills of employees at home and abroad
- Promote awareness of the underlying values of a culture
- Reduce culture shock
- Build rapport, trust, and confidence
- Increase individual effectiveness and overall profitability

TABLE 5.1   Four Types of Recruitment Approaches

Approach	Attribute
Ethnocentrism	Assignment of key positions to home country executives Found in highly centralized firms
Polycentrism	Assignment of key positions to host country nationals, who bring knowledge of the local market, people, and government policies
Regiocentrism	Assignment of key positions to a specific region Used when products are similar all over the world
Geocentrism	Assignment of key positions to qualified people of any background and culture Staffing, manufacturing, and marketing done on a global basis

RECRUITMENT PHILOSOPHY

An objective selection process should be used when hiring from a global pool of applicants, which means that the best-qualified applicant should be chosen for each job. However, research indicates that a major influence on hiring decisions is the attitude of top executives toward host country nationals. There are four approaches to recruitment that are used by MNCs (Table 5.1).

The first approach is **ethnocentrism**. Management staffs all key positions, both at home and abroad, with home country executives. This approach is found in firms that are highly centralized and that rely on low-cost production of products.

The second approach is **polycentrism**. The attitude here is that host country management should be done by host country nationals. It is based on the belief that home country nationals are better able to understand their own markets.

The third approach is **regiocentrism**. This means that global markets should be handled regionally. For example, the main headquarters for all European markets might be located in France, or headquarters for all markets in North and South American would be in the United States. This style is used when similar products are sold all over the world and only the marketing is tailored to meet different cultural needs.

The fourth approach is **geocentrism**. According to this approach, qualified people can come from any background or culture. Resource allocation, staffing, manufacturing, and marketing are done on a global basis.

SELECTION CRITERIA

Selecting a manager to operate a corporation in a foreign market is a major decision. To the people of a host country, the manager represents

TABLE 5.2   **Managerial Selection Criteria**

Criteria	Definition	Example
Technical and managerial skills	The capability of a manager to do his or her job	At the start of his employment, a manager walks around and greets every employee
Motives and desires	The reason why a manager is interested in an overseas assignment	A manager is sent to Germany because she is fluent in the language and has studied German business techniques
Social skills	How a manager interacts with people	On weekends, a manager goes to the marketplace by himself to do his shopping
Diplomatic skills	The ability of a manager to interact with business associates, government officials, and political leaders	A manager is invited to attend a government function
Maturity and stability	The ability of a manager to react logically to situations	A manager is able to handle unexpected surprises
Family factors	How a manager's family adapts to a new country	A manager's family takes weekend trips in their new country
Other attributes, such as age and gender	Indicates maturity and authority level; differentiation between male and female roles	Women cannot perform certain tasks in some countries; an older gentleman is president of an overseas division

both the MNC and its home country. The impression a manager leaves lasts a long time, long after the manager returns home. Therefore, choosing the right manager to go abroad could mean the difference between success and failure.

What criteria should be used when selecting a manager for a foreign assignment? What characteristics should a manager possess? Opinions differ as to what makes a good manager, but the following seven criteria are among the most frequently mentioned (see also Table 5.2):

1. **Technical and managerial skills:** These skills are usually based on past performance at the managerial level. The technical, administrative, and managerial skills that make a manager successful at home are applicable in a foreign assignment.

2. **Motives and desires:** Motivation for wanting a job is an important factor. The best candidates have a genuine interest in the host country, rather than just a financial incentive. A good candidate should know something about the host country, preferably through travel or by learning the language.

SAMPLE INTERVIEW WORKSHEET
FOR OVERSEAS CANDIDATES

1. **Motivation**
   A. Why is the candidate interested in the job?
   B. Does the candidate know what is involved in living abroad?
   C. Why does he or she want to go abroad?

2. **Language Ability**
   A. Can the candidate speak another language?
   B. Does he or she want to learn another language?
   C. Does his or her spouse know another language?

3. **Adaptability**
   A. Is the candidate able to interact with others?
   B. How does he or she react to new situations?
   C. Does the candidate understand and accept his or her cultural bias as well as those of others?
   D. Can the candidate accept criticism?
   E. How patient is the candidate when problems arise?
   F. If setbacks do occur, can the candidate bounce back?

4. **Health**
   A. Are there any current medical problems which might interfere with the assignment?
   B. Is the mental health of the candidate good?

5. **Family Considerations**
   A. Has the candidate moved in the past?
   B. Did any problems occur in the last move?
   C. How many children does the candidate have?

3. **Social skills:** This may be the most important attribute. A manager must be able to interact with and understand people in the host country. He or she must be able to form relationships and understand the norms of the society in order to effectively deal with the people, whether on a business or social level. Social activities, such as attending a sporting event or eating out, often provide an opportunity for interaction.

4. **Diplomatic skills:** A manager's ability to interact with business associates, government officials, and political leaders.

5. **Maturity and stability:** The ability of a manager to deal with a situation logically.

6. **Family factors:** The ability of a manager's family to adapt to a new environment is a major factor in the success or failure of a MNC in a foreign country.

D. Is everyone willing to relocate?

E. How close is the extended family?

6. **Resourcefulness and Initiative**

A. Is the candidate resourceful?

B. Does he or she need constant supervision?

C. Does the candidate stand behind his or her decisions?

D. Can he or she get the job done with the manpower and resources available?

E. Will the candidate be able to communicate company policy and goals to the workers?

F. Is the candidate a confident and disciplined individual?

G. Is he or she able to solve problems?

H. Will he or she be able to perform overseas without supporting services?

7. **Financial**

A. Is the candidate financially able to accept the assignment?

B. Are there any current financial problems which might affect the move?

C. Are there any special expenses to consider (such as housing, education, etc.)?

8. **Career Planning**

A. Is the assignment part of the candidate's career plan?

B. What is the candidate's feeling toward the organization?

C. Does he or she have any previous history of a bad performance?

D. Is the overseas job considered anything but temporary?

Source: David M. Noer, *Multinational People Management: A Guide for Organizations and Employees* (Washington, D.C.: The Bureau of National Affairs), 1975, pp. 55–57.

7. **Other attributes:**   Less specific criteria that may vary from culture to culture. For example, age is a sign of authority in some countries. Women may find it difficult to deal with host country nationals, subordinates, colleagues, or clients in some countries due to societal restrictions.

Managers should be fully aware of differences in culture and ethics. They should be fluent in their host country's language and aware of its traditional business practices.

The process of selecting host country and third country national managers is time consuming. Technical expertise, adaptability, flexibility, communication, and decision-making skills are key ingredients in the process.

There are many reasons for hiring qualified international managers. Host country personnel may not have received the professional training that would allow them to assume managerial roles. A combination of poor educational opportunities and depressed economic conditions in a host country may limit the number of talented and qualified people available for employment.

Many countries go abroad because of inexpensive and plentiful labor and find that local employees are quite friendly and loyal to foreign investors and managers. Foreign investors and managers may find that work settings and employee attitudes in foreign countries are, in some instances, more conducive to business. Obedient employees are less likely to confront employers or managers. Labor disputes, which are common in Western countries, are rare overseas.

Managers should understand that emphasis on technical skills, which is considered very important in measuring the success of organizations in the West, may not be quite as appealing in foreign countries.

Foreign managers and investors should understand that workers in other countries like to know that they are appreciated by the organization as demonstrated through its HRM practices. These practices include selection and training geared toward overall concern for employees and collective negotiation in the workplace. In order to suit local organizational philosophy, foreign managers should consider using a relationship-oriented approach to performance appraisal.

EASING THE ADJUSTMENT

Workshops, employment information, and mentor programs are a few of the ways in which a MNC can assist a manager and his or her family in adjusting to life in their new home country. Workshops should include language training and information on health, safety, and medical needs, in addition to tips on managing a household in the host country. Companies should think of spouses as an asset and take their needs into consideration.

Mentors in the home country and host country can be helpful in making the adjustment to the new country and making the readjustment upon return home. This type of program can help managers to overcome their biases and acquire a truly global perspective. A culturally diverse staff can also improve a manager's understanding of the business and management philosophies of different nations. The more contact a manager will have with people of other cultures, the more in-depth training he or she will require.

Typically, a documentary approach is used to acquaint a manager with a foreign culture. This can include lectures, films, and literature. The manager learns the history, geography, and sociopolitical and economic systems of the foreign country. This type of education may not be sufficient, however. The best way for a manager to learn about a country and its culture is by interacting with people from the host country.

European and Japanese managers are better trained than Americans to deal with other cultures. Some U.S. companies have started programs to identify future managers for global operations. They learn about the

CASE STUDY
Preparing the Family

The following scenario is a good example of why the spouse of an expatriate should be included in the training program prior to a transfer overseas.

Prior to her husband's transfer, Emily was not interested in her husband's job or the company that employed him. She was aware of how much he made and the basic work he performed on a daily basis, but work was not discussed at home or when she and her husband were out socially.

When the actual move took place, the situation changed drastically. Emily became very dependent on the company and felt that it was responsible for taking care of her and her family. After all, the company had sent them abroad.

Emily came to rely heavily on the allowances and incentives provided by the company as compensation for the difference in housing and the standard of living. She lived in a community with other expatriate families. When they got together, it was only natural for them to discuss their jobs and company policies. They worked for a number of different companies, and jealousies began to surface when some realized that they were not receiving the same benefits as other expatriates.

Emily began to resent the company and the fact that she had become so dependent on it. She became so upset that she sat down and wrote a letter to the wife of the company president. She did so without her husband's knowledge, and when he found out, it was too late. Emily's letter did bring about a more detailed explanation of the company's expatriate policies, which was provided by a manager who was visiting the country at the time. After their discussion, Emily was better able to understand the policies and realized that the company was treating her family fairly. If the company had provided Emily with this information prior to her departure, some of her resentment could have been avoided and it would have been easier for her to cope with the situation.

Source: David M. Noer, *Multinational People Management: A Guide for Organizations and Employees* (Washington, D.C.: The Bureau of National Affairs), 1975, pp. 66–68.

corporation's operations and the firm's overall purpose and mission. The norms and values of the corporate culture are thoroughly discussed so that future managers know what to expect. Topics includes salary increases, promotion packages, and other financial considerations.

Part of this orientation should include discussion of repatriation problems or problems after returning home, which most MNCs tend to ignore. Expatriates often find themselves feeling like foreigners in their own country. They need time to adapt to changes that may have occurred while they were gone. They may have lost out on promotions or, even worse, may be returning from foreign assignments that were not successful.

The cost of living difference or loss of benefits may also be a shock, particularly because benefits are an important incentive to expatriates. It is important to explain that expatriates will pay the same taxes. Compensation for expatriates should be comparable to similar domestic positions. The company should, however, cover the cost of transferring expatriates and their families between various locations. It is important that this package be similar to those offered by competitors in the industry.

In most cases, one or more of the following approaches to compensation are used:

1. Domestic scale plus an allowance for affiliate differential: This system takes the base pay from the home country and adds a foreign service allowance. It includes a cost levying adjustment, tax equalization, currency devaluation, and a hardship bonus.

2. Citizenship compensation scale: This system is designed primarily for managers from Third World countries. For example, an Iraqi manager's compensation would differ from the salary of an American. A company needs to be careful that such a situation does not cause resentment among employees.

3. Global compensation scale: This system uses the same salary for the same job regardless of citizenship. It requires a global pay scale and global ranking. An affiliate difference is added to the base pay to account for differences in local economies. It is a difficult approach but seems to be the most accepted way of doing things.

Most host country employees are paid the typical local salary. MNCs can use a variety of methods to help compensate their host country employees. Problems arise when qualified personnel are not satisfied, especially when they move from a local to an international status. A company can adjust the salary of a host country manager who agrees to move to a Third World country. A second approach is to put the manager on the home country pay scale when he or she reaches a certain level. A third approach is to use management by objectives.

In the near future, we will see an expanded need for managers with a global attitude. The challenge is to recruit young, talented people for future global assignments. As global opportunities increase, a clear message will be sent to all MNCs: there is a need for talented employees who are prepared to this undertake this responsibility.

STRATEGIC INTERNATIONAL HUMAN RESOURCE MANAGEMENT

The process of developing a plan for international HRM is briefly discussed in this section. The technical, human, and conceptual skills needed by managers to develop a strategic plan are emphasized. Other related issues are also investigated.

When a company decides to expand overseas, a corporate strategy must be developed. A carefully designed plan can help to minimize the chance of failure, the incidence of which is high in overseas ventures. The strategy should include a master plan for HRM. Corporations need to develop their employees to be able to assume more diverse tasks and assignments. A better understanding of cultural differences is also needed. Developing an awareness of these differences and finding the right mix of managers and employees to run a MNC is the focus of HRM strategy.

There are six basic steps or activities in developing a multinational HRM strategy: planning (human resource planning and forecasting, career management, work scheduling, and job design), staffing (recruitment and selection), compensation (wages and benefits), employee development (training and career path planning), labor relations (labor–management relations, collective bargaining, and codetermination), and performance management (performance appraisal, policies and program evaluation).[8]

As with any strategy, HRM needs a **plan of action** before it can be implemented. Two important steps in developing a firm's human resource strategy are assessing future managerial and nonmanagerial needs and choosing a workable combination of personnel management and development programs that enables an organization to accomplish its stated goals. There are two steps in assessing future managerial needs. The first step is a quantitative forecast to determine the number of managers that will be needed to staff the organization. This is followed by a qualitative forecast to determine the special skills that will be needed in order for a firm to accomplish its objectives. This allows a firm to identify and develop the right people for the right tasks. Three types of skills are critical for managers: technical, human, and conceptual.

Technical skills are proficiency in specific types of methods, processes, procedures, or techniques. They involve the knowledge, skills, and abilities needed to solve specialized problems. Examples of technical skills are operating a machine, working on a computer, and drafting a financial statement. These skills are most important at the operating (supervisory) level of management; however, other managerial levels should also be technically proficient.

Human skills are the ability to work with as well as interact with individuals and groups of people. These skills involve the way an individual is perceived by his or her co-workers, subordinates, and superiors, as well as how an individual behaves. Human skills are relevant to all managers because their main job is to get the job done through working with people. Communication is an important part of human skills. It involves the transfer of information within the organization to keep internal operations functioning smoothly and the transfer of information outside the organization to nurture reliable relationships with the external world.

Conceptual skills allow a manager to visualize the relationship of the individual business to an industry, community, and the political, social, and economic forces of a nation as a whole. Managers should be able to understand the relationship of the parts to the whole and how a change in one affects the other. These abilities are cognitive in nature. Such skills are more important at the top level of management than at the operating level. When hiring, a company should consider the conceptual skills of a candidate. A manager should be able to think in relative terms rather than certainties. Factors such as job experience and technical expertise are part of the future forecast when deciding on a managerial candidate. When an international firm hires, it must determine whether a candidate is willing to relocate to a foreign country. This complicates the task, because a company has to find someone with the necessary managerial skills who is also willing to relocate. A company should also consider whether a candidate has any skills that might be helpful in training others, such as knowledge about a host country or its language or any other intangibles that would help make the decision easier.

The next step is to **staff the organization**. It is not always easy to find someone who is familiar with the foreign country where the firm intends to conduct business. Such people may not be available. Therefore, a MNC may need to develop its own personnel. Once an organization has developed its structure for expanding, management must staff those positions with people capable of completing the specific tasks. The staffing process starts with a review of the firm's personnel needs. These needs are generally determined by corporate headquarters. Subsidiaries are surveyed about their human resource needs, but ultimately headquarters is responsible for putting it all together. Subsidiaries are brought into the staffing process as the specifics of job analysis, job design, work schedules, and career management are further determined. When recruitment targets have been specified in terms of positions to be filled, their location, and the type of personnel required, an international firm can follow conventional recruiting practices.

Robock and Simmonds identify some of the decisions a multinational firm must make when selecting staff. The first is in what countries to recruit. The second is what new techniques and sources will have to be used when recruitment is planned outside the home country. The third is whether or not to centralize recruiting activities in the home country or decentralize activities in foreign subsidiaries.[9]

Once these decisions have been made, a pool of candidates is assembled. At this point, a human resource manager decides on the mix the firm wants its management team to have. Should it staff key management positions with people from the home country, host country nationals, or some combination of the two? In filling these positions, a firm must follow its host country's rules. Countries such as Canada, Mexico, the former Soviet Union, and most developing countries require the head of a subsidiary of a foreign enterprise to be a citizen of that country.[10] This is generally to the benefit of a firm, because the head of a subsidiary should be familiar with the nuances of the host country, which an expatriate would not.

Hays[11] classifies overseas jobs into four categories: chief executive officer (CEO), functional head, troubleshooter, and operatives. The CEO oversees the entire operation, the functional head establishes departments in a foreign affiliate, the troubleshooter analyzes and solves special problems, and the operative is the rank-and-file worker.[11]

According to the **ethnocentric** view of staffing overseas, the primary positions are held by citizens of the home country. The main problem with using expatriates is the enormously high rate of failure among them. People are generally not willing to adapt to a culture that is new to them. With this in mind, the following three factors should be considered when selecting an international manager: failure, success, and training.

The main causes of expatriate failure have to do with adjustment, family, culture, and personality problems. Adjustment-related problems stem from several factors: self-orientation, orientation toward others, and perceptual and cultural biases. An expatriate should try to enjoy the local entertainment, develop local relationships, and be willing to communicate with locals. He or she should be able to recognize the differences between the home and host cultures. Family problems center on adjusting to a lifestyle to which a family is unaccustomed. The severity of family problems usually depends on the circumstance of the overseas assignment. It can either bring a family together or pull it apart. An expatriate's success depends on a three-dimensional construct which consists of job satisfaction, job performance, and adjustment to the local culture. If the job goes well, the family likes its new surroundings, and the person is satisfied with his or her job, success is more likely. To achieve success, however, an individual should be trained properly. Proper training should cover both language and cultural training and can be in the form of instruction or a visit to the host country.[12] Expatriates can achieve success, but they need good training and an open attitude toward the host country.

According to the **polycentric** view of staffing overseas, the primary positions are filled by nationals from the host country. Employing host country nationals tends to reduce personnel problems and can help a company shed its foreign image. A host country manager can protect a MNC from hostile treatment by the host government, in addition to the knowledge he or she brings about the local market, people, and government policies.

According to the **regiocentric** view of staffing, the primary positions are filled by people from countries with similar cultures, experiences, and management practices. This approach assumes that host countries can be grouped geographically, and, therefore, culture, experiences, and practices can be transferred within each regional group.

In the **geocentric** view, the best qualified individuals are hired for positions at home and abroad, regardless of nationality. This approach assumes that all countries have some similarities and some differences in terms of culture, experiences, and practices and that it is, therefore, more important to match the individual with the goals and objectives of the organization. A MNC with this outlook considers the whole world as its market.

In review, in designing its staffing policies, a firm first determines its needs. It then identifies its approach to hiring: who, how, and from where. Finally, if necessary, recruits are trained for life in a foreign land.

In conjunction with hiring policies, a **compensation plan** must be formulated. For obvious reasons, different jobs have different pay rates, but firms must also make allowances for such factors as sending people abroad. In order to entice employees to go to a foreign nation, special incentives may have to be offered. A firm must also take into account any rules or regulations of a host country. It is important that incentives are appropriate and fit within the mainstream of an industry.

An effective compensation policy for expatriates should meet the following criteria:

1. Attract and retain employees qualified for overseas service

2. Facilitate transfers between foreign affiliates and between home country and foreign affiliates

3. Establish and maintain a consistent and equitable relationship in the compensation of all employees, whether at home or abroad

4. Provide reasonable compensation, in the various locations, in relation to the practices of leading competitors

Most U.S. companies construct their policies for expatriates based on three components: base salary, premiums for working abroad, and overseas allowances.[13] The base salary of an expatriate transferred to a foreign nation usually stays the same. This is largely because all personnel are tied to the home country payroll, no matter where they work.[9] It also allows for compensation upon reassignment to the home country. What happens when the base salary is retained but the going rate for the position differs from the base salary? A company may to decide to raise the salary. On the other hand, some companies actually lower the salary to bring it more in line with local compensation rates. This means that some expatriates may work side by side with expatriates from other countries but at different rates of compensation. Due to fluctuating exchange rates, expatriates can find themselves with lower incomes if the value of their home country's currency falls below that of the country in which they are posted. The situation becomes even more complicated if overseas employees are paid in the home country's currency.[9] For example, some major league baseball players have a clause in their contract that grants them an automatic increase in base salary if they are traded to a Canadian team. While this may not be a perfect example, it gives a general idea of the problems created by the values of different currencies.

Premiums are also offered as an extra incentive to live abroad. There are two basic types of premiums: those that encourage mobility and those for the hardship of living abroad. Hardship premiums are usually 10 to 20% of the base pay and are generally paid for the duration of the stay. The main problem with this type of premium occurs when a person is sent back to the home country. Because repatriates stand to incur a substantial cut in pay, many tend to want to stay in one place or are reluctant to move from country to country.[9]

The final part of the compensation package is allowances. These are designed to allow personnel assigned to foreign posts to continue their normal patterns of living.[9] The most common allowances are for cost of living, housing, education, and tax protection. There are many ways to personalize a compensation policy, depending on the individual and the country in which he or she will live.

After deciding how to pay the employees, there may be a need to train and develop them. The purpose of **employee development** is to align employee aspirations and capabilities with organizational goals. The basic objective of training and development for international assignments is to cultivate cultural sensitivity. In a survey of Americans and nationals, both groups ranked human relations skills as most important. The education, training, and development of expatriate international managers is becoming a multibillion dollar business.[10] The need for cultured, educated, and knowledgeable managers is increasing, and big business in the international market is the proving ground for talent.

Labor relations is the next part of the HRM structure. This encompasses collective bargaining between management and the unions that support the needs of employees. Unions usually negotiate such issues as wages and salaries, working conditions, and industrial relations (rules and regulations between management and labor).[10] The nature, role, and power of unions vary from country to country depending on a multitude of factors. The first is the level at which bargaining takes place (enterprise or industry level). In the United States and Japan, the local or company level is preferred. In most European countries, the employer's representatives bargain with union representatives at a national or regional level. The second factor is the centralization of union management. In the United States, the AFL-CIO does not bargain directly with employers. Its role is to act as a coordinating body and resolve disputes among its member unions. In Europe, confederations have more decision-making power. The third factor is the scope of bargaining. The fourth factor is the degree of government intervention. The final factor is the percentage of the work force represented by unions.[14] These factors determine mobility of workers, level of unemployment, homogeneity of the labor force, and the educational level of the work force. Perhaps the most pressing reason for headquarters involvement in labor–management affairs is the move toward internationalization of the labor movement, which in itself is a direct reaction to the growth of the MNC. Unions around the world have been increasingly threatened by powerful multinational employers. MNCs have ways of shutting out unions. They can impose an investment strike in which they simply do not reinvest in a particular subsidiary, thus making the subsidiary obsolete. This forces the union to lower its demands in order to retain any level of employment. Unions also claim that MNCs are so big that they can weather any strike and continue to make a profit even though union strikes may shut down operations in one country.[9] Anyway you look at it, a union is going to satisfy only half of the people—either management or the employees.

Labor relations patterns differ markedly among countries. The varying patterns reflect the unique cultural, legal, and institutional settings in

CASE STUDY
Advice for Newcomers

If you think you would be or are interested in working overseas, it would be wise to start planning now instead of waiting to be offered a job and having to make a hasty decision.

Your marital status will play a role in your decision. Being single will probably make a move overseas easier. If you are married, your spouse should definitely be consulted prior to making any decision. Do not assume that moving to another country will be fine with your spouse. It might also be helpful to talk to other expatriates who have returned home.

Accepting a position overseas can cause unforeseen problems. Therefore, if your family is currently having problems (financial, personal, etc.), do not think that moving will solve them. One person who owed $14,000 on credit cards thought his debt would just disappear when he was transferred overseas. Eventually, the bills caught up with him. He started writing bad checks, which affected not only him but many other people as well. The foreign bank stopped honoring the checks of all U.S. citizens.

Assuming you are next in line for an overseas position, you should check into your company's policies regarding relocation. First, make sure that the company has a policy in this area. Mr. Nicholson, the author of an article about expatriate life, recommends getting all the guarantees made by the company regarding benefits in writing.

Mr. Nicholson advises visiting the new location prior to making the actual move. One of the first stops that he and his wife would make was the local grocery store to see what items were available. Then, when they packed for an overseas assignment, they would take with them those items that they used quite frequently but would not be able to purchase. Another area that needs to be investigated is host country regulations. There may be restrictions on or requirements for moving certain items. The Nicholsons ran into problems in moving some of their antiques and artwork.

Your housing choices may be limited depending on the host country. More often than not, the company will assist you in making the move. Be careful in choosing the people who will move you. If you do not speak the language, definitely get someone who does to help you, so you will be better able to communicate with the movers.

different nations, which reflect labor relations through varying social values. Recognizing these realities, MNCs have to delegate the task of managing the work force to the managers of foreign subsidiaries.[9] This puts decision making in the hands of the local leaders, who know the problem firsthand. The importance of labor relations on the international level is immeasurable because of the need to keep host country nationals happy. The field is expanding and only the future holds the answer to management-labor relationships.

One issue the Nicholsons came to realize is that having a maid to help run the household may be a necessity in underdeveloped countries. If few conveniences are available, it is sometimes difficult to get by without help. Hiring local help also made the Nicholsons realize they were providing jobs for people who were then able to help their families survive. During the interview process, be sure to investigate and check the references of prospective household employees. Use common sense and do not tempt the hired help by leaving valuables lying around. The Nicholsons experienced the loss of some jewelry, which is why they warn you to be careful.

It is a good idea to read articles about the host country to gain some background about the area and the people. When the Nicholsons moved to West Germany, at first they found their neighbors to be cold and unfriendly. Then, a friend suggested that they go around and introduce themselves to their neighbors. Once they did, they made many friends. Another piece of advice they offer is to become friendly with the local merchants, who can help obtain items that are in short supply.

When working overseas, Mr. Nicholson advises trying to learn the language, trying not to transfer your prejudices (learn to accept things the way they are), trying to blend into the local community, and participating in local activities.

Mr. Nicholson mentions two regrets: (1) not taking enough pictures (he said he felt silly doing so) and (2) not doing enough sightseeing. His wife and daughter would take side trips on weekends, but he was not always able or willing to go along. Afterward, he realized that he had missed an opportunity to see things that other people only dream about.

His last comment was, "know when it is time to go home." In some cases, expatriates really enjoy the job and do not want to return home. Companies sometimes agree to let them stay, if it is to their advantage and will save them money in the long run. In other instances, expatriates and their families have made no real friends in the host country and have been away for so long that they have also lost touch with their friends and families at home. Do not let this happen to you! Know when it is time to leave.

Source: William Nicholson, "On the Far Side: Stories About Expatriate Life," The *Expatriate Observer,* pp. 26–27, January 12, 1989.

The final part of a MNC's HRM strategy is **performance management and control**. In this day and age of downsizing, either you perform or you are out of a job. Big firms are cutting costs, and that includes cutting dead weight. Getting a manager to perform his or her specific tasks is no longer a chore. Controls are built into corporate policy to help evaluate management's performance. These controls make it easier for upper-level management to keep tabs on foreign subsidiaries as well as the home base. With today's communication links, information is available in minutes and performance does not take weeks or days to evaluate. The MNC now has the resources to keep track of itself and its employees, which makes performance a very important factor in management.

In conclusion, a MNC must develop a six-step strategy for its human resource needs. The need for more culturally diverse workers has resulted in an increase in HRM awareness. When developing its strategy, a MNC should keep in mind that the world is very diverse and that only by developing its workers can this diversity be harnessed to benefit the company.

SUMMARY

1. Human resource management encompasses the decisions that enhance employee effectiveness and that help to achieve organizational goals.

2. An international human resource department must deal with more functions, more involvement in the employee's personal life, and more external influences.

3. To be successful, managers must familiarize themselves with the differences in culture, social beliefs, customs, language, philosophies, religious beliefs, and work habits of the market in which they will function.

4. The most important factor in achieving economic progress is understanding the host culture.

5. Recruitment philosophies range from ethnocentrism (home country managers) to polycentrism (host country nationals) to regiocentrism (regional managers) to geocentrism (any background or culture).

6. Selection criteria are based on a wide range of skills and family factors, in addition to the necessary business knowledge and experience.

7. Compensation policies for international personnel are very complex due to the many factors involved.

8. Critical types of managerial skills are technical, human relations, and conceptual.

9. The six steps in developing a human resource management strategy are planning, staffing, compensation, employee development, labor relations, and performance management.

REFERENCES

1. T. Leap and T.A. Oliva, "General Systems Precursor Theory as a Supplement to Wren's Framework for Studying Management History: The Case of Human Resource/Personnel Management," *Human Relations,* 36:627–640, 1983.
2. F. Acuff, "International and Domestic Human Resources Functions," *Innovations in International Compensation,* pp. 3–5, September 1984.
3. Philip R. Harris and Robert T. Moran, *Managing Cultural Differences* (Houston: Gulf), 1991, p. 215.
4. Keen, Benjamin, and Aztec, *Image in Western Thought* (New Brunswick, N.J.: Rutgers University Press), 1990.
5. F. Murray and Ann Murray, "SMR Forum: Global Managers for Global Businesses," in *Selected Readings in Business,* Myra Schulman (Ed.) (Ann Arbor: The University of Michigan Press), 1986, pp. 247–252.
6. Avivah Wittenbert-Cox, "Delivering Global Leaders," *International Management,* 46:52–55, February 1991.
7. Natalia Wolniansky, "International Training for Global Leadership," *Management Review,* 75:27–28, May 5, 1990.
8. V. Scarpello and James Ledvinka, *Personnel/Human Resource Management: Environments and Functions* (Boston: Kent), 1987.
9. H. Stefan Robock and Kenneth Simmonds, *International Business and Multinational Enterprises,* 4th edition (Homewood, Ill.: Irwin), 1981.
10. A.G. Kefalas, *Global Business Strategy* (Cincinnati: Southwestern), 1990.
11. R.D. Hays, "Expatriate Selection: Insuring Success and Avoiding Failure," *Journal of International Business Studies,* 5:25–37, 1974.
12. Parviz Asheghain and Bahman Ebrahimi, *International Business* (New York: Harper & Row), 1990.
13. S. Davis, "Career Paths and Compensation in Multinational Corporations," in *Managing and Organizing Multinational Corporations* (New York: Pergamon), 1977.
14. R. Robinson, *Internationalization of Business: An Introduction* (Chicago: Dryden), 1984.

BIBLIOGRAPHY

Howard, Cecil G., "How Best to Integrate Expatriate Managers in the Domestic Organization," *Personnel Administrator,* pp. 27–33, July 1982.

Howard, Cecil G., "Expatriate Managers," in *Proceedings of the International Academy of Management and Marketing,* Washington, D.C., 1991.

Nicholson, William, "On the Far Side: Stories About Expatriate Life," *The Expatriate Observer,* pp. 26–27, January 12, 1989.

Young, John, "An American Business Perspective of the Single Market," *Europe,* pp. 27–29, February 1993.

6

DIVERSITY OF THE WORK FORCE: VARIABLES AFFECTING MANAGERS AND EMPLOYEES

ABSTRACT

In the 1990s and beyond, multinational corporations will face increasingly turbulent pressure emanating from various components of their surrounding environments, i.e., competition, domestic and international trade, and sociocultural factors. Technology transfer will help them to better position themselves in the ever-changing global market. The importance of developing the relevant skills to appropriately apply technology in the marketplace, which can give a company a competitive edge, is explored in this chapter.

CHAPTER OBJECTIVES

1 To distinguish among the work ethics of various countries

2 To describe the changes that have taken place in the field of international management, including changes in the diversity of the work force

3 To describe the recruitment process for overseas assignments and to discuss the reasons for expatriate failure

4 To understand the five levels of human resource management training and to describe the strategies for integrating returning expatriates

5 To describe the skills that 21st century expatriate manager will need

6 To discuss other related human resource management issues

CASE STUDY
Born To Be Real

Based in Milwaukee, Harley Davidson's Richard Teerlink recognized that the only way to successfully manage a diverse work force is to start with management. Teerlink says that many companies try to place the blame for ineffective management on other factors such as unions, customers and their demands, and competition. The only ones who should take the blame are management.

In order to manage its diverse work force, Harley Davidson had a specific recipe for success. Harley's "close to the customer" marketing philosophy created an opportunity for employees to receive direct input and feedback from both dealers and end customers. Another important aspect was to have appropriate technology. Harley also sides with the customer in another crucial area: pricing.

Teerlink feels that the leaders of a diverse work force have three responsibilities: to define the reality, to be a servant, and to say "thank you." Managers must empower their employees to make decisions. By following these rules, Harley was transformed into a successful business with long-term planning and growth. As Teerlink put it, "We are in the business of [producing and selling] motorcycles *by* the people and *for* the people. We must never forget it because the last owner forgot the people and they could not find a buyer for the business when they put Harley up for sale."

Source: Bryan S. Moskal, "Born to Be Real," *Industry Week,* pp. 14–18, August 2, 1993.

INTRODUCTION

In the rapid paced of today's world, the pressure on companies to produce, expand, develop, and advance is overwhelming. Acquisition of new technology seems to be a never-ending battle for every company. Lack of technology can threaten the survival of any company, whether domestic or international.

Observers have witnessed that technological innovation can lead to increased productivity. Therefore, it is essential for every organization to develop its human resources in order to acquire the skills needed to adopt the appropriate technology. This can given an organization an edge over its competition.

In order for technology transfer to be successful, the culture of the transferee must be compatible with that of the transferor. This means that the transferee and the transferor have to be similar in certain respects.

Technology transfer from one individual to another or from one company to another in a less developed country must include the appropriate abilities and skills as a prerequisite for success. Technology is not transferred unless it is actually received. Hence, the development of management skills becomes important. This issue will be discussed in greater detail in Chapter 13. Technology transfer as it relates to human resource development is the focus of this chapter.

The challenges that management faces today because of the diversity of the work force within an international environment are thoroughly investigated in this chapter. More specifically, emphasis is on such issues as work ethics, job descriptions, motivation and incentives, the roles of managers and employees, and other related human resource management issues. There is no doubt that future managers will have to deal with the different attitudes and cultural values of a diverse work force. Future managers can educate each other in new ways of thinking about these differences as they relate to business practices and management philosophies.

ROLES OF MANAGERS AND EMPLOYEES

Different cultures have different levels of expectations for how employees and managers should do their jobs. What one culture encourages as participatory management, another views as managerial incompetence. What one values as employee initiative and leadership, others may consider selfish and lack of teamwork.

In many countries, authority in business or government is inherited, vested in the person rather than the position. This may be a holdover from the influence of feudalism, as is the case in the Arab world. In this culture, a manager commands respect by virtue of position, age, or influence.[1] In China, the oldest member of the family is often the head of the family business, and usually the wealthiest family member.[1] American managers, on the other hand, tend to believe that respect must be earned. In terms of decision making and delegation, some executives believe that a tight rein and close supervision are necessary for adequate job performance. Other managers feel that there is more prestige in directing than persuading. In India and South America, those with authority believe that employees want a strong boss who gives orders and that workers should not question a manager's word.[1]

Because of the mobility of the global economy, employees often travel to other countries. When employees travel abroad, they should be prepared to handle the culture shock. Culture shock is the trauma of facing the different rituals and expectations of a foreign land. A comparison of the work ethics in the United States, Japan, and Latin America is provided in Table 6.1.

TABLE 6.1 Different Work Ethics

	Perception of foreigners	Job/company oriented	Perceived by others
United States	Poor workers	Job oriented	Lazy
Japan	Hard to make Americans work	Company oriented	Hard-working Lean and hungry
Latin America	Want American products but not their lifestyle	Individual	Rich and money-hungry

EMPOWERING THE WORK FORCE

The traditional roles of American managers and employees are changing. American companies are beginning to realize, although slowly, that they can become successful if they focus on empowering the work force. One successful strategy for creating an empowered work culture is the use of **self-directed teams** (SDTs), which are small groups of employees who have day-to-day responsibility for managing themselves and their work. Members of SDTs typically handle job assignments, plan and schedule work, make production-related decisions, and take action on problems. SDTs are formal, permanent organizational structures and require minimal direct supervision. They operate with fewer layers of management than do traditional organizational structures. SDTs take on tasks that were once reserved for supervisors or managers, including hiring, firing, conducting appraisals, and setting schedules.

In a recent survey, it was estimated that about 25% of U.S. companies are implementing SDTs somewhere in their organizations. Companies that already use SDTs include Corning, Toyota Automotive, Texas Instruments, Digital Equipment Corporation, Procter & Gamble, and Colgate-Palmolive. An organization must focus on five major issues in order to make SDTs work:

1. Designing teams for success

2. Selecting team players

3. Training for success

4. Initiating leadership transitions

5. Rewarding team performance

The SDT is one of the most powerful tools available to today's companies. Hundreds of organizations are using SDTs to some extent, with great success. They can prove to be an exciting innovation for the improvement of employee participation, productivity, and quality of life in the workplace.[2]

WORK ETHIC

Understanding the meaning of **work ethic** is essential in order to achieve a high level of performance. Ethics is the study of the general nature of morals and of the specific moral choices made by an individual in his or her relationships with others. Relating this to the work force, ethics is the rules or standards that govern the conduct of the members of a profession.

While Americans often perceive foreigners as poor workers in terms of work ethic and motivation, Japanese and Swiss who have taken over American firms find that getting the American labor force to produce is a perpetual problem. In Japan, employees consider themselves a part of the company and are loyal to it. Their daily personal life is their company life, and its future is their future. Americans, however, tend to be more job oriented than company oriented. When displeased with salaries, company policies, or working conditions, they often resign. Whereas the Japanese are perceived as hard working, lean, and hungry, Americans are often seen as lazy.

Latin Americans, on the other hand, work not for a company or a job, but for an individual. Here, managers can get performance only by effectively using personal influence. Among Middle Easterners, the influence of feudalism is still dominant. The individual is supreme, and employees tend to be evaluated based on their loyalty to superiors more than actual job performance. Australians have the shortest working hours in the world and take frequent smoking breaks. The French cling to their free time and vacation time and resist overtime. German firms also are moving in this direction. However, both the French and Germans are productive during work hours.[1]

JOB DESCRIPTIONS

Corporate policies, procedures, and job descriptions in the United States are specific and leave little room for flexibility. This reduces uncertainties and also permits job mobility among organizations. In Japan, corporate descriptions are vague and flexible to allow for uncertainties and to strengthen the bond between the individual and the company.[3]

In the United States, evaluation and compensation, in general, are based on performance, abilities, and skills and not on traits or personal characteristics. Other factors, however, also play a significant role. Concrete results are the criteria for selection and promotion in the United States. Among Arab corporations, policies, procedures, and job descriptions are vague and ever-changing and adhere to the desires of the people at the top, whether in government or business. Evaluation of performance in the Middle East is based on loyalty to the government and a close relationship with top management.

MOTIVATION AND INCENTIVES

Incentives and rewards that are appropriate in the United States are not necessarily acceptable in other countries. In America, money is the driving force. In the Arab world, for example, family considerations, job status, respect, job security, a good personal life, social acceptance, professional advancement, and job satisfaction act as incentives. The importance of family is paramount in the Middle East. Elsewhere, managers are more likely to emphasize respect and power.

Individualism in the United States means that people tend to look after their own interests rather than the interests of the group. A self-made person has more self-respect and feels proud of what he or she has accomplished. Incentives that support the team instead of the individual are more appropriate in Japan. American top executives, on the average, make 84 times what an average employee makes. In Japan and Germany, executives make 17 times what an average employee makes. The incentives usually match the values of the culture. The factors that influence employees are listed in Table 6.2.

Managers working overseas typically face both domestic and host country tax liabilities. Tax equalization policies must be designed to ensure that there is no tax incentive or disincentive associated with a particular overseas assignment. The administration of tax equalization policies is

TABLE 6.2 Differences in Job Descriptions, Motivation, and Incentives

	United States	Japan	Latin America
Key incentive(s)	Money	Respect and power	Family considerations, respect, job status, security, good personal life, social acceptance, professional advancement, job satisfaction
Corporate policy and procedures	Specific	Vague and flexible	Vague and ever-changing
Evaluation and compensation	Performance, ability, skill	Company's success	Government loyalty and relationship with top management
Promotion and selection	Performance	Predefined	
Self- or group interest	Self-interest	Group interest	Interest of employer
Executive pay rate to employees	84 times average	17 times average	

complicated by the wide variation in tax laws across host countries. The fact is that there may be a considerable time lag between the completion of an overseas assignment and the settlement of domestic and international tax liabilities. Recognizing these difficulties, most large international companies retain the services of a major accounting firms for overseas tax advice.

Another major area of activity for international human resource departments is relocation and orientation. International relocation and orientation addresses the preparation of managers for overseas assignments. It includes a wide range of activities, such as training for departure, travel plans, immigration details, housing, and schooling information.

An additional major area of activity is finalizing the details of the compensation plan, such as delivery of salary overseas, determination of various overseas allowances, and tax advisory services. An international company usually requires the services of an international human resource department or group in the host country in which it operates. Their advice is particularly important in providing expatriates with administrative services and information on government relations.

As mentioned earlier, money is the driving force in the United States. An employee incentive program is one of the best ways to motivate employees. Companies looking for ways to boost business usually overlook the most obvious frontier: their own people. Companies should look for ways to get their employees to not just work harder, but to work more intelligently.

There are a number of ways in which employee incentive plans can be created and carried out for maximum benefit to the company and the participants. The following guidelines can help motivate employees:

1. Involve the very people who will be motivated in planning the program.

2. Attempt to inspire the majority of the employees instead of only the top level, because they are already motivated. It is important to reward all those involved, particularly if they achieve their goals.

3. Provide merchandise rather than cash as an incentive, because commodities have more value as recognition.

4. Focus attention on actions that will lead to employee success. Develop two to three goals to focus on.

5. The objectives selected must complement each other. Success in one objective should promote success in another.

DECISION MAKING

Approaches to decision making vary across cultures. In Arab countries and Latin America, decisions are made at the top. Deals are never concluded over the phone; rather, they are made in person. In Arab countries, connections are a key to conducting business. Good connections mean faster and easier progress. Negotiations and bargaining are also commonplace. Decision making is usually done by the top person, who relies heavily on personal impressions, trust, and rapport. The Japanese consider proposals in silence. Their silence is often misconstrued by Americans, who consider silence in negotiations as a sign that the offer was not acceptable.

DIVERSITY OF THE WORK FORCE

The workplace of the 1990s and beyond can be described as high-tech, knowledge-intensive, global, complex, and diverse. Today's organizations face unprecedented challenges. Fierce competition, restructuring, globalization, deregulation, and technological change can create new opportunities as well as new challenges. Organizations need to build diverse work forces in order to create team members who will be ready to face these challenges. The dramatic increase in the complexity and diversity of the workplace means that managers must be able to perceive problems from a broader, deeper perspective.

Increased diversity during the recent past has changed the makeup of both management and the general work force. The number of women in the work force has increased 57% and 68% in management. Racial minorities have increased 53% in the work force and 36% in management. The number of immigrants in the work force has increased 31% and 7% in management positions. Disabled workers have increased 25% in the work force and 5% in management.[4]

Structuring a multicultural work force is not an easy task. Diversity of the work force begins at home, whether an organization is for-profit or not-for-profit. A top priority is recruiting and retaining a work force that reflects the diverse culture of the community in which an organization operates. Corporate and local government managers are being selected because of their commitment to diversity in the work force. For example, many local government programs for awarding contracts include policies that mandate diversity in hiring and support for minority- and female-owned business enterprises.

Managers have to deal with the problems of diversity from social, legal, and political standpoints. They have to cope with change and respond flexibly to the unexpected. Human resource management in a domestic environment usually deals with a single national group of employees. These employees are covered by a uniform compensation policy and are taxed by a single government. On the other hand, international human resource management deals with employees from diverse cultural backgrounds. The fact is, however, that even domestic human resource management in the United States has to deal with a diverse work force due to the melting pot nature of the American population. Because of this diversity, management should take a global perspective in recruiting, selecting, training, and compensating personnel, whether domestic or expatriate. Greater involvement in employees' personal lives may be

---

CASE STUDY
Kinney Shoes Steps into Diversity

Through training and hiring, Kinney Shoes Corporation, a subsidiary of Woolworth Corporation with headquarters in New York City, is ensuring that its employee base reflects its diverse customer base. To serve cultural diversity better, the company has embarked on a proactive training program to ensure that its work force mirrors its customer base through the hiring practices of its store managers. Kinney's Office of Fair Employment Practice was created to promote a fair and equal opportunity employment arena based on education instead of numbers or filling quotas.

Kinney also conducts eight-hour seminars, called *Valuing Diversity,* for its executives. This program focuses on managing persons in the workplace who are from different cultural backgrounds. The Kinney program also teaches how different people react to different situations in the workplace.

---

necessary in discharging these functions. Companies might consider establishing a multicultural committee to promote positive attitudes toward diversity. In a multicultural environment, it is not enough to focus on similarities among individuals. Programs and policies must be established to ensure that all members of an organization are treated with respect and are encouraged to share their diverse cultural experiences.

CULTURAL SENSITIVITY

Sensitivity to different cultures is of immense importance in managing cultural diversity. Asian Americans make up the fastest growing, most affluent minority group in the U.S. population. Many U.S. companies are using cultural sensitivity training to eliminate and reduce conflicts that occur between employees who speak only English and those who converse in other languages. Examples of how cultural sensitivity affects different types of professions are provided in Table 6.3.

Cultural awareness is essential in getting a product accepted and understanding consumption patterns. The way a product is sold must not be offending to the host environment. Flexibility in attitude is essential to the success of any global organization. There is no one approach that a company should use to effectively perform in a global market. Each company must design a strategy that matches the needs of its work force operating in a particular environment.

A successful manager must be creative, responsive, and tolerant. Managers should understand and respect the organization and be able to coordinate complicated issues, work with diverse behaviors, and solve organizational problems. Through a commitment to teamwork, managers should try to find ways of integrating the various units of the organization.

TABLE 6.3   Effect of Cultural Sensitivity on Various Professions

Profession	Cultural sensitivity
Law enforcement	In the Asian culture, lack of eye contact with persons in authority is considered a sign of respect. If a police officer in the United States were to stop an Asian on the highway, this behavior would be interpreted as that of a guilty person.
Social services	The cultural upbringing of Asians dictates that they do not divulge personal feelings or communicate too directly. Therefore, discussing personal feelings with a stranger, such as a social worker, is an alien concept to an Asian.
Emergency services	Fire departments constantly interact with businesses to conduct inspections. Many emergency services located in California have found it very helpful to include translations in educational materials provided by fire and police departments.

In order for cultural training to be effective, all levels of workers must be involved. It must start from the top and everyone must buy into it, hearing the same thing at the same time.

Source: "Cultural Training Benefits Many Industries," *Personnel Journal,* pp. 83–84, May 1993.

HUMAN RESOURCE MANAGEMENT AND RECRUITMENT

As firms become more international, the need for better human resource management techniques increases. Corporations need to develop their employees to handle more diverse tasks and assignments. A better understanding of the variety of cultures that exist in the world is also needed. Employees contribute positively when they feel that their contributions are valued and that they have future career opportunities within the organization. A plan is required in order to help employees develop the skills they will need. Such a plan is most helpful when it is created for a specific department or job category within a department. A program can be provided for all staff or for all departments. A successful business leader must learn to uphold instinctively the values that the native population respects and cherishes. Developing an awareness of these differences and finding the right mix of managers and employees to run a multinational corporation (MNC) is the focus of human resource management.

One way to identify managers for some or all of the senior positions in an overseas subsidiary is to recruit them from the home office or the home country. These managers are called **expatriates** or **home country nationals**. There are four advantages to using this method. First, the manager would be familiar with the goals, objectives, policies, and practices of the home office. Managers must know one another and their company. Second, the manager is more likely to be technically and managerially competent (otherwise, the person should not even be considered for an overseas assignment). Third, the manager is more likely to be an effective liaison with home office personnel. This is useful in communicating effectively. Fourth, it is easier to exercise control over operation of the subsidiary.[5]

Another way to recruit managers of foreign subsidiaries is to appoint someone who is a native of the host country. These people are called **host country nationals** or **local nationals**. According to a study conducted by *Forbes,* most companies prefer to hire native employees from the country where the foreign subsidiary is located, although it may be difficult to find local nationals who are capable of managing a complex business operation.[6]

Hiring **third-country nationals** is another possible recruiting approach. This manager is from neither the home nor the host country. For example, a U.S. company with a subsidiary in France employs a manager from England to manage the operation in France. This approach is sometimes used for a promotion from one part of the company to another, for example promoting a national who is career oriented and an international business manager. Sometimes, this happens by chance, as when a foreign executive is promoted to the main office or as the head of a new subsidiary because of a special talent.

Another recruiting approach is **international grade**, which is a modification of the third-country national policy to deal with salary problems. By agreeing to accept a transfer to anywhere in the world, an executive is promoted to international grade at a higher salary.

The last recruiting approach is **transferring a manager** for specific or limited duties, such as for a fixed period of time or a special assignment. New and changing locations of manufacturing facilities has created a shortage of certain skills and types of experience. For this reason, there is an increased demand for specialists on foreign assignments.

Understanding the link between strategy and human resource management is useful for several reasons: it provides a clear explanation of why such management should be linked to strategy, it provides a parameter for expected behaviors within an organization, and it helps researchers apply traditional human resource theories, such as role behavior, to the strategic posture of firms.[7] Strategic responsibilities of the human resource manager include continual monitoring of trends relating to the human resource function, assessing staffing needs and costs for alternative strategies proposed during strategy formulation, and developing a plan for effectively implementing a strategy. The human resource department must develop performance incentives that clearly link performance and pay to strategies.

When developing a multinational human resource management strategy, as with any strategy that has to be implemented, a company must first create a plan of action. In order to plan effectively, a company must assess its managerial and nonmanagerial needs for the future. A company must choose a workable combination of personnel management and development programs that enable the organization to accomplish its stated goals.

Normally, control is an administrative function connected to the implementation of a strategy. Control in a MNC is much the same as in a local company; however, multinationals face four additional areas of control which parallel their multinational status. The first relates to foreign exchange rates, and the second is linked to the fact that the firm operates in multiple environments. The third area relates to risk assessment. The last area of control, which is very complex, is the basic conflict between a MNC and its host government in terms of which will control certain key aspects of the company's activities. As a firm grows and operates in a larger geographical area, it must hire managers who can work in this broader arena. Global management means transforming an international perspective into a global perspective. A global manager must be able to change the way he or she thinks. Thinking in global terms means taking ideas and concepts from one situation and using them in a more complex global situation. For example, a manager from the United States will be required to know more than just his or her domestic language and culture. He or she will have to deal with foreign companies in conducting business transactions. To be effective, a global manager must develop the ability to use global strategic skills; to manage change, transition, and cultural diversity; and to design and function in a flexible organizational structure. A global manager should be able to work with a diverse group of people both individually and in teams, to communicate effectively, and to acquire and transfer knowledge in an organization.[8]

For top managerial personnel, the evaluation of performance is critical. As with all other dimensions of a firm, the process of evaluation becomes increasingly complex as a firm becomes increasingly involved internationally. All financial figures will be subject to the problem of currency conversion, and some currencies cannot be converted to other currencies. These problems are directly related to accounting and financial operations. An extremely important function of both of these disciplines is to provide accurate feedback, so that managers know exactly what they are doing and can properly plan for the future.

The government and the economy of the host country in which a business operates are the two main factors that influence international human resource management. In developed countries, labor tends to be more expensive and better organized and government regulations require compliance with guidelines on a wide range of issues such as labor relations, taxation, and health and safety. In less developed countries, labor tends to be cheaper and less organized, and government regulation is less pervasive and, therefore, less time-consuming. The basic functional areas of human resource management do not change substantially between domestic and international environments, but international human resource management involves a more diverse set of activities, with a more diverse population in a more complex external environment. Some managers tend to minimize these differences and overemphasize the similarities. Failure to recognize the differences in managing human resources in foreign environments—whether due to ethnocentrism or simply poor information and lack of an international perspective—frequently results in considerable difficulties for an international operation.

OVERSEAS ASSIGNMENTS

According to Harris,[9] there are more than two million expatriates currently on duty. International companies that use expatriate managers understand the importance of preparing those expatriates. The issues that surround expatriates make up a comprehensive area, called international human resource management. In 1987, Mendenhall et al.[10] identified 50 publications "in the areas of expatriate personnel, selection, training, and career pathing."

One of the major problems that requires special attention is preparation for foreign assignments. Predictions of a fundamental cutback in the number of manager transferred overseas have not proven true. In fact, the number of expatriate managers has held about even during the past few years.[11] Many companies, such as Ford, Exxon, Coca Cola, and Dow, consider international managerial experience as a must to get to the top. Those companies should also pay close attention to the issue of managing their expatriates. In addition, there is a growing belief that international transfers constitute a valuable strategic tool, as affirmed in several instances by Tung[12] and by Edström and Galbraith.[13]

The most noticeable issue is the inability of a significant proportion of expatriates to adapt. The recall rate is astonishingly high, as is the cost per failure for an international company.

Job Satisfaction

It is clear that one of the most thoroughly researched concepts in business is worker attitudes toward job satisfaction. Job satisfaction is a key factor in the turnover rate. Many studies have shown that job satisfaction is negatively related to domestic turnover. Although few of the domestic findings have been extended to the study of expatriate turnover, the fact is that expatriate turnover is much higher than domestic turnover. Studies show that 20 to 50% of all expatriates who transfer are dissatisfied, which results in the high turnover rate. Several factors that are under the control of an organization can increase expatriate job satisfaction, such as job task characteristics, organizational characteristics, and worker characteristics.[14]

Cost of Failure

Managers who plan to work in a foreign atmosphere should not only have a good understanding of the foreign culture, but must also develop an appreciation of it. This ensures a smooth relationship between the two countries involved and leads to a successful business venture. Drastic cultural differences are a main contributor to the risk of employing expatriates. If human resource management does not prepare expatriates appropriately for the job, there is every possibility that they will fail to adjust to the new environment. Expatriate failure can cause an international company thousands of dollars. One source indicates that the direct cost per failure to the parent company is between $55,000 to $80,000, depending on currency exchange rates.[15] Another source suggests that the cost of expatriates returning from overseas assignments can be around $150,000.[7] A more recent source suggests that expatriate failure costs a company anywhere from $250,000 to $1 million, depending on the employee's salary, the location, and whether a family transfer was involved.[16] When an expatriate fails, the company suffers a major economic loss. After returning home, a failing repatriate may choose to leave the company. The company will then need to recruit, train, and support a new global leader.[17] Indirect costs such as loss of market share, time consumed in finding a new expatriate manager, and damage to overseas customer relationships should also be taken into consideration.

Reasons for Expatriate Failure

There are many reasons why expatriates fail overseas. One of the main reason is their families, especially their spouses. According to one study, spouses are the reason why 90% of expatriates come back early.[18] The problems that spouses face are isolation, loneliness, and boredom, which can lead to alcoholism and mental and physical problems. This could result in an unexpected early return for the expatriate. Overseas assignments have been dominated mainly by male expatriates. However, recently the number of female expatriates, as well as nonheadquarters nationals, has begun to increase.

Another reason why spouses face these problems is because many companies do not consider them to be an important factor in selecting employees to go overseas. Some companies do not take the time to train the spouses of expatriates. As a result, spouses are uncertain of their mates' success, what they want, and what they will find upon going overseas. A spouse may have to put his or her career on hold while living overseas, because it is likely that he or she will not find employment in the host country. Some countries do not allow a spouse to obtain a work permit.

Finance is another major reason for expatriate failure. The cost of living in a foreign country can be much higher than in the home country. In 1981, maintaining the standard of living based on an income of $30,000 to $60,000 in America cost $90,100 in Ireland and $173,800 in Japan.[19] Businesses invest between $150,000 to $250,000 per annum to maintain a U.S. family overseas.[20] When the dollar is weak, it costs more to live in another country. Moreover, in countries with a high currency exchange rate, such as Germany and Belgium, the cost of living is higher. In Belgium, the tax reform act of 1976 made working in that country less attractive for expatriates.[19]

Another problem in the selection of expatriates is the misconception that they will work as efficiently as they did in their home country. Companies should design programs to carefully select individuals for overseas assignments and culturally prepare them to face the uncertainties.

They should select only those individuals who would be able to relate to, live with, and work with people with different values and beliefs.

Unfortunately, some MNCs do not have appropriate training programs for expatriates before they begin their foreign assignments. The feeling that such programs are ineffective, the dissatisfaction of expatriate trainees, and the short time between the training and actual departure are some of the reasons why companies do not have well-established training programs.

Such training programs would expose expatriates to various cultural nuances. For example, shaking your head in different ways means "yes" in different countries. Any type of touching is unacceptable in India and Pakistan, where people bow to one another. Crossing your legs and showing your heels is an insult and a sign of disrespect to the host in Arab countries. Expatriates need to be aware of these differences beforehand.

Shock upon reentry is another equally important problem faced by expatriates and their families. A different job, a new manager, the loss of a spouse's job, new schools for the children, increased housing expenses due to inflation, and loss of authority are all factors that create problems upon returning home.

An expatriate working in a host country can cost a company as much as or even more than hiring a local manager, which is why some MNCs have attempted to replace expatriates with local managers from the host country. According to a 1989 study, 88% of companies that responded planned to reduce their number of expatriate managers.[21]

There are also problems associated with using a host manager rather than an expatriate, in particular finding a qualified person to run the overseas operation. Also, by using a host manager, a company does not gain the international expertise that an expatriate brings upon returning home. This expertise includes language skills and knowledge about the social, political, and cultural systems of a country.

LEVELS OF TRAINING

The training provided to expatriates has been criticized as insufficient. The evaluation process is also considered to be inadequate and short-term performance oriented. Furthermore, the possibility that an expatriate will not find a position upon returning home is very stressful for both the company and the manager. International companies must develop overall training programs that can help them select those candidates with the greatest likelihood of success as expatriates. Companies should clarify what they expect from each expatriate selected. Training programs should be conducted in a systematic way so that companies can be better prepared for the expatriate experience. MNCs should conduct different levels of training to ensure the success of overseas assignments.

The first level of training should focus on learning about the host country's culture, language, politics, business, geography, religious values, and history. This should be done months before an overseas assignment begins. The tools used to acquaint an expatriate with a host country's culture can include written materials about the country, seminars conducted by experts in the region, videos, meetings with citizens of the country, and a visit(s) to the country before an assignment begins.

The second level of training deals with information about the assignment itself, such as the requirements of the position and the technical, managerial, and legal knowledge that are needed. This level of training should be conducted before an expatriate leaves for the actual assignment. Company officials in the home country can conduct this level of training.

The third level of training deals with better preparing an expatriate for the new job and should be conducted after an individual has transferred to his or her new location. It is similar to the training given to all new employees at any company, except that it is done in the host country in order to familiarize an expatriate with his or her new job. This training is usually conducted by the person whom the expatriate is replacing.

The fourth level of training actually continues for as long as an expatriate is in a host country. It involves keeping a close eye on how he or she adjusts and adapts to the new location and can be as simple as providing assistance to help an expatriate fit into the new environment.

The fifth level of training addresses reentry. The shock can be minimized by encouraging an expatriate to keep in contact with people at home and visit home during vacation. It is important to include an expatriate's family in the first, fourth, and fifth levels of training.

STRATEGIES TO INTEGRATE RETURNING EXPATRIATES

When an overseas assignment has been completed, a company can choose from among a number of strategies to integrate a returning expatriate.

Utilize the Experience of the Expatriate

An organization should make the best use of the experience of an expatriate upon his or her return. This can be done by supplanting domestic employees to make room for the returning expatriate. Such a policy would be encouraging to those considering an overseas assignment. Moreover, it would provide the expatriate with economic security and the company with a ready-made solution to the problem of finding a job for the expatriate upon his or her return. However, this policy is not without certain disadvantages. Displacing one employee to make room for another can affect the morale of both the expatriate and existing employees. No conscientious expatriate, no matter how desperate for a job, would want to be the cause of another individual losing his or her job. The new job may not offer the expatriate the professional challenge and opportunity for growth that he or she expects or wants, which can create additional problems, such as boredom, frustration, and disenchantment.

There should be a general understanding between the expatriate and the employer that the expatriate will be provided suitable employment upon return, provided the overseas performance was satisfactory. Many multinational corporations make a sincere effort to suitably place a high performer in the domestic organization. Such a strategy would encourage overseas expatriate managers to consider domestic career opportunities after completing overseas assignments, in addition to providing them with economic security and an incentive to stay with the organization. It may also encourage other employees to opt for overseas assignments. Every effort should be made to provide a returning expatriate with a job that is both professionally satisfying and financially rewarding.

Create a New Position

If an appropriate position for a returning expatriate is not currently available, a company should consider creating a new position that would be suitable. Sometimes an existing position can be altered to suit the newly acquired qualifications and experience of an expatriate. Letting an expatriate know that his or her services are valuable promotes loyalty to the organization, which also reduces hiring costs. A professionally and financially satisfied employee tends to stay with an employer unless an extraordinary new opportunity arises. Moreover, this strategy attracts competent domestic managers for foreign assignments. Keep in mind that creating a new job or modifying an existing one can lead to resentment and dissatisfaction among other employees, who may view it as unwarranted favoritism toward expatriate personnel.

Keep the Expatriate on Hold

In the event that an appropriate position is not available for a returning expatriate and a company is not in the position to create one, the expatriate can be kept on hold. An expatriate placed in this status usually receives some form of compensation, but must provide some appropriate, professional service to the organization. An expatriate who is considered to be potentially valuable to an organization may stay in this status as an adviser, provided that such an arrangement is acceptable to him or her. The benefit of this strategy is to provide the returnee with economic security. However, placing a returnee in a holding pattern is obviously a short-term solution to a permanent problem. It can create some new problems and compound existing ones, such as uncertainty about one's professional future in the organization and the frustration of doing something that is not challenging. Moreover, someone in a holding position may not know what exactly he or she will be doing when and where. Because of this uncertainty, an expatriate may look for a job with another organization, which means that the valuable experience gained from the overseas assignment will be lost to the organization that provided the opportunity. This strategy should be used only if management is confident that a meaningful position for the expatriate will be found in the very near future.

Postpone the Expatriate's Arrival Until a New Position Is Found

Another strategy used by companies that face the problem of finding meaningful jobs for their returning expatriates is to postpone the return. When this method is used, an overseas expatriate is notified of his or her transfer back to the United States, but is not physically repatriated until an appropriate position is available. This strategy has the same benefits and inherent weaknesses as the holding pattern.

Force-Fit the Expatriate into a Position

If an appropriate job is not available or cannot be created, a company can offer an expatriate a different job, which the returnee may accept or reject. While this strategy provides the expatriate with economic security, the professional challenge may fall below his or her expectations. Although this option does not guarantee a continued source of income, it does keep the expatriate professionally occupied. It is preferable to keeping a returnee in a holding pattern, even though the position offered may not meet the expatriate's professional expectations, which may result in extreme dissatisfaction.

INCENTIVES FOR EXPATRIATE MANAGERS

More experienced managers seem to be influenced by a variety of factors, such as a new job experience, better compensation, and a sense of obligation to the company. Therefore, MNCs are well advised to provide diverse types of incentives for both newer as well as more experienced managers. Expatriates tend to accept overseas assignment for the job experience, attractive compensation, possibility of advancement upon return, improved lifestyle (especially in less developed countries), exposure to a new culture, and greater professional responsibility.

Analysis of the current literature on expatriate managers reveals that most studies concentrate on the selection, training, and evaluation policies of MNCs. The literature also includes some studies of the cultural differences between home and host countries and the adaptation of expatriate managers to local cultures. Most studies, however, are from the MNC's point of view. How expatriate managers feel and behave is equally important in understanding how they adapt to overseas assignments.

The literature treats expatriate managers homogeneously so that differences in personalities, attitudes, and experience tend to be overlooked. Distinguishing between new or less experienced managers and more experienced managers can be useful in understanding the disparity between them. Experiencing a new culture may be appealing to some new expatriates but uncomfortable for those with less experience. The less experienced, however, may be attracted by the possibility of promotion upon their return. Such information can be valuable to an MNC in formulating different incentive packages for expatriates and can eventually lead to more effective international human resource management.

MNCs should develop personnel plans, policies, and procedures for integrating expatriates and utilizing their experience. All expatriate managers should not be treated homogeneously. Each has different motives, expectations, abilities, and skills, and an MNC should tailor its human resource policies to meet these individual needs. in doing so, an international firm will be able to develop profiles of its expatriate managers and then develop policies accordingly.

WAYS TO INTEGRATE A RETURNING EXPATRIATE MANAGER

Temporary replacement is one method whereby an expatriate manager is not relieved of his or her domestic job permanently. Instead, a temporary replacement is found to officiate in the expatriate's position while he or she is on an overseas assignment. Upon return, an expatriate can go back to his or her own job or can accept another suitable position. The individual who temporarily occupied the expatriate's domestic job goes back to his or her own job or to some other job within the organization. If the expatriate finds a better job, the employee who served as a temporary replacement could stay in the job on a permanent basis. All three parties involved in this transaction stand to benefit.

A MNC that utilizes a temporary replacement does not encounter a staffing problem. It does not have to worry about finding a suitable job for a returning expatriate, because the expatriate returns to his or her own job. Even though the individual is relocated abroad, his or her job back home is secure. The expatriate continues to enjoy both job and economic security while working abroad. Acting as a temporary replacement provides an employee a real professional opportunity to prove himself or herself in a new position. Satisfactory or superb performance may open up new professional opportunities for the temporary replacement in the organization when the expatriate returns. The temporary replacement also continues to enjoy job security, since the replacement can always go back to his or her own job. The expatriate manager also continues to enjoy both job and financial security while abroad.

The use of a temporary replacement to fill an expatriate's job presents two major problems. First, there is bound to be some disruption to a department whose employees fill positions in other units. Second, a temporary replacement may be professionally dissatisfied with the temporary job or, on the other hand, may not want to go back to his or her own job.

Co-equal arrangement is another method that might be used to solve the problem. This method can be utilized when it is difficult to find a position for a capable and valuable domestic employee upon his or her return from an overseas assignment, especially when the organization is afraid of losing the services of the expatriate because of his or her dissatisfaction. In this case, the overseas position is assigned to two individuals who alternate the assignment until the project is completed. While one employee is overseas, his or her responsibilities at home can be spread among other employees temporarily.

MNCs stand to benefit from a co-equal arrangement in two ways:

1. It reduces their overseas operating costs significantly, because the colleagues' families do not have to go along, and management is relieved of the major task of finding a suitable job for the returnee since the employee should return to his or her own position.

2. There is less room for hard feelings between the expatriate and company management since neither was promised anything.

The individual also benefits by this system because his or her job and economic security are not threatened by accepting an overseas assignment. It is only an alternative assignment and thus does not affect an employee's permanent position in any manner. Despite these benefits, the main weakness of a co-equal arrangement is that it disturbs the expatriate's family life.

Another method of integration is to develop a **career plan** by which an employee who possesses the right kind of management ability is prepared for increased responsibility as an expatriate manager. This involves matching an expatriate's career goals with the managerial opportunities available in an organization. It requires the development of a career path for each expatriate manager. Both career plans and career paths should be developed simultaneously. Career planning gives an expatriate manager a clear picture of his or her future in the organization. It also promotes loyalty to the organization and keeps the turnover rate low. Career paths provide expatriates with the job satisfaction and professional challenges that many seek. Further, if these plans are professionally and financially attractive, they can attract other domestic employees to foreign assignments.

Career planning would be ineffective in a situation that calls for mass repatriation of expatriates. For example, calling back all the expatriates who were working in Libya, Iran, and Iraq might not be appropriate for a MNC that operates exclusively overseas on discrete projects. A MNC in this category can sign short-term employment contracts with the employees who will serve abroad on a specific project. The MNC is then in no way responsible for the future careers of these employees or for providing employment in the United States after the project has been completed. Each returnee is on his or her own in terms of finding future employment. On the other hand, an organization may not want to appoint an outsider because he or she may not be as effective as an insider. In order for the plan to be successful, it must have the support of top management.

It is important to mention that even the most carefully developed and executed repatriation and job placement program can be an ineffective solution to the problem of no job upon return under certain conditions.

Factors such as political chaos, a highly fluctuating economy, and deteriorating business conditions abroad may force repatriation of an exceedingly large number of expatriates to the United States. In this case, even career planning, which is usually a logical remedy to the problem of no job upon return, will not help.

If management truly wants to prepare a company for the next century, it should start developing career planning that includes career pathing in order to accommodate overseas assignments. MNCs need to take a hard look at both their present and future overseas staffing policies.

SKILLS NEEDED BY THE 21ST CENTURY EXPATRIATE MANAGER

Personnel managers are expected to master a range of managerial and interpersonal skills to fulfill their mission. The future also demands from them a global vision. It is important for an organization to realize that successful domestic managers do not necessarily become effective global managers. Organizations need to expand their recruitment policies and procedures in an effort to secure successful global managers.[22]

Future global managers need an innovative spirit and excellent interpersonal and communication skills, combined with an understanding of a host country's culture. If a MNC wants to remain competitive and succeed in the global market, it must reevaluate its recruitment, selection, and development policies in order to accommodate the changes that will take place in the next century. Two crucial issues need to be addressed immediately:

1. The new criteria for expatriate managers of the 21st century, such as how they deal with people of varied backgrounds, as well as their selection and training

2. The multidimensional skills and knowledge that these managers should possess in order to succeed, including professional skills, experience, and management orientation

Future managers should be prepared to deal with different cultures, variable functions, other companies and industries, and varying backgrounds. The job of future managers, as well as the risks involved, will be particularly challenging.

Managers need to understand that the American way is not the only way. Business practices in foreign countries may be more complicated than in the United States. International managers are encouraged to be more patient and sensitive when working overseas.

The need for a new breed of expatriate managers with multicultural exposure and a broad base of education and experience is growing enormously. It is therefore important to educate managers in the global marketplace about the cultures and languages of a variety of host countries. In view of this compelling need, MNCs should subject their overseas staffing policies to serious scrutiny and determine the professional skills and training that their future expatriate managers will need.

It can be concluded that MNCs should develop personnel policies that take into consideration differences among expatriate managers. All expatriate managers cannot be treated homogeneously, because each has different motives, expectations, abilities, and skills. MNCs must tailor their human resource policies to meet the variety of needs and qualifications of expatriate managers. In doing so, international firms should be able to develop profiles of their expatriate managers and then develop policies accordingly.

REFERENCES

1. L. Copeland and Lewis Griggs, *Going International: How to Make Friends and Deal Effectively in the Global Marketplace* (New York: Random House), 1986.
2. Richard S. Wellins, "Building a Self-Directed Work Team," *Training & Development,* pp. 25–28, December 1992.
3. Susan C. Schneider, "National vs Corporate Culture: Implications for Human Resource Management," *Human Resource Management,* 27:231–246, Summer 1988.
4. Dawn Gunsh, "For Your Information," *Personnel Journal,* pp. 16–17, October 1992.
5. A.R. Negandi and P.A. Donhowe, "It's Time to Explore New Global Trade Options," *The Journal of Business Strategy,* 10:27–31, January–February 1989.
6. Cecil G. Howard, "How Best to Integrate Expatriate Managers in the Domestic Organization," *Personnel Administrator,* pp. 27–33, July 1982.
7. Cecil G. Howard, "Expatriate Managers," *Proceedings of the International Academy of Management and Marketing,* 1991.
8. Henry W. Lane, Joseph J. Distefano, and Brian Hollocks, "International Management Behaviour—From Policy to Practice," *Journal of Operational Research Society,* 41:646, July 1990.
9. James E. Harris, "Moving Managers Internationally: The Care and Feeding of Expatriates," *Human Resources Planning,* 12:49–53, 1989.
10. Mark E. Mendenhall, Edward Dunbar, and Gary Oddou, "Expatriate Selection, Training, and Career-Pathing: A Review and Critique," *Human Resource Management,* 26:331–345, 1987.
11. *World Executive Compensation and Human Resources Planning* (New York: Business International), 1982.
12. R.L. Tung, cited in L. Copeland and Lewis Griggs, *Going International: How to Make Friends and Deal Effectively in the Global Marketplace* (New York: Random House), 1986.
13. A. Edström and J.R. Galbraith, "Transfer of Managers as a Coordination and Control Strategy in Multinational Organizations," *Administrative Science Quarterly,* pp. 248–263, 1977.
14. Earl Nauman, "Organizational Predictors of Expatriate Job Satisfaction," *Journal of International Business Studies,* pp. 61–64, 1993.
15. M. Mendenhall and G. Oddou, "The Dimensions of Expatriate Acculturation: A Review," *Academy of Management Review,* 10:39–47, 1985.

16. Dhari Caudron, "Training Ensures Success Overseas," *Personnel Journal,* 70:27–30, December 1991.

17. Gilbert Ruchsberg, "As Costs of Overseas Assignment Climb, Firms Select Expatriates More Carefully," *Wall Street Journal,* 9:B1, B4, January 1992.

18. Charles Hill, "The Pitfalls in Diversity," *Management Today,* pp. 80–83, December 3, 1984.

19. Nadeem Shahzad, "The American Expatriate Managers: Present and Future Roles," *Personnel Administrator,* 29:23–25, July 1984.

20. F. Murray and Ann Murray, "SMR Forum: Global Managers for Global Businesses," in *Selected Readings in Business,* Myra Schulman (Ed.) (Ann Arbor: The University of Michigan Press), 1986, pp. 247–252.

21. "Expatriate Staff Cuts," *Personnel Journal,* p. 106, March 1989.

22. N.J. Adler, R. Doktor, and G.S. Redding, "From the Atlantic to the Pacific Century: Cross Cultural Management Reviewed," *Journal of Management,* 12:295–318, 1986.

BIBLIOGRAPHY

Cava, A., "Evaluating the Professional: New Perils for Management," *Business & Economic Review,* 35:27–29, 1989.

Cuneo, Alice, "Diverse by Design," *Business Week,* 72:18–19, October 23, 1992.

Dalton, D.R. and I.F. Kesner, "Composition and CEO Quality in Boards of Directors: An International Perspective," *Journal of International Business Studies,* pp. 15–32, Fall 1987.

Desatnick, R.L. and M.L. Bennett, *Human Resource Management in the Multinational Company* (New York: Nichols), 1978.

Heenan, David A., "A Different Outlook for Multinational Companies," *The Journal of Business Strategy,* 9:51–54, July/August 1988.

Hoffman, Richard C. "The General Management of Foreign Subsidiaries in the USA.: An Exploratory Study," *Management International Review,* 28:41–55, February 1988.

Hughes, Robert, "Navigating the Differences," *Training & Development,* pp. 29–33, April 1993.

Pesmen, Sandra, "Going the Quality Route," *Business Marketing,* pp. 18–19, 1992.

Pozniak, Julia, "Getting the Most Out of Employee Incentive Plans," *Business Marketing,* pp. 44–45, May 1992.

7

MANAGERIAL SKILLS AND THE FLOW OF TECHNOLOGY

ABSTRACT

The previous chapters in this book dealt with the transfer of managerial skills. This chapter addresses international technology transfer. In order to successfully transfer technology across countries, certain characteristics are necessary, including adaptation of the corporate culture of the recipient. The appropriateness of the technology is a vital issue that most countries, but especially less developed countries, must deal with. Competitive forces as they relate to technology transfer are discussed in this chapter. In addition, the elements that need to be understood before the transfer can take place, i.e., technical expertise available locally and exporting laws and practices, are addressed.

CHAPTER OBJECTIVES

1   To understand the concept of international technology transfer

2   To understand the keys to successful technology transfer

3   To understand the technology transfer process

4   To measure product potential in an overseas market

5   To discuss Kotler's four industrial structures to identify the economy of a country

CASE STUDY
The Success of the Swiss Watchmaking Corporation

The revitalization of the Swiss watchmaking industry and the launch of the Swatch watch in the Italian market provides an interesting insight into a successful transfer of technology by a global company. Nicolas Hayek (CEO) and his colleagues at the Swiss Corporation for Microelectronics and Watchmaking (SMH) engineered one of the most spectacular industrial comebacks in the world.

The dimensions of the turnaround were amazing. SMH took shape in 1983, when Hayek recommended that Switzerland's banks merge the country's two giant watch manufacturers. That year, the newly formed company generated revenues of $1.1 billion and lost $124 million. In 1992, SMH generated revenues of about $2.1 billion and posted profits of more than $286 million.

Hayek's management philosophy and strategic thinking are at odds with the prevailing views of how companies should compete in the new economy. Prevailing views suggest that global companies should become "stateless." They should seek low-cost production and build operations in many national markets. Yet SMH is committed to its Swiss home base. The major portion of SMH's technology, people, and production are anchored in the traditional center of Swiss watchmaking, the towns and villages around the Jura Mountains on Switzerland's border with France.

Companies also hear endless advice to become niche players by focusing on narrow market segments—but SMH is everywhere. Its brash and playful Swatch watch has become a pop cultural phenomenon. Last year, SMH sold an estimated 27 million Swatch watches.

In addition, managers increasingly believe that they should dismember their companies and retain only those core activities that are crucial to success. SMH, however, is a vertically integrated fortress. It assembles all the watches it sells, and it builds most of the components for the watches it assembles. Presently, 40% of the watches sold in the Italian market are made by Swatch, but the watch was not introduced in Italy until 1986. In fact, Italy was the last major European country to receive the watch. This seems odd in view of the fact that Italians love fashion and watches in particular. Even the Italians began to wonder when the watch would be marketed in their country. Then, when Swatch was launched in Italy, the market took off and

INTRODUCTION

With expanding global markets, practitioners of international management have observed that the technological innovations that have led to increased productivity in particular organizations in some countries have failed in other places. The supposedly erratic reactions of organizations to new technologies have prompted some researchers to has kept growing ever since. The average Italian customer owns six Swatch watches.

The delay in introducing the Swatch watch in Italy was due to the company's unhappiness with the distribution situation there. The company decided to wait until they could do it properly and then looked for the perfect opportunity. For example, when Milan was chosen by Sotheby's as the site of one of its first Swatch auctions, no one knew quite what to expect. It turned out to be an intense and emotional event, with many people pushing their way into the store and ready to buy. The employees at Sotheby's were amazed.

Design, communication in the broadest sense, quality, and price are the four pillars of the appeal of the Swatch watch. However, few people can ultimately appreciate the importance of price. The Swatch watch is sold at a very reasonable price throughout the world. Quite simply, it is affordable. For example, the watch costs $40 in the United States, SFr 50 in Switzerland, DM 60 in Germany, and ¥ 7000 in Japan.

The price of the Swatch has not changed in the first ten years of the product's introduction. Price is also a reflection of other characteristics of communication. It creates a sense of uniqueness for the company. The affordable price is hard to match and, therefore, consumers are unlikely to spend much time deciding whether or not to buy.

This sensibility is also reflected in the great cultural diversity that is behind the Swatch designs. There are close to 20 people in the Italian Swatch lab. The designers come from all over the world, including Italy, Japan, Germany, France, America, and Australia, among other countries. Some are right out of the university, trained in architecture or industrial design.

In conclusion, the success of the Swatch watch has had a major impact throughout the world. With proper willpower and dedication, other companies in Switzerland, France, Germany, or America can also be successful. Swatch was a major accomplishment at a time when the Swiss watch industry was declining and ready to fold. People thought that Nicolas Hayek and his associates were ridiculous when they invested SFr 1.1 billion in such a high-cost region of the world. For as risky as the situation was at the time, Swatch certainly came through as a technological success.

Source: William Taylor, "Message and Muscle," *Harvard Business Review*, pp. 99–110, March–April 1993.

speculate that few organizations hold the characteristics that govern all innovations.

International technology transfer has traditionally been regarded as a diffusion process by which innovations, knowledge, and the operational behaviors necessary to sustain the new technology are transmitted. However, in order for technology transfer to be successful, the culture of the transferee must be compatible with that of the transferor. In cases where such compatibility does not exist, human resource policies that intentionally change the corporate culture of the transferee are needed. In other words, for technology transfer to be successful, both the transferor and the transferee may need to adopt a similar culture so that compatibility between the two is achieved.

Although international technology transfer has been extensively studied from a macroeconomic perspective, the human elements involved in the process have only generated fragmentary theories. The ultimate goal of technology transfer is to establish and ensure the continued existence of a system that assists the transfer of managerial skills needed to carry on the project undertaken as an operating industrial organization."[1] For technology transfer to be successful, the management of technology, the project, and human resources must be integrated.

ADAPTATION OF TECHNOLOGY

Recipients of technology have two options: either adapt the new technology to use with the existing culture or modify the existing culture to be compatible with the new technology. The choice depends on a cost/benefit analysis. The final organizational behavior is determined by both technology and organizational culture. Hence, successful transferees often focus on both aspects.

Change in organizational culture can be achieved through organizational development interventions. Technological behavior and ceremonial behavior jointly determine the specific behaviors exhibited by organizations. If this framework is expanded to explore the assimilative behavior of an organization in transferring technology, it can be said that technological behavior and ceremonial behavior interact to determine the success of the transfer. Ceremonial behaviors are manifestations of organizational culture. Technology determines how instrumental functions are performed.

Kedia and Bhagat[2] suggest that the success of technology transfer may partially be determined by the fit between the organizational and national cultures of the transferor and the transferee. However, their classification of nations into developing, industrialized, and moderately industrial countries does not capture the variance among organizations within particular countries. Countries that deal with technology transfer can be classified as follows.

Technological creators. These organizations spend considerable money on research and development (R&D) and devise new ways and means of doing business. They are technologically venturesome and are sensitive to the other cultures. These organizations could be described as initiators. Because they spend huge amounts of resources on R&D, it is likely that these organizations expect good returns for their innovations from underdeveloped countries that want to utilize their modern technology. In this regard, they have two options: they can either internalize the technology or externalize it for a huge profit. As innovators, these organizations discover new technology and thereby differentiate themselves from existing cultures and technologies. Swatch was a technological creator in the sense that they researched and developed their product and became an initiator of a new style of watch which was an instant success.

Primary adopters.   These people and organizations are sensitive to and interested in adopting the new technology with a view toward development. On an individual level, these people are courageous enough to take the initiative and set an example for others who may adopt the technology later. Organizations that have ample resources and whose products are at the saturation stage also look for a breakthrough technology. These organizations adopt the new technology easily because they have no constraints relative to adopting it. These countries usually share a similar culture, standard of living, and environment with the transferor country and thus have no problem accepting the new technology. These people, organizations, and countries have an influence on those who adopt the technology later.

Traditionalists.   This group dreads change and is therefore resistant to it. However, their lack of development and decline of market share forces them to adopt the new technology. Since they are not by nature risk takers, they wait to see the benefits of the new technology being adopted by others. Usually under public pressure, and in order to automate themselves, they then implement the advanced technology.

Late recipients.   Groups that fall under this category adopt the new technology much later than others due to many reasons. The most significant reason is their financial position. Adopting new technology involves changing the existing technology, purchasing new equipment, employing newly trained personnel, training existing employees, and dealing with cultural differences and governmental restrictions. Since this requires expenditures that an organization may not be prepared to make, this group tends to delay adopting the new technology. A small section of this group can be described as *last* recipients. This group is tradition bound. Trapped in the past, they are not prepared to see the future or what the advanced technology holds in store for them. This group is a negligible minority in any field and is therefore not considered to be a serious influence.

It can be concluded that all companies in developing countries have cultures similar to the traditionalists and late recipients. From the preceding definitions, it is obvious that only late recipients and traditionalists are influenced by national culture in terms of the diffusion of technology. Culture is a construct that integrates strategy, structure, reward systems, skills, and human resource management in a company.[3] Successful technology transfer is facilitated by low commitment to the current frame. Many alternative frames also need to be available to a company for the healthy change of culture that will allow successful technology transfer. One alternative available to an organization that does not possess the culture of the innovators and early adopters is to change its process in order to alter its culture.

The main reason for marketing products internationally is to obtain greater profits. Four factors will encourage product adaptation:

1. **Differing conditions:** The conditions that affect the use of a product include culture, climate, user skills, geography, etc.

2. **Other market factors:** These factors include income and consumer tastes. For example, people may not have the money to buy a Cadillac or Mercedes in some countries. In France, people prefer four-door cars over two-door cars. These factors may require that a product be modified.

3. **Government influences:** Certain goods may be prohibited from being marketed in some countries. Some governments require that a product be manufactured locally rather than imported. Taxation policies can also determine which products are offered in what countries. Governments can impose restrictions on product packaging and labeling, especially in areas of food and drugs. For example, product ingredient requirements or the number of units in a medication may differ from country to country. Government specifications may also affect industrial goods such as trucks, tractors, and tires.

4. **Company history and operations:** Some multinational corporations have had foreign subsidiaries since before World War II. Those firms with established foreign subsidiaries will find product adaptation much easier. One reason is that the cost of product adaptation will be much less.[4]

Some researchers have proposed that interim transactions will be more attractive if the receiving country is similar to the exporting country in its demographics, tastes, cost of resources, religion, and language.[5] When such similarities do not exist, an organization must be receptive and make the changes necessary to facilitate a smooth transfer and understanding of culture. According to Adler and Jelinek,[6] the facets of national culture that affect transferability are dominance, desirability of change, individualism versus collectivism, and past orientation versus future orientation.

Hofstede[7] also shared a similar impression in defining national culture as power distance, uncertainty avoidance, masculinity/femininity and individualism. Kedia and Bhagat[2] considered lower uncertainty avoidance, high power distance, and masculinity as ideal conditions for successful technology transfer across nations. Therefore, it is imperative that the cultures of the transferee and transferor match.

TECHNOLOGY TRANSFER PROCESS

Traditionally, technology transfer has been an ad hoc failure in terms of addressing the overall success of the transfer process. Usually, the only type of training provided is the education of the initial foreign personnel to utilize the technology. However, successful international technology transfer needs to be a self-sustaining, ongoing system, and that requires the regeneration of skills and technology to guarantee the extension of the acquired innovation. Past failures in international technology transfer have been the result of providing only a small group of personnel with job skills training. Furthermore, although international managers have stressed the "appropriateness" of the technology to be transferred for the success of the operation, they have not developed an approach that would be applicable in cases where adapting the technology is not feasible.

The first step in such an approach is to identify the aspects of the transferee's organizational culture that may require adaptation. That is, once a company has decided to transfer technology from a foreign organization, the very first task of the human resource manager should be to determine whether the organization is an innovator, early adopter, early majority, late majority, or laggard. At this stage, it is also important to determine the level of commitment to or the fluidity of the current frame. The next step in identifying the aspects of the organizational culture that need to be changed is to conduct a management climate survey. Management's values and beliefs are not the only factors that constitute organizational culture. Evaluations of the ambiguity that is associated with the transfer and the clarity about the ultimate goals of the transfer are usually quite accurate.

A management climate survey can reveal the actual degree of openness in the organization and the satisfaction of the employees with existing technologies. If the employees are dissatisfied with the existing technologies and they regard any innovations favorably, then the task of the human resource manager is relatively easy in the transition from the old technology to the new. Although employees may be dissatisfied with existing technologies, the uncertainty surrounding the new technology tends to create resistance. For example, employees may fear layoffs or elimination of whole job categories if the new technology involves automation.

THE ISSUE OF TECHNOLOGY TRANSFER

Three key issues encompass technology transfer from developed countries (DCs) to less developed countries (LDCs): price, appropriateness of technology, and the ecological aspects of technology transfer.

Price of Technology

The issue of price attracts much attention because of ongoing negotiations between DCs and LDCs. Owners of advanced technology have long been accustomed to having their own way with LDCs. Only recently have LDCs developed technology transfer legislation designed to protect their interests. The laws are very controversial and have generated intense feelings on both sides, even resulting in impasses that have seriously hindered the flow of technology.

Because technology is generally patented, the seller is in the position of power. This allows sellers to choose who they will sell to, for what price, and under what conditions. On the other hand, LDCs must not adopt transfer legislation that is so rigid as to drive away multinational corporations (MNCs) and their wealth of technological knowledge. Several issues must be addressed when dealing with technology transfer:[8]

1. How much and what kind of technology will be transferred. The MNC in the position of power and may decide to withhold some information. A LDC that does not have all the information is operating in a partial vacuum and may not recognize the full implications of the technology or the lack of it.

2. The MNC controls what products will be produced with the technology.

3. The MNC can control the distribution of the product.

4. Sometimes a LDC will be required to purchase and use trademarks for the technology. This represents an additional cost to the LDC.

LDCs should continuously develop new technology legislation to protect their own interests in terms of price, transfer agreements, and appropriateness of the technology. However, legislation that is too restrictive will keep MNCs away.

Appropriateness of Technology

Only since the early 1980s have MNCs begun to realize the importance of transferring appropriate technology. The appropriateness of the technology has become the center of serious and fundamental problems that most LDCs must solve in order to escape their state of underdevelopment. There are two sides to this issue: supply and demand.

On the demand side, MNCs must produce products that allow LDCs to maintain important aspects of their cultures and traditions. On the supply side, technology must be compatible with the resources of LDCs in order to reduce poverty, unemployment, and uneven distribution of income. It is essential that LDCs develop appropriate technology norms. MNCs can assist in the development of technology norms in the following ways:[8]

1. MNCs can provide technical assistance in developing policies that will satisfy both sides.

2. MNCs can research directly through funded projects or indirectly through incentives to the private sector.

3. MNCs can restructure technology which may be obsolete for DCs and make it appropriate for LDCs.

The private sector of the home country can also contribute by producing products that are suitable for LDCs.

Technology and Ecological Issues

Ecology is an issue that has plagued DCs, MNCs, and LDCs. The ever-increasing search for technological advancements has created a surge of new problems due to the side effects of pollution and congestion. Thus, companies have had to devote considerable attention to modifying the manufacturing process in order to lessen the pollutive and congestive effects. Another aspect of this problem is that technology advancement requires heavy utilization of nonrenewable resources. All parties involved must learn to use technology that has less congestive and pollutive effects and low requirements for exhaustible resources.

DCs, MNCs, and LDCs must collaborate on all three issues. Given the need for technology transfer for all parties involved, it is in their collective best interest to work together. Although conflicts in price and terms will arise from time to time, sufficient commitment to help one another will serve to resolve these conflicts more easily.[8]

TECHNOLOGY TRANSFER AND THE ENVIRONMENTAL CHALLENGE

Changes in political, social, and economic forces have revolutionized the way MNCs are managed. These forces are continuing to create a global market which requires the standardization of products in order to compete in a global economy.

The phenomenon of globalization has not been a sudden, nor will it be a discontinuous, development. Globalization has been a product of change caused by economic, technological, and competitive factors. A hundred years ago, these same factors transformed companies from a regional to a national scope.

Three principal economic forces have driven companies and industries toward globalization: economies of scale, economies of scope, and national differences in the availability and cost of resources. These forces have caused companies to specialize and standardize their products. This competitive strategy has become known as *global chess* and can only be played by companies that message their worldwide operations as interdependent units implementing a coordinated global strategy.

Only since the early 1980s have MNCs adopted this "global chess" strategy. In the past, the approach of most MNCs was based on the assumption that each national market was unique and independent. With the advent of a new global strategy, MNCs quickly discovered that they could use funds generated in one market to subsidize their position in other markets, thereby increasing their competitive advantage.

TECHNOLOGY TRANSFER AND COMPETITIVE FORCES

As the international market becomes more and more competitive, those companies that can most effectively develop, diffuse, and implement innovative products and processes on a worldwide basis will be the ones that prosper. MNCs are recognizing that they can gain a competitive advantage by sensing the needs in one country, responding with capabilities from a second country, and diffusing the innovation to markets around the world.

No longer can U.S. companies assume that they have the most sophisticated consumers and the most advanced technology. No longer does the United States have the most innovative environment in the world. Today, new technology and new consumer needs are emerging worldwide.

Managers of MNCs must develop the skills that will allow them to learn from many different environments to benefit the host country, the home country, and the corporation. The 1990s and beyond will present both strategic and organizational challenges to managers of MNCs. On the one hand, MNCs are being forced to develop strategies that will allow them to be efficient, responsive, and innovative. At the same time, they must continue to practice traditional strategic approaches to ensure other aspects of their operations.[9]

NATURE OF ORGANIZATIONAL CULTURE

A collectivist culture that is masculine in nature can assimilate new technology very well. According to Hofstede,[7] an individualistic national culture is more open to innovation. He also points out that masculine cultures are adept at transferring technology because of their achievement-oriented, aggressive nature. Status and symbolic rewards are important in such cultures. Moreover, an abstractive culture is also hospitable to new technologies because of its dominant rationality and the cause–effect relationship.

In the case where a transferee possesses unfavorable cultural characteristics, the intervention of organization development can be sought. In addition, organizational development mechanisms can be used to establish a new and more favorable climate toward technology transfer. The very first step in adopting any new corporate culture starts with combating the lack of information and the sense of insecurity about the new situation. Because technology transfer potentially brings changes in jobs and roles, compensation, career paths, and co-workers, it is possible that an identity crisis may arise in an organization. To deal with the feelings of frustration and helplessness on the part of employees, the corporate culture should be adapted to be more hospitable to the new technology. To this end, the human resource manager could identify strong opinion leaders within the organization and try to use them as agents of change. This process could be facilitated if these opinion leaders or change agents exhibit in their behavior cultural characteristics appropriate for technology transfer.

Human resource managers can play an important role in clarifying ambiguities with regard to cultural aspects in order to reduce uncertainties. International human resource managers are expected to design policies and procedures that will facilitate employee performance. They are also expected to design a corporate culture that will facilitate a successful transfer of technology. In doing so, international human resource managers need to set certain performance standards, develop some incentives, and provide employees with the necessary guidance to utilize the new technology. These measures would facilitate the absorptive capacity of the recipients. The international human resource manager should also consider the cost factor and make sure that the cost is less than the benefit of the cultural adaptation.

The changing environment is always a concern for every manager. Not properly adjusting to environmental changes could be the difference between success and failure in any organization. These changes are not exclusive to government regulations, changing markets, or the prime rate. The CEO of a MNC also needs to understand that negotiating cross-culturally is as important to the organization as meeting consumer demands.

The conflicts that often arise between American and Japanese businesspeople and how these conflicts can be avoided is the focus of this section. The Japanese usually attempt to resolve a conflict by using methods that have proven successful in their own country, while Americans turn to methods that are used in the United States. This clash of cultural differences usually aggravates the condition. Americans assume that harmony is at one end of the spectrum and conflict is at the other. Westerners believe that harmony among a group comes only after conflict has been resolved. In a public setting, the Japanese, on the other hand, usually refuse to confront conflict head-on or even pretend that it does not exist. This approach minimizes obligations and offers more flexibility in fulfilling any obligations that have been incurred. In Japan, obligations are a critical influence in daily behavior. For example, when two Japanese businesspeople negotiate a contract, the party that gives in is not necessarily the loser. The other party is usually in debt to the person who gave in.

Understanding this key difference in thinking is extremely critical for American companies attempting joint ventures. Most joint ventures with American firms are held in a public forum in Japan, and the American firm is viewed as an outsider. Americans tend to rely on direct questions and logical persuasion as a means of influence in contract negotiations. The Japanese tend to deflect these direct and confrontational tactics with vague responses or periods of silence. American negotiators usually misinterpret this silence to mean "no" and adjust their offer or try to forcefully persuade the Japanese to accept the original offer. This increased pressure usually just aggravates the Japanese.

The general strategy of the American negotiator should be to manipulate the situation into a more private setting in order to gain some kind of insider status. By talking with the Japanese leader more privately and becoming more personal, he or she is less concerned about obligations incurred. Therefore, by reducing the number of eyes and ears that are involved in the discussion, the American negotiator is breaking into the in-group. As a member of the in-group, the Westerner can meet with the Japanese leader in a more private setting that will be conducive to flexibility, such as a restaurant or golf course. The private setting does not mean that the Westerner should confront the Japanese leader directly or make huge demands. This setting is simply the best tactic to resolve conflicts and to attempt small changes and compromises. The increased privacy should be used to build a relationship of insider status.

The U.S. investment in Japan has tripled since 1980 to $17 billion, and Japan is buying U.S. assets at a rate that totaled $70 billion in 1989. The number of firms that are forming joint ventures is increasing rapidly. A better understanding of the cultural and negotiating practices of other countries by American firms could provide the framework for a more competitive America.

MEASURING PRODUCT POTENTIAL IN OVERSEAS MARKETS

There are several ways to measure a product's potential in overseas markets. One of the most important is its success in domestic markets. If a product can be successfully sold in the U.S. market, there is a good chance that it will be successful in markets abroad, wherever similar needs and conditions exist. In markets that differ from United States, some products may have limited potential. If a product is successful in the United States, its success in export markets may necessitate a careful analysis of why it sells domestically and then the selection of similar markets abroad. This way, little or no product modification is required. "Think global and act local" is an important concept for international managers. However, they must also think locally and apply their knowledge on a global basis.

METHODS OF EXPORTING

Once a company has determined that it has exportable products, it must still consider other factors, such as what the company wants to gain from exporting, the demands that exporting will place on the company's key resources, whether the expected benefits are worth the costs, and whether company resources would be better used in developing new domestic business. Once these questions have been answered, a company is ready to continue the exporting process.

The next logical step is to research the targeted foreign market. Find out if the needs of the people fit the service that the product provides. Would the product be able to survive in this type of atmosphere? Answers to the questions can be determined by finding out specific information about the country targeted as a new market. For example, a company considering marketing in the Middle East should examine the trade aspect there. Trade is and has long been a major part of the economic scene in the Middle East. The region is very rich in resources that are scarce elsewhere. Therefore, it will continue to be an important market for future trade. Middle Eastern cities of ancient and medieval times were great commercial and trading centers. Twentieth century trade has been dominated by the petroleum industry, and manufactured goods are a major part of Middle Eastern imports. Despite the large role of agriculture in local economies, foodstuffs are another major import. Jordan's imports include foods, machinery, textiles, and military equipment, and its imports consistently exceed its exports. Israel's imports are uncut diamonds, fuel, lubricants, and consumer goods, and its imports usually exceed its exports in value. Beirut's trade center, which once was the most important port on the eastern Mediterranean and the hub of trade for all of southwest Asia, has been disrupted by violence. In addition to trade, normal life and essential services have been disrupted as well. This information alone is revealing when considering exporting a product.

Another important factor that needs to be addressed is the transportation available to move a product from one area to another. Because of its central location, the Middle East has long been an important region in terms of intercontinental transportation. The Silk Route from China and water travel in the region's seas have been significant since ancient times and are still being used. In recent years, the Middle East has also become an important interregional air route because of its location, and a number of major international airports are located there. Transportation within countries is not as well developed. Traditional means of transport are still widely used, such as camels, donkeys, and other draft animals, although they are gradually being replaced by motor vehicles. Great river boats which haul freight, such as the feluccas of the Nile, are becoming motorized. Although the first railroads were built as early as 1851, the rail systems are not well developed. This information reveals that the two main means of transporting a product into the Middle East are by plane or by boat and that transferring a product within a country can be difficult.

Another important factor that must be taken into account is foreign government product regulations. These regulations can take the form of high tariffs or nontariff barriers, such as regulations on product specifications. Tariffs are not the only way to control trade. A commonly used device is the import quota, which specifies the maximum amount and sometimes the maximum value of a commodity that can be imported in a given period. All of these factors must be taken into consideration before exporting a product.

In order for a U.S. company to successfully enter a foreign market, it may have to modify a product to meet government regulations, geographic and climatic conditions, buyer preferences, or differences in standard of living. A company may also need to compensate for possible differences in engineering or design standards. For example, parts of the Middle East that are mostly dry and barren are more underdeveloped. Some of the higher technology that the United States has to offer would probably not be of great use in these areas.

Buyer preferences in a foreign market may also lead a U.S. manufacturer to modify a product. Local custom, such as religion or the use of leisure time, often determines whether a product will sell in a market. The sensory impact of a product may also be a critical factor.

Another element which should be considered before exporting a product is the ease of installation. Find out whether technicians or engineers will be needed overseas to assemble a product. If so, is the technical expertise available locally or will the extra costs of assembly have to be incurred?

Once the decision to export a product has been made, familiarity with exporting laws and processes is imperative. The United States has a variety of strict export controls. First is the general control against trading with communist countries such as Albania, Communist China, Cuba, North Korea, and North Vietnam. The bans are so strict that they even prohibit the sale of components to a foreign firm that produces products destined for a prohibited market.

Another export control relates to the nature of the product being exported. The United States controls exports through a licensing program. A general license, available from the Department of Commerce, covers products that are generally obtainable from many other countries and those products that are no significance to national security.

Restricted goods or goods being exported to certain countries require a validated license. This license is more difficult to obtain and more restrictive. For example, the license may require that exported goods be shipped within a certain time period.

There are many restrictions against exporting products considered strategic or sensitive, including technical data or commodities related to nuclear weapons, explosives, armaments, various copper goods, and electrical, mechanical, or other devices used for surveillance. These controls have been imposed on grounds of national security.

Another restriction on exporting is in the area of pricing. The IRS has minimum transfer pricing limitations which it will not allow MNCs to go below because it will lower a corporation's tax base.

The North Atlantic Treaty Organization (NATO) imposes other export controls. NATO was designed to prevent the export of strategic goods and technology to communist countries if the sale would jeopardize national security. Although the United States is a member of NATO, it is not really affected by NATO controls because its own controls are more stringent.[4]

Indirect Exporting

There are two methods of exporting: indirect and direct. The principal advantage of indirect marketing for smaller U.S. companies is that it provides a way to penetrate foreign markets without getting involved in the complexities and risks of exporting. Several types of intermediary firms provide a range of indirect exporting services. Each type offers distinct advantages for a company.

The first is **commission agents**, or buying agents, which are "finders" for foreign firms that want to purchase U.S. products. They buy a product from a U.S. firm and then resell it abroad in several ways:

1. Foreign department stores, wholesalers, or retailers with buying offices in the United States may stumble across a product and find it desirable for a foreign market.

2. American and foreign manufacturers in extractive industries often have American offices to supply equipment and supplies for their foreign operations.

3. A MNC that purchases supplies domestically for foreign subsidiaries becomes a buying agent.

Another type of firm is an **export management company**, which acts as the export department for one or several manufacturers of noncompetitive products. It solicits and transacts business in the names of the manufacturers it represents or in its own name for a commission or salary. In other words, the producer gets the advantages of an export department without actually having one. Working with an export management company generally means closer cooperation and more control. There are several advantages to an export management company:

1. The manufacturer gains instant foreign market knowledge and contacts.

2. Export management companies often offer variable costs, which can be much easier for small or medium-sized companies to meet.

3. The manufacturer does not have to develop exporting expertise, which saves time and costs.

4. Consolidated shipments offer freight savings.

5. A line of complementary products can get better representation than just an individual product.

A third type of indirect exporting firm is an **export trading company**, which is an organization designed to facilitate the export of U.S. goods and services. It can be either a trade intermediary, providing export-related services to producers, or an organization set up by producers themselves. Export trading companies are very important in some markets. European and Japanese trading companies are usually the largest and most stable and offer the broadest market coverage, which makes them very attractive to potential distributors. In addition, many trading companies can also service the products they sell. However, there are some disadvantages to using trading companies:

1. They sometimes carry competing lines.
2. The latest product added might not get full attention.
3. Some developing countries do not accept trading companies.

Sales derived from indirect exporting are generally as good as direct exporting, but can be less stable and reliable. Indirect exporting tends to cause gaps in distance, information, and control.

Direct Exporting

The advantages of direct exporting include more control over the export process, potentially higher profits, and a closer relationship with the overseas buyer and marketplace. These advantages do not come easily however, since a company needs to devote more time, personnel, and other corporate resources than are needed for indirect exporting. With direct exporting, market research and control, actual distribution, export documentation, pricing, etc. become the responsibility of a company's exporting department. Direct exporting usually achieves greater sales than indirect exporting, provided the profits are greater than the cost of operating an in-house exporting department.

There are several different approaches to direct exporting. The first is using **domestic sales representatives** or agents to introduce a product to potential buyers. A MNC should select several representatives for each target market.

Another approach is the use of **foreign distributors**, who are merchants that purchase merchandise from a U.S. exporter and resell it at a profit. The foreign distributor generally provides support and service for the product, relieving the U.S. company of these responsibilities. An in-house exporting department can be both helped and hindered by foreign distributors because the distributor's interests do not always coincide with those of the MNC. Also, a MNC cannot control a distributor.

The first step in control is the proper selection of the distributor. Next, an appropriate contract must be drawn up. Most importantly, the export department must make sure that the foreign distributor is acting in the best interest of the MNC. Cooperation can be obtained through appropriate margins, marketing assistance, cooperative advertising, and good communication.

A third approach is **direct sales** to end users, whereby a U.S. business sells its products or services directly to end users in foreign countries. These buyers can be foreign governments or institutions such as hospitals, banks, schools, or businesses. The last approach is locating foreign representatives and buyers. A company may choose to use foreign representatives.

After the method of exporting has been chosen and the sales have been made, it is important that an exporter does not ignore its customers. Feedback and customer relations should be maintained. Rarely should an exporter rely entirely on secondary sources for information critical to business. There are several advantages to visiting the country involved in exporting. First, it is important to get the feel of the market. Find out how the products are being received, what the competition is doing, and if the customers are really happy. Flexibility and cultural adaptation should be guiding principles when traveling abroad on business. Acquire an understanding of the business culture, management attitudes, and business methods.

Exporting can be a risky business if not researched carefully. All items of importance must be studied and examined thoroughly before executing a plan to export a product overseas. Many companies fail because they overlook something important. Exporting requires thought and planning, but it can pay off if assessed properly.

THE RELEVANCE OF HUMAN RESOURCE MANAGEMENT TO LESS DEVELOPED COUNTRIES

The term *Third World* means a "loose designation originated in the 1950s for Asian and African countries emerging from colonial status or for nonindustrial and developing countries in general; originally used in the sense of a 'third bloc' distinct from the communist and western countries" (*Encyclopedia Britannica*, 1982), The Third World includes a wide range of countries, customs, and conditions. Latin and South America as well as the Middle East are included under this definition. Countries in these areas are considered nonindustrial and developing. Recently, some countries in Asia have started to develop faster and are now considered newly industrialized countries. The following four industrial structures have been suggested to distinguish among countries:[3]

1. **Subsistence economies:** In these economies, the vast majority of people are engaged in simple agriculture. They consume their output and barter for simple goods and services. These markets offer few opportunities for exporters.

2. **Raw material exporting economies:** These countries are rich in one or more natural resources but poor in other respects. Most of their revenues come from exporting resources. These countries are good markets for equipment and machinery which help them to gather their natural resources. Also, they enjoy Western-style commodities and luxury goods.

3. **Industrializing economies:** Manufacturing accounts for 10 to 20% of a country's gross national product in these economies. These countries now become markets for raw materials, steel, and heavy machinery. Industrialization brings a middle class which demands consumer goods.

4. **Industrial economies:** These economies have become major exporters of manufactured goods and investment funds. The large manufacturing activities of these industrialized nations create markets for all types of goods and raw materials.

In the past, only three of the four types of industrial structures were found in the Third World. Today, however, such countries as South Korea, Taiwan, Singapore, and Hong Kong fit the fourth classification. While some Third World countries have massive debt problems, others are using the wealth accumulated from the sale of their natural resources to enter the industrial category. No longer are all Third World countries considered to be underdeveloped and nonindustrialized.

A MNC needs to adapt to the culture of its host country. The word *culture* refers to the beliefs, morals, customs, language, and other habits or ways of life which have been acquired through tradition and which are distinct from those of other countries. Culture is acquired as opposed to innate. The cultural uniqueness of a country should be of particular concern to a MNC. Although cultural awareness has increased due to modern methods of travel and communication, the physical and cultural differences among countries need to be understood and appreciated. Sound business decisions are made when a MNC takes the cultural uniqueness of a country into account.

Women play a very strategic role in today's business world. Although the Middle East is taking steps toward liberating women, most men from the Middle East are not used to working with women as equals. Women expatriates should be aware of these conditions before going to the Middle East, where they may face opposition from both men and women.

Middle Eastern men working in the other cultures, particularly the United States, must realize that women are respected there. They cannot disregard what a woman says and must learn to show respect to their women superiors. The ideal situation would be for Middle Eastern men to realize how much women have to offer and take this new attitude back to the Middle East.

TECHNOLOGY TRANSFER AND THE NEW CONSUMER OF THE FUTURE

The past several years have been very traumatic for the global economy. The collapse of communism in Eastern Europe and the Soviet Union has altered the social, political, and economic landscape of the world, bringing new hopes and fears for global business leaders. Continuing trade tensions in the world community and the emergence of economic blocs in North America, United Europe, and the Asia–Pacific region have raised the specter of protectionism and insularity in global markets.

Despite these economic problems, a growing number of economists and business experts see a turnaround for the global economy. They predict that the world is on the verge of one of the greatest economic booms in modern history. The engine that will drive the great boom is the Baby Boom generation. Harry Dent, a Harvard-educated economic forecaster, predicts that the 80 million baby boomers will move into their peak spending years between 2006 to 2010. They will turn their sports cars in for station wagons and luxury cars. They will buy different products than they did in the 1980s. Toys, babysitters, and aerobics will be out. Trade-up homes, health care, and savings will be in. According to Dent, "The Baby Boom generation has different values than the Bob Hope generation. The Bob Hope generation was perfect for the standardized economy: they all bought the same toasters, wore the same suits, lived in the same homes and played on the same basketball courts. The baby boomers see value differently: they want to have it their own way. They are individualistic, and they demand customization." The new generation has less patience and demands what they want when they want it, the way they want it, and at the price they want it. The customer is no longer king—the customer is dictator.

Millions of consumers are eager to make the change to a capital market oriented global economy. This is partly because industrialized countries are becoming more interdependent, the needs of developing countries are continuously growing, and many of the walls that blocked the flow of information have been dissolved. The flow of money and technology across borders has further accelerated the trend toward globalization.

All these new developments will force companies worldwide to re-evaluate their marketing assumptions, further define their management strategies, shift to higher value-added production, customize their products and services, and generally reposition themselves in the global market in order to be prepare for the business opportunities that will come about in the years ahead.[10]

REFERENCES

1. Abdalla Hayajneh, Semere Haile, and Bobby Cunningham, "The Challenge of Diverse Work Force in American Organizations: Suggested Techniques and Competitive Advantages," in Abbass F. Alkhafaji, *Business Research Yearbook: Global Business Perspectives,* Vol. 1 (Lanhan: University Press of America), 1994, pp. 263–269.

2. Ben L. Kedia and Rab S. Bhagat, "Cultural Constraints on Transfer of Technology Across Nations: Implications for Research in International and Comparative Management," *Academy of Management Review,* 13(4):559–571, 1988.

3. Rauf R. Khan, "Japanese Management: A Critical Appraisal," in Abbass Alkhafaji, *International Management Challenge* (Acton, Mass.: Copley), 1990.

4. Vern Terpstra, *International Marketing* (New York: Holt, Rinehart & Winston), 1972.

5. W.H. Davidson and D.G. McFetridge, "Key Characteristics in Choice of International Technology Transfer Mode," *Journal of International Business Studies,* 6(2):5–21, 1985.

6. N.J. Adler, and M. Jelinek, "Is 'Organization Culture' Culture Bound?" *Human Resource Management,* 25:73–90, 1986.

7. G. Hofstede, *Culture's Consequences: International Differences in Work-Related Values* (Beverly Hills, Calif.: Sage), 1980.

8. Subhash C. Jain and Lewis R. Tucker, Jr., *International Marketing: Managerial Perspectives.* (Boston: CBI), 1979, pp. 283–288.
9. Christopher A. Bartlett and Sumantra Ghoshal, *Transnational Management: Text, Cases, and Readings* (Homewood: Ill.: Irwin), 1992, pp. 104–120.
10. Harry S. Dent, Jr., "Global Alliances 1993: Special Advertising Section," *Fortune,* pp. S.2–S.3, August 23, 1993.

BIBLIOGRAPHY

Aldag, R.J. and T.M. Stearns, *Management* (Cincinnati, Ohio: South-Western), 1991.

Ali, A. and Mohammed Al-Shakhis, *The Meaning of Work in Saudi Arabia,* (Hays, Kans.: Fort Hays State University), 1987.

Asheghain, Parviz and Bahman Ebrahimi, *International Business* (New York: Harper & Row), 1990.

Brenton, Schlender, "Are the Japanese Buying Too Much?" *Fortune,* p. 99, Fall 1990.

Carroll, S.J. and C.E. Schneier, *Performance Appraisal and Review Systems* (Glenview, Ill.: Scott, Foresman), 1982.

Caudron, Dhari, "Training Ensures Success Overseas," *Personnel Journal,* 70:30, December 1991.

Cohen, R.B., "The New International Division of Labor and Multinational Corporations," in *The Transformation of Industrial Organization: Management, Labor and Society in the United States,* Frank Hearn (Ed.) (Belmont, Calif.: Wadsworth), 1988.

Cole, W.E. and J.W. Mogab, "The Transfer of Soft Technologies to Less-Developed Countries: Some Implications for the Technology/Ceremony Dichotomy," *Journal of Economic Issues,* 21:309–319, 1987.

Das, Gurcharan, "Local Memoirs of Global Manager," *Harvard Business Review,* pp. 38–47, March–April 1993.

Edström, A. and J.R. Galbraith, "Transfer of Managers as a Coordination and Control Strategy in Multinational Organizations," *Administrative Science Quarterly,* pp. 248–263, 1977.

Ellsworth, P.T., *The International Economy* (New York: Harper & Row), 1990.

Friberg, Eric G., "1991: Moves Europeans Are Making," *Harvard Business Review,* pp. 85–89, May–June 1989.

Godiwalla, Yezdi H., "Multinational Planning—A Global Approach," *Long Range Planning,* 19:110–116, April 1986.

Helfgott, R.B., *Computerized Manufacturing and Human Resources.* (Lexington, Mass.: Lexington Books), 1988.

"Meet The New Consumer," *Fortune,* p. 6, Autumn/Winter 1993.

Taylor, William, "Message and Muscle," *Harvard Business Review,* pp. 99–110, March–April 1993.

Tung, Rosalie L., "Strategic Management of Human Resources in the Multinational Enterprise," *Human Resource Management,* 23:129–143, 1984.

SECTION IV

COMPARATIVE MANAGEMENT

A comparative analysis of decision-making practices in various nations is presented in this section. This cross-cultural analysis applies the following correlates of managerial decision-making practices across various countries: organizational structure, human resource management, involvement of the private sector, participant motivation, manager–subordinate interaction, corporate governance, and temporal factors. This comparison of decision-making practices raises the question of the transferability of management skills from a universal and an environmental perspective.

Comprehensive theoretical models for cross-cultural research are conspicuous by their absence from the field of comparative management. The few existing theoretical frameworks invariably treat culture as a residual factor (e.g., Ajiferuke and Boddewyn[1] and Lammers and Hickson[2]) rather than an independent variable and thereby fail to address the need for congruence or fit among cultural, structural, behavioral, and environmental factors that determine managerial effectiveness. In the absence of valid theoretical models, we can only speculate that productivity, profits, and employee satisfaction are high when there is congruence between organizational structure and the external environment and when structure and environment mesh with the cultural values of the operating system.

Longenecker[3] stated that culture in the United States developed from what different cultures left. More specifically, Longenecker argued that the things produced (i.e., food, clothing, housing, transportation devices, technology, etc.) are part of culture. However, despite a wealth of material culture, the United States developed primarily because it was blessed with abundant resources, a strong Protestant work ethic, and a legendary self-sufficient, entrepreneurial spirit, thereby substantiating Longenecker's distinction between material (artifact) and nonmaterial (i.e., organizations, status systems, rituals, etc.) culture.

Other values critical to American managerial effectiveness are individualism and time orientation. In the American culture, individualism, which motivates personal and professional accomplishments and self-expression, is considered to be of great worth. In contrast, individualism is not considered to be important in cultures that emphasize collectivism. In Japan, for example, the group is preeminent in work and family life, and conformity and cooperation outrank individualism. In view of the differences in cultural and decision-making practices in the United States, Japan, Brazil, Europe, the Middle East, and Africa, the question arises as to whether or not management technologies are transferable form one country to another. In other words, can Japanese or American decision-making strategies be practiced by managers in Middle Eastern or African countries? Do the latter's managers offer solutions for their Japanese or American counterparts?

This question may be approached from two divergent perspectives: the universalist (i.e., McFarland[4] and Haire et al.[5]) and the environmentalist (i.e., Gonzales and McMillan[6] and Oberg[7]). From the universalist perspective, it has been argued that there is a fundamental management philosophy or way of doing business. The environmentalists, on the other hand, believe that constraints such as local education, politics, law, and economic conditions are the primary determinants of managerial effectiveness.

This means that the way in which managerial effectiveness is defined may determine the universality of management practices. For example, the findings of Gonzales and McMillan[6] appear to support the environmentalist view. These researchers found that American management practices were not universally applicable in Brazil, specifically in the area of interpersonal relationships, which includes interactions between management and workers, suppliers, customers, community, competitors, and government. On the basis of similar research, Oberg[7] agreed with the finding of Gonzales and McMillan. Oberg expressed the belief that management principles are inapplicable not only between cultures but between subcultures as well.

In support of the universalist view, McFarland[4] discussed the similarities and differences between managerial practices in different cultures. He stated that some researchers affirm that management, because it is a science, should be universally applicable. According to McFarland, this is a controversial issue which has been applied in two contexts: (1) to search for principles and laws that work under different circumstances in varying cultures and nationalities and (2) to search for a fundamental administrative theory as evidenced by the transferability of administrative skills among firms, industries, and types of organizations within a given culture.

McFarland[4] found confirmation for his propositions in a study by Haire et al.[5] which supported the existence of universality of managerial thought, philosophy, and conceptualization. Haire et al. surveyed 3641 managers from 14 countries to assess the assumptions and attitudes underlying management practices, cognitive descriptions of the managerial role, and the need for satisfaction. According to these authors, "managers are so similar that countries find themselves, perforce, in the same region of the scale. However, in this considerable unanimity a real diversity among countries exists." Only 25 to 30% of the observed differences in the Haire et al. data were accounted for by national origin, which indicates that cultural differences were present but accounted only for a portion of the variance.

The author concluded that being a manager is a way of life and that managers across the spectrum of countries sampled in their research expressed similar beliefs, values, and perceptions about management.

The validity of the findings of Haire et al.[5] was, however, questioned by Massie and Luytjer,[8] who noted that generalizability of the universality of managerial practices was limited to Western cultures (10 of the 14 countries included in the Haire et al. research were Western nations). In addition, questionnaire items were open to numerous interpretations as a result of linguistic and cultural differences.

REFERENCES

1. M. Ajiferuke and J. Boddewyn, "Culture and Other Explanatory Variables in Comparative Management Studies," *Academy of Management Journal,* 13:153–163, 1970.
2. C. Lammers and D. Hickson, "Are Organizations Culture-Bound?" in *Organizational Alike and Unlike,* C. Lammers and D. Hickson (Eds.) (London: Routledge & Kegan), 1979.
3. J.A. Longnecker, *Principles of Management and Organizational Behavior* (Columbus, Ohio: Charles Merrill), 1973, pp. 339–349.
4. D.E. McFarland, *Management: Principles and Practice* (New York: Macmillan), 1974, pp. 627–628.
5. M. Haire, E.E. Ghiselli, and L.W. Porter, *Managerial Thinking: An International Study* (New York: John Wiley & Sons), 1966.
6. R.F. Gonzales and C. McMillan, Jr., "Universality of American Management Philosophy," *Journal of the Academy of Management,* 4:39, 1961.
7. W. Oberg, "Cross-Cultural Perspectives on Management Principles," *Academy of Management Journal,* 4:142–143, 1963.
8. J.L. Massie and J. Luytjer, in *Management in the International Context,* N.W. Hazen (Ed.) (New York: Harper & Row), 1971.

8

JAPAN'S ECONOMIC COMPETITIVENESS: A CRITICAL APPRAISAL

ABSTRACT

For the past half century, Japanese industries have acquired an economic strength and influence over the world economy. In fact, the literature is full of examples of the uniqueness of Japanese management systems and how critical that uniqueness has been to the country's phenomenal economic success. At the same time, it is apparent that it is essential for the United States to strengthen its economic competitiveness in the world or it will continue to lose ground to Japan. How Japan achieved this remarkable economic success in recent years is analyzed in this chapter. Those aspects of Japanese management that are not generally given much attention are examined. Why America seems to have difficulty retaining its position as a world-class competitor is discussed. Finally, suggestions are offered as to how the United States can meet the economic challenge of the mid-1990s and beyond.

CHAPTER OBJECTIVES

1 To study the economic competitiveness of today's global market

2 To understand how the Japanese management system differs from the American system

3 To review the factors contributing to Japan's economic success

4 To analyze the shortcomings of the Japanese management system

5 To examine Japan's attitude toward foreigners

6 To compare how the Japanese view Americans and vice versa

CASE STUDY
The Strength of the Japanese Economy
at the Bargaining Table

Following the collapse of the U.S.–Japan trade summit in early February 1994, the yen soared against the dollar. The Clinton administration stated that it was not their intention to let the yen rise just so Japanese goods would be more expensive in the United States and the Japanese consumer would have more buying power to purchase U.S. products. The U.S. government decided to launch a two-pronged attack aimed at the Japanese economy: to categorize Japan as a "Super 301" and subject it to retaliation by imposing trade sanctions on Japanese cellular telephones. Most of corporate America was happy about the administration's stance.

U.S. automakers claim that their Japanese counterparts are flooding the market with automobiles in order to maintain their market share rather than make a profit. Likewise, Eastman Kodak accused its major rival of flooding the U.S. market with film paper below market price. To remedy this, Fuji decided to produce film paper in the United States, a move that would allow Fuji to set its own price in the United States.

The supercomputer industry is another area of contention. U.S. agencies rarely, if ever, buy foreign supercomputers, partly because they know that such purchases will cause them political grief. U.S. trade officials complain that Japan is trying to buy off the U.S. supercomputer industry by awarding small quotas of American-made supercomputers to be sold in Japan. U.S. companies have not been able to beat their Japanese competitors and probably never will. If the U.S. government were to impose sanctions on Japanese supercomputers or take retaliatory actions against the industry, companies like Cray Research, Inc. would suffer the most. Cray imports many of the components, amounting to about $100 million, for its supercomputers from Japanese suppliers. If trade sanctions were imposed, the Japanese would increase tariffs on Cray's imports. Although the United States has a weak case with the supercomputer issue, the case for the cellular telephone is strong.

The cellular telephone dispute centers on an area south of Tokyo, where the telecommunications ministry paired Motorola with a company that also represents Motorola's major Japanese rival, Nippon Telegraph & Telephone Corporation (NTT). Motorola has said that its partner spends most of its time pushing its own technology. Now, Motorola wants NTT to pledge to promote Motorola's system and the telecommunications ministry to police that pledge.

Source: Wendy Boundis, "Fuji Co. Color Photographic Paper Set for U.S. Production, Challenging Kodak," *Wall Street Journal*, p. A7, February 7, 1994; Bob Davis and David P. Hamilton, "U.S. Set to Press Japan in Trade Fight; Tactics Include 'Super 301' Provision," *Wall Street Journal*, p. A3, February 15, 1994.

INTRODUCTION

Since the late 1970s, Americans have shown great interest in Japanese management. The difficult economic conditions of the 1970s resulted in the closing of many U.S. plants, a soaring unemployment rate, and a recession that reached new depths. At the same time, Japanese goods dominated American markets. Many people felt that the Japanese way of doing things could be used to cure America's economic and productivity problems. Many books, journal and newspaper articles, presentations at professional meetings, and television programs have focused on understanding the Japanese way of doing business. These forums have discussed various aspects of Japanese management, such as decision making, lifetime employment, the union–management relationship, total quality management, just-in-time inventory, and quality control circles. Many questions have been raised as to why Japanese companies have been so successful in the U.S. market and why U.S. firms have had problems penetrating the Japanese market. Japan's success is also attributed to the fact that the Japanese have succeeded in blending their human resource management practices with a system of efficient production. Integration of their unique sociological and cultural characteristics is what makes the Japanese human resource management approach workable. It is these very characteristics that have made it possible for Japan to effectively adapt Western management and technology.

JAPAN'S ECONOMIC SUCCESS

According to the U.S. Department of Commerce, the U.S. trade deficit with Japan grew from $10 billion in 1980 to $52 billion in 1988.[1] In the 1950s and 1960s, the label "Made in Japan" suggested poor quality, while "Made in the U.S.A" meant just the opposite. Today, Japan has rapidly become an impressive competitor of the United States. The United States and Japan are the two most powerful industrial countries in the free world today.[2] Japan in the 1990s projects the image of a producer of quality goods. In fact, Japanese-made goods have become the standard against which other countries now measure their productivity and quality. Japan's phenomenal economic performance has had an unparalleled impact on the United States and the world.

In the 1950s, the Japanese Union of Scientists and Engineers invited two American quality experts, Dr. W. Edwards Deming and Mr. J.M. Juran, to Japan to teach statistical quality control techniques and the secrets of managing for quality. At that time, many American firms were not interested in what Dr. Deming and Mr. Juran were preaching, but the Japanese business community enthusiastically promoted the quality improvement techniques and ideas of these two experts. The result was that Japanese managers adopted quality circles and encouraged workers to make suggestions. By the 1970s, customer perceptions of many Japanese-made products (such as consumer electronics, automobiles, and machine tools) had made a 180-degree turn for the better.[3] Nevertheless, U.S. productivity continued to dominate into the 1980s. Today, however, the story is different. The United States was in a recession until 1993 and Japan is booming.

Today, Japanese goods dominate not only U.S. markets but world markets as well (Table 8.1). While the Japanese economy is growing larger and stronger every year, the U.S. economy is moving in the opposite direction. This is evidenced partially by the huge annual U.S. trade deficit, the rapidly growing U.S. foreign debt, and the continuous decline of the U.S. share of world exports. Billions of dollars in annual trade deficit cannot be absorbed forever, even by an economy as developed as that of the United States. Protectionist sentiments, which have already resulted in milder trade sanctions than in previous years, are on the rise. There is a clamor for tougher and more punitive measures against Japan.[4] The significance of Japan's progress becomes apparent in view of the fact that the United States has become the world's largest debtor nation, while Japan has taken its place as the world's largest creditor nation. Japan's claims against other countries exceed $1 trillion.[5] Japan has seized the position of the world's leading industrial power, surpassing the United States in the production of both steel and automobiles. On a per capita basis, Japan's gross national product (GNP) is about even with that of the United States, and Japan has the edge in terms of growth. The United States is ahead only because of the sheer size of its economy.[6]

The economic success that Japan has achieved requires little documentation. Even a cursory look at its accomplishments is evidence that Japan is in a battle for supremacy with the greatest economic power in the world—the United States. Some Japanese have even begun to express the attitude that the United States has "taken the place of Japan's prewar colonies, supplying agricultural products and raw materials to a superior modern industrial machine."[7]

Comparing the GNP of Japan and the United States becomes extremely significant in view of the fact that Japan has virtually no natural resources

TABLE 8.1   Share of World Exports (in Percent): An International Comparison

	1970	1975	1980	1986	1987
United States	15.4	13.6	12.1	11.4	11.1
France	6.4	6.7	6.3	6.4	6.5
West Germany	12.1	11.4	10.5	12.2	12.9
United Kingdom	7.0	5.6	6.0	5.5	5.8
Japan	6.9	7.1	7.1	10.8	10.1

Source: U.S. Department of Commerce, "Current International Trade Position of the United States," *Business America*, pp. 18–23, December 5, 1988.

and only about half the population of the United States. Equally important is the fact that Japan has already surpassed the United States in the production of automobiles. The competitiveness of Japanese automakers has had a profound impact on the U.S. auto industry and has resulted in some fundamental changes in it. For example, Japanese automakers captured a record 26% of U.S. auto sales in 1990. Japanese transplants accounted for 22% of the cars built in America in 1990, up 53% from the previous year.[8] Transplants allow the Japanese to avoid trade barriers. Therefore, the Japanese can produce cars that will still be priced competitively in the U.S. market. Production of these transplants is expected to grow 44.4% between 1990 and 2000.[9]

Since 1987, Japanese auto manufacturers have opened five new plants in the United States, while General Motors (GM) has closed five and Chrysler has closed three plants during the same period. The only new plant opened by a U.S. firm was the Saturn plant, which opened in 1990. In addition, Japanese companies are now setting up engine factories, engineering centers, design studios, and research facilities in the United States. In effect, they have everything necessary to create, produce, and sell a car in the United States. Honda's first station wagon was designed, produced, and sold in America. Most U.S. firms cannot say the same for their cars. For example, the 1991 Ford Escort was engineered for Ford by Mazda. Ford's Taurus SHO engine is made by Japan's Yamaha Motor Company. Why are U.S. firms looking to the Japanese to engineer their cars? The answer lies in the technology.

GM purchased 38.6% of Isuzu Motors Ltd. of Japan and unabashedly imports and sells Isuzus at its own dealerships. Even more importantly, GM's joint venture with Toyota, which resulted in the establishment of New United Motors Manufacturing, Inc. (NUMMI),[10] started a new trend by which the auto industry in the United States is fast becoming a global partnership. There are already a few hundred deals between U.S. automobile companies and companies from other countries. Examples include Ford's Probe, which was designed and built by Mazda, and the Pontiac Lemans, which was engineered by Opel (GM's West German subsidiary) and built in South Korea. The Corvette's high-performance transmission comes from West Germany.

Another factor that attests to Japan's economic success is the ever-increasing level of Japanese investment in the United States. The number of Japanese companies in the United States is in the hundreds and covers a wide range of industries, employing more than 100,000 American workers.[11] Japanese investments in the United States are no longer confined to manufacturing and are becoming greatly diversified. Of special concern to Americans is real estate, particularly residential real estate. Japanese purchases have inflated the price of housing for U.S. customers.[12] In California alone, Japanese investment totaled $1.5 billion in 1985. In 1982, Japan's investment in the United States was $0.6 billion. The figure for 1988 is $14.2 billion.[13]

Japan's use of robots and plant modernization is rather impressive, to say the least. Japanese firms continually redesign and improve their cars. For example, Honda has a four-cylinder engine that is 10 to 15% more powerful than the six-cylinder engines of GM, Ford, and Chrysler. This type of continuing improvement will give Japanese firms an advantage in the future, when tougher fuel economy standards are imposed.[8] The Japanese invest two to three times more money on plant modernization than their U.S. rivals.[13] Both Japanese and U.S. automakers use robots in production. The Japanese, however, have installed new robots to make production more automated and more flexible. The use of robots allows firms like Honda and Nissan to produce hundreds of variations on a given model by simply reprogramming the robots.[14] Honda has taken the assembly line workers displaced by robots and employed them as engineers in its U.S. and British plants. Robots are more than a substitute for human labor. They do some things better than humans. Robots work at a precise speed, are clean, and do not make mistakes. The use of robots may be one reason why Japanese auto firms were able to reduce the number of defects per car from 2 to 1.2 between 1980 and 1990.[14]

Other indications of Japan's success can be found in such areas as global banking. It seems that after conquering large sections of the world market for manufactured goods, Japan has also assumed the role of a world banker. According to a report from the Bank of International Settlements in Switzerland, the share of international banking business held by Japanese banks exceeded the portion held by U.S. banks for the first time in 1986. The international assets of Japanese banks totaled $640 billion, while the figure for U.S. banks was $580 billion.[15]

FACTORS CONTRIBUTING TO JAPAN'S ECONOMIC SUCCESS

Some of the primary factors contributing to Japan's economic success can be seen at both the macro and micro levels.

Macro Level

First, Japan is considered to have an effective political system, wherein bright, competent, and dedicated government bureaucrats plan and coordinate all the developments within the society. The relationship between business and government in Japan is said to be cooperative, while in the United States the relationship is classified as adversarial. The Japanese Economic Planning Agency has been involved in formulating multi-year plans for the entire Japanese economy since 1955. The Ministry of International Trade and Industry (MITI) is responsible for gathering relevant information, developing and implementing long-term plans, and doing whatever possible to quicken the pace of industrial growth in the country. MITI officials give special attention to those industrial areas in which they think Japan can compete successfully with other countries in the future, help purchase foreign technology at the lowest possible price, promote the construction of modern plants and the use of modern equipment, encourage Japanese companies to cooperate in order to penetrate promising foreign markets, and so forth.[16] The Japanese government is also credited with creating a favorable economic and business environment for Japanese firms. For example, the Japanese tax system encourages personal savings, which means that Japanese firms are able to obtain low-interest capital easily. Government regulations and bureaucratic practices encourage the Japanese public to purchase from Japanese producers and distributors. Before 1985, Japan had successfully managed to keep the value of the yen at an artificially low level for the purpose of boosting its exports.[17]

Second, Japan is considered to operate with a long-term view, while the United States typically operates on a short-term basis. To be competitive, there has to be a continuous supply of faithful employees:

> For many U.S. business leaders, the monthly, weekly, or even daily sales chart is the key indicator of success...While U.S. managers think only in terms of sales, Japanese executives think in terms of everlasting customers...There is a world of difference between cultivating an everlasting customer and making a one-time sale. One does not sell an everlasting customer defective products or fail to meet his delivery schedules. A manager with a long-term view of customer relations would see a sale as the beginning, not the end, of the marketing process.[18]

Third, Japan is considered to have a well-rounded, educated, well-trained, and highly disciplined work force. Top management in Japan is promoted internally from among the company leaders. Everyone starts at the bottom of the ladder and has an equal opportunity. The Japanese government views education as one of the most important factors in economic development. Over 90% of the population are high school graduates and 60% are college graduates.[19] About 85% of top managers in America and Japan and 65% in Germany and France have university degrees. A 1975 survey found that only about 25% of British top managers had degrees. Even today, about half of Britain's top managers leave school before earning a degree.[20]

Management education varies widely among countries. In America, for example, 70,000 students earn MBAs each year compared with about 1200 in Britain (although the number is rising rapidly), none in Germany, and only about 60 in Japan. In fact, Japanese schools are credited with educating a diligent, loyal, cooperative, dependable, highly literate work force equipped with superb knowledge and skills in math and science.[21] Professor Jerry Fisher, an East Asian history expert, reports, "When you sit with Japanese blue-collar workers in a quality-control circle, you hear discussions at levels you'd expect from Americans who had gone through four years of engineering school."[22] Japan currently trains about 9% more engineers than the United States does each year.[22] There are 120,000 qualified accountants in Britain compared to just 6000 in Japan; that is because accountancy in Britain is seen as a way into general management.

More than 40% of the top 300 American firms and most big firms in Germany and Japan provide more than five days of off-the-job training each year for every manager. The statistics for Britain are somewhat vague, but it is estimated that the average British manager receives only one day of training each year.[20]

Fourth, the Japanese use a system called *keiretsu,* which basically is an overall product work group. *Keiretsu* refers to a number of companies that cooperate with a commitment to buy and sell from each other. *Keiretsu* companies constitute less than 1% of all Japanese companies; however, more than half of the Japanese-affiliated manufacturing facilities in California are fully or partly owned by *keiretsus.*[23] Japan's strategy involves a combination of cultural traits and the willingness to compromise in order to achieve consensus in all phases of business. The traditional Japanese way of thinking values devotion to an organization, and this is reflected in the overall style of Japanese management and the way that Japanese companies manage their employees. Coupled with Japan's sense of competitiveness, this is what has made Japan so successful. Americans would call it collusion. The Japanese call it *keiretsu* or business alliance. The Japanese see *keiretsu* as an agenda to protect their national security. *Keiretsu* is critical to Japan's special brand of capitalism and is the reason why Japan has an edge in the global market. The difference is a system that includes government, industry, capital, and the best technical information in the world.[23] This could be how Japan is closing the gap on America. Three of the Japanese Big Six corporate families come from the pieces of *zaibatsu* (or family-owned industrial groups) that the U.S. forces dismantled after World War II. Members of the Big Six own each other's stock, top executives may sit on each other's boards, and they give preferential treatment to each other as customers and vendors.

Micro Level

First, the Japanese are credited with having established a rather simple way to manage a complex organization, which is to eliminate conflicts between human needs and organizational demands. Harmony in the work environment is an important part of the Japanese business ethic. A Japanese company makes a total commitment to its employees and thereby gains their loyalty. The company is also committed to sharing knowledge and understands the value of its employees' ideas. The company involves its employees in all aspects of the organization's processes. Therefore, Japanese employees participate in decisions relating to quality, quantity, and even planning and operating policies. These functions are normally performed only by managers in the United States.[24] Also, the Japanese are considered to be the hardest-working people among the leading nations. They have managed to retain their work ethics and have a strong desire for progress. Japanese workers are praised for their dedication. They work long hours for their low pay and work overtime without extra pay if they fall behind. American employees, on the other hand, expect to be paid for every minute they work.

Second, the essence of Japanese management in large companies is a focus on human resources. This is accomplished through (1) a desire for quality, (2) a company philosophy that considers employee needs and emphasizes cooperation and teamwork, and (3) close attention to hiring people who are a good fit with company values and who can work as a team with members of the organization. Teamwork is prominent in Japanese companies because operations are based on human ties. The Japanese are inclined to conform to the general trend even without complete group consensus. Conforming to the group can be positive in that intragroup conflict can be avoided. In a recent survey of Japanese workers, 70% identified human relations as their top priority in life.[25] This emphasis on human resources is manifested in long-term employment, a unique organizational philosophy, and intensive socialization. The job security offered to employees confirms a company's commitment to its workers through good times and hard times. Japanese companies use various strategies to ensure permanent employment, such as hiring new employees fresh out of college, hiring temporary employees, reducing staffing levels through attrition, and across-the-board cuts in pay or hours instead of layoffs.[26]

Third, the Japanese strongly emphasize productivity and quality and continually look for new ways to simplify production and cut costs. One example is the Japanese use of a U-shaped assembly line whereby workers inside the U can reach a longer segment of the line. The U-shaped assembly line allows tasks to be grouped, which means fewer workers and an efficiently balanced line.[27] This is part of the reason why the Japanese need only three employees per day to produce a single car.[9] In comparison, GM, Chrysler, and Ford require 5, 4.4, and 3.4 employees, respectively, to produce a car.

Fourth, consensual decision making, or the *ringi* system (i.e., the Japanese decision-making process), differs significantly from decision making in the Western world. It is based on bottom-up decision making and involves the participation of a large number of people who do not have the authority to make decisions on their own. The basic steps in the process are (1) origination of a proposal, (2) research and horizontal coordination, (3) approval and vertical coordination, and (4) action. The principal benefit cited is that a decision and its implementation are fully integrated and, therefore, no one has to be convinced that a decision is the right one. The main drawbacks are that it is inordinately time consuming and can be used only for major decisions.[28]

Fifth, the Japanese system of lifelong employment provides stability and security. Employees are seldom fired or laid off, even when business is stagnant. Most employees are covered by a system that provides complete job security once they pass a probationary period. Wage increases are based on length of service and seniority. The company is committed to its employees and provides a sense of belonging, personal support, and a guarantee of employment until an employee is ready to retire. The worker in turn gives the company his best in terms of effort, loyalty, and devotion.

However, this system is not as comprehensive as it is usually understood to be. It covers only about 60% of the industrial labor force and excludes temporary workers and most women.

The relationship between employer and employee, as discussed earlier, is bound together by Japan's history, traditions, and culture. When an employee becomes a member of a company, he becomes a member of a "family." A company hires a person not only for his labor, but for the "total man" or *marugakae* in Japanese. This concept of the "total man" provides a sense of cohesion, identification, and loyalty and is the basis of an individual's total emotional participation in a Japanese company. The concept of *marugakae* leads to congruence between the objectives of the company and the objectives of the individuals working in that company.

A Japanese worker, whether in an office or a factory, basically believes that he is a member of the same team as the head of the company. He may like it or may hate it, but he sees that there are returns for his cooperation. Japanese firms are rigidly hierarchical, where every individual knows his place and where people enter according to educational background and are promoted according to age. There is only one hierarchy, as opposed to two or even three separate hierarchies as in Britain or the United States. Although status is important, it is not accentuated by such symbols as clothing, parking places, or dining rooms.

DISADVANTAGES OF THE JAPANESE SYSTEM

The success of Japanese management has been remarkable; however, it has not been without sacrifice. The system has many drawbacks, which are not always apparent. Workers endure significant social and personal suffering in return for the overall economic benefit to the country. For example, on one hand, the Japanese have created a unique approach to human resource management and have succeeded in blending it with a fundamentally efficient system of production. The resultant surge in the quality and quantity of Japanese goods and services is quite well known. On the other hand, this process does not appear to have been built purely with the workers' interests in mind. Rather, the main concern is the benefit to the society as a whole, for which a large number of individuals have had to sacrifice. Also, the practice of lifetime employment usually covers only a limited portion of an employee's life. The number of temporary workers is almost as large as those who have lifetime or permanent status. Perhaps the most inequitable aspect of this system is that the Japanese use female workers as buffers for the benefit of their male workers. Women are always considered to be temporary workers and can be laid off whenever necessary to keep the system of lifetime employment intact for men.[29]

Promotion and compensation structures are such that individuals are forced to retire at an early age, usually 58. Once they retire, they more or less have to provide for themselves. Retirees in Japan face severe hardships and often are forced to seek low-level jobs to maintain their standard of living. This is a serious social consequence in a country whose population is projected to be the oldest in the world by the end of the century. Whereas workers in many other countries view retirement as a reward for a job well done, the Japanese usually fear it. Even in companies where the retirement age is past 55, "elderly" workers are excluded from pay raises and in some cases are even required to take cuts in pay. In this sense, perhaps the retirement programs in the United States and other industrialized nations of the world actually come much closer to the idea of lifetime employment, where individuals are able to spend the later years of their lives in relative ease. The Japanese, on the other hand, exhibit a cold indifference toward their older and retired people.[30]

The Japanese system has also been criticized for not giving the individual the freedom to show initiative. People with initiative are not valued, because initiative is indicative of individualism, which is synonymous with immaturity. Autonomy is not the freedom to take initiative but rather the freedom to comply with one's duties within the context of the group. In addition, the basic element of Japanese culture is conformity and group orientation. The Japanese are taught to imitate and are discouraged from being distinctive.

Other weaknesses in the system can be seen in the promotion process, which is based solely on seniority. No one who enters a Japanese company ever serves under a person who entered the company after him. Merit has no place in this system. Salary increase is also linked to seniority. People usually get the same increases during the first few years, regardless of their performance. It is assumed that such a system avoids competition and jealousy among peers. Also, promotions are usually given only to those individuals who enjoy the respect and approval of their peers.

The *ringi* system of Japanese decision making, which is very well known in the United States for its positive motivational implications, has its drawbacks as well. First, it can be used only for major decisions. Second, the amount of time required for a successful *ringi* process is inordinately long. This system of comprise can mean the loss of corporate resources, can discourage bold decisions, and can lead to mediocrity and lack of innovation, creativity, and leadership, which is incompatible with today's ever-changing world.[31]

Japanese overtime policies demand that workers stay on the job beyond the assigned hours without extra pay and demonstrate a lack of concern for employees. It is estimated that an average work year in some Japanese companies is 20 days longer than in U.S. companies. This means that companies are able to get almost a month of extra work without paying overtime.

In addition, the demands made by Japanese companies on their employees' off-duty hours can contribute to economic and social hardship. Japanese employees are expected to spend a certain number of off-duty hours socializing with colleagues and subordinates in bars and restaurants, usually under company support. They often get home very late in the evening, and the time thus taken away from the family becomes a common cause of conflict between husband and wife.[32]

THE YOUNGER GENERATION OF JAPAN

The key ingredient in Japan's ability to integrate modern production operations with its human resource management approach is the unique Japanese cultural values. Japanese workers are becoming increasingly aware of the inequalities that are the result of the exploitative use of these values. The younger generation of Japan has become increasingly dissatisfied with the traditional values of the country, and this dissatisfaction is surfacing in their attitudes as well as their work behavior. Young men in their twenties are especially critical of what they call Japan's "mindless groupism."[33]

The concept of loyalty to the company has also been challenged by the new generation. Current surveys of the younger generation in Japan show that more people are oriented toward home rather than the company. According to Lee Smith, in 1984 the Japanese work ethic seemed to be shifting toward the American style. The new generation in Japan appears to oppose working long hours, whether on job-related activities or socializing outside the work area.[34] Japanese workers are becoming more time oriented and are observing the clock, even to the point of stopping in the middle of a job. As soon as the clock strikes the closing hour, workers expect to go home, and they often resent being asked to stay beyond normal working hours. The Japanese are taking more interest in leisure activities and the general concept of leisure, as evidenced by sales of sports equipment. Today, Japanese workers are actually using and taking greater advantage of vacation time than ever before. Traditionally, no Japanese worker would ever enjoy the full vacation time he had earned. Workers would often voluntarily surrender vacation time to the company. Today, however, a new trend is taking place in Japan concerning extended vacation time. The trend is a definite departure from tradition and is a sure indication of the change in attitude toward work and leisure in Japan.[35]

The value placed on lifelong employment is being questioned as well. Japanese employees do not demonstrate the same desire for or the same attitude toward this concept as they have in the past. Mobility is becoming increasingly visible. Younger workers no longer feel obligated to continue working for the same company. Until a few years ago, such an attitude was unheard of, but people are now moving freely from one company to another. The appearance of Western-style "head-hunting," or *heddo-hantaa*, is another phenomenon developing in Japan. Bright workers are receiving unsolicited job offers from other companies. Fearful of this growing trend, many large companies have begun to take steps to retain their employees by offering such incentives as bigger bonuses and long-term loans for housing and education. Companies are also being forced to rethink their traditional policies based solely on seniority.[36]

The end of loyalty and perhaps of the traditional system of life-long employment may be in Japan's near future. Not only are workers exhibiting changes in their attitudes and work behavior, Japanese managers themselves are violating the traditional patterns of management practices.

Some of the largest Japanese companies are being run by managers who have authoritarian attitudes at best and who are downright dictatorial at worst. Important decisions are being made individually, and the consensus process is nowhere to be found. The Japanese system has been characterized by a uniquely harmonious relationship between management and organized labor. It has been said that trade unions do not exist in Japan. The truth is that they do not exist in the Western sense of the term. Contrary to popular belief, however, strikes do occur in Japan. For example, there were 938 strikes and lockouts in Japan in 1983, which cost the economy 507,000 working days.[37]

FOREIGNERS THROUGH THE EYES OF THE JAPANESE

A prevailing form of social inequality in Japan is the treatment of non-Japanese members of its society. The level of acceptance of foreigners is so low that even third-generation foreigners—whether Asian, European, or American—are not treated as equals or as full citizens. This attitude translates into discriminatory attitudes in employment as well as in social contexts.[38]

A large number of Japanese feel that if they remain silent, they will be understood. Generally speaking, the Japanese consider it best not to talk too much and no more than is necessary in any situation. Although eloquent, the outspoken speaker during a conference often is not respected and sometimes even despised. This custom may originate in the tradition of acknowledging another's superiority over oneself, which the Japanese view as modesty or politeness.[18]

Although the Japanese have developed a reputation as the epitome of courtesy and politeness, such hospitality is not applied universally. For example, the Japanese make a clear distinction between a visitor to their country, who is considered a guest, and a foreigner, who takes up residence and tries to become a part of Japanese society. The latter no longer has the status of a guest. While guests are treated with the utmost courtesy, foreigners living in Japan are not. Some foreign residents in Japan have become so disillusioned that they plan to move to "a less falsely polite country."[39] Foreigners generally find it virtually impossible to become integrated into Japanese society.[40]

Japanese View of Americans

The Japanese criticize American workers as being too preoccupied on Fridays with the coming weekend and unable to throw themselves back into their work on Mondays. Typically, Americans are depicted as lazy and laid back. Americans concentrate on themselves as individuals and what they can accomplish today for themselves rather than for a friend or their country. This attitude has prompted the Japanese to say that there is a

Monday car and a Friday car. Both types of cars are thought to be defective because on Mondays the workers are plagued with hangovers and on Fridays they are in a hurry to leave work for the weekend.

Yoshio Sakurauchi, speaker of the Lower House of Diet, has referred to America as Japan's subcontractor. It has been noted, however, that the more the Japanese criticize America, the more incensed the Americans become and the harder they work. The Japanese believe that Americans should act more like they do, but not by copying their system. They think that Americans should adopt parts of their system and become more knowledgeable about how it works. Shoicha Saba, former chairman of Toshiba (a member of the Mitsui group), stated that Japan as a system is "not a closed society, but one of long-term relationships."[23] Many of these relationships stem as far back as World War II.

HOW THE UNITED STATES VIEWS JAPAN

A recent survey by *Time* magazine indicated that 21% of the Japanese viewed American workers as lazy. In another poll conducted by *Time*, 66% of Americans surveyed felt that the main reason that the U.S. trade deficit is so large is because American products are unfairly kept out of Japan.[41] The same survey found that 51% of Americans polled thought that the United States would be the strongest economic power in ten years and 27% thought that Japan would be. The survey also found that 4% of Americans viewed the Japanese as lazy.

Americans view the hard-working Japanese in five different ways: as sarcastic, prejudiced, frightening, having a superiority complex, and as a learning opportunity.[25] Few Americans actually want to learn from the Japanese.

The Japanese are becoming concerned about how Americans view their country. Japanese executives view these negative attitudes toward them with alarm, because Japan has a big stake in the American market. Foreigners claim that Japanese participants at conferences are silent and "smile and sleep." Silence may be the custom in Japan, but it may not be an effective means of communication outside of Japan. This is an example of a custom that should be modified in order to promote better communication in business relations in foreign countries where the opposite is common practice.

Haniyasa Osumi states, "We must change ourselves, even though our way of business is good for Japan." Keikichi Honda, president of the Bank of Tokyo's research arm, states, "The reality is that the United States needs greater Japanese collaboration, it is not a joke. We need to recognize our responsibility and to share the burden." As of yet, no program has emerged, but it is predicted that the "Japanese problem" will take center stage in future American presidential elections.[42]

One such program might include technical and financial support for U.S. auto and electrical parts suppliers that want their products to be designed into Japanese products. Bureaucrats might agree to purchase more U.S. glass and paper products and to contribute money to the $8 billion American supercollider project. It seems that the Japanese are willing to try to work things out with the United States. According to Akio Morito, the Japanese would find managed trade easier to swallow if they felt that it would result in a more competitive America, because they continue to depend on the United States as a vast market for their products.[43]

MANAGEMENT PERFORMANCE

Management performance incentives are the most important tools available to top management and boards of directors in influencing managers to pursue corporate goals. Compensation includes financial returns, tangible services, and the benefits employees receive as part of an employment relationship. Compensation excludes promotions, recognition for outstanding work, feelings of accomplishment, and choice of office location.[44]

There are six basic forms of compensation: cash bonuses and profit sharing, stock bonuses, deferred compensation, stock options, stock appreciation rights, and performance shares.[45] Modified forms of compensation can be either indirect or direct. Americans use direct forms and the Japanese use indirect forms. Recently, considerable attention has been given to the differences in compensation between chief executives in America and in Japan. "American CEO's are grossly overpaid, earning about 160 times more than the average employee. In Japan, by contrast, CEO's earn only sixteen times more than the average worker."[46] A prime example of a Japanese corporate executive is Shoichi Saba, CEO of Toshiba. Mr. Saba did not bring up the issue of a raise once between 1980 and 1986. It was estimated that he was making approximately $320,000. This compares as follows:

Country	Compensation
United States	$3,200,000
Britain	$1,100,000
France	$800,000
Germany	$800,000

A *Time* magazine comparison of the salaries of the CEOs of Detroit's Big Three automakers (GM, Ford, and Chrysler) versus Japan's top three automakers (Toyota, Nissan, and Honda) showed an enormous difference in favor of the U.S. dealers, who were less productive.[47]

As can be seen, the wages of Japanese CEOs are not comparable to the wages of other CEOs.[48] The Japanese do not understand why U.S. businesses generously reward their top executives during hard times. In Japan, top managers are expected to take a voluntary cut in pay when their companies get in trouble. Executive pay is cut before jobs are eliminated. The irony of the situation is that there are no long-term incentives in Japan, even though long-term behavior is more prevalent. The only solution to this problem is to limit the salaries of CEOs in America. However, pay limits, which are really price controls, never work. The salary of a CEO is expected to increase at least 5% this year, and bonuses are expected to jump as much as 10%. Many Americans feel that U.S. executives make more than Japanese CEOs, even though they have done less to earn their pay.[47]

FINAL REMARKS

International economic competitiveness is attracting much attention. America's industrial leadership is being put to the test by Japan. During the past few years, Japanese management practices have become well known in the United States. They are generally perceived positively. Japanese production operations are acknowledged for their efficiency, productivity, and quality, and Japanese human resource management policies are praised for their concern for workers, their emphasis on participation and motivation, and their overall humanitarianism.

The Japanese strongly emphasize productivity and quality and continually look for new ways to simplify production and cut costs. Japanese firms continually redesign and improve their products. The Japanese invest two to three times more money in plant modernization than their U.S. rivals.[13] While both Japanese and U.S. automakers use robots in auto production, the Japanese have installed new robots to increase automation and flexibility.

Although Japan has had great economic success, a more thorough investigation reveals the sacrifice in human and social terms, often at the expense of workers. Even Japanese executives admit that Japanese companies have grown by sacrificing the health of their employees. The frustration felt by Japanese workers is evident in many forms today. For example, emotional breakdowns, alcoholism, and the divorce rate are growing at an alarmingly rapid rate.[49] Policies such as lifelong employment do not symbolize what they did in the past. Only a small number of workers benefit from such policies now. People who have been persuaded to retire are left to fend for themselves.[50] Discrimination against women is a very conspicuous characteristic of the system. The beneficence of Japanese management is limited to a minority rather than every worker, as exaggerated descriptions imply.

The seniority-based system of promotion is frustrating and often stifles creativity. The emphasis is on conformity, group orientation, and the concept of lifelong employment. The Japanese demand for unquestioning obedience and loyalty borders on servitude. Using tradition as a force, unreasonable time demands are placed on employees, which inevitably fosters family problems. However, the way the system is designed influences even family members to stay in line. The newer generation of Japanese are becoming dissatisfied with the system, as reflected in their actions. Their blatant disregard for the traditional patterns of behavior worries older mangers. Although no one is speculating that the Japanese work ethic is collapsing, there is a fear that changing attitudes toward work, leisure, company loyalty, individuality, and such traditions as lifetime employment may ultimately lead to decreased productivity.

Japan seemingly disregards the human and social costs associated with economic growth. Not surprisingly, the Japanese have been called "economic animals."[51] However, these trends may be changing with the emergence of the younger generation, which appears to no longer be willing to be taken advantage of in the name of culture. Perhaps Japan has recently begun to realize that there is a price for prosperity.

American political and business leaders should seriously consider taking the following actions:

1. Give top priority to international economic competitiveness and establish distinct long-term and short-term national economic goals.

2. Build an educational system that is second to none.

3. Aid U.S. companies that aggressively enter foreign markets with a well-thought-out policy for the export of technology. Companies that transfer technology to foreign competitors in contrast to this policy should be warned by the government about the long-term consequences.

4. Adopt a new, positive outlook concerning the management–labor relationship.

U.S. managers make very different assumptions about their employees than do their Japanese counterparts. Japanese managers view everyone at all levels of the organization as equal and credit everyone with the ability to contribute to the organizational goals. U.S. management, on the other hand, sees itself as the decision maker and sees the role of labor as simply following directions. In essence, Japanese managers have a Theory Y approach to management, and U.S. managers have a contrasting Theory X set of assumptions about their work force.

REFERENCES

1. U.S. Department of Commerce, "U.S. Trade with Leading Partners in 1988," *Business America,* p. 6, September 11, 1989.
2. "Potential Power: Two Germanys United Would Be an Economy to Rival U.S., Japan," *Wall Street Journal,* p. A1, November 13, 1989.
3. Allan S. Baillie, "The Deming Approach: Being Better than the Best," *SAM Advanced Management Journal,* 4:15–23, Autumn 1986; Otis Port, "The Rush for Quality," *Business Week,* pp. 130–135, June 8, 1987.

4. "Challenging the System," *Los Angeles Times,* p. 6, May 29, 1989; "Trade: Will We Ever Close the Gap," *Business Week,* p. 22, February 1987; Rauf R. Khan, "The Changing US–Japan Trade Relationship: Causes and Implications," Proceedings, Academy of International Business Southeast Asia Region, Taipei, Taiwan, 1986.

5. Sam Jameson, "Japan's Claims Against Other Nations Increased 47% to a Record $1 Trillion," *Los Angeles Times,* p. 4, May 25, 1989.

6. John Naisbitt, *Megatrends* (New York: Warner Books), 1984, p. 54

7. Ezra F. Vogel, *Japan as Number One: Lessons for America* (Cambridge, Mass.: Harvard University Press), 1979, p. 13.

8. Paul Ingrassia, "Auto Industry in U.S. Is Sliding Relentlessly into Japanese Hands," *Wall Street Journal,* pp. 14–17, November 6, 1990.

9. Eva Pomice, "Can Detroit Hold On?" *U.S. News and World Report,* pp. 51–53, April 15, 1991.

10. "Driving Towards a World Car," *Newsweek,* p. 35, May 1, 1989.

11. "The Japanese Manager Meets the American Worker," *Business Week,* p. 128, August 20, 1984.

12. Louis B. Richman, "The Japanese Buying Binge," *Fortune,* p. 77, December 7, 1987; Toy Stewart, "Japan Buys into the American Dream," *Business Week,* p. 42, November 7, 1988; William J. Holstein, "Japan's Bigger and Bolder Forays into the United States," *Business Week,* p. 80, November 17, 1986; John H. Makin, "Japan's Investment in America: Is It a Threat?" *Challenge,* p. 8, November–December 1988.

13. Jim Impoco and Terri Thompson, "Reversal of Fortune," *U.S. News and World Report,* pp. 42–44, February 17, 1992.

14. Andrew Tanzer and Ruth Simon, "Why Japan Loves Robots and We Don't," *Forbes,* pp. 150, 151, April 16, 1990.

15. "Japanese Pass U.S. in Share of the Global Bank Business," *The Asian Wall Street Journal Weekly,* p. 7, February 3, 1986.

16. Ezra F. Vogel, *Japan as Number One: Lessons for America* (Cambridge, Mass.: Harvard University Press), 1979, pp. 68–78.

17. Paul Kennedy, *The Rise and Fall of the Great Powers* (New York: Random House), 1987, pp. 459–464.

18. Cecil G. Howard, "Expatriate Managers," *Proceedings of the International Academy of Management and Marketing,* 1991.

19. Arthur M. Whitehill, "America's Trade Deficit: The Human Problems," *Business Horizons,* 31(1):21, January–February 1988.

20. "The Model of the Modern British Manager," *The Economist,* 27:26–28, May 20, 1989.

21. Thomas P. Rohlen, "Why Japanese Education Works," *Harvard Business Review,* 65(5):42–43, September–October 1987.

22. Lewis J. Lord et al., "The Brain Battle," *U.S. News and World Report,* pp. 58–65, January 19, 1987.

23. Carla Rapopo, "Why Japan Keeps On Winning," *Fortune,* 124:77, July 15, 1991.

24. Eugene Hunt and George Gray, "Participative Approach—Time to Catch Up," *Management World,* pp. 30–31, May 1981.

25. Tsuji Ken, "Are The Japanese Workaholics?" *Japan Quarterly,* p. 25, 1991.

26. Nina Hatvany and Vladimir Pucik, "An Integrated Management System: Lessons from the Japanese Experience," *Academy of Management Review,* 6(3):469–470, 1981.

27. Everett E. Adam, Jr. and Ronald J. Ebert, *Production and Operations Management,* fifth edition (Englewood Cliffs, N.J.: Prentice-Hall), 1992, p. 277.

28. Kazuo Noda, "Traditional Management Decision Making," *Management International Review,* 8:128–129, 1968.

29. Ezra F. Vogel, *Japan as Number One: Lesson for America* (Cambridge, Mass.: Harvard University Press), 1979, pp. 141–142.

30. Mitsuo Tajima, "Japan's Cold Indifference Toward Old People," *Wall Street Journal,* p. 14, November 8, 1982.

31. "America vs. Japan: Can U.S. Workers Compete?" *U.S. News and World Report,* p. 43, September 2, 1985.

32. Ezra F. Vogel, *Japan as Number One: Lessons for America* (Cambridge, Mass.: Harvard University Press), 1979, pp. 240–244.

33. William M. Fox, "Japanese Management: Traditions Under Strain," *Business Horizons,* pp. 76–85, August 1977.

34. Lee Smith, "Cracks in the Japanese Work Ethic," *Fortune,* pp. 162-168, May 14, 1984.

35. John F. Lawrence and Sam Jameson, "Japanese Workers Learning to Relax," *Los Angeles Times,* p. 14, May 30, 1985.

36. Kim Foltz and Nancy Okai, "Head Hunting in Japan," *Newsweek,* p. 110, November 7, 1983.

37. Tadshi Hanami, *Labor Relations in Japan Today* (New York: Kodanshi), 1981, pp. 52–59.

38. Bradley K. Martin, "Big Cheese at Japan McDonald's Won't Mince His Words," *The Asian Wall Street Journal Weekly,* p. 16, February 10, 1986.

39. Urban C. Lehner, "Are the Japanese the Rudest People or the Most Polite?" *Wall Street Journal,* p. 22, July 23, 1982.

40. L. Becklund, "Japanese Student in US to Defy Her Country's Rules for Koreans," *Los Angeles Times,* p. 16, May 31, 1988.

41. Barry Hillenbrand, "America in the Mind of Japan," *Time,* p. 10, February 10, 1992.

42. Ted Holden, "Japan Just May Be Ready to Change Its Ways," *Business Week,* p. 30, January 27, 1992.

43. Akio Marito, "A Japan That Can Say No," *Newsweek,* p. 9, October 14, 1989.

44. George T. Milkovich and John W. Boudreau, *Human Resource Management,* 6th edition (Homewood, Ill.: Irwin), 1991, p. 453.

45. Stephen Butler and Michael W. Maher, *Management Incentive Compensation Plans* (Florida: National Association of Accountants), 1986, pp. 5–8.

46. Paul Gigot, "Potomac Watch," *Wall Street Journal,* p. A8, January 10, 1992.

47. Thomas McCarrol, "Motown's Fat Cats," *Time,* p. 35, January 20, 1992.

48. Robert Neff, "How Much Japanese CEOs Really Make," *Business Week,* p. 31, September 3, 1990.

49. "The High Cost Japan Pays for Success," *Business Week,* pp. 52–55, April 7, 1986.

50. Karl Schoenberger, "Skid Row Homeless a Dark Spot in Japanese Success," *Los Angeles Times,* p. 10, May 22, 1988.

51. Takamitsu Kumasaka, "Nakasone Sets Japan's Course in International Waters," *Business Japan,* p. 26, March 1985.

BIBLIOGRAPHY

Adam, Everett E. Jr. and Ronald J. Ebert, *Production and Operations Management,* fifth edition (Englewood Cliffs, N.J.: Prentice-Hall), 1992.

Adams, D., "The Monkey and the Fish: Cultural Pitfalls of an Educational Advisor," *International Development Review,* 2:17–23, 1969.

Ajiferuke, M. and J. Boddewyn, "Culture and Other Explanatory Variables in Comparative Management Studies," *Academy of Management Journal,* 13:153–163, 1970.

Barney, J., "Organizational Culture: Can It Be a Source of Sustained Competitive Advantage," *Academy of Management Review*, 11:656–664, 1986.

Boundis, Wendy, "Fuji Co. Color Photographic Paper Set For U.S. Production, Challenging Kodak," *Wall Street Journal*, p. A7, February 7, 1994.

Davis, Bob and David P. Hamilton, "U.S. Set to Press Japan in Trade Fight; Tactics Include 'Super 301' Provision," *Wall Street Journal*, p. A3, February 15, 1994.

Farmer, R. and B.D. Richman, "A Model for Research in Comparative Management," *California Management Review*, 7:55–68, 1964.

Gonzales, R.F. and C. McMillan, Jr., "Universality of American Management Philosophy," *Journal of the Academy of Management*, 4:39, 1961.

Haire, M., E.E. Ghiselli, and L.W. Porter, *Managerial Thinking: An International Study* (New York: John Wiley & Sons), 1966.

Hodge, D. and R. Johnson, *Management and Organizational Behavior: A Multidimensional Approach* (New York: John Wiley & Sons), 1970.

"How Americans Feel about Their Future," *Business Week*, p. 175, September 25, 1989.

"Japanese Schools: There Is Much We Can Learn," *U.S. News and World Report*, p. 43, September 2, 1985.

Kennedy, Paul, *The Rise and Fall of the Great Powers* (New York: Random House), 1987.

Kolchin, Michael G., "Borrowing Back from the Japanese," *SAM Advanced Management Journal*, 52:27–28, Spring 1987.

Lee, Sang M. and Maling Ebrahimpour, "An Analysis of Japanese Quality Control Systems: Implications for American Manufacturing Firms," *SAM Advanced Management Journal*, 50:24–31, Spring 1985.

McFarland, D.E., *Management: Principles and Practice* (New York: Macmillan), 1974, pp. 627–628.

Naisbitt, John, *Megatrends* (New York: Warner Books), 1984.

Nussbaum, Bruce, "Needed: Human Capital," *Business Week*, pp. 100–103, September 19, 1988.

Patton, Mark A., "What Happened to the Export Trading Company Act of 1982?" *The Journal of Midwest Marketing*, 3:337–343, Spring 1988.

Tong, Hsin-Min and Timothy J. Walters, "The Export Trading Company Act," *Louisiana Business Review*, 48:35–37, Summer 1984.

Vogel, Ezra F., *Japan as Number One: Lessons for America* (Cambridge, Mass.: Harvard University Press), 1979.

9

CORPORATE GOVERNANCE IN DEVELOPED COUNTRIES: A COMPARATIVE STUDY

ABSTRACT

The issue of corporate governance has become increasingly important over the past few years. The ideological differences among corporate governance systems of the United States, Britain, Germany, Japan, Sweden, France, Turkey, and Canada are presented in this chapter. The implications of these differences in international markets are also discussed.

CHAPTER OBJECTIVES

1 To understand corporate governance

2 To understand the role of the board of directors

3 To compare the corporate governance systems of various countries

4 To understand the trends in corporate governance

CASE STUDY
American Corporate Governance:
Shareholders Call the Plays

The role of the shareholders is slowly increasing in some companies. In such corporations as General Motors, IBM, American Express, and Westinghouse, the shareholders have had a hand in ousting the chief executives.

This increase in shareholder power is a result of two rule changes by the Securities and Exchange Commission, America's securities regulator. The first rule change requires fuller disclosure of executive compensation packages, which has put managers on the defensive. The second change has made it easier for shareholders to communicate with each other and with managers by removing the barriers to effective shareholder action.

More and more shareholders are becoming interested in corporate governance. This is most apparent in the area of public pension funds. One reason is that public pension funds are often run by political appointees. Other investors are following the path of public pension funds, including banks, insurers, mutual funds (unit trusts), and corporate pension funds.

Shareholders in public pension funds have tried to change company boards and procedures. Changes include not re-electing the whole board every year, scrapping golden parachutes and poison pills, electing a majority of independent directors to the board, splitting the jobs of chairman and chief executive, setting up shareholder advisory committees, and instituting confidential voting at annual meetings. Some major shareholders, however, believe that these changes are not worth their cost. Robert Pozen of Fidelity, America's largest mutual fund company, feels that independent directors, confidential voting, and annual board elections are needed, but shareholder advisory committees are not. Shareholders must remain strong for the long battle still ahead of them.

Source: "Shareholders Call the Plays," *The Economist,* pp. 83–84, April 24, 1993.

INTRODUCTION

After having been ignored for quite some time, corporate governance has recently received attention from both critics and friends of business. The Advisory Board of the National Association of Corporate Directors has agreed upon the following definition:

> Corporate governance ensures that long-term strategic objectives and plans are established and that the proper management structure (organizations, systems and people) is in place to

achieve those objectives, while at the same time making sure that the structure functions to maintain the corporation's integrity, reputation, and responsibility to its various constituencies.[1]

In other words, corporate governance is simply the mode of structure and power that determines the rights and responsibilities of various groups involved in running an organization.[2]

A BRIEF HISTORY OF CORPORATE GOVERNANCE

Over the years, corporate governance has undergone massive change due to societal, environmental, and government influences. In late 18th and early 19th centuries, American corporations were chartered with the purpose of serving the public interest. Corporations that supplied transport, water, insurance, and banking among other activities incorporated to such a degree that state legislatures were forced to pass laws that gave the state the right to grant incorporation by issuing a charter.

In the early 1900s, the fiduciary role of the board of directors could be summed up by three criteria: (1) courts recognized the underlying central public interest of early corporate charters; (2) the directors' duty was to act in the best interest of the corporation, which was synonymous with maximizing the current value of the stock; and (3) the directors must consider the interest of all stakeholders when taking any action so as not to leave the shareholders entirely without protection.

In the mid-19th century, state legislatures began passing laws of incorporation that were very general. Corporate promoters had the freedom to write their own corporate charters. Because noncontrolling shareholders were oppressed and exploited, the federal government passed legislation to protect their interests. The 1900s ushered in the modern concept of fiduciary duties for the board of directors. No longer could the board do what it felt was in the best interest of the company. The board now had to consider the effect of its decisions on all stakeholders of the company.

Corporations in America flourished after World War II, when managers controlled organizations. Modern corporations are owned by absentee owners and operated by professional managers. Adam Smith found that the latter type of system did not work effectively because of conflicting interests: management is interested in daily operations and their own self-interests whereas stockholders are interested in profitability. However, because ownership is dispersed, capital is often taken for granted and no real challenge exists from the owners or the board of directors.

The corporation has been through some major changes, including information technology, flexible manufacturing, worldwide markets, morality in the workplace, and corporate capitalism. These changes have enabled management-controlled corporations to manipulate and dominate employee pensions in order to upgrade the company and ultimately the economy. Included in corporate capitalism are institutional investors.

Those who meet certain criteria of the 1933 Securities Act can buy large blocks of stock without public disclosure. These investors are entitled to a voice in management changes, but many do not bother and just sell their stock.

THE BOARD OF DIRECTORS

The board of directors consists of shareholder-elected representatives. The primary functions of the board of directors are to hire the chief executive officer and to oversee management and company performance. Recent developments have redefined the responsibilities of a member of the board of directors and what is involved in managing a corporation. These developments are changing the relationship between the board of directors and management in many different ways. The board of directors is becoming more liable for its decisions than ever before.

Laws governing the operation of a multinational corporation (MNC) differ in each country. Because of the expansion of MNCs, there has been an increased focus on the issues of governance in these corporations. Each country has its own set of laws concerning the board of directors. Some of these laws are ambiguous, but where there is limited liability, MNCs are required to have a body to oversee the company and to protect the interests of the stockholders.

Responsibilities of the Board

The board of directors should set policies and oversee management. However, the chief executive officer (CEO) plays a major role in the decisions made by the board of directors. Directors must realize that their job is not to satisfy the CEO but instead to satisfy the stockholders. Benjamin M. Rosen, former chairman of Compaq Computer, states that the board should be a check on management: "I think that the owners of the company should be represented by the directors. That has ceased to happen at lots of companies where management dominates the board."[3] Harold S. Geneen, former chief of ITT states: "The role of the board is not to be a contender against management. Its role is to help management."[3]

The directors need to be aware at all times of what is going on in the company they represent. If board members believe that the firm is not performing up to their expectations, and that it is top management's responsibility, then the board should probably dismiss the CEO. "The mere presence of dissenting expectations and attributions within the Board increases the likelihood for dismissal."[4] A good example of a board that was not aware of what was going on is Allegheny International. Robert J. Buckley, who was CEO at the time, generously helped himself to corporate money. In 1984, he paid himself $1 million in compensation when the company's total earnings were only $14.9 million. He spent millions more without the board's knowledge. In 1986, when the situation became public, the stockholders sued the board for "waste of corporate assets and grossly improper business decisions."[3] Many well-known people who were on the board later resigned. This case shows that even well-known people on the board does not guarantee that a company will be run properly.

The legal environment is somewhat changing the relationship between the board of directors and the stockholders. Federal law is a factor in this relationship, because it is vague as to the directors' responsibilities. Some states have gone so far as to specify that directors should act with loyalty, honesty, and care. The law has been changing since the 1960s, when shareholder litigation exploded. In 1985, a ruling on a shareholders' suit against ten board members of Trans Union Corporation sent a wave of terror through the boards of many large corporations. The court ruled that the directors were "negligent when they agreed to sell the Railcan-Leasing Company to the Pritzer family's Mommon Group in a hasty, two hour meeting dominated by the CEO."[4] However, the board members did not pay one cent, because an insurer paid $10 million of the settlement and the Pritzers came up with the rest. Although the board members' insurance covered this liability, people began to worry about serving on a board of directors, since they could face personal bankruptcy.

Today, many top executives and others will not serve on boards of directors for fear of lawsuits being brought against them. The insurance premiums for members are astronomical, and many companies have reduced the size of their board. A 1993 survey conducted by the author showed that about 90% of companies that went private also reduced the size of their board. Some say that this whole situation has been blown out of proportion and that there were only a few actual instances in which a board was sued. In either case, the board of directors should be held accountable for its actions when the stockholders are not notified and decisions are made that are not in the stockholders' best interest.

CORPORATE GOVERNANCE SYSTEMS

The major changes in corporate governance in both the United States and Western Europe occurred during the 1970s. However, the two areas used different approaches based on their ideological beliefs and their definition of the problem. For example, the priority in the United States is to make a corporation more accountable to its stockholders. This is clearly seen in the emphasis on property rights for stockholders. A second concern is corporate social performance. A third concern is corporate morality or the ethics of business practices.

In Western Europe, the difference in corporate governance basically reflects the difference between capitalism and socialism. The dispute continues as to who should control the property of a corporation. This dispute has divided Europe into two different ideologies, the left (socialism) and the right (capitalism).

The United States does not experience such ideological conflict because it began as an open frontier society with continual westward movement. This effectively drew off the problems of surplus population. Also, there is a materialistic approach to problems in the United States. "While populism has been a strong strain, particularly in the midwest, in American thought, it too still regards the solving of problems in a pragmatic way. Thus, the approach to the corporation has not yet been an ideological one."[5] The case in Western Europe is different because modern industrial development stemmed from the feudalistic society and the existence of a class structure. This gave rise to much concern about organizing property and resulted in strong ideological differences, such as pitting capitalism against socialism in most countries in Europe.

Because of this ideological difference, the approach to corporate governance in the United States is government regulation. This approach is based on the idea that any problem can be solved by regulating it.

CORPORATE GOVERNANCE MODELS

The Traditional Model

The traditional model of corporate governance, which is the prevalent model in the United States, holds that shareholders' property rights are paramount. The shareholders, or owners of the corporation, elect the board of directors. The board acts as an intermediary between the owners and the management of a corporation. The board appoints the officers who run the corporation on a daily basis. Management exercises its authority over the firm's employees in order to achieve the corporate objectives.

In theory, the stockholders exercise their legal right by voting at an annual stockholder meeting. The stockholders evaluate management's corporate performance and then elect their representatives to sit on the board of directors. The board selects the officers of the corporation to run the business on a daily basis and meets periodically with management to resolve the issues that need stockholder approval. The board also oversees management to ensure that the stockholders' interests are looked after. Management chooses the employees necessary to run the business and accomplish the corporate goals and objectives.[6]

It is clear that in this type of organization, the main emphasis is on the stockholders' interests. Management is more concerned with production and their own rewards. Employees are concerned with wages and benefits. This model relies on the ability of the CEO to run the company efficiently and effectively.

Berle and Means,[7] Larner,[8] Eisenberg,[9] Mace,[10] Williams and Shapiro,[11] and others believe that even though the traditional corporate statutes require that the business affairs of a corporation be managed by the board of directors, in practice the board rarely performs either as management or policymakers of a corporation. According to Buchholz,[12] the reality is that ownership of most major U.S. corporations is so dispersed that most stockholders hold an amount of stock that is too small to make any difference. They think of themselves as investors rather than owners of the corporation. When they do not make enough return on their investments, they prefer to sell their stock because they have little power to effect change individually.

The Codetermination Model

Codetermination is a two-tiered system in which there is a division between supervision and management. This system originated in Germany and has spread to many European countries.

The codetermination, or European, model maintains that both capital and labor should be represented in the process of corporate governance. Representatives of both ownership and the employees comprise the board of directors. One practical version of this model promotes a two-tiered structure, with a supervisory board and a management board. The supervisory board oversees the operation, and the management board is involved with daily operation of the corporation. The supervisory board has ultimate authority in that it can select and dismiss members of the management board.

The major feature of this system is not that it creates two levels of administration where only one existed before or that it recognizes management as a separate organ, but that it makes a clear distinction between those who manage and those who monitor. This results in a system of checks and balances which avoids conflicts of interest.[1]

Who monitors the upper tier in a two-tiered board? Here, the implication is that the supervisory tier does not need external supervision, because it consists of two distinct interests—the shareholders' and the workers' representatives—and that each side will not let the other get away with anything unprofessional.[1] Mining and steel corporations fall under a special code of regulation. In these industries, the formula was and still is equal representation for shareholders and for employees, plus one additional neutral outside member acceptable to both sides.[1] Some critics of the two-tiered system are skeptical of its motivation. They believe that it is put into effect primarily to ensure that worker representatives are not elected to the essential management body of a company. Some companies in Germany have gotten into trouble due to the inability of their boards of directors to provide effective measures to influence the governance process. Lack of ability, information, and authority gives the board little opportunity to effectively monitor management's performance in corporate affairs.

Other Models

In the stakeholder model of corporate governance, all constituencies that have a direct stake in the performance of a corporation are represented

**TABLE 9.1   Comparison of Corporate Governance Models
with American Law Institute Proposals**

Traditional model	Codetermination (European) model	Stakeholder model	ALI proposals
Stockholders (owners)	Capital and labor	Social, political, and economic interests	Independent monitoring by board of directors
Board of directors	Supervisory board	Stakeholder participation in board of directors	Audit committee
Officers and managers	Management board	Management	Nominating committee
Employees	Management	Employees	Compensation committee

in the governance process.[2] The constituents include more than just the employees and owners. The interests of all stakeholders are taken into account when employees, major customers, major suppliers, major creditors, environmentalists, bankers, and other affected parties are represented on the board of directors of a corporation. Objectives are achieved by balancing the often-conflicting interests of the different constituents. The participation of these various stakeholder groups in the governance process ensures that a wide range of interests will be taken into account in corporate decision making.

The American Law Institute (ALI) has proposed an independent board of directors whose function is to monitor as opposed to manage. Under the ALI proposals, the board would focus on auditing functions, reviewing management, operations, staffing, and execution, to assess the competency of the CEO and senior staff of an organization. The monitoring board would actually be a new level of top management. In addition to the monitoring board, the ALI recommends an audit committee, a nominating committee, and a compensation committee. The models of corporate governance are summarized in Table 9.1 and their use in various countries is indicated in Table 9.2.

The United States and Britain: Single-Tiered Model

The United States and Britain use the single-tiered or traditional model, which is comprised of external and internal directors. The directors are usually selected or elected by the shareholders. In this system, the board is expected to make major policy decisions and monitor these policies. In the United States, corporate decisions are almost always made by top management, with little or no input from workers. The main concern in

TABLE 9.2 The Spread of Better Governance Beyond the United States

	Traditional model	Codetermination model	Other models
Owners	Stockholders	Stockholders and labor	Stockholders with direct interest
Overseers	Board of directors	Supervisory board	Board stakeholder and management representative
Daily operations	Management	Management	Management
Users	United States Great Britain Japan France Turkey	Germany Sweden	Theory

American firms is to maximize the wealth of the shareholders.[2] For more information on the growing role of shareholders in U.S. companies, refer to the case study entitled "American Corporate Governance: Shareholders Call the Plays" at the beginning of this chapter.

Germany: Two-Tiered Model

In Germany, all employees have a voice in a firm's decision making at two levels: on the shop floor and at the supervisory level. The Works Constitution Act of 1972 allows for a works council elected by employees to represent their interest in company decisions that may affect them. Codetermination in Germany can be traced back to 1834, when consultative work councils were first introduced, and to 1881, when they were first instituted. Most Germans strongly believe in codetermination, which means that an employer cannot make a decision on an operational matter without the approval of the works council. Codetermination applies to both the works council and the supervisory board, which appoints the board and monitors its decisions.

The Works Constitution Act of 1976 dealt with labor–management relations at the shop floor and plant level. Worker councils were established to represent workers' interests in personnel, social, and economic issues related to working conditions.

The Codetermination Act of 1976, which covers all enterprises with more than 2000 employees, provides for "near parity codetermination" for labor. Near parity codetermination means that while labor is formally equally represented on supervisor (director) boards, in case of a tie vote, the chairman (always a representative of the shareholders) casts the deciding vote. Also, employees in managerial positions are entitled to elect,

CASE STUDY
One Share, One Vote

Heribald Naerger, a supervisory chairman of Siemens, Germany, silenced a critic by proposing the "one share, one vote" amendment to Siemens by-laws. Naerger was angry about questions asked by shareholders and decided to take action against giving into their requests for more information. When he commented that the board would refuse to respond, one shareholder shouted, "Sauerei," which means that stinks.

Welcome to Germany, where a self-serving management routinely runs roughshod over its external shareholders. This real-life example of how the chairman and shareholders interact at annual meetings provides a view of corporate governance overseas. Both sides are outspoken, without concern for etiquette or respect for upper management.

Source: Friedo Meyer, "Corporate Governance in Europe," *Management Magazine,* 4(1):26.

within the allotted number of labor seats, a special representative to the board. American trade unions emphasize collective bargaining, which is a private contract between a corporation and a union. German unions, on the other hand, emphasize codetermination of working conditions and legislative recourse. This involves industry-wide agreements between employers and unions instead of individual agreements.

Germany has more long-term shareholders, such as banks and large institutions. These institutions play an active role on corporate boards. In this centralized system, decisions are made without public disclosure.

Recently, German managers have begun to oppose codetermination because they feel it infringes on basic ownership rights. In response to this tension, labor unions are moving toward the American system of collective bargaining. The United States, on the other hand, has been moving slowly toward a form of codetermination by allowing a representative of labor on the board of directors. Many are opposed to this and feel that if there must be a representative from labor, it should be on a lower management level. Neither management nor labor, however, sees the codetermination model in America's near future because labor unions in the United States are opposed to it.

Japan: Single-Tiered Model

Boards of directors of Japanese corporations are distinct in many respects. Most corporations in Japan are owned by shareholders. The Japanese seem to have larger boards than do other countries. As many as

20 to 40 board members participate in the decision-making process. Japanese boards are primarily composed of internal directors, most of whom are company executives. Fewer than 10% of the directors are not full-time employees or union members. The external directors are major shareholders or agents. Members of the board of directors are selected by the corporate shareholders or top management and sometimes even the government. A board member generally serves a two-year term of office. Retirement from a company often disqualifies a person from serving on the board of that company. The board meets monthly, which is unusual in most other countries. It is also interesting to note that although the board rarely establishes any committees, those committees that do exist can meet as often as 50 times a year.

Sweden: Two-Tiered Model

A set of laws governs the board of directors in Sweden. There is no other form of business organization with limited liability share capital in Sweden. The rights and duties of the directors are set out in the Companies Act of 1975. Board members have authority only as a group, although they can pick a member to represent them. The board is responsible for managing all the activities of a corporation. The board is elected at a general meeting of the shareholders. Worker representation on Swedish boards is similar to the German model.

The size of the board ranges from 14 to 21 members and is made up of both external and internal directors. Women serve on boards of directors in Sweden. Directors serve an average of one year, and the board meets about 12 times a year. The basic role of the board of directors in Sweden is to make decisions regarding financial and policy matters and to deal with management. It is the responsibility of the shareholders and the business community to appraise the board's performance. It is obvious that boards of directors in Japan and Sweden operate under different frameworks. In fact, no two countries are exactly the same. Each has different laws that govern the board of directors, and the size of the board also varies. It is important to note that changes take place regularly, and laws that are in effect today can easily become outdated tomorrow.

France: Single-Tiered Model

There is considerable government involvement in France. The government sets many of the rules and laws by which businesses must abide. Boards must have between 3 and 12 members. No more than six may be salaried employees. A salaried employee must work at a company for two years before becoming eligible as a board member.

No one may serve on more than eight boards. Each director must own a specified number of company shares. There are no restrictions on the residence or nationality of board members. The board meets an average of five times per year. Workers do not serve as voting directors.

Turkey: Single-Tiered Model

Turkish law requires that board members manage the business affairs of a corporation. In many companies, directors are involved in daily operations. A director must own shares equal to 1% of the paid-in capital (about 5000 Turkish liras). There is no restriction on the nationality of board members, but directors who are not employees or shareholders are rare. The size of the board ranges from 3 to 11 members, and the board meets about 16 times a year. There is no worker representation on a Turkish board unless a company is government owned.

Canada: Single-Tiered Model

Corporate law grants authority to the board of directors in Canada. This means that the board's role can vary among companies. Directors do not have to be shareholders, but the majority of board members are Canadian citizens. Most companies have two outside directors who are neither officers nor employees.

The size of the board ranges from 5 to 18 members in manufacturing and 5 to 53 members in nonmanufacturing companies. A term is normally one year, but three years is also common. There is no law limiting the number of boards on which one is allowed to serve.

International Similarities

For all of their differences, boards of directors have some basic similarities, including:

1. The basic legal concept is that the board of directors is elected to represent the owners of a corporation. Board members are expected to be loyal to the company and its shareholders and to exercise prudent judgment.

2. The major areas of responsibility are to:
   - Identify long-range corporate objectives
   - Develop long-range planning to meet those objectives
   - Allocate a corporation's major resources
   - Make major financial decisions
   - Make decisions regarding mergers, takeovers, and divestments
   - Govern management, including succession and compensation

3. The views and influences of each board member establish their commitment and integrity. Most boards view the CEO as having the greatest influence.

4. In cases of conflict, the employee director is expected to adopt a company-wide perspective.

THE FUTURE OF CORPORATE GOVERNANCE

Globally, stockholders are finally demanding that they be heard. Shareholders are increasingly asserting themselves and are calling for reforms in how companies are being run. The current wave of proxy battles at annual meetings is a sign of shareholder discontent. "Big investors are demanding international standards of corporate behavior, accounting clarity, and disclosure."[6] Boards of directors have been sued and found liable for their actions (or nonactions). Shareholders in some companies have had a hand in the dismissal of the CEO and other management. For a look at the situation in Britain, Japan, Belgium, the Netherlands, and Australia, see the case study entitled "The Future of Corporate Governance."

EVALUATION

There are differences between the one- and two-tiered board systems, although they are similar in many respects. Germany and the United States incorporate both systems. U.S. corporations tend to use the two-tiered model in their corporate governance, and Germany is moving toward the one-tiered system.

The German supervisory board consists of frontline managers, workers, union representatives, and nonexecutives such as bankers. Bankers add a special dimension to the supervisory board. It has been argued that the supervisory board's judgment on almost any kind of proposal, including investment proposals, is based on little more than intelligent ignorance. This is because about 15% of all supervisory board members hold mandates on six or more supervisory boards.[1] In Germany, a person can accept a seat on up to ten boards, plus a seat on the boards of five subsidiaries. This leaves little opportunity to effectively monitor management's performance and corporate affairs.

MULTINATIONAL EFFECTS OF THE SUBSIDIARY BOARD

The board of directors of a subsidiary is called the subsidiary board. Its members are chosen by the board of directors of the parent company. A subsidiary board can be either a dummy board or an active board. A dummy board operates only according to the letter of the law and not the spirit of it. An active board operates as a subsidiary's highest authority. It governs, discusses local policies, and in general is proactive. Host country legislation addresses the structure and composition of the board and is applied to local subsidiaries' board composition.

Subsidiary boards are legally required by most host countries. Their duties are the same as a board of directors. Active subsidiary boards provide governance, advise management in key situations, assume legal

CASE STUDY
The Future of Corporate Governance

Britain

Shareholders have helped to force the ouster of several top executives. The Cadbury Report on corporate governance recommends splitting the jobs of chairman and CEO, installing a majority of outside directors, and more complete disclosure of directors' pay.

Japan

The Ministry of Justice has proposed rules to force companies to use independent auditors and to allow suits against directors for poor performance. Investors are clamoring for higher dividends.

Belgium

Laws that limit the voting power of the shareholders make it easier to take over a company. Demeanor, a shareholder activist company, was formed to give small investors a voice.

The Netherlands

Anti-takeover poison pills are prohibited in new companies. The Dutch Shareholders Association, which represents small investors, pressured NMB Postbank to raise the price in a recent takeover.

Australia

Major institutions have joined forces to monitor corporate performance—and shake up the laggards.

Source: Richard A. Melcher and Patrick Oster, "Yankee-Style Activists Strike Boardroom Terror Abroad," *Business Week,* p. 74, March 15, 1993.

responsibility, and meet a specified number of times per year. The absence of an active board is perceived by host governments as a lack of concern for their interests.

By serving as an intermediary, a subsidiary board can be a helpful link between the foreign subsidiary of a MNC and a host country. A subsidiary board is an additional structure intended to help a MNC deal with a highly turbulent and heterogeneous environment.

A subsidiary board offers operational and strategic advice to subsidiary

CASE STUDY
Corporate Governance Uprisings

Since 1990, shareholders have removed the chairman of the Burton Group and Barclays Bank in Britain. Shareholders are voicing their concerns about falling profits and dividends and exercising their rights.

Shareholders in other countries are following suit. Five top managers of large Danish corporations were fired in 1992. A change in values plus the recession is causing a normally docile group of shareholders to become assertive. These shareholders are challenging top management, firing them when necessary, and demanding to be consulted about any mergers. Institutional shareholders prevented the merger of Hafnia with a Swedish competitor.

In Japan, restless shareholders are being backed by a bill sponsored by a ministry of justice committee that would force companies to hire auditors who have no previous company link. The bill would give shareholders with a 30% interest the right to inspect management accounts. It would also be easier for shareholders to sue the board of directors due to poor performance.

The Netherlands prohibits anti-takeover poison pills. While the Dutch Shareholders Association could not stop the merger of Nationale Nederlanden and NMB Postbank, it was successful in getting the price increased.

Source: Richard Breeden, "Fight for Good Governance," *Harvard Business Review*, pp. 76–77, January–February 1993; Leif Fallesen, "Corporation Purges," *Europe*, p. 38, February 1993; "In Search of Better Boardrooms," *The Economist*, pp. 13–14, May 30, 1992; Richard Melcher and Patrick Oster, "Yankee Style Activists Strike Boardroom Terror Abroad," *Business Week*, pp. 74–75, March 15, 1993.

management. It also relays local information to the parent company. An active subsidiary board can provide proactive knowledge of local economic, political, and social conditions. In fact, many joint ventures fail due to a lack of understanding of cultural and behavioral factors. This is often the result of inadequately trained managers. It appears to be to a company's advantage to have an active subsidiary board.

Strategic uses of an active board are as follows:

1. **Strategic windows:** A subsidiary board immediately learns of environmental changes in the host country and informs the parent company.

2. **Windows of understanding:** A subsidiary board uses prominent locals to promote understanding between a MNC and a host country.

3. **Windows of influence:** Prominent local members of the board influence stakeholder groups to think in ways that benefit the MNC.

Japanese MNCs have the highest use of active subsidiary boards. They view subsidiary boards as very important in future dealings and as an important means for understanding local conditions. Japanese subsidiary boards are primarily utilized to (1) approve the subsidiary's budget, (2) monitor the subsidiary's performance, (3) participate in strategic planning, (4) ensure local legal compliance, (5) relay knowledge about the local environment, and (6) minimize local political risks. Japanese MNCs are well structured to take advantage of active subsidiary boards because of *ringi* or consensual decision making. The Japanese are concerned with all stakeholders and receive input from them, and this attitude flows over into their subsidiary boards. The Japanese subsidiary board provides information about the local environment, participates in decision making, and serves in an advisory capacity.

Sweden is the second highest user of active subsidiary boards. The Swedish view subsidiary boards as important in future dealings in host countries. Swedish subsidiary boards are a source of information about the local environment, participate in decision making, and play an advisory role. Sweden has mandated the use of active subsidiary boards to cope with local situations.

A number of factors can influence the use of active subsidiary boards among countries:

1. The parent company's home country
2. The type of industry the company is involved in
3. The local legal and economic conditions of the host country
4. The formal and informal structure of the parent company
5. The management styles of the parent and the subsidiary
6. The degree of internationalization of the parent company

MNCs with active subsidiary boards generally view their efforts as valuable and a worthwhile investment.

Subsidiary boards in U.S. MNCs play a less active role. The future role of subsidiary boards is seen as of moderate importance. The United States lags behind in the use of subsidiary boards to cope with strategic and operational uncertainties. Subsidiary boards are primarily utilized to advise local management and to provide information about the local economy, politics. and social conditions.

Two factors can affect a company's use of active subsidiary boards:

1. Greater national responsiveness, which implies that country-level operations will be more independent and that decision making be more decentralized
2. Pressure for more integrated operations and centrally controlled decisions, resulting from the strategic imperative for increased global efficiency.

Many MNCs retain dummy boards and apparently do not recognize the strategic uses of an active board. Some MNCs are not structured to take advantage of active subsidiary boards. Some MNCs do not want active boards because of the decentralization, the apparent loss of power, and the cost to control them. U.S. management appears to be opposed to the loss of power and control that comes with active boards. This shows the fear of MNCs with respect to decentralization and the apparent loss of power when local boards try to engage in a management of the company.

A subsidiary board is chosen by the parent company board to help an MNC succeed in a foreign country. The evolution of the role of foreign subsidiary boards in selected situations is closely tied to the increasing scope of activities of MNCs around the world and increased host country involvement in controlling the direction of those activities. Most countries continue to request that subsidiaries of MNCs take national development policy objectives into account when mapping out corporate strategies.[13] The absence of actively participating directors is interpreted by many host countries as a lack of concern for local needs and requirements.

The board is responsible for ethical issues when faced with making decisions. It is up to the directors to guide management in the application of ethics to decision making. Subsidiary executives and directors in the field must show strong support for ethical conduct. The liability of directors in Japanese MNCs is one reason behind the changing role of subsidiary boards.

Economic patterns in developing countries affect subsidiaries, their boards, and their relations with their parent company. Subsidiaries have to be particularly careful with regard to their performance and actions so that they can survive when the parent company is unable to provide assistance.

In addition to economic factors, local laws also play an important role in the operation of subsidiaries. The Organization for Economic Cooperation and Development (OECD) voluntary guidelines for MNCs in Europe stress the need for MNCs to give due consideration to the economic and social progress of member countries. These guidelines deal with disclosure of information, taxation, financing, employment and industrial relations, and science and technology. Legislation in many countries increasingly addresses the structure and composition of the board of directors and has been applied to local subsidiaries of MNCs. Worker representation on the supervisory board in Germany's two-tiered system is one example of the national differences that are emerging in the laws of host countries. Canadian law requires that a majority of board members of a corporation be residents of Canada.

IMPLICATIONS FOR
INTERNATIONAL BUSINESS MANAGEMENT

There are many implication of corporate governance in international markets, three of which are discussed here. The first implication is concerned with the recruitment and selection of international managers. American-based MNCs may find it difficult to compete in the international market without acquiring and developing international managers. In addition to possessing all the qualities that make a good manager in a domestic corporation, these managers must also be mobile, receptive, and at ease in cultures other than their own.[14,15] Emphasis should be placed on selection rather than just training. Belief in worker participation is not intuitive; rather, it develops over a period of time. This implies the need for a responsible policy, which is sensitive to other cultures, in recruiting international managers. The failure of many MNCs can be attributed to a lack of understanding and conflicts in decision making. This means that a MNC can be successful in international markets only if the orientation and values of its overseas managers are consistent with the values of the local society. In other words, a MNC should blend with a culture and not conflict with it. Familiarity with and sensitivity to a host country are prerequisites for a successful operation.

The second implication is related to human resource planning in the international arena. People with appropriate skills and knowledge are a scarce commodity. For many years, MNCs have tended to rely on expatriate managers for overseas assignments. Unfortunately, experience indicates that this policy is usually costly and inappropriate. A long-term perspective for the recruitment and development of indigenous personnel to assume managerial responsibility is imperative and should not be left to chance. Furthermore, developing international managers gives a MNC a competitive edge and can strengthen its position in a market.

The third implication relates to maximizing a company's resources for success. What can a company do to ease into a foreign culture? A subsidiary board should be chosen carefully and should include nationals from the host country. This board can be helpful in creating a spirit of friendship between the home and host countries.

CONCLUSION

The framework for managing a board of directors varies among countries. No two countries are exactly the same. Each has different laws that govern the role, conduct, and size of the board of directors. It is important to note that changes take place regularly, and laws that are in effect today can easily become outdated tomorrow.

The concept of codetermination is alien to American culture, as are the German and Japanese governance models. Their closed nature contradicts the demands of American shareholders for openness and accountability. U.S. corporations would not be successful under such a closed system. Forms of participation which have been adopted in North America seem to have their roots in economic necessity rather than higher ideals, commitments, or pursuits. In fact, the preference for some type of participative model flows from the nature of work or the structure of an organization. In contrast, the concept of codetermination in Western Europe stems a belief in the distribution of power and organizational social responsibility. This belief has its roots in the historical and economic development of European societies. Even though codetermination is not practiced in the United States, managers should understand the concept when dealing with countries where it is practiced. This would help a company to fit in with the local culture.

A firm should consider three major points when doing business in another country. First, an American manager in a foreign country should be at ease with and receptive to that particular culture. Second, the orientation and values of the managers should be consistent with those of the host country. Finally, it would be to a firm's advantage to hire as a manager a qualified foreign national who knows the country and its culture. A firm that keeps these points in mind improves its chance for success in another country.

REFERENCES

1. K. Bleicher, "Corporate Governance Systems in a Multinational Environment: Who Knows What's Best?" *Management International Review,* 3:4–15, 1986.
2. Abbass F. Alkhafaji, *A Stakeholder Approach to Corporate Governance: Managing in a Dynamic Environment* (New York: Quorum Books), 1989.
3. S.P. Sherman, "Pushing Corporate Boards to Be Better," *Fortune,* p. 18, July 1988.
4. J.W. Fredrickson, D.C. Hambreck, and S. Baumron, "A Model of CEO Dismissal," *Academy of Management Review,* 13:255–270, 1988.
5. Joseph Moson, "Directions in the United States and European Corporate Governance," paper presented at the AACSB Conference on Business Environment and Public Policy, Summer 1979, pp. 1–2.
6. Rogene A. Buchholz, *Business Environment and Public Policy: Implications for Management and Strategy,* 4th edition (Englewood Cliffs, N.J.: Prentice-Hall), 1992, pp. 241–270.
7. Adolf A. Berle and Gardiner C. Means, *The Modern Corporation and Private Property* (New York: Macmillan), 1932, pp. 89–93.
8. Robert J. Larner, *Management Control and the Large Corporation* (New York: Dunellen), 1971, pp. 9–24.
9. Melvin Eisenberg, *The Structure of the Corporation: A Legal Analysis* (Boston: Little, Brown), 1976, pp. 14–18.
10. M.L. Mace, "Director: Myth and Reality," by the President and Fellows of Harvard College Press, Boston, 1971, pp. 78–79.

11. Harold M. Williams and Irving S. Shapiro, "Power and Accountability: The Changing Role of the Corporate Board of Directors," *Benjamin F. Fairless Memorial Lecture* (Pittsburgh: Carnegie-Mellon University), 1979, p. 11.
12. Rogene A. Buchholz, *Business Environment and Public Policy: Implication for Management* (Englewood Cliffs, N.J.: Prentice-Hall), 1992, p. 104.
13. Mark Kriger, "Strategic Governance: Why and How MNCs Are Using Boards of Directors in Foreign Subsidiaries," *Columbia Journal of World Business,* pp. 39–46, Winter 1987.
14. A. Ali and D. Horne, "Problems and Skills in International Business: Tri-City Executives' Perspectives," *SVSC Economic and Business Review,* 7(1), 1986.
15. J. Maisonrouge, "The Education of Modern International Managers," *Journal of International Business Studies,* Spring 1984.

BIBLIOGRAPHY

Andrews, K.R., "Rigid Rules Will Not Make a Good Board," *Harvard Business Review,* pp. 34–35, 1982.

Bacon, Jeremy, *The Board of Directors: Perspectives and Practices in Nine Countries* (New York: Conference Board), 1977.

Delaware, General Corporation Law of the State of Delaware, revised April 9, 1941, Art. 1, Chapter 65, Section 9.

Dunn, D.J., "Directors Aren't Doing Their Jobs," *Fortune,* p. 60, March 16, 1987.

Lewis, R.F., "What Should Audit Committees Do?" *Harvard Business Review,* pp. 22, 26, May–June 1978.

Low, Murray B., "Farsighted Corporations Focus on Long Term Gains," *Business and Society Review,* p. 40, Summer 1988.

Mitchell, T.H , "Chairman and Chief Executive Officers: A Conflict of Rules?" *Canadian Business Review,* 15:30–32, Spring 1988.

Patton, A. and J.C. Baker, "Why Won't Directors Rock the Boat?" *Harvard Business Review,* pp. 24–26, November–December 1987.

Pawling, J.D., "The Crisis of Corporate Boards: Accountability vs. Misplaced Loyalty," *Business Quarterly,* p. 26, Spring 1988.

Randall, R.F., "Audit Committees Strengthen Boards," *Management Accounting,* p. 12, February 1989.

Tricker, R.I., "Improving the Board's Effectiveness," *Journal of General Management,* p. 460, September 1987.

Winckles, K., "The Responsibility of the Board Is Indivisible," *Accountancy,* May 1987.

10   CULTURE IN THE MIDDLE EAST

ABSTRACT

Because of the strategic importance of the Middle East and because many Americans are not familiar with this area, a brief discussion of culture in the Middle East is provided in this chapter. The importance of the region, its human resource developments, the dominant religion in the area, and the economic and political environment are examined.

> *If the Day of Resurrection has approached and any of you is holding a seedling in his hand, he must plant it, if possible, before he stands up.*
>
> Prophet Mohammed (peace be upon him)

This saying highlights the importance of utilizing all opportunities to make use of natural resources for the benefit of mankind. The Islamic way of life considers all natural resources as provisions for the benefit of everyone. In Islam, human resource work is to explore, develop, and use all available natural resources to enhance the well-being of all human beings in this world and in the hereafter.

CHAPTER OBJECTIVES

1 To understand the Middle Eastern culture, politics, and economy

2 To understand the Islamic way of life

3 To understand how the Arabs and Moslems develop and use their natural resources

4 To understand the relationship between Arabs and the West

5 To understand how Islam is viewed in the eyes of the Western media

6 To compare Middle Eastern women and Western women

CASE STUDY
Islamic Banking

Islamic banking is a system of finance based on the sharing of risk and profit rather than the payment of interest. The few Westerners who do know what it means do not take it seriously as a way for a modern economy to do business. In some respects, this is a mistake. In 1992, Pakistan's federal Sharia court ruled that all forms of interest paid or charged by banks and other financial institutions were un-Islamic. In some ways, Islamic banking is better suited than Western banking to capitalism. The errors that have led Western banks and economies into their financial troubles are exactly the mistakes that Islamic banking aims to avoid.

Islam considers it an injustice to charge interest, but interest is used as a measure of economic conditions in Western countries. "Western economists talk of an interest rate that reflects, among other things, 'pure time-preference'—i.e., the notion that consumption today is worth more than consumption tomorrow. Islamic scholars point out that mere hoarding of cash ought, in that view, to warrant an economic reward. But an economic reward becomes available for distribution only if consumption foregone is translated into investment that yields a real economic return. Lenders are entitled to part of any such return, according to Islam, but only to the extent that they help to create wealth." In general, contracts in Islamic law mandate that risks be shared. When there is uncertainty, contracts that assure one party of a fixed return come what may are discouraged.

Many Muslim banking systems follow Islamic principles. Different partnerships have developed, allowing lending without interest. Under ideas

INTRODUCTION

About eight million Americans practice the Islamic religion. Some Americans have practiced Islam since the 1800s.[1] There are 1.2 billion Muslims around the world. No one in business or politics can afford to ignore the importance of Islam. According to an article that appeared in *The Plain Truth* in June 1983,[2] "Few topics have created as much misunderstanding in the Western world as that of Islam. Most Westerners do not begin to comprehend even the most basic tenets of that important faith. They view it largely from a standpoint of ignorance and uninformed impressions." According to Gibbs, people in the West know very little about the Arabs. "People in the U.S. and Europe do not know that Arab thinking is in harmony with Western espoused values. People in the U.S. do not know that a significant number of Arabs are educated in the west and that these Arabs believe that they have a Western orientation."[3]

The work environment in Middle Eastern and Western countries differs such as *mudarabah* (equivalent to short-term commercial credit) and *musharakah* (longer term equity-like arrangements), banks receive a share of the profits or share in the profits created by a particular investment project, depending on the contract.

There are many advantages to this approach to finance. It discourages debt and encourages equity. The principles of Islam oblige lenders to be concerned with profitability rather than the credit worthiness of the firms they are lending to. This helps them to be more conservative when making decisions and to monitor their borrowers more carefully.

Some of the alleged disadvantages of this banking system can be overcome. One disadvantage is that the monetary authorities have no control over monetary policy without interest rates. However, control can still be maintained through limits put on the cash base of an economy or through reserve requirements for banks. Another disadvantage is that a government that cannot pay a fixed rate of interest on its bonds has a hard time financing its deficit. One answer is to pay a rate that varies according to the growth of the economy and the inflation rate.

The adoption of interest-free banking must take place gradually to be successful. "Pakistan's reforms may yet prove to be the disaster that some have predicted—not because Islamic banking makes no sense, but because the Shariat court appeared to call for the sudden conversion of all existing financial contracts. That seems an impossible task. But Pakistan's more gradual moves towards Islamic banking since the mid-1980s seem to have worked quite well—as, in principle, you would expect."

Source: "Banking Behind the Veil," *The Economist,* p. 49, April 1992.

from the American work environment. This is particularly apparent in Arab countries, where Islamic doctrine does not allow for the separation of the spiritual and lay spheres of life, in contrast to U.S. tradition.[4] Any kind of analysis of the environment in Islamic countries will provide a window to understanding Islamic society. The resurgence of Islam has grabbed the attention of Western nations, although it is marked by considerable ignorance in the United States.[5]

THE MIDDLE EASTERN ECONOMY

Before we begin our discussion of Middle Eastern culture, it is important to get a feel for the Middle Eastern economy. The Middle Eastern economy is divided into two main periods: before and after World War II.

The Middle East was an economic backwater for the half-century preceding World War II. The operations of Levantine traders and bankers in Beirut, Aleppo, and Haifa were inconsequential compared to the big firms of England and Western Europe.[6] Even the extractive industry was weak compared to other countries.

By 1930, petroleum had been fully utilized in the Middle East. In the decades after World War II, petroleum exports earned huge sums for some Middle Eastern countries and Western oil companies. Oil changed the distribution of economic power by channeling it to the oil-exporting countries, such as Saudi Arabia, Iran, Iraq, and Kuwait.[7] Another stimulus for the economy came from the agricultural use of the Jezira region in northeast Syria, which created a post-war wave of prosperity in Lebanon and Syria. Another thrust came from the creation of Israel and the resultant influx of more than a million new immigrants to the Jewish state. Its speedy development was financed by more than $3 billion from abroad.

Many other events also helped the Middle Eastern economy. The Korean War pushed up cereal and fiber prices to the great benefit of Egypt, Turkey, and Syria. The growing intensity of the Cold War led to economic and military aid from the United States in the annual sum of more than $100 million each to Turkey and Iran. The flow of Muslims to Mecca permitted Saudi Arabia to earn millions annually from the *hajj,* or pilgrimage. Finally, a large sector of citizens reacted to the economic challenges. Government officials put enormous sums of money to work and people worked harder.

In retrospect, one can point to a record of enormous post-World War II economic expansion in the Middle East. This has been mainly due to expanded commerce, services, and government. All things considered, the relationship between the West and the Middle East has grown beyond all expectations.

ISLAMIC COUNTRIES

The Middle East is a particularly distinctive region that has many cultural differences in comparison to the United States. If a company is to expand globally into this region, it must explore the culture in order to understand how it will affect business strategies.

The term "Islamic countries" is used to denote more than 40 countries in which Muslims constitute the majority population. Muslims form almost the entire population of North Africa and they are the majority population in Egypt, Sudan, Turkey, Afghanistan, Syria, Jordan, Saudi Arabia, Iraq, Iran, all of the Gulf States, and Yemen. They are present in all other countries of the region as well. In the mid-1980s, 26 countries in the Middle East had a total population of approximately 340 million, or about 7% of the world population. Although these countries are comprised of many races and cultures, there are significant similarities which allow some generalizations about the region as a whole. This is especially helpful to companies researching the region for possible expansion into it. The growing trend toward global expansion makes the study of these cultures especially relevant.

The differences in language, religion, logic, notions of truth and free-dom, honor, trust, family, friendship, and hospitality all contribute to the misunderstandings that persist between Arabs and the West. These differ-ences alone, however, do not account for all the misunderstanding. Westerners do not seem to understand the history that has always been a major force in Arab life. An Arab's life is built on the glorious history that has preceded him. Americans in particular have very little sense of their own past and virtually no sense of Middle Eastern history.

At one time, some Arabs thought the answer to their own economic advancement lay with the West. In the midst of modernizing and adapting many of the Western ways, the traditions that had served as reference points for centuries were being lost among all of the changes. The general criticism of this era made by Islamic activists focuses on the loss of Islamic history and values with the incorporation of Western strategies. Along with Western technology and management efficiency came new and sometimes unwelcome ideas concerning individualism, materialism, sexuality, family, and politics. For some time, these ideas were seen as a threat to Islamic tradition and basic values, but they were tolerated simply because of the hopes and aspirations associated with Western methods. Most Muslim governments courted Western protection for their unpopular regimes by promoting Western systems.

In the 1970s, things began to change in the Middle East. Resentment developed and tensions rose as the Islamic people perceived the West as arrogant and repressive. The process of modernization was seen as an attack on the Islamic basic values. What followed was a resurgence of religious values and a marked return to the basic value system of Muslims. There was increased concern for protecting Islamic countries from Western influences in social and cultural behavior. Because of this resurgence, American companies that conduct business in the Middle East must first understand this culture. They may be forced to change some of their business policies if they want to be accepted in these countries. There is a reluctance in the Middle East to accept some of the fundamental principles of capitalism, and the religious resurgence has led to the rejection of many fundamental American ideals.

The most marked difference in understanding Islamic culture is the lack of separation between church and state, which is in direct contrast to U.S. practices. Islam enters virtually every aspect of individual and collective life and is the basis of the norms and moral codes according to which Islamic societies function.[8] Anything like a wall of separation between the secular and the religious is simply inconceivable, given the culture of the region and despite the pervasive forces of secularization and Westernization. The interaction of religion and politics is a far more powerful force in the Middle East than in any other part of the world.[9] Political differences within the Moslem world and even within individual states are extensive. Nation-alism has superseded Islam as a political identity in most Moslem coun-tries.[10] However, to understand culture in the Middle East, one must have a basic understanding of Islamic principles.

THE FAITH OF ISLAM

The Prophet Mohammed introduced the faith of Islam to the world. Islam translates as "submission to the will of Allah (God)." A Muslim is a person who submits to the will of God, an adherent of Islam. Muslims believe in the oneness and justice of Allah, the Arabic name for God used by all Muslims and by Arabic-speaking Christians and Jews. The relationship with Allah is direct and open (without the intervention of church, priests, or other intermediaries).[11] There are approximately 1.2 billion Muslims in the world today, accounting for about one-fifth or one-fourth of the world's population.

Muslims see themselves as an extension of Judaism and Christianity, as a reaffirmation, correction, and consummation of the earlier religions. The book of Islam is the *Qur'an,* and the recitations contained in it were revealed by God to the Prophet Mohammed. It includes 114 chapters, called *suras,* and is the main source of the religion and religious life. The general moral teaching of the *Qur'an* urges men to be generous and to care for the poor, the weak, and the orphans in society. It calls for fairness and justice in commercial transactions and forbids hoarding. It contains fairly detailed stipulations for marriage, divorce, and inheritance and the various religious duties.[11] It is the only holy book in history that was memorized and written down from the mouth of the prophet in his lifetime, under his supervision, and in the original language of its revelation.[12] Islam is international in its outlook and approach and does not allow barriers and distinctions based on color, clan, blood, or territory. It strives to unite the entire human race under one banner.

Pillars of Islam

There are five basic religious duties of every Muslim, derived from the *Qur'an* and set out in the Traditions. The first is a declaration of faith asserting the unity of God and the truth of the message (the *Qur'an*). This is done by making the assertion, "I testify that there is no God but Allah, and that Mohammed is the Messenger of God." When this is said with sincerity, a person is a Muslim. The second duty is that a Muslim must perform the *salat* (formal prayer) five times a day. Prayer times are dawn, mid-day, mid-afternoon, sunset, and evening. The prayers are a constant reminder of Allah's presence in one's life, a perpetual cleansing of sins and the highest direct expression of mutual love, submission, humility, and petition. In each prayer, portions of the *Qur'an* are recited. These prayers can be performed in such a way that they do not interfere with working hours. Third is *zakat* (alms tax); Muslims who are able should pay from their wealth a certain amount for specified purposes. *Zakat* means purification. It asserts social justice and security. Fourth, the *Qur'an* requires all mature Muslims to fast during the month of Ramadaan. The fast begins the day after the new moon and lasts until the new moon is seen for the ninth month. The fast is from dawn to dusk, and during that time a Muslim should not eat, drink, or smoke, and should abstain from any sexual relationship and all evil intentions and desires. The last pillar is a pilgrimage, or *hajj*, to Mecca, if affordable, once in a lifetime to strengthen one's ties with Allah and previous prophets.[11]

ISLAMIC WORK VALUE AND ETHICS

A study by Kuroda and Suzuki[12] compared Arab, American, and Japanese cultures. It indicated that Arab culture is industrialist, rational, efficiency oriented, selection oriented or decisive, and tradition oriented. American culture is characterized by its individual orientation, optimism, post-industrialism, and paternalism in the workplace. Japanese culture is seen as collective, nondirection oriented, indecisive, and fuzzy to Arabs and Americans.

The study further indicated that Arabs are serious about their work. Favoritism, give-and-take, paternalism, and the like have no place in the Arab workplace. In comparison, the Japanese and Americans consider the workplace to be an atmosphere of friendship. The study also concluded that the Arabs adhere more closely to their own values even when they think in English.

A study conducted by Ali[13] suggested that Arab managers are highly committed to the Islamic work ethic. The study showed a moderate tendency toward individualism (i.e., good work benefits both self and others, life has no meaning without work, and work gives one the chance to be independent). The Islamic work ethic is an orientation toward work and is evident in the actualization of ideals, justice, and generosity. In the Muslim mind, work is considered a quality in light of the need to establish equilibrium in one's individual and social life. In 1992, Siddiqui[14] argued that the Islamic work ethic is a commitment toward fulfillment and indeed holds business motives in the highest regard.

> *On the day of judgment, the honest Muslim merchant will stand side by side with the martyrs.*
>
> Prophet Mohammed (peace be upon him)

Indeed, the Islamic work ethic has its roots in the Muslim holy book, the *Qur'an,* and the sayings and practices of the Prophet Mohammed. The Prophet preached that hard work caused sins to be forgiven and that "no one eats better food than that which he eats out of his work." Imam Ali, the fourth successor to the Prophet Mohammed, stated, "Persist in your action with a noble end in mind…Failure to perfect your work while you are sure of the reward is injustice to yourself."

PROTESTANT WORK ETHIC

The Protestant work ethic is a relationship between Protestantism and capitalism as proposed by Max Weber. In 1961, McClelland[15] initiated the linkage between the Protestant work ethic and the need for achievement. Ali[13] discussed how the Protestant work ethic has attracted the attention of students of cross-cultural psychology and management. Many researchers, such as Aldag and Brief,[16] Blood,[17] Furnham,[18] Furnham and Bland,[19] and Furnham and Muhuideen,[20] have examined the Protestant work ethic and its impact on human behavior and economic development. In 1991, Congleton[21] implied that cultural work ethic promoted economic development. Researchers including Fodor[22] suggested that a good work ethic motivates employees to be highly involved in their jobs.

Individualism is another important factor that contributes to organizational performance and success in the West. However, in Asian cultures, individualism is considered to be a liability.[23]

Research on work ethic and individualism has been conducted mainly in the West. Few studies in these areas have been carried out in the developing nations. The instruments used in what research there is were developed mainly to measure work orientation in Western culture and therefore may be less suitable for developing countries.

Industrialized nations placed special emphasis on the Middle East as oil played an increasingly strategic role in economic growth and political domination in the West. This emphasis led to the increased interest of politicians, journalists, and researchers. Understanding Arab executives and their work ethic is extremely important for multinational corporations and for cross-cultural negotiations.

The work ethic varies from one culture to another, and this variation is obvious when observing Islamic and Christian work forces. The Islamic view work as an obligation, compelling them to work harder. This led to the Middle East becoming a commercial and cultural center.[13]

INTEREST-FREE BANKING

The payment of interest is in line with the value systems of most societies in today's world. Societal values are those norms, mores, guidelines, and policies that bind a group of people into a cooperative whole or society, where individual activities are directed either for the good, or at least not against the good, of the society. This stems from the religious value that if you borrow from your neighbor, you should repay him with something of greater value than that which you deprived him of the use of for the period of borrowing, thus enriching your neighbor's existence. This implies that "money" has value, and herein develops the conflict among societies.

With the establishment of Islam as the dominant religion of the Orient in the sixth century A.D., the societal norm of paying interest on borrowed money came under fire. In Islamic Sharia law, "money" is only a means of facilitating exchange and has no value in and of itself. Therefore, the payment of interest for borrowing money is not necessary. Sharia law prohibits the payment of interest on borrowed money. (For more information on this issue, read "Interest Free Banking" by Ajami et al.[10])

THE IMPORTANCE OF RESOURCE DEVELOPMENT

The utilization of a country's resources is important in the spectrum of overall development, including economic, social, political, spiritual, or material aspects. Islam encourages learning and interaction among different people:

> *O mankind! We created you from a single soul, male and female, and made you into nations and tribes, so that you may come to know one another. Truly the most honored of you in God's sight is the greatest of you in piety. God is All-Knowing, All-Aware.*
>
> *Qur'an* (49:13)

Even though spiritual matters seem to be noneconomic in nature, their inculcation and development involve the use of resources. Hence, God (Allah) commands mankind to invest in the development of spiritual values. For example, the spread and establishment of Islam around the world requires travel, dissemination of knowledge, education, publication of literature, use of media, protection of Islamic societies from non-Islamic forces (i.e., internal and external defense), and the administration of institutions intended for the implementation of Islamic obligations, norms, and the like. Each of these functions requires tremendous material and human resources.

Economic growth requires investable resources for producing capital goods, hiring workers and managers, acquiring raw materials, improving technology, and organizing the production process. In particular, capital formation and technological change are considered key factors in economic development; the availability of adequate investable resources is a prerequisite for the smooth supply and use of these factors.

Utilization of Natural Resources for Development

Islam provides enormous incentives for mobilizing resources, both material and human. It also provides an institutional framework conducive to the efficient use of resources for development. The Islamic way of life considers all natural resources as provisions for the benefit of mankind. In Islam, the purpose of human resources is to explore, develop, and use all available natural resources to enhance the well-being of all human beings in this world and in the hereafter. Human resource management should develop technology that promotes a better use of natural resources.

Consider the following Qur'anic verses, which are only a few of the many passages that discuss natural resources:

He it is Who created for you all that is in the earth.

Qur'an (II:29)

And there is an abode and a provision for you for a time in the earth.

And the earth we have spread out, set thereon firm mountains, made to grow all kinds of things in due balance. And we have provided therein means of subsistence for you...

And we sent down iron wherein is hardness and advantages for men.

And it was He who made the sea subservient that you may eat flesh that is flesh from it.

We shall show them Our Signs on the horizons and within themselves until it will be manifest unto them that it is the truth...

Qur'an (XXXXI:53)

Muslims therefore believe that (1) all natural resources are given by Allah, (2) the objective of providing the natural resources is to benefit mankind to build a better future, and (3) human resource managers are encouraged to explore and develop natural resources by every available means, within Islamic laws, and to use them for the benefit of humanity.

The incentive to mobilize and use natural resources is connected to an instruction from Allah: "And when the prayer is over, disperse in the world and search for the bounty of Allah" (LXII:10). This does not refer merely to trade; it refers to the utilization of all provisions, including natural resources, that are made by Allah.

The Prophet Mohammed stated that if the *Qiyamah,* or day of resurrection, is approaching, one will not be able to make use of the fruits of the land or the land itself, which is a natural resource. However, leaving it unused is discouraged. This emphasis received legal status in the early Islamic state. It was declared that if a person did not cultivate his land for more than three years, the land would be confiscated and transferred to someone who would cultivate it.

A question may arise concerning the use of exhaustible natural resources, such as petroleum and tin. Excessive use of these resources deprives future generations and causes an imbalance in the intertemporal distribution of exhaustible resources. It is the Islamic point of view to avoid all waste and excess, but at the same time to use whatever is needed for the welfare of the present generation. Whatever is not required by this generation will be left for future generations. Added to this is the knowledge that Allah, who created them in the first place, can increase the stock of so-called exhaustible resources.

Thus, there are two dimensions to the utilization of natural resources. First is the mobilization of natural resources, which is simply exploring and owning them. Second is developing and using natural resources for the benefit of mankind. Islam provides all motivations and instructions to both explore and use natural resources for human welfare.

ISLAMIC LAW

The Sharia, or Islamic law, literally means "a path to water." It is the sacred law and embraces all aspects of life, not just religious practices, that are described as the Islamic way of life. The Sharia has four sources: the *Qur'an,* the practice as laid down by the Prophet, Consensus (which is concerned with implementing the meaning of the requirements of the *Qur'an*), and Analogy (using parallel cases to apply Islamic law). In specific cases, where no laws have been formed, analogy is used. There are five categories of laws that can be formed: obligatory (for some Muslims or for all), recommended, permitted, disapproved of, and forbidden. In previous times, schools of law were formed in different cities in the expanding Islamic empire. Although the differences in these schools are actually fairly small, recent practices encourage Muslims to adopt the legal practice of individual schools according to the appropriateness of their teaching on specific issues, and not to follow one school rigidly.

The Sharia also lays down the rules concerned with areas that would be covered by law in the Western sense of the word. This is perhaps the area that has received the most attention in the Western world. Marriage, divorce, inheritance, alcohol consumption, and diet are all mentioned. Contrary to popular belief, Islam neither degrades women nor establishes their inferiority in any way. The *Qur'an* states only the obvious, namely that men and women are distinguishable.[11] Women have the fullest freedom to choose their life partners, and they cannot be forced into marriage.[11] When a contract for marriage is made, a dowry is given to the bride or the family of the bride. Divorce is accomplished by repudiation of the marriage by the husband. If a woman wants a divorce, it must be granted with the consent of her husband, or it can be dissolved by a judge in certain cases. There are also established laws regarding the custody of minor children in the case of divorce. The drinking of alcohol is prohibited. Laws of inheritance limit the amount of an estate that can be given to nonfamily members and specify how an estate can be divided. A man has the primary responsibility for providing for his family, and inheritances are meant for that purpose. A woman's primary responsibility is caring for the family. She has the right to own and retain property and is not necessarily obligated to use money earned or inherited to provide for her family. Although women are expected to dress modestly in public, there is not a big difference between what Muslim women wear today and what Western women wear. Women exercise more leadership roles. Recently, Arab women have fought for their rights, with considerable success. For example, women are paid equally and have political rights such as the right to vote and the right to hold public office.[11]

The preceding is only a partial listing of the laws of Islamic life. To understand Islamic laws fully and how they are applied, thorough research on the *Qur'an* and its teachings is necessary. The laws must be understood in their complete context. With so much Western influence, Muslims had hoped that the use of Western technology would help them to develop and advance. Before World War II, they wanted to follow the path set by the Europeans in order to be their equals and partners in civilization. They hoped to take what was good from the West and add it to what was good in the East. However, the influences were later seen as a detriment to Islamic traditions, and this spurred the current religious resurgence. Middle Eastern countries became particularly suspicious of feminism. Muslims saw this Western influence as an attack on the family structure, which is the strongest social unit. Work and family are seen as the most important values for Arabs. A worker is defined by his or her commitment to family, and work is seen as the means to enjoy an adequate social and family life. Thus, the commitment to Islamic values and tradition is especially important in this sense.

MIDDLE EASTERN VERSUS WESTERN WOMEN

Women constitute a large percentage of the Middle Eastern population. It is imperative that foreign organizations understand the position of women in a society that is so conservative and religious. There is a sense of rapid change in the position of women in Middle Eastern society, and this is in part due to Western influence. Multinational corporations needs to be aware of this fact in order to keep up with the dynamic changes and their impact on Middle Eastern society. The misconceptions that Westerners have about the position of women in society and religion are clarified to some extent in this section.

American women have a unique place in their society. They are independent in nature and compete with men in every aspect of life. American women expect to get an education, find a job, and select a husband without parental interference. American women, like their husbands, are supposed to be able to earn a living, manage money, and hold a full-time job. Many American women no longer want to just take care of the home and have come a long way in expanding their role to be similar to that traditionally assigned to men. Throughout the world, women who never envied their husband's position now want to emulate the American woman. For example, during the Gulf War, women in the American military stimulated Saudi Arabian women to protest for the right to drive a vehicle for the first time in history.

The status of women in the entire Arab world is inextricably interwoven with the Islamic religion. Moslem men may marry not only Moslem women, but Jewish or Christian women as well. Moslem women, on the other hand, may marry only Moslem men. These religious barriers, however, can be removed by conversion. Women also have the fullest freedom of choice in marriage and cannot be forced into marriage. Male Muslims are permitted to have up to four wives according to the *Qur'an,* but it is *specifically* stated that all wives must be treated equally. If this is not possible, only one wife is permitted. A Moslem woman is entitled to one-quarter of her husband's estate. Moslem daughters inherit half as much as sons, mainly because daughters, unlike sons, do not have to share their inherited property with other family members if necessary.

Educational norms and institutions are becoming less conservative than ever before. Men and women study together in academic institutions, and women study farming, engineering, exploitation of oil, and medicine, among other fields.

There has been a drastic change regarding the woman's role in the family and society. Women are seen increasingly outside their homes. In fact, some women exercise the prerogatives of American women and are genuinely in control of the family. This applies largely to the middle class and the less conservative portion of the upper class. In terms of public life, Moslem women are exercising more leadership. Arab and Moslem women in general have fought, with considerable success, for the recognition of women's right. They have won political rights, such as the right to vote and the right to hold public office. Women such as Prime Minister Khaleda Zia of Bangladesh and Benazir Bhutto of Pakistan serve as the heads of Islamic states. Moslem women also increasingly hold high-level diplomatic positions.

The status of women invariably arises in any discussion of Islamic society or Arab countries. Contrary to popular belief, Islam neither degrades nor establishes the inferiority of women. Islam emphasizes equality in many rights and duties of both sexes and gives a woman absolute authority over her property. Furthermore, women have the fullest freedom of choice in marriage as well as the right to divorce with reasonable grounds. Islam does not require women to be veiled or to remain indoors; it merely asks that they be moderately dressed in public.

Islam encourages modesty for men and women and does not encourage unnecessary mingling between males and females. This is misconstrued in the West as mistreatment and subjugation of women. Islam emphasizes the education of both women and men. A better understanding of Islam's emphasis on modest dress for men and women to preserve its ethical and moral foundations may reduce tensions when Westerners come into contact with Muslims. Family is the cornerstone of Islamic society. By assigning to women responsibility for the family, stability, well-being, happiness, and unity, Islam emphasizes the importance of and high regard for women in its ethical and social systems. Muslims contend that the real power is with God almighty. The individual is an agent of God on earth and is a part of a family and a community. Anything he or she does will affect the society at large. The goal is not to glorify yourself but to glorify God. Western philosophy, on the other hand, is based on individualism.

Everyone wants to be independent. Focus is on the individual rather than the family or community.

It has often been said that one learns from the experience of others. This is true not only on an individual basis but applies on a societal basis as well, such as when examining the tremendous differences and changes in American and Arab societies.

ISLAM THROUGH THE EYES OF THE WESTERN MEDIA

It is imperative that multinational corporations understand the present political situation in the Middle East, because politics is an important issue for success in a host country. The following discussion shows how the Western media has depicted the Islamic world and what is really behind this portrait.

The Islamic world is poorly represented in the West in terms of press and media coverage. Language problems, the absence of developed news agencies with international networks, and inadequate or biased accounts by some reporters and analysts from the West contribute to this poor representation. The Arabs believe that many factors have contributed to the biased or inadequate reports. Some biases come from the historical animosities left over from the Crusades and the Ottoman domination of Eastern Europe until World War I.[1,3]

Some of the events in the Muslim world are often misunderstood, misinterpreted, and blown out of proportion to their significance. For example, Imam Khumayni's sentence of death to Salman Rushdie was regarded by the Western media as Iran's total disregard for basic human rights and international law. However, the West does not seem to realize the tremendous insult that the book *Satanic Verses* leveled at the entire Muslim world. Had the situation involved a Western country, the media would have responded from a different perspective.

There is a worldwide yearning among Muslims to reorder their political, social, and economic institutions according to Islamic principles. Unfortunately, this has been perceived by the Western media and foreign policy experts as a threat and a rise in militant or fundamentalist Islam.

CONCLUSION

When examining the culture of the Middle East, American managers must attempt to fully understand the implications and importance of Islamic values and traditions and how they apply to the lives of Middle Easterners as well as the companies with which they are involved. This is a crucial first step. Only a small minority of Westerners actually try to understand Arabs. Visitors and military personnel should be briefed on customs and courtesies before entering Arab countries (this was especially true during the Gulf War). Westerners in general know very little about the culture of these countries. They need to learn about Middle Eastern business customs in addition to Islamic law. The most effective way to initiate this understanding is to work with agencies or consultants that specialize in Middle Eastern culture. Kumar[4] suggests that the negative impressions of Islamic societies can be modified by being sensitive to the customs that local societies consider important and cultivating long-term relationships in the host environment. It is important not to offend the people in a host country. Experts specializing in this area can help a company tremendously because they know the important aspects of a country's culture and are familiar with its business practices. Understanding this unique culture will enable American companies to succeed in the region.

REFERENCES

1. Charly Reese, "Islam Offers No U.S. Threat," *New Castle News,* p. 2, September 3, 1993.
2. Keith Stump, "Seeing the World Through Islamic Eyes," *The Plain Truth,* pp. 5, 6, June 1983
3. Manton C. Gibbs, "A Refocused Strategy for Arab's Effective Business Operation: Dealing with Western Orientation," *The International Journal of Commerce and Management,* p. 34, Fall 1993.
4. Kamelesh Kumar, *American Multinational Enterprises in Islamic Countries,* (Dallas: The International Academy of Management and Marketing), 1990.
5. S. Mohammad Tabataba'i, *Islamic Teachings: An Overview,* translated by R. Campbell (Canada: John Deyell), 1989, p. 175.
6. Georgiana G. Stevens, *The United States and the Middle East* (Englewood Cliffs, N.J.: Prentice-Hall), 1964, pp. 49–69.
7. Lauren S. Bahr and Bernard Johnston, *Collier's Encyclopedia* (New York: Macmillan), 1992, pp. 150–177.
8. S. Mohammad Tabataba'i, *Islamic Teachings: An Overview,* translated by R. Campbell (Canada: John Deyell), 1989, p. 200.
9. L.R. Bolling, "Religion and Politics in the Middle East Conflict," *Middle East Journal,* 45:125–130, Winter 1991.
10. Riad Ajami, D. Khambata, and M. Kavoossi, "Interest Free Banking," in D. Siddiqui and A. Alkhafaji, *The Gulf War: Implications for Global Businesses and Media* (Apollo, Pa.: Closson Press), 1992, pp. 133–135.
11. A.F. Alkhafaji, *Toward a Better Understanding of Islam* (Slippery Rock, Pa.: Slippery Rock University), Spring 1990.
12. Yasumasa Kuroda and Tatsuzo Suzuki, "A Comparative Analysis of the Arab Culture: Arabic, English and Japanese Language and Values," paper presented at the 5th Congress of the International Association of Middle Eastern Studies, Tunis, September 20–24, 1991.
13. A. Ali, "The Islamic Work Ethic in Arabia," *Journal of Psychology,* 126:507–519, 1992.
14. D. Siddiqui and A. Alkhafaji, *The Gulf War: Implications for Global Businesses and Media* (Apollo, Pa.: Closson Press), 1992, pp. 133–135.
15. D. McClelland, *The Achieving Society* (New York: Free Press), 1961.

16. R. Aldag and A. Brief, "Some Correlates of Work Values," *Journal of Applied Psychology,* 6:757–760, 1975.

17. M. Blood, "Work Values and Job Satisfaction," *Journal of Applied Psychology,* 53:456–459, 1969.

18. Adrian Furnham, "A Question of Competency," *Personnel Management,* 22:37, June 1990.

19. A. Furnham and K. Bland, "The Protestant Work Ethic and Conservatism," *Personality and Individual Differences,* 3:205–206, 1982.

20. A. Furnham and C. Muhuldeen, "The Protestant Work Ethic in Britain and Malaysia," *Journal of Social Psychology,* 122:157–161, 1984.

21. R. Congleton, "The Economic Role of a Work Ethic," *Journal of Economic Behavior and Organization,* 15:365–385, 1991.

22. George M. Fodor, "Attitudes Anchor Harbor Sales," *Industrial Distribution,* 79:20–22, June 1990.

23. C. Chow, M. Schields, and Y. Chan, "The Effects of Management Controls and National Culture on Manufacturing Performance," *Accounting, Organizations and Society,* 16:209–226, 1991.

BIBLIOGRAPHY

Ahmad, K., *Islam: Its Meaning and Message* (London: Islamic Council of Europe), 1976.

Buchholz, R., "An Empirical Study of Contemporary Beliefs About Work in American Society, *Journal of Applied Psychology,* 63:219–227, 1978.

Dickey, C., "Why We Can't Seem to Understand the Arabs," *Newsweek,* pp. 26–27, January 7, 1991.

Hautman, Kenneth J. and Rose Ann Sullivan, "Intellectual Property: Maximizing Protection of an Employer's Rights," *Employee Relations Law Journal,* 15:253–265, Autumn 1989.

Hennessy, Colleen M. and Kay W. McCurdy, "RRGs Grapple with Vague Application of Securities Laws," *Risk Management,* 37:46–50, July 1990.

Jackri, Ernest, *Background of the Middle East* (Ithaca, N.Y.: Cornell University Press), 1952, pp. 145–157.

Nolte, Richard H., *The Modern Middle East* (New York: Atherton), 1963, pp. 124–140.

Peretz, D.T., "The Middle East," *Pension World,* 10:70–74, 1991.

Razi, G.H., "Legitimacy, Religion and Nationalism in the Middle East," *American Political Science Review,* 84:70–85, March 1990.

Sajjad, Waseem, "Political Comments on Islam and Communication I," *Media, Culture and Society,* 15:81–83, 1993.

Wittenberg-Cox, Aviah, "France's Age of Reason," *International Management* (European edition), 45:52–55, September 1990.

11 MULTINATIONAL COMPANIES AND LESS DEVELOPED COUNTRIES/ COMMODITY-DRIVEN SOCIETIES

ABSTRACT

The impact of multinational corporations in Third World countries is examined in this chapter. The factors that make foreign investment desirable to host countries are discussed. The relationship between multinational corporations and Third World nations is explored. The discussion is based on the short-term, high-profit strategies that are often used by multinational corporations in doing business with developing countries. The conflict between the real social needs of less developed countries and the short-term profit-maximizing policies that multinational corporations require is also discussed.

CHAPTER OBJECTIVES

1 To discuss the rationale for foreign investment

2 To explore the effects of multinational corporations in Third World nations

3 To examine the conflict between multinational corporations and less developed countries

4 To identify the needs of less developed countries

5 To examine the problems caused by multinational corporations

6 To explore how less developed countries can protect themselves

CASE STUDY
Local Color

"We are not an American company. We're a Thai company." This is what C. William Carey, chairman and CEO of Town & Country Corporation, the largest U.S. jewelry manufacturer and wholesaler, said about his Thailand subsidiary Essex International Company Ltd. Carey has built a successful jewelry operation on the basis of respect for native customs and cultural transition. Carey proclaims, "I don't believe in Americanizing them. You have to go to a place and understand its strengths and massage them." He goes on to say that people "don't want outside influences coming in that distort their values and work ethic."

"If you take a cookie-cutter approach and stay open on a Buddhist holiday, workers will be resentful and feel you're disrespectful of their culture. They don't care if you're closed on the Fourth of July, but they do care if you close for the Queen's birthday in April." Carey's views are shared by the majority of CEOs, who feel that adapting to local culture is the biggest problem in globalization.

Carey has apparently accomplished his goal of cultural awareness to its full extent. When Town & Country established a subsidiary in Hong Kong, he spent $15,000 on fortune-tellers to tell the workers the fate of the company. Carey also gave off all local holidays after his purchase of Little Switzerland, based in the Caribbean.

Thailand is where Carey has proven himself to be most culturally sensitive. Essex enjoys being ranked in the top 5 of over 800 jewelry manufacturers in Thailand, with net annual sales of $19.4 million U.S. dollars. Carey chose Thailand, which ranks second in the world in jewelry exporting, because of the people's tradition in stone cutting, the low labor cost, and the work ethic. Also, Thailand's pro-business attitude gave Essex a four-year tax holiday and permission to build a warehouse free of restrictions and duties.

Carey's original goal with Essex was to make it acceptable to the people of Thailand, who are motivated by security and respect from their employer. Carey had to do many things to gain their confidence, including sitting cross-legged for a three-and-a-half-hour ceremony, inviting nine Buddhist monks to bless the seven-story factory, and building a Buddhist spirit house at the factory for daily prayers and offerings.

After using 15 expatriates to help set up the company in the first year, Carey sent them all back and used a polycentric recruitment policy to fill all

INTRODUCTION

As discussed earlier, the concept of a multinational corporation (MNC) is relatively new in the field of business. The creation of such entities was the direct result of the need for businesses to expand outward as opportunities in local markets began to shrink.

positions. Essex's initial 200 workers were between the ages of 17 and 22 and had previously worked in rice paddies. Essex lured women from 500 miles away with rent-free dormitories and the opportunity to learn a trade and increase their standard of living. The women receive on-site medical care and exams, three meals a day, and uniforms. Courses for high school equivalency diplomas are offered, as are classes in home economics and self-improvement. There is a library, and a number of recreational programs have been started. These benefits are intended to both help the workers develop and keep them occupied. "We wanted to give them esprit de corps...to mold them into what we wanted...by getting them to excel," Carey stated. These women, who at one time had nothing, were able to open bank accounts, send money home, and join the profit-sharing program. They were offered company stock in 1991, and these workers now own approximately 10% of the 30% of publicly held stock.

The total cost is hard to figure, but Carey estimates that these benefits add around $250 a month per employee. Essex employees are paid on the average $500 to $1500 per month; in comparison, the average jewelry company in Thailand pays $220 to $550 per month according to *American Jewelry Manufacturer* magazine.

Recognition is another major factor in Essex's and Carey's success. There are both team and individual incentives. While at first people were reluctant about individual incentives, the recognition is now welcome. As their performance improves, workers can move up the line and earn more money, relocate to a semi-private dormitory, be named employee of the month, or receive a pat on the back in a formal ceremony. "Recognition in front of one's peers is the most important thing next to money," Carey explains.

Carey's cultural sensitivity knows virtually no bounds. In the beginning stages of Essex, he allowed a work schedule that started much later in the day than in the Western world. After the employees were comfortable with the company, he was able to slowly move the starting time up to 8 a.m.

To sum up, 95% of Essex employees have stayed, unlike the Thai average. There is a low level of absenteeism and a waiting list for job applicants. When there is a large order, Essex has no problem getting workers to stay late. "The workers feel proud of the company," Carey says. "They are proud and appreciative of working in a company where they are recognized."

Source: Carol Steinberg, "Local Color," *World Trade,* p. 4, December 1992.

In order to fully understand the relationship between MNCs and developing countries, each must first be defined. A developing country is a nation with a low level of income and technical development. At least three criteria must be met in order for a corporation to be considered multinational. The first is that a company's operation must be a direct investment in a foreign land and that a company must have control over decision making in that foreign enterprise. The second element is the collective transfer of resources, including such inputs as knowledge, entrepreneurship, and capital. The third element is that the income-generating assets acquired by this process must be located in a number of countries.[1]

The phenomenon of the MNC is quite common in today's business world. These institutions are an integral part of the globalized economy. The impact of large MNCs has been so tremendous that many argue that these large organizations have become too powerful and that they cause more harm than good. These criticisms are largely directed toward the impact and influence that MNCs have in Third World nations.

When the overall result of operating internationally has a negative effect on a host nation, MNCs are pointed to as the culprit. A relevant issue is the legitimacy of MNCs in Third World nations. Various factors such as culture, customs, language, and law differ among countries, as do the expectations of host nations in terms of the overall performance of MNCs.

The issue of the impact of MNCs in the Third World is also of importance. Some factors make foreign investment very attractive to host countries. However, the long-term effect of the existence of MNCs in Third World countries is that they result in more damage than good. The lives of many people change when a MNC enters a new market, while it operates there, and when it leaves. This is a critical component in analyzing the impact of MNCs in Third World nations.

THE RATIONALE FOR FOREIGN INVESTMENT

The development of MNCs did not just happen by chance. It grew as the result of several factors that forced firms to expand their operations to an international scale. Both domestic and external factors serve as primary motivating influences that affect the need to expand a business operation to foreign lands.

Domestic factors include the existence of an oligopoly in a MNC's respective industry in its homeland, which limits the ability of a corporation to grow. General Motors, with factories in Mexico, is one such example. Firms that seek continual growth in both absolute size and market share are forced to expand their horizons into foreign markets. PepsiCo is one company that expanded due to this reason. The need for access to raw materials affects the expansion process in the form of investments, as in Alcoa's bauxite mines, as does the need to build production facilities rather than export goods. Another important factor is the improvements in technology and telecommunications that allow corporations to have better, faster, and more efficient control over their foreign investments. All MNCs benefit from such improvements, which have created a new interest in global opportunities as corporate managers recognize the ever-increasing possibilities.

External factors also spur the outward expansion of major corporations in their search for continual growth. On the one hand, the barriers to restrict exports that are imposed by foreign governments, such as trade barriers, trade restrictions, and tariffs, serve as incentives for a corporation to enter a foreign country and establish its own production plant. Goods produced in a foreign production plant are not affected by these trade restrictions. On the other hand, the tax incentives, tax breaks, and tax holidays that foreign governments provide also serve to induce foreign investment.

Low-cost labor is attractive to many MNCs, especially those in labor-intensive industries. Because of the extremely low cost of labor in Third World nations, most foreign investments in these countries are in such labor-intensive industries as consumer electronics, clothing, footwear, and toys.

THE LEGITIMACY ISSUE

Foreign investment has played an important role in international economics only since the latter part of the 19th century. Although MNCs come in all shapes and sizes, they often generate some fairly common reactions in the developing nations in which they operate. The problem of corporate legitimacy is an extremely important and complex issue. Due to their global outlook, MNCs encounter a wide variety of environments. The legal, political, social, and cultural constraints they face in different countries vary dramatically, depending on how a society tries to manage these institutions to meet its own goals.[2] This can create conflicts of interest, and the failure to resolve such issues results in unnecessary tension between MNCs and their host countries. Therefore, in order to function successfully in the long term, MNCs must behave in a socially responsible manner in the countries in which they operate.[3]

Corporations from industrialized nations operating in their home countries are very familiar with the issues that surround legitimacy and social responsibility, but the practice of such concepts on an international scale has been limited in scope and very often unsatisfactory. The 1984 Union Carbide incident in Bhopal, India, which caused almost 3000 deaths, is an example of a MNC that did not take the same precautionary measures that it would have taken in its home country. The result of this irresponsibility was devastating in terms of both loss of life and permanent damage to the environment.

The Bhopal Settlement

The mayor of Bhopal compared the destruction that hit his city in December 1984 to chemical warfare. The worst industrial accident of all time resulted in a death toll of over 2000 and tens of thousands more seriously injured after a Union Carbide plant ran amok.

Four years after the accident, Union Carbide and the government of

India reached a settlement of $470 million, $425 million from Union Carbide and $45 million from its Indian subsidiary. The settlement will be paid to the Indian government, "the sole representative of the victims of the tragedy."

Numerous criticisms can be leveled against the settlement itself. Many in India saw it as a sellout. Many felt that the price tag was far too low and that Union Carbide was not punished severely enough for what some considered gross mismanagement of the plant in Bhopal.

Even without a full appraisal of the accident, some positive elements can be derived from the incident. Worldwide, chemical manufacturers have learned a valuable lesson, and the chances of a similar accident occurring are very small. The need for government regulation of the environment, safety, and zoning became obvious to the MNC as well as the host country.

The importance of corporate legitimacy and social responsibility is unavoidable for a number of reasons. First, because MNCs are basically outsiders operating in a foreign environment, they are seen as somewhat suspect by both the local people and the local government. This is largely because the goals and objectives of MNCs often reflect maximization of profit, whereas local governments seek to improve the local economy. An added pressure is that local governments often expect more from MNCs than from local corporations. The expectations are high when a large MNC moves into a Third World country. The MNC is often seen as a savior who will solve the various problems that the host country faces. This feeling is not only concentrated in the upper ranks of society, but permeates throughout the general public. To most Third World governments, foreign investment provides quick revenue that can be used to upgrade the economy of the country. Unfortunately, it is also an opportunity for government officials to accept bribes, and corruption has proven to be a problem in some countries. The entrance of large MNCs into Third World nations creates a chain reaction that provides new job opportunities—from the construction of the plant to the ultimate production of goods and services. Some host governments tend to overreact to the potential problems that can arise due to the difference in objectives and goals, which they perceive as a negative influence on the development of their interests.

Corporate legitimacy becomes an issue when there is a real or perceived conflict that would require a MNC to cope with conflicting priorities.[4] The inability to resolve these conflicts means that the MNC and the host government are unable to cooperate, which results in a failed venture. More serious situations can result in abrogation of agreements, expropriation, confiscation, and nationalization on the part of the host government and withdrawal on the part of the MNC.

The situation is different in less developed countries because of the considerable power that MNCs have over them. With widespread corruption, Third World nations become fairly easy targets for large corporations.

These companies enter the new market, reinforce their position over a period of time, and inevitably take advantage of the various options that are open to them. The Bhopal incident exposed the widespread corruption in the Indian justice system that gave Union Carbide the power to escape legal consequences.

THE EFFECTS OF MULTINATIONAL CORPORATIONS IN THIRD WORLD NATIONS

In most Third World nations, the large gap between the upper and lower income groups has eradicated the middle class. As a result, there is a concentration of wealth at one extreme. Therefore, it is not surprising that this group ultimately controls the political, economic, and social climate of a country. As MNCs enter new markets, they develop an understanding with these powerful individuals. Widespread corruption is common among government officials, which benefits both parties. The relationship between a MNC and the host country elite is based on short-term, high-profit strategies. This relationship damages the balanced development of Third World nations and creates political instability, which damages the relationship between the MNC and the host country in the long term.

A MNC enters a foreign market with the promise of employment, investment, and hope. These promises go unquestioned. However, in the process, all of the benefits are consumed by the ruling elite of the country. This so-called "cream" of society has no desire to act for the well being of the nation as a whole. They do not operate fairly and give preference to their own well being over that of the nation. This increases their income exponentially, and the gap between the rich and the poor widens. An additional problem is that a MNC's operation is often located in isolated enclaves that are not linked to other sectors of the economy.[5] This reduces balanced development and increases the revenues of the elite, which further widens the gap in terms of income distribution. The social cost of this disparity becomes so great that employment increases and other benefits are minimal and of little significance. The petroleum industry in many Middle Eastern countries is a representative example of this problem.

MNCs in general have no intention of improving the conditions in any country in which they have business interests. The few benefits that do reach the lower income groups are often offset by the inflation that is the result of the unequal distribution of wealth. MNCs make and sell products throughout the world without taking into account the needs of consumers in Third World nations. This is accomplished by producing goods designed for Western consumers and using marketing methods that make the usage of these products seem socially desirable.[6] This process is even more effective when the goods are first introduced to the elite of a country and finally to the general public. The direct result of this approach is to change

CASE STUDY
The New World Market

General Electric is one of the American multinational companies that, after retrenching, quickly learned the new rules to follow in the worldwide globalization process. After closing several plants in the United States and simply purchasing what it needed from foreign markets in the early 1980s, GE changed its focus to foreign market penetration. This change in emphasis is the main reason why GE exported $5 billion more than it imported— "twice as much as it had five years ago."

One of the primary means GE used to accomplish this turnaround was joint ventures. A sampling of this broad-based success story can be seen in the diverse areas in which GE operates. In the appliance sector, GE has established joint ventures with Godrej in India for the production of low-cost ovens and with Mabe in Mexico to produce gas ranges for export to the United States. A new research center has also been established in Mexico. In the plastics division, GE started a joint venture in Mexico, where commercial resin is produced. Another joint venture was set up in China with GE's medical systems division, and it has struck deals to do the same in India and Thailand.

Contrary to the anti-free trade rhetoric that permeates many sectors today, GE is a testimony to free trade. It has a $250 million trade surplus with its Mexican operations, and its "total exports of $8 billion help support some 160,000 jobs in the U.S., based on Commerce Dept. assumptions."

In a developing world where a multinational's intentions are viewed with great skepticism, GE has become a welcome partner. It has accomplished this with a tremendous effort to adapt to the new world market. GE realized that developing countries view multinational corporations as exploiters— and set out to prove them wrong. The only way to do so was to offer a truly beneficial package. In Indonesia, GE is part of a $2 billion power plant project, and it has also "offered an array of technologies to help upgrade the manufacturing base." The GE Technology Indonesia division, with its technology transfer operations, is setting up joint ventures in Indonesia. These deals will serve as models for further advances into even lesser developed countries such as Vietnam.

Another change in focus can be seen in Mexico, where GE is attempting

the consumption patterns and lifestyles throughout Third World nations. However, the real problem is that the majority of the population in the lower ranks of society is not in a position to purchase these desirable items. The increasing gap between what people have and what they want contributes to political instability in the Third World.

As problems in Third World nations increase, so does the awareness of "to recruit and develop global brains in its management ranks." A major component of this new venture is the export of the training programs that GE considers mandatory in its U.S. operations. Those tapped for the new positions created by expansion overseas are rotated every two years and given different assignments. Newly hired managers are given courses in global issues, while senior executives are sent on four-week missions to foreign markets, after which they are debriefed at headquarters. GE's CEO, John F. Welch, Jr., hopes that when all these ideas are put together, GE will become a "multipolar and multicultural company."

Let's take a closer look at one of GE's joint venture operations in Mexico. The joint venture between GE and Organizacion Mabe, in Queretaro, central Mexico, is "a model of the north–south cooperation that supporters of the North American Free Trade Agreement like to quote." At a new $7 million research and development center, GE has access to Mexico's low-cost labor and a fast-growing appliance market, while Mabe gains the advantage of GE's purchasing power and its state-of-the-art technology. The success of the joint venture can be seen in the mini-refrigerator market. Sanyo Electric exports most of its 1.1 million units to the United States from its plant in Tijuana. Mabe has been able to cut into that market drastically by taking over almost 30% of the export market. Mabe's strongest product, however, is gas ranges. Here, we see how mutually beneficial joint ventures can be. GE had never manufactured gas ranges and, ironically, the multinational giant, which provided the manufacturing technology and production schemes, was given the know-how by Mabe. Together they now supply 33% of all gas stoves purchased in the United States. This has been achieved by using 80% American-made components, which created 2500 jobs in the United States, the same number created in the Mexican operation. It also created a $20 million trade surplus for the U.S. division.

GE maintains a very low profile in the management area. Mabe's executives "report directly to GE's appliance chiefs in Louisville, not to a country manager in Mexico." This allows Mabe to experiment with multiskills training and just-in-time systems simultaneously with GE in the United States, proof that a truly mutually beneficial joint venture is the way to go in the new global economy.

Source: Tim Smart, Pete Engardio, and Geri Smith, "GE's Brave New World," *Business Week,* p. 42, November 8, 1993.

the damage created by the entrance of MNCs into these markets. Although MNCs provide better wages in comparison to local corporations, improvements in lifestyle do not keep up with inflation.[7] As social awareness increases, so does the cost of operation, which can force a MNC to relocate. A MNC that decides to move its operation to another untapped paradise leaves a gap which, if not filled, can deplete the local economy.

It used to be far simpler for foreign corporations to enter Third World countries and function in whatever way they chose. However, the situation is slowly changing as the current generation is no longer sheltered from the rest of the world and seeks a better tomorrow for themselves and the next generation. They are questioning policies and demanding respect.

MULTINATIONAL CORPORATIONS VERSUS LESS DEVELOPED COUNTRIES

There are some lessons to be learned about the relationships between MNCs and Third World host countries. MNCs enter developing countries based on short-term, high-profit strategies. It is important to note that there is a contradiction between the real social needs of less developed countries (LDCs) and the short-term profit-maximizing policies that MNCs require. MNCs should understand that these policies can damage their own long-term interests and their very survival.

MNCs in LDCs often focus on pure economic factors based on their own values and objectives and discount the values and interests of the LDCs in which they operate. Furthermore, most Western MNCs define the problems of LDCs in economic terms, such as market share, price, and rate of return on investment. These factors are actually far removed from the lifestyles and values of the majority of people in LDCs.

The relevancy of Western-style management and education in underdeveloped countries has been debated for decades. One argument is that management is culturally constrained and that it would be impossible to adjust and apply American management techniques in foreign environments. However, the basic concepts of management constitute a useful analytical tool that is applicable in other environments. American management techniques are largely based on assumptions that involve simplifications. Examples of these assumption include a closed economy, perfect competition, government noninterference, precise information, and an all-out effort to optimize.

Such simplifications may not be practical in day-to-day applications, nor are they necessarily valid under all conditions, even in Western economies. Their inadequacies increase as they are applied to underdeveloped economies. For example, in Brazil, where there is tremendous fluctuation in market performance, an inflation rate that varies from 20 to 80% per month, constant government interference in pricing and regulations, a very strong labor movement, and a general distrust of multinational intentions, an unprepared manager can feel totally helpless. As a result, whole bodies of theory and even entire fields such as marketing, finance, and international trade are not universally applicable. Market research is a must for MNCs as they try to find new consumers for their products in LDCs. In some cases, MNCs may find similarities among countries throughout the LDCs. The Arab or Muslim countries, with their many similarities, are a good example of a situation that would allow a MNC to develop a marketing plan that can be applied, with minimal changes, in a number of countries.

THE ROLE OF THE INVESTOR IN LESS DEVELOPED COUNTRIES

Former President Jimmy Carter, through the Carter Center in Atlanta, Georgia, has set his sights on international investment markets, and one of his primary targets at the moment is Zambia. Here, we see some of the classic dilemmas that face both MNCs and LDCs with regard to globalization. "With Carter looking on, Zambian ministers announced they will privatize the country's majority state-owned copper mines, and invited U.S. investors to bid. While details were noticeably vague, the audience of business executives, academic types and Beltway regulars recognized a major repositioning under way: A generation ago the rallying cry was 'Africa for the Africans.' Today it's 'Africa welcomes the capitalists.'"[8] It is wrong, however, to think that all the changes necessary to establish global business on the African continent should come from the African continent itself. There are many changes that need to be made in the United States as well. Americans should realize that other countries are highly competent and should make the effort to become educated about the different kinds of markets in Africa.

The following is an excerpt from an interview with Mr. Carter conducted by *World Trade* reporter Warren Strugatch:[9]

After considering Africa's colonial history, what role do you foresee for investors, what kind of citizen should they be, and what can be expected from the politics and policies of the African governments?

We must be "honest and fair." We must recognize that all new business contracts will need the inclusion of government ministers and the presidents. These new contracts need to be compatible with Zambian law and benefit the people of Zambia. We must stop exploitative type ventures where all the profits are exported.

Should the decision to invest depend solely on the return on investment?

No. Return on investment is not enough. Dependability over a long period of time is important; we must also start paying proper attention to environmental issues and to health care for employees and their families; we need to help these countries strengthen democracy; we must prove freedom and a free-market economy are advantageous to the country. These are all vital things to be considered—as well as the bottom line for the first year.

RESERVATIONS OF LESS DEVELOPED COUNTRIES

There are two major criticisms of the application of management theory in underdeveloped countries. The first involves the differences in the social and institutional environments between developed and underdeveloped countries. This can be described as attacking the substance of management theory. The second line of criticism suggests that the interests of Western management theory differ from the interests of underdeveloped countries. For example, Western economies are more concerned with optimum allocation of resources, maintaining full employment, inflation, and national debt. Thus, traditional theories are likely to be out of focus and not necessarily relevant to the needs of LDCs, whose central problem is to initiate and accelerate sustained growth.[9] Such criticism can be described as attacking the relevancy of management theory.

LDCs have come to realize that they must protect their strategic natural resources. Their central issues are the development of human resources, economic infrastructures, and industrial and agricultural self-reliance. In addition, LDCs want to preserve their unique cultural heritage. Therefore, MNCs have to be very sensitive to these cultural differences when formulating their strategies for working with LDCs.

The North-South Model is a theory used by MNCs doing business in developing countries. It is the perceived division of the world on the basis of economic criteria, including gross national product and all factors that go into its progress (i.e., technology, capital, and human skills). While the model appears to be one-sided, its implications are important because of the widespread belief in the model among the people of many developing countries.

MNCs are often viewed as hindering rather than helping the progress of developing countries. Proponents of the North-South Model argue that MNCs do not bring in new capital but instead use existing capital in such countries.[9] It appears that MNCs often send the profits to other areas which offer the promise of better profitability (i.e., their home country or other global locations).

THE RULING ELITE

There is always conflict between the modernization of developed countries and the traditionalism or culture of developing countries.[9,10] One assumption according to the North-South Model is that developing countries want modernization because of such benefits as the transfer of capital, education, and technology and improvements in employment opportunities and the standard of living. However, the benefits are often accompanied by social, cultural, and political problems. These problems are caused by the misuse of power and the inherent political role of the elite in a society. Dissatisfaction and frustration arise as the slow rate of progress does not fulfill the initial promise of development and material prosperity for the people.

The real domain of MNCs is the privileged sector of society in host countries—the elite—whose interests, privileges, and status are derived from their ties to MNCs and their home countries. Historically, the governments of LDCs have rarely been representative of the majority interests in their societies. The ruling elite in these countries generally have no desire to pursue national priorities that may jeopardize their own short-term interests. Typically, a LDC adopts a bureaucratic authoritarian model in order to maintain a climate that includes generous tax provisions, few restrictions on repatriation profits, and suppression of organized labor.

The operations of MNCs in LDCs are concentrated in manufacturing and extraction, each of which provides different benefits to LDCs. Manufacturing for markets in LDCs is interested in the buying power of consumers and can be expected to support limited redistribution policies by the governments of LDCs. MNC manufacturing operations in LDCs produce intermediate goods for shipment to other facilities in other countries for future processing. These operations are only concerned with factors that relate to keeping operating costs down in LDCs. Extractive operations are the least beneficial to LDCs. They generally significantly increase the wealth of the elite and therefore widen the gap in distribution of income.

In general, MNCs (and the elite in LDCs) have no intention of or interest in modernizing the local society, and few economic benefits ever trickle down to the lower sectors of society in LDCs. The only ones who benefit are the elite and the MNCs, who channel the flow of wealth from these countries back to their home nations. MNCs have been criticized for distorting consumption patterns by producing the same type of goods throughout the world without reference to consumer needs in LDCs. In South America, for example, most of the goods produced by multinationals are primarily for export, and what is sold in local markets is far too expensive for the average person to purchase. As the elite further advance their own standard of living by purchasing these goods, a deeprooted resentment forms toward them as well as toward MNCs. Somehow, the lower classes find a way to purchase these good, often by foregoing a better diet or school supplies for their children, just to take part in the illusion that they have improved their standard of living. MNCs selling goods designed for Western consumers in the markets of LDCs start with the elite and then move on to the masses. However, because only a small segment of the population in LDCs can afford these goods, most of the people feel deprived. The increasing gap between what people have and what they want contributes to political destabilization in the Third World.

THE ENVIRONMENT OF LESS DEVELOPED COUNTRIES AND MULTINATIONAL CORPORATIONS

When dealing with LDCs, MNCs typically face different environments, as determined by political, legal, economic, technological, social, and cultural factors. The political and legal environments in a LDC are critical to a MNC during the entry stage. In order to deal with the local society, a MNC must understand the social and cultural variables (markets, employees, community, etc.). The economic and technological variables affect market size, market share, product design, the manufacturing process, and distribution channels. Godiwalla[11] points out that strategic decisions (such as basic mission, primary purpose, and product lines) are often imported into a host country by a MNC in order to accomplish its goals. Instead, the managerial philosophies of the parent organization should be transferred to the local corporate culture. This is usually difficult, but MNCs generally attempt to transfer these philosophies to the extent that the local culture will accept them.

Technology transfer by MNCs to LDCs faces similar problems. It is usually faster and easier to transfer technology than to transfer managerial expertise. It is important to modify the technology in order to suit the particular needs of a developing country. For example, developed countries typically evolve capital-intensive technologies. Before transferring such technologies, however, it is vital that they be modified to meet the employment needs of populous developing countries.[12]

Sophisticated technological transfers are often criticized on the grounds that they are irrelevant to the needs of developing countries. Critics argue that they stunt a country's drive toward self-reliance and growth. Although most MNCs provide good training for new workers, problems still exist. On the one hand, MNCs provide technical job-specific training and general educational improvements. On the other hand, the jobs created by their subsidiaries require unskilled labor with minimal training and offer only limited career opportunities.[12]

The creation of a worker elite widens the gap between the wages of trained workers and the income of the large number of untrained and rural workers. An important role for a U.S. MNC is to achieve equity between these two groups. MNCs pursue those developing countries that seek manufacturing plants for import or export purposes, but overreliance on the subsidiaries generates a number of problems. Prominent among these problems are the choice of technology, managerial values, and operational methods transferred and the lack of local R&D facilities.

Cultural considerations must be taken into account in such issues as centralization versus decentralization, compensation, level of responsibility, family versus company loyalty, work-related values, and the timetable. An example of the influence of culture on decision making took place in Taiwan, where a U.S. company set up a plant without understanding that the structure of the society is based on the military hierarchy. The company employed a manager who seemed to be well qualified, but he consistently bowed to a subordinate who had outranked him in his military career.[11]

THE NEW ROLE

Exploitation, domination, and pumping out profits were the past approaches used by U.S. MNCs in dealing with developing countries. U.S. MNCs need to modify their role, and many have already begun to do so. Advanced technology, managerial expertise, brand loyalty, and capital resources are some of the advantages that MNCs offer. Countries at varying levels of development are hungry for the technology and know-how that MNCs can provide.

The strategies of MNCs, such as decentralized autonomy for the local organization, need to be culturally modified. Also, the attitude that what works well in the United States will work well everywhere should be abandoned. The goals and objectives of MNCs should take into consideration the national goals and problems of developing countries. A joint venture in which a MNC is not dominant but instead provides technical expertise and may prove less suspicions to LDCs. As MNCs cooperate by offering to play a significant role in achieving the national and regional goals of a host country, trust and acceptance will increase.

The North-South Model explains the nature of the conflicts between MNCs of advanced countries and developing countries. The stage of a country's development provides the framework for acquiring a particular technology. It helps to explain the reason for conflict in such issues as excessive control of commerce by MNCs, the widening gap between the elite or trained workers and untrained workers in LDCs, and transplanting the values and culture of the parent organization into the subsidiary organization. U.S. MNCs, like MNCs in other advanced countries, must carefully analyze the overall situation before formulating their strategies.

Developing countries continue to show increased demand for Western products, equipment, and services. More and more developing countries are indicating a new pro-business attitude toward Western companies. Privatization and fewer government restrictions are now beginning to emerge in these countries. Even some countries long known for their difficult business environments are changing their ways. Chile, Argentina, and Mexico are good examples of countries that created tremendous obstacles to the entry and operation of MNCs, especially with their firmly entrenched state-owned companies. Today, they have divested themselves of most of these state-owned companies, opened their markets to accept free trade, and are making great strides toward improving their economic future. The following four factors have brought about this change in policy:[13]

1. Government leaders now recognize the severe limitations of socialism in advancing their economic interests.

2. The enthusiasm of foreign governments for state-owned enterprises has diminished. Countries with massive debt problems can no longer afford the drain from these enterprises on the national treasury.

3. The growth of Third World multinationals is proof that emerging nations can adopt the free market system.

4. International lenders and creditors are no longer comfortable pumping money into failing economies. These institutions insist on economic efficiency as the primary lending criterion.

The governments of Tanzania, India, Malaysia, Brazil, China, and most of the Middle Eastern countries have announced plans to permit foreign companies to increase their stake in these economies. U.S. MNCs need to find better ways to pursue these expanding opportunities. A MNC that wants to conduct business in a Third World country may have to find a local partner with which to do business. A MNC should be willing to enter into countertrade agreements or joint venture partnerships with local firms and state-owned enterprises. Today, many countries are using countertrade all over the world, including the Third World. Countertrade can be defined as "the exchange of goods for other goods or exchanges involving parallel, but linked, cash purchases."[14] A company must also be aware of the competition that exists in Third World markets from other MNCs, which may mean that a company will have to accept lower profits.

RECOMMENDATIONS

The various problems facing Third World nations can be largely attributed to the exploitation of industrialized nations. Large MNCs from these economically powerful countries enter new markets with the hope of optimizing profits by reducing costs. MNCs have been accused of exploiting low-cost labor, increasing corruption, and changing consumer demands in the Third World to their benefit. However, part of the blame rests with the local governments and the ruling elite of these Third World countries. By allowing MNCs to infiltrate their countries through corrupt and irresponsible business practices, which inevitably strengthen their own position in their country, they have set a precedent that has spread throughout the Third World.

The increasing level of education, health, and social awareness among the lower string of society within the Third World has brought about changes. These changes have led to a larger middle class society, which in turn has reduced the power of the ruling elite. The present social structure will continue to change over time, and as these changes take place, the relationship between the elite and MNCs will require better control. The biggest problem that needs to addressed is corruption. As a country begins to develop economically, issues of business ethics become increasingly important. With increased development, the problem of corruption would be reduced by the increased participation of the growing middle class in the decision-making process. As the expectations of societies increase, MNCs would be forced to behave in a more responsible manner.

Governments must be more aware of the long-term effects of the participation of MNCs in local economies. Governments need to set far stricter guidelines for acceptable business practices of these large corporations. The situation could be further improved if Third World nations would begin to diversify their economies and identify multiple opportunities for growth. This would provide these countries with additional options, because a broader based economy would not be dependent on one particular industry. This approach has worked well for many developing nations that were once considered Third World nations.

Third World governments can also protect themselves from being taken advantage of by multinationals in terms of profit. Governments should require MNCs to establish joint ventures with local corporations in which a particular portion of the assets must be owned by local entities. Third World nations can also help themselves by requiring MNCs to provide technical training to their employees. This transfer of knowledge would benefit host nations and would force MNCs to accept their social responsibilities in terms of the interests of the residents of Third World nations in which they do business.

CONCLUSION

The social impact of MNCs in LDCs should not be viewed only from the perspective of the elite. Social progress that guarantees a long-term beneficial relationship between MNCs and LDCs can only be accomplished by changing the present trend and by integrating the interests of the citizens of LDCs into the decision-making process. Failure to do so will result in uneven development and lead to hostilities between the citizens of LDCs and MNCs and their home countries. MNCs must move beyond a narrow economic approach to their activities and use strategies that include a commitment to meet the needs of host country populations. This transformation is necessary in order to secure long-term profitability in developing countries. If the relationship between MNCs and LDCs is managed wisely and cooperatively, it can constitute a win–win situation for both parties.

MNCs must blend their modernism with the traditionalism of developing countries in formulating ways of doing business. The social problems caused by the drive to improve the standard of living in LDCs must be dealt with. World competition will continue to increase in the future, and European and Japanese MNCs will no longer be the only competitors that American corporations face.

REFERENCES

1. M. Hood and S. Young, *The Economics of Multinational Enterprise* (London: Longman), 1979.
2. L. Zurawicki, *Multinational Enterprises in the East and West* (The Netherlands: Sijthoff and Noordhoff), 1979.
3. Kamalesh Kumar, "American Enterprises in Islamic Countries: Understanding and Resolving the Corporate Legitimacy Dilemma," *IABD Proceeding*, 1991.
4. L.D. Solomon, *Multinational Corporations and the Emerging World Order* (National University Publications), 1988.
5. G.R. Bassiry and M. Jones, "MNC Strategies in the Third World: Lessons to Be Learned," *IABD Proceeding*, 1990.
6. Abbas Ali, "Human Resource Problems and Development in the Arab World: A Challenge to Multinational Corporations," paper presented at the Academy of International Business, Southeast Region, Atlanta, Georgia, November 13—15, 1986.
7. A. Teichova, M. Leboyer, and H. Nussbaum, *Multinational Enterprise in Historical Perspectives* (London: Cambridge University Press), 1988.
8. Warren Strugatch, "Africa Does the Eastern European Thing," *World Trade*, pp. 12–15, October 1992.
9. Karen Paul and Robert Barbato, "The Multinational Corporation in the Less Developed Country: The Economic Development Model Versus the North-South Model," *The Academy of Management Review*, 10:8–14, January 1985.
10. Paul W. Beamish, "The Characteristics of Joint Ventures in Developed and Developing Countries," *The Columbia Journal of World Business*, 20:13–19, Fall 1985.
11. Yezdi H. Godiwalla, "Multinational Planning—Developing a Global Approach," *Long Range Planning*, 19:110–116, April 1986.
12. Lee A. Tavis, "Multinationals as Foreign Agents of Change in the Third World," *Business Horizons*, 26:2–6, September–October 1983.
13. David Heenan, "A Different Outlook for Multinational Companies," *Journal of Business Strategy*, 9:51–54, July/August 1988.
14. Anant R. Negandi and Peter A. Donohowe, "It's Time to Explore New Global Trade Options," *Journal of Business Strategy*, 10:27–31, January–February 1989.

12

ACADEMIC TRAINING TO PREPARE MANAGERS FOR A GLOBAL ECONOMY

ABSTRACT

Today's managers, as well as those in the future, have a much more difficult job than managers in the past. American companies are competing in a global marketplace. Therefore, there is a vital need to better prepare managers for the 21st century. Universities usually address this challenge of preparing future managers by providing the educational leadership necessary in this environment. The skills needed by a global managers are discussed in this chapter. The role of the university in preparing future managers is also explored.

CHAPTER OBJECTIVES

1 To understand the effects of ignorance and arrogance on American businesses

2 To identify appropriate teaching methods that encompass experience in the real world.

3 To identify the roles of business and academia

4 To clarify the role of international professors as an asset to the business and academic communities

5 To identify ways that universities can encourage faculty to learn a new language, incorporate new materials into their teaching, or begin a new research stream

CASE STUDY
The INSEAD Education

The European Institute of Business Administration, or INSEAD as it is called, exemplifies the teachings of international business and multicultural studies. Americans seek to acquire formal management education at INSEAD for two primary reasons. First, INSEAD promises to equip them with the global and multicultural tools they will need to succeed in the business world of the present and the future. Second, INSEAD is geographically and intellectually on the leading edge of Europe's eastward expansion into the former Warsaw Pact countries and the republics that were once part of the former Soviet Union.

INSEAD requires a lot from its students before they even begin their studies. INSEAD requires students to be fluent in both English and French and to acquire a third language if they do not already know one. Students must also have at least four years of experience in the business world before they are admitted.

INSEAD runs a very tough regime in order to better train its students. Students learn in groups of six or seven people from very diverse backgrounds. INSEAD seeks to have students "clash and then work together in spite of differences of age, culture, nationality, and work experience." A typical student group might include a German advertising executive, an American management consultant, a French engineer, a Lebanese banker, and a Japanese marketing manager. These groups enable students to understand that there is more that one way of doing things. INSEAD's intent is for students to learn to understand each other, utilize each other's expertise, and discover ways to work together.

INSEAD provides students the opportunity to gain knowledge of foreign languages, cultures, traditions, and means of conducting business on an international level. This gives their students an edge in the world of international business.

Source: James Bredin, "Inside INSEAD Multiculturalism Is Basic at Europe's Best B-School," *Industry Week,* pp. 51–52, July 20, 1992.

INTRODUCTION

Because American businesses are competing in a global marketplace, there is a vital need to better prepare managers for the 21st century. The global economy has elevated competition to a level that threatens business survival as never before. The internationalization of business includes many facets. Competitive activity has assumed an international dimension in trade, investment and ownership, manufacturing and sourcing, markets and customers, finance, technology, and research and development. Universities usually address the challenge of preparing future managers by providing the educational leadership needed in this environment.

America's businesses are not prepared for their potential involvement in the global market due to both ignorance and arrogance. Ignorance is evident in a company's decision not to export its products because of the perceived difficulties involved in the transaction. It also results in accepting unsolicited requests for information and products from foreign companies. Arrogance induces American companies to ignore the global marketplace altogether and expect to conduct business on their own terms. Some businesses believe that buying American is patriotic. Some believe that the U.S. government will protect their inefficiencies from foreign competition.

The university must serve as the conduit to change the international perceptions in American society. Unfortunately, a university's resources are often stretched too thin to provide long-term solutions. A university provides services to its various stakeholders, including students, alumni, the community in which it is located, and the country as a whole. While a college of education serves the needs of an educational system within a particular state, a college of business serves the needs of the business community. Because universities have limited resources to devote to this task, companies should be actively involved financially as well as academically. Business and academia should cooperate in order to better prepare managers.

SKILLS A GLOBAL MANAGER NEEDS

New requirements for a global manager simply means transforming the international perspective to a global perspective. A global manager must change the way he or she thinks. Thinking in global terms means taking ideas and concepts from one environment and using them in the more complex world of global management. For example, this means that a manager from the United States will be required to know much more than his or her domestic language and culture. The following is a list of the skills and abilities a manager should have or develop in order to be effective on the global level:

1. The ability to perform in a team setting

2. The ability to manage change and transition

3. The ability to manage work force diversity

4. The ability to communicate in various cultural settings

5. Proficiency in developing global strategic skills and turning ideas into action (implementation)

6. The ability to change the way he or she thinks and operates

7. The ability to be creative, learn, and transfer knowledge

8. The expertise to form joint ventures or strategic alliances and to operate with a high degree of personal integrity and honesty

A new global economy is emerging, and managers of MNCs have no choice but to adapt. A company's resources must be effectively allocated at all levels of management. Managers must recognize the changes in the global market and prepare themselves to deal with them. Management needs to establish a crucial link between the formulation and the implementation of a global strategy. In order to ensure the successful transition to a global operation, managers in both home and host countries should be in agreement with the strategic design. Effective global managers will also need the skills to manage the transition from independence/dependence to interdependence. On a personal level, global managers will need to act more as equals and less as dominant decision makers operating from a powerful headquarters. They must be able to persuade their bosses, peers, and subordinates in allocating corporate resources. They must learn how to balance local and global influences under changing competitive conditions. They must establish a team relationship with their customers, suppliers, and distributors.

Managers must learn how to deal with cross-cultural influences, which requires flexibility. Global managers will require a working knowledge of international relationships and foreign affairs, including global financial markets and exchange rates.

Abell[1] recommends five guidelines for managing the change:

1. Organize business units and subunits to reflect major lines of business and key market segments.

2. Promote organizational processes and personnel policies that encourage individual initiative, promote entrepreneurship, and orient the company toward its market and the needs of chosen market segments.

3. Redefine marketing management so as to bring the market into manufacturing, research and development, and human resources.

4. Recognize the key differences in leadership requirements.

5. Detail the specific tasks required of each leader in the new organization.

Managers need to understand how to manage a diverse work force. This will enhance their cultural awareness. Top management should develop an appreciation of this diversity, which should be communicated throughout the rest of the organization. This will help to achieve high product acceptance, because culturally rooted differences can have a significant impact on a product's success in a global market. Management needs to understand that a product might not succeed if old consumption patterns are assumed to hold true. Standardizing a product might not be acceptable in a global market. A competitive edge can be gained through manufacturing flexibility and by identifying universal themes segmented according to similarities instead of geographical differences.

The new global managers will be team players who understand and respect the role of each function in an organization. Even before the advent of global companies, effective teamwork was becoming essential for managerial success. As specialization of individuals and differentiation of organizations increase, there is an increased need to integrate these specialized units to serve the objectives of an organization. Teams, committees, and task forces are among the structures that can be used to accomplish this integration.

The increased complexities of global operations require the ability to function in work teams, principally in multicultural groups. The experience of 30 major MNCs in building teams to increase their global interests was summarized in a Conference Board Report. The report included the following observations:

1. Teams that are used only for advice and counsel or for communication are still in existence, but an increasing number of firms are utilizing teams in distinct and more participative and powerful ways.

2. In addition to improved market share and technological intelligence, global teamwork can provide additional benefits. It can yield more flexible business planning, a stronger commitment to achieving world-wide goals, and closer collaboration in carrying out strategic change.

3. Teams that span the internal boundaries of an organization or that span a company's external boundaries are often required.[2]

Communication is one of the main elements of culture. It is also the cause of many problems between cultures. MNCs and their executives should be able to establish good communication with customers, suppliers, employees, the public, and the governments in the countries where they do business. Language is the key to any culture. It is the primary means of communication and penetrates all dimensions of a culture. It is also a reflection of human behavior. Learning the language indicates an interest in the culture and the people of a particular country. In order to effectively communicate with diverse groups of people, managers will require multilingual skills and high levels of cross-cultural awareness and sensitivity. Styles of communication vary among different people and at different times. Communication takes place at a certain time, at a specific place, using a specific medium, and in a specific cultural context. Effective communication requires an understanding of and sensitivity to all of these contextual elements. People also use nonverbal forms of communication, such as gestures, which add meaning to the spoken message.

THE ROLE OF BUSINESS COLLEGES

Business colleges cater to the different needs of the establishment, whether domestic or international. Depending upon their state of development, companies may need assistance with market research and distribution.[3,4] Business schools can help marketing managers identify potential markets for their products. They can also help businesses decide whether or not a demand exists for their products and can help identify the available channels of distribution. Other issues such as language, culture, exchange rates, financing, licensing, trade barriers, and transportation also vary by company, product, and experience.

The rich experience of international professors can be an asset to both the business and academic communities. Schools of business sometimes utilize their foreign professors to provide managerial assistance to companies doing business globally. Universities should encourage companies to make use of this inexpensive and knowledgeable source of information.

Companies are stepping up the services they provide to the employees they select. For example, many companies are bolstering the language and cultural training they offer to employees and their families headed overseas. As companies become more involved in international trade, they will require assistance in very specific issues. Management is troubled and sometimes confused by the different rules and regulations that are issued at the state and federal levels simultaneously. Some of these regulations seem too complicated to be understood and implemented. To compound the problem, not all services are equally available in all communities. In preparing marketing managers, universities must determine which international marketing management problems they can and will address.

FACULTY REQUIREMENTS

The task of finding qualified faculty to develop and teach courses in international business is an important issue. The situation is similar to the problem of job training that the U.S. business community faces. Faculty, like the workers on the assembly lines of the past, must be prepared to face the challenge of the future. Many of the faculty who are teaching today received their academic training without being exposed to a foreign culture or language, and some have not had the opportunity to travel abroad. In addition, most are not involved in training or research in international business.

However, things have changed in the last 15 years. The increase in the number of foreign companies with manufacturing operations in the United States posed a challenge to American products in foreign markets and forced companies to develop managers with a broader understanding of the global market. These managers are required to have technological expertise as well as managerial abilities. Universities have been forced to meet this challenge. Consequently, faculty must be able to upgrade the skills of the diverse work force.

In response to this situation, many faculty have engaged in international research. Expertise among individual faculty exists in the disciplines of marketing and management. Some faculty members have developed an effective educational infrastructure to meet the challenges of the changing world.

International business faculty usually deal with individuals who represent the small business community in America. These people must be exposed to the global market, know how to enter it, and have realistic expectations about the result of their efforts. Faculty also work with executives in large corporations with existing international and multinational operations. These executives require a different level of informational training. They need to be taught how to coordinate their efforts in the international market, how to be better competitors, how to prepare expatriates and their families, and how to consummate the flow of technology into their subsidiaries overseas.

The main customers that offer the greatest challenge to marketing and management faculty are students. Undergraduate and graduate students are curious about how the market is changing globally. Upon graduation, they are enthusiastic about working for a company that offers overseas opportunities. They require a broad-based education, including language skills and cultural competence. Universities will have to meet the challenge of preparing students and community members to be the future leaders and managers of the global economy. To incorporate real-world experiences, educators can use such techniques as inviting international experts to speak, encouraging class discussions about world events, and utilizing actual cases from around the world. Exchange programs offer another useful way to actually give students hands-on experience. Individuals who receive diplomatic and interpersonal training generally have a more cosmopolitan outlook than those who do not.

The role of business and academia should be to provide faculty with the resources necessary to incorporate the international aspect into their existing classes. While this would allow faculty members to develop a basic knowledge of the subject, only by learning a foreign language and visiting other countries can they develop true expertise. Faculty members currently have little incentive to learn a new language, incorporate new materials into their teaching, or begin a new research stream. Universities must develop programs that encourage faculty to engage in such activities. Providing travel expenses to attend appropriate international meetings would represent a step in the right direction. Interested faculty should be given sabbatical time to attend other universities for course work or research. They should also be supported by grant money for research on international issues.

Universities must develop plans for integrating the international experience into a student's education. Students can be required to take core courses that examine the differences between domestic and international cultural, political, and economic systems. Students in management should be encouraged to take courses that deal with international applications within their respective disciplines. Management courses should incorporate the international dimension in a way that is relevant to the subject area.

Students can take internships or independent studies to investigate specific international issues in greater depth. An international component needs to be added to many of the mainstream training courses offered today in negotiation, communication, and supervisory skills. Furthermore, students should be exposed to community organizations or businesses that are involved in international trade in order to get a better sense of the real application of the issues. International students enrolled in a university could be invited to host cultural events that would expose students to other cultures. Exchange programs between faculty and students of universities in different countries would also be beneficial in this sense. Such programs could offer the opportunity to attend school and live in a foreign country for an intersession, a summer, a semester, or even an academic year. While each of the preceding suggestions requires a different level of involvement and expense, collectively they provide a range of alternatives available to universities.

Regardless of what approach is followed, education must have some practical relevance. This applies to both domestic and international education, because much of mainstream management theory is irrelevant to experience in less developed countries. Entertaining and informative lunch-time presentations can be offered on various international topics. Including international articles in company newsletters can also be effective. Irrelevancy is largely due to the unrelated curriculum, scarcity of teaching materials and textbooks, and lack of quantitative preparation of future managers. Most students do not have a clear concept of what managers do. Murray and Murray[5] are of the opinion that students with no previous experience of market exchange in business and who entertain traditional beliefs about management theory have difficulty dealing with the basic concepts of management. The aim of education should be to instill an objective view of and share an analytical and fair-minded approach to practical issues. While transferring technology is not always difficult, transferring the expertise with which to approach issues in a practical way is rather complex.

SUMMARY

Students need to study foreign history, cultures, work ethics, economies, markets, politics, governments, business philosophies, and management styles. Students must develop written and verbal fluency in another language, at the least. They should be able to communicate using the appropriate dialect, gestures, behaviors, and etiquette. In order for students to develop a better understanding of the international arena, faculty need to be better trained as well. With appropriate teamwork and organizational support, the process of increasing global skills can be viewed as a challenge rather than an impossibility. Support for the improved education of students and faculty will prove to be to the benefit of the international business community.

REFERENCES

1. Derek Abell, "Multinational Management Strategies," *Multinational Business,* pp. 44–46, Summer 1990.
2. Henry W. Lane and Joseph J. Distefana, *New Requirements: The Global Manager* (Boston: PWS Kent), 1992.
3. Pradeep A. Rau and John F. Preble, "Standardisation of Marketing Strategy by Multinationals," *International Marketing Review,* pp. 18–28, Autumn 1987.
4. Peter W. Turnbull, "Interaction and International Marketing: An Investment Process," *International Marketing Review,* pp. 7–19, Winter 1987.
5. F. Murray and Ann Murray, "SRM Forum: Global Managers for Global Businesses," in *Selected Readings in Business,* Myra Schulman (Ed.) (Ann Arbor: University of Michigan Press), 1991, pp. 247–252.

BIBLIOGRAPHY

Asheghran, Parvez and Bahman Ebrahimi, *International Business* (Philadelphia: Harper Collins), 1990, p. 3.

Bredin, James, "Inside INSEAD Multiculturalism Is Basic at Europe's Best B-School," *Industry Week,* pp. 51–52, July 20, 1992.

Cavusgil, S. Tamer, "Internationalization of Business and Economics Programs: Issues and Perspectives," *Business Horizons,* pp. 92–100, November–December 1991.

Coon, C.S., "Pique Performance," *The Economist,* 321:44–45, 1991.

Derderian, Stephanie, "International Success Lies in Cross-Cultural Training," *HR Focus,* pp. 70–79, April 1993.

Early, P. Christopher, "International Training for Managers: A Comparison of Documentary and International Methods," *Academy of Management Journal,* pp. 685–698, December 1987.

Fuchsberg, Gilbert, "As Costs of Overseas Assignments Climb, Firms Select Expatriates More Carefully," *Wall Street Journal,* January 9, 1992.

Johnson, H.G., "One Vacant Chair," *The Economist,* 320:30–32, 1991.

Labich, K., "Making Over Middle Managers," *Fortune,* pp. 58–64, May 8, 1989.

Schonberger, R.J., *Japanese Manufacturing Techniques: Nine Hidden Lessons in Simplicity* (New York: Free Press), 1982.

Stoddard, Philip H., *Change and the Muslim World* (Syracuse, N.Y.: Syracuse University Press), 1988.

White, Timothy, "On the Road to Respect and Revenue," *HR Focus,* pp. 70–79, April 1993.

SECTION V

TECHNOLOGY TRANSFER

Technology is a vital component of development. Marketing technology is a complicated business. Enriching life in less developed countries through the transfer of technology becomes, therefore, a complex and difficult task. Technology is not a magical formula with which local managers can enrich life in their countries. Rather, technology for the vast majority of goods and services is known or knowable. The difficulty is overcoming the hurdles in the transformation. Basically, there are three general ways to acquire new technology: develop it internally, purchase it, or license it. In a study of technology transfer, the first method, to develop it internally, obviously is not included.

The issue of technology transfer has generated much controversy. It is frequently asserted that the transfer of technology to less developed countries is not appropriate to their relative level of development. Throughout the management literature, numerous researchers have investigated the issue of technology transfer from different perspectives and have arrived at different, sometimes contradictory, conclusions.

The supply of technology, the role of multinational corporations, and the impact on the development of host countries are discussed in this section. The roles of recipients and intermediaries and the negotiations that take place in the process are also explored.

13 INTERNATIONAL TECHNOLOGY TRANSFER

ABSTRACT

The importance of the technology transfer process, the debate between developed and less developed countries, and the roles of the participants involved in the transfer are discussed in this chapter. The information is compiled in a style that facilitates the adoption of appropriate strategies by less developed countries. A framework is provided at the end of the chapter to show how technology can be acquired and put into practice in less developed countries.

CHAPTER OBJECTIVES

1 To establish a working definition of technology transfer

2 To understand the importance of technology transfer

3 To understand the classifications and phases of technology transfer

4 To discuss the problems of technology transfer

5 To understand the modes through which technology transfer takes place

6 To identify and discuss the different strategies that facilitate the transfer process

7 To develop a better understanding of the technology transfer environment, including internal and external factors

8 To examine the different theories behind technology transfer and their respective weaknesses

9 To develop a strategic framework for determining the technological needs of a less developed country

CASE STUDY
IBM in Mexico

Mexico has undergone a dramatic change from a strongly nationalistic Third World nation, with strong state intervention in the regulation of foreign investment and the control of technology transfer, to lead the developing world in liberalizing foreign economic policy. This transformation has changed the relationship between the United States and Mexico. Some say that Mexico had no other choice, while others credit Mexican president Carlos Salinas de Gortari. Van R. Whiting, a senior research fellow of U.S.–Mexican studies, states that the "changed opportunity structure of global markets provides the necessary context for liberal policy choices in Mexico." The case of the Mexican government accepting IBM's proposal in 1985 for a 100% IBM ownership of the computer plant in Guadalajara is clear evidence of these changes. The liberal policy in Mexico includes a strategy for free trade as well as policies to force the flow of capital and technology.

IBM's Gain in Mexico

In addition to access to cheap labor, by operating in Mexico IBM was also able to gain entrance into the microcomputer market in Mexico and other parts of Latin America. Due to the Latin American free market treaty, IBM was guaranteed preferential treatment, i.e., IBM products exported from Mexico would be subjected to fewer tariffs than goods produced outside Latin America. IBM was also interested in showing other less developed countries the benefits of less government control in the computer industry.

Mexico's Interest in IBM

IBM's operation in Mexico will bring in a needed source of foreign exchange. IBM's name recognition and market prestige will give Mexican-made IBM computers instant recognition. IBM will also commit resources to develop the supply industry. Access to state-of-the-art IBM PCs within Mexico could also encourage the development of a wider range of related industries, such as software and other peripherals. IBM has promised the Mexican government the following projects as part of the package: development of an international distribution center to support export operations to over 30 countries, a software center to distribute software to Spanish-speaking Latin America, an international purchasing program to assist local industry in developing products for IBM manufacturing facilities worldwide, partnership programs with Mexican universities and technical schools, and scholarship programs for Mexican scientists to study at IBM plants and laboratories worldwide.

Source: Steve Lohr, "Beefing Up Seen at IBM Marketing," *New York Times,* p. D3, July 30, 1993; Lori Valigra, "Big Blue's Mr. International," *Asian Business,* 29:6–7, March 1993.

INTRODUCTION

For many years, economists have concentrated on the importance of investment as a means of economic growth. While technological change is considered to be an important determinant of growth, it has been viewed as a passive exogenous variable rather than an endogenous factor that could be modified through policy. Recently, however, the rate of technological innovation and development has been considered a major endogenous factor in determining economic growth. This new concept has caused many nations to consider new technology as a way of developing their economies. In an attempt to spur economic development, less developed countries (LDCs) look to multinational corporations (MNCs) to provide them with the necessary capital, technology, and skills that will serve as their link to world markets.

In today's rapidly paced world, the need for countries to produce, expand, develop, and advance has become overwhelming. The acquisition of technology seems to be a never-ending battle for every nation. In fact, this battle has reached the point where a lack of technology can threaten the survival of an underdeveloped country amidst many technologically advanced countries. Today, technology is treated as a commodity, and, consequently, it has great value in the international trade arena. International technology transfer, as this type of trading is called, has become one of the most important and controversial elements of international business. Technology transfer can "contribute to the ability of a receiving country to develop new technology and to the capability for maintaining existing machinery, equipment, or tools."[1] The issue of technology transfer is important to both home and host countries. Much of the technology transfer is handled by international firms, but an increasing number of noncommercial organizations also participate in the process. Clearly, the subject of technology transfer is also of great importance and interest to international management students. Therefore, the management of international technology transfer is discussed thoroughly in this chapter.

This chapter has three purposes. The first is to discuss technology transfer and the debate that surrounds it. The second purpose is to answer two important questions: (1) From a LDC's point of view, what are the economic, social, political, and technological factors that affect transfer process? (2) How does the international environment affect the transfer process? The third purpose of this chapter is to present a strategic theoretical framework that can be used as a guideline by LDCs in determining their need for new technology.

DEFINITION

Before discussing technology transfer, it is crucial to establish a working definition. Technology transfer can be defined in many different ways. For the purpose of this chapter, technology transfer involves the following perishable resources: the knowledge, skills, and means to use and control the elements of production for the purpose of developing, delivering to users, and maintaining goods and services for which there is an economic and/or social need.

Technology, then, makes practical use of scientific and empirical information. (It should be noted that this definition includes both social goods and economic goods.) The proposed definition also encompasses managerial technology, which is simply the know-how necessary to manage the productive functioning of an enterprise. The transfer of technology is the process of connecting the supplier of technology to the user. (Only international technology transfer will be dealt with in this chapter.)

Although the knowledge, or technology, is usually transferred by a learning process, the term technology transfer can imply three different meanings:

1. It can be used to indicate the process whereby technical information originating in one institutional setting is adapted for use in another institutional setting.

2. It can refer to moving something from one person to another.

3. It can specifically indicate that technology has been transmitted, received, and applied.[2]

THE IMPORTANCE OF TECHNOLOGY TRANSFER

Technology transfer was not considered a major issue for either developed or developing countries until the last two decades. In 1967, the concept of technology transfer was articulated and "science and technology were incorporated in the political language and decisions of the inter-American system."[3]

This articulation, however, did not extend immediately to a focus on science and technology in public discussions between developed and developing countries until 1972. At the Conference on the Application of Science and Technology, held in that year, the issue of technology transfer was discussed for the first time.[4] Since then, technology transfer has become of significant interest to developed and developing countries, which led to a series of inter-American working groups in 1974–75. Participants included government ministries, and important issues were isolated as a basis for discussion, including:

1. Problems stemming from the transfer and development of technology through multinational enterprises

2. The responsibility of developed nations to participate with LDCs in the development of scientific and technological infrastructures

3. Promotion of institutional mechanisms to improve the flow of technology to developing countries

4. The responsibility of host governments to develop local structural environments to facilitate the absorption of technology

The identification of these issues is evidence of the importance of technology transfer and the complexity of the transfer process, in which governments of developed and developing countries have a common responsibility to strengthen the technological infrastructure in the Third World.

Additional evidence of the increasing importance of technology transfer is the formation of the International Executive Sessions Corps (IESC), which was founded in 1964. The IESC is committed to technology transfer throughout the world by assisting firms in developing countries to overcome specific problems that demand specialized expertise on both the conceptual and technical levels.

TECHNOLOGY TRANSFER CLASSIFICATIONS

Technology can be classified into four general groupings and four specific groupings (Table 13.1). The four general classifications are self-explanatory: process technology, product technology, application technology, and management technology.

The first of the more specific classifications includes hard and soft technology. **Hard technology** refers to the capital goods, blueprints, technical specifications, knowledge, and support necessary to use the technology listed above. **Soft technology** refers to management, marketing, finance, and administration.

The second specific classification of technology is proprietary and nonproprietary. As the name implies, **proprietary technology** is owned by a certain group or organization. **Nonproprietary technology** can be freely reproduced without infringing on proprietary rights.

The third specific classification of technology is front-end and obsolete technology. **Obsolete technology** is outmoded, while **front-end technology** is state-of-the-art.

The fourth specific grouping is bundled and unbundled technology. **Bundled technology** is controlled, in that the owner transfers it only as

TABLE 13.1   Classification of Technology

General	Specific
1. Process technology	1. Hard and soft technology
2. Product technology	2. Proprietary and nonproprietary technology
3. Application technology	3. Front-end and obsolete technology
4. Management technology	4. Bundled and unbundled technology

part of a package. **Unbundled technology** can be accessed independent of a package of resources.[1]

THE TECHNOLOGY TRANSFER PROCESS

The actual transfer process is very complex. There are many transfer modes available, and many parties can participate in the process. "Many distinct phases are involved, ranging from planning and product and facilities design to personnel training, engineering for quality control, and technical support to local suppliers."[5] In very general terms, the first phase of technology transfer is the **material transfer**, where new materials or a new product is exported from one country to another. The second phase, **design transfer**, represents the ability of a firm to manufacture the new material or product in the user country. The last phase, **capacity transfer**, is reached when the capacity to adapt the new item to local conditions is transferred. "The nature of the technology transferred, the characteristics, capabilities, and objectives of the parties involved, and the absorptive capability of specific economic and social sectors within the recipient country all affect the time required, the expense necessary, and the effectiveness of technology transfers."[1] For example, the transfer of technology from a U.S. firm to a developing country may be slow, ineffective, and expensive, whereas a similar transfer to a developed nation may be rapid, effective, and relatively inexpensive.

PROBLEMS IN TECHNOLOGY TRANSFER

The key aspect of any strategy or policy is the final step in executing it, or implementation. There is no question that technology transfer has the potential to be an incredibly helpful tool to LDCs, if planned and implemented appropriately. One purpose of technology transfer is to provide aid in development. Well-endowed MNCs use their resources to develop technologies that will help LDCs cope with today's problems. However, this seemingly foolproof idea has not worked as well as it should have because of various inefficiencies in the implementation of technology transfer. There are a broad range of problems, each of which is important, because the transfer of technology must be problem-free in order to be successful.

Many experts have offered reasons as to why technology transfer is so often unsuccessful. All explanations have to do with the many differences between the environment of MNCs in developed countries and the environment in LDCs, as well as the conflicts of interest between the two. Fan[6] states that much of the controversy is the result of the divergent views of the process between the sender and the recipient. This divergence appears in terms of goals and objectives, the projected benefit versus cost in the

short and long term, the time frame for completion, and the basic understanding of technological innovation and its diffusion. According to Finnegan,[7]
home governments cannot force MNCs to produce technology for LDCs
without a sufficient return. Watanabe[8] asserts that technologies developed
in advanced countries are not appropriate for developing countries because they do not take into account the needs of LDCs based on local
conditions. Crastner and Naiman[9] indicate that the problem of technological compatibility in transfers can be solved only by removing the barriers
to compatibility and developing incentives to stimulate the technology
transfer process.

According to Driscoll and Wallender,[4] barriers to compatibility are
caused by a lack of communication of both the needs and constraints of
each party involved in the process of technology transfer. The conflict of
interest that occurs in technology transfer pits the profit motive of MNCs
against the development needs of LDCs. MNCs are constrained by the laws
of their home countries, the laws of their host countries, and the conflict
between the two. Host country constraints have to do with the fact that a
host country must try to maximize employment while attempting to
balance economic and social advances. When one party does not take the
constraints and needs of the other party into account, as often is the case,
incompatibility results.

Another reason for failure in implementation is that LDCs often do not
have the expertise to be able to implement the technology supplied by a
MNC. LDCs often do not have the capability to manage or plan for the new
technology. Moreover, they often do not have personnel trained to utilize
the new technology. Further, management is frequently incapable of
identifying or resolving problems caused by the new technology.

Another potential obstacle to technology transfer arises when more than
the two traditional agents—sender and receiver—are involved. For example, a third party, known as the technology transfer consultant, may be
involved. The job of the consultant is to design a system for the transfer,
which is usually accompanied by the creation of a new plant or the
beginning of a new industrial project. This means that a fourth party, such
as the engineer of the new building, the builder, or other businesspeople,
may be involved. As the number of parties involved in an exchange
increases, the chance for dispute naturally increases, as does the probability that something will be lost in the exchange of technology.[10]

The major problems in technology transfer can be summarized as
follows:

1. Sender and recipient have divergent views about the process in terms
   of goals and objectives, expected benefits and costs, time frame for
   completion, and general understanding of the technology.

2. MNCs expect a return for their investment.

3. The same technologies are not appropriate for developed countries and
   LDCs. Some farm equipment cannot be directly transferred because of

the tougher grains and plants in LDCs. LDCs often lack trained technicians to service the equipment.[11]

4. Problems can only be solved by removing the barriers to compatibility, which are caused by lack of communication.

5. LDCs may not have the expertise to implement the new technology.

6. The possibility of dispute increases when more than the two traditional agents are involved.

HOW THE TRANSFER TAKES PLACE

The principal modes of technology transfer are foreign direct investment, sharing technology, licensing technology, turnkey projects, and strategic alliances. Each is discussed in the following sections.

Trade can be in the form of goods and services, contracts and agreements, research and development, and personnel. Research and development can be located in a foreign country as a research subcontract or as a joint R&D project. Personnel strategies for technology transfer are very flexible. Technology can be transferred when foreign firms employ nationals, foreign technicians, or migrating trained personnel or by utilizing internal or commercial training programs.

Much of existing technology is freely available or nonproprietary. Free donations are used only in the case of noncompetitive technology for which there is no genuine commercial value to the owner. Relevant technologies can be found in education, health, and food production.

In the past, industrial firms have focused on those market segments that could pay for their technology rather than those that needed it. Firms can use current products, new products, and simplified products in basing their profits on the needs of LDCs. **Current products** are existing technologies that serve to raise the technological level of LDCs. An example is communications equipment geared toward specific sectors such as manufacturing, distribution, or government. **New products** can be developed with the needs of LDCs in mind. Products designed for one market segment may not be compatible with another. A firm must reevaluate its strategies and goals in order to be successful. **Simplified products** deal with transformation of technology so as to simplify it for LDCs. Modifying an electronic device so that it requires hand or foot power is an example of a simplified product.

It is critical that the potential product user identify the appropriate mode of technology transfer (current, new, or simplified) that meets its need. "Whether a potential user is able to exploit that technology depends upon a number of factors. The user must be able to define the need for the technology. The user must also have qualified personnel available who have access to scientific and technical publications and an ability to apply that information. Also, the receiving country must have an infrastructure adequate to support the absorption, translation, and utilization of the technology."[1]

Direct Transfers

In direct investment, traditionally a new technology is transferred as a collection of capital, management, and marketing. Direct investment lowers unemployment and increases technological sophistication. In the future direct, investments will decrease as LDCs increasingly insist on control and ownership. Although direct investment may satisfy the market needs of a company, it generally ignores the needs of host countries.

Sharing Technology

A recent issue under discussion in Japan is sharing technology. According to Taizo Yakashiji, a professor of international relations at Saitama University, technology must be shared and transferred for the success of any firm in international business. For a nation to become a top power, or a "technohegemon," it must freely exchange its knowledge. This point is illustrated by countries that have copied or imitated technologies and eventually improved upon them. Yakashiji attributes Britain's downfall in the 19th century to its failure to study the improvements in technology in the textile industry.[12]

Licensing Technology

In managing international technology transfer, various strategies under which to operate must be considered. The goal, of course, is to choose a strategy that will allow a firm to realize its potential and earn the greatest return. Two very general strategic choices are to internalize by extending operations or to operate in external markets. Obviously, we are interested in operating in external markets in the context of technology transfer. Because government policies have become increasingly restrictive and opposed to direct investment, licensing and selling turnkey in external markets have become increasingly important methods of technology transfer.

Licensing as a means of technology transfer has gained importance over time. While licensing is profitable, its low risk factor also makes it attractive. Licensing is better suited to small companies that may lack the capital, management, or general experience to opt for direct investment. Licensing also allows the licensor to take an ownership interest in the foreign operation. If trademarks are included in the licensing agreement, they remain the property of the licensor. Therefore, the licensor maintains its bargaining power because of the "perishable nature of technology and the licensor's ability to supply new technology in the future to the licensee."[1] Licensing may be a preferred strategy where host countries restrict imports or direct investments.

Another reason why licensing is used is corporate technology feedback, which gives the licensee access to the technologies developed. The risk to

EXAMPLE
Digital Equipment Corporation

Digital Equipment Corporation (DEC) considers its intellectual technology an asset, just like property, equipment, and money. This rationale has led to the formation of a corporate licensing office. DEC makes a practice of licensing its technology to other companies as a way of exploiting it. This method of exploitation is emphasized in DEC's development of a new computer chip. In order for the chip to be successful, DEC thought it had to be licensed through other companies to gain massive market penetration. Profit maximization and recovery of large research and development expenditures were other licensing motives.

An estimated 75 to 85% of DEC's efforts deal with finding and creating optimal technological partnerships. DEC's opportunity licensing agreements must be evaluated through seven activities: (1) commercial or outside benefit is determined, (2) relative technological value is estimated by identifying and contrasting comparable technologies, (3) the rate at which technology is being absorbed and its future reach are examined, (4) the price of the newly developed technology and the licensing rights are determined, (5) negotiation with future licensees, (6) licensing agreements are audited so that both sides are satisfied, (7) infringements by unlicensed competitors are identified. When an infringement is discovered, a licensing agreement may be offered if the technology is relatively new.

Some of DEC's licensing strategies have developed out of international pressure to make its technology more accessible. One of DEC's vice-presidents feels that this actually enables DEC to utilize its assets more effectively.

Source: John Sheridan, "Technology: Manage It as an Asset," *Industry Week,* 241: 47–48, September 21, 1992.

---

the licensor is small because the licensee will probably not become a fierce competitor in the future. There is also a rush to exploit the technology before it becomes obsolete.

A company's global reputation can be damaged if the licensee does not maintain the licensor's standards. Unfortunately, there is no way to know this until after the fact, when it is too late.

Licensing does not maximize profits, because a company deals indirectly with the licensee. There are also additional costs associated with licensing. Establishing a licensing agreement includes finding an optimal licensee, communication, and training. A firm also has to incur maintenance costs, such as back-up services and market research.

Some countries require government approval for licensing. Some governments do not allow an exclusive license for fear of decreasing competition. In addition, governments may impose taxes on royalty payments to the licensor.

Turnkey Projects

In a turnkey project, a contractor is responsible for every detail of a project, so that upon its completion the user is handed a key and operations can begin immediately. The contractor may even have the option of taking an equity interest in the project. More specifically, turnkey is a construction project in which a contractor promises to build a project or facility (it could be a factory, bridge, highway, etc.). After the project is completed, the buyer's personnel are trained to run the facility efficiently, and only then is it considered to have been "delivered" to the customer. This type of strategy is very common in the chemical, petrochemical, and petroleum refining industries. The sale of newly developed technology replaces the sale of end products. Firms generally reinvest some profit in the development of new technology. Thus, the turnkey method can be quite successful for end-product companies.[1] Turnkey projects can dramatically increase exports with one sale. These projects can be either self-engineered or constructed to specification:

- **Self engineered:** The exporter is in charge of the plant and equipment design, but the specific performance requirements are left up to the importer.

- **Constructed to specification:** The specifics of the project are left up to the importer.

Both of these approaches can be implemented on a fixed price or cost plus basis. On a fixed price basis, the risk is associated with the exporter; on a cost plus basis, the risk is associated with the importer.

Turnkey projects may be so large that they are implemented through a joint venture by two or more firms. However, this can cause confusion when it comes time to split the profits.[13]

Strategic Alliances

Certain variables should be avoided when choosing a partner for a strategic alliance. Alliances should not be formed to correct a weakness, because the weaker party ends up at the mercy of the stronger. An example is GM's alliance with Toyota. GM entered the alliance with an inability to manufacture high-quality small cars. Ten years later, GM still was not able to strengthen this weakness. Alliances should also not be formed when *both* parties are trying to correct weaknesses. For example, when Interfirst and Republic banks merged in 1987, the newly formed alliance was set up for failure because both participants had problems in the area of real estate loans.

Proprietary technology should never be licensed in strategic alliances.

The goal is not to let the other party know your technological secrets. For example, Sony acquired transistor technology from Bell Laboratories for the small price of $25,000, and now, a few years later, there are literally no radio manufacturers left in the United States. Many companies enter into alliances with the expectation of increasing competition, but they end up relinquishing control of their technology.

Alliances *should* be formed when one or both parties have a unique strength. If both parties have a unique strength and these strengths are merged, the chance for success improves. A good example is 3M's merger with Squibb Corporation. 3M had developed a pharmaceutical technology that Squibb could not replicate. Squibb, however, had a well-developed distribution system. This was an ideal situation in which both parties reaped the benefits of a strategic alliance.[14]

Technology Transfer to Small Firms

The primary sources of technology transfer to small firms are through universities and networking. These networks consist of mostly informal, personal contacts, although as they grow and become more organized they can encompass research centers and financial institutions. Networks serve two purposes: to reduce the amount of money spent to obtain useful information and to ensure that the information is reliable.[15]

Small firms must use strategic alliances to remain competitive. Strategic alliances consist of short-term and relatively temporary agreements between firms. These firms collaborate with top universities where highly qualified people are located. Small firms use **inward licensing**, which is an agreement between a small firm and another company for the use of the other's technology for a fee, or **outward licensing**, in which their patents are shared with other small firms in return for a royalty.[16]

THE CHOICE OF TECHNOLOGY

While choice of strategy is important, so is the choice of technology. When a technologically advanced firm expands into another firm with similar technological capabilities, normally a similar type of technology is transferred with only minor adaptations. The situation is different, however, when technology is transferred from an advanced country to an underdeveloped country. The appropriate technology to be transferred is the subject of international controversy.

Many believe that an underdeveloped host country should utilize technology that differs from the technology of the supplier country. This usually means that the technology should be more labor intensive and smaller scale. Whether or not this adaptation is possible depends on the availability of technological alternatives, the cost of developing a more appropriate technology, and a mix of other factors.[5] In general, the nature of the product will be indicative of the available alternatives. The nature of the industry also affects the cost and availability of technical information needed to make choices on alternative technologies. While a greater emphasis on labor is desirable in developing nations, this does not imply that the trade-off between capital and labor is the only criterion. Quality control, waste minimization, response time to market fluctuations, training costs, labor relations, and the prestige of having the latest equipment may influence management to choose a method of technology that is more automated. Host governments can also influence the choice of a more capital-intensive technology.[1]

PRICING

An interesting facet of international technology transfer is its pricing. Very little public information is available on negotiating the price of technology. Different transactions warrant different types of payment. There is general agreement, however, that the price paid for technology is too high, and it has been argued that the weak negotiating position of developing countries has affected pricing. Patent monopolies on technology also lead to excessive pricing. Patented technology, however, can face competition in the market where substitution technology is available. In short, there is no standard pricing model for international technology transfers.

THE TECHNOLOGY TRANSFER ENVIRONMENT

Several factors affect the technology transfer process. These factors fall into three categories: external environmental factors, internal factors, and consultation (Table 13.2). External factors include all the economic, political, and technological influences. Internal factors include managerial capabilities, reliability of information, planning, and financial resources. Consultation factors encompasses a variety of problems, including mismatches between problems and solutions, uncertainties caused by the lack of

TABLE 13.2   The Technology Transfer Environment

External environmental factors	Internal factors	Consultation
Economic factors	Lack of managerial capabilities	
Political factors	Lack of reliable information	
Infrastructure factors	Lack of long-term planning	
	Lack of financial resources	

adequate information about the external environment, lack of expertise, and inadequate criteria for problem solving. The involvement of participants other than suppliers and users also affects the transfer of technology. Many private as well as government groups function as expediters or controllers of operations. They therefore can have a significant effect on such areas as timing, the type of transfer, and terms negotiated.[5]

External Factors

Economic factors include the market and the demand it creates for products. If both are large, a firm will be more inclined to take a risk in a LDC. Competition is also a factor in the external environment. In certain industries, competitors are exposed to technological innovations and development by one another and are forced to take risks in order to keep up with changing market patterns. A firm may also be affected by instability in its industry. Some industries are more severely affected by shifts in market demand than are more stable industries, such as equipment manufacturing. The general economic environment may also encourage or discourage risking limited resources in new technology. For example, rapid deterioration in the balance of payment discourages many firms from committing themselves to new programs that involve long-term technological change.

Moreover, when new products are introduced into the markets of LDCs, their level of sophistication is almost always a negative factor. The vital positive elements that make up appropriate technology are low initial cost, simplicity of operation, and minimum maintenance requirements.[17]

Political factors include turbulence, degree of predictability, and regulations. Entrepreneurs in developing countries are not always free to choose their suppliers of technology. In some cases, they are forbidden from importing technology from certain countries or are forced to import technology from "friendly" countries due to political influences.[8] Turbulence refers to how rapidly or radically the political environment is changing and how well a firm understands these changes. Predictability of change in the environment and stability are often perceived as being as pervasive as competitive or market forces. Governments of LDCs usually enact regulations to organize the process of technology transfer in a way that they believe will allow them to achieve national objectives. Regulations and commercial laws, therefore, may either impede or encourage the transfer process, depending upon their complexity and permanence.[18]

Infrastructure factors include the availability of support systems, direct supplies, and diffusion systems. The availability of support systems is essential to a firm in acquiring and using technology. For example, financial institutions, government offices, and communication systems are in many cases important sources of financial counsel and general information to aid a firm in its technological development. The absence of such support systems may mean that a firm will be unable to implement its plans to develop and adapt new technologies. The availability of manpower and supplies is also of concern to any company. Diffusion systems are necessary to link different parts of technological infrastructures. An active patent office serves to make more information available to investors, businesspeople, and government technicians.[8]

Internal Factors

User organizations in the Third World are equally affected by internal factors as they are by the external environmental factors already discussed. Four major elements affect the process of technology transfer internally.

Lack of managerial capabilities is a major obstacle to improving the process of technology transfer. These capabilities are required to diagnose the need for technology. Without such management skills, it is impossible for a firm to utilize and exploit technology improvements or to establish long-term goals and match them to specific situations.

Lack of reliable information about the external environment imposes some severe limitations on the technology transfer process for the user firm. This information may concern population growth, industry trends, consumer purchasing power, and inflation. Where such information is not available, planning for the future can hardly be appropriate.

Lack of long-term planning is one important reason why firms in LDCs have such problems defining their need for new technology. In the absence of planning capability, executives focus only on the short term. In many cases, particularly when a firm is new, most energies are directed toward organizing resources so as to ensure at least short-term survival.

Lack of financial resources affects the ability of a firm to receive and utilize technology. The history of acquisition in a firm appears to be one of the most important elements in terms of the capability to absorb technology. Thus, those firms that have experience in acquiring new technology, and in the process have learned to diagnose their technological needs, are better prepared to exploit opportunities for technology transfer.

Consultation

Consultation also influences the receipt and utilization of technology. Because of special knowledge or a unique position with respect to buyers and sellers, a consultant can facilitate the technology transfer process.[19]

Ginsberg[20] identified a number of major problems that may be encountered in the consultation process:

1. Mismatch between problems and solutions

2. Failure to deal adequately with power relations within a firm

3. Perceived threat from the uncertainties of change

4. Unsatisfactory manager/consultant working relationship

5. Inadequate criteria for problem selection and solution evaluation

6. Environmental factors

THEORY OF TECHNOLOGY TRANSFER

Four important theories of technology transfer can be found in the management literature.

Oligopoly/Monopoly Theory

The oligopoly/monopoly theory depicts MNCs as the owners of most of the world's technology. Accordingly, MNCs are the leading channel for the transfer of technology to LDCs.[21] The oligopoly/monopoly theory, therefore, is based on the following assumptions: the primary holder of technology is MNCs, MNCs are unwilling to share their expertise, and the long-term objective of MNCs is to maintain control over their technology.

This explains why MNCs have been reluctant to employ host country manpower in high-level management positions. Available data and evidence indicate that key managerial and technical positions in the international hierarchy are still largely controlled by source country personnel.[21] However, in applying the general model of oligopoly/monopoly behavior, a number of studies have focused on various aspects of these practices. One study emphasizes the "proprietary protectionism" of a MNC in its desire to maintain control over its technology.[22] Another study stresses the "discriminatory monopolist" behavior of MNCs, which results in direct investment in those countries with the greatest potential for profit. Another variation of the general theory is that MNCs invest abroad in order to exploit new markets after their domestic markets have been saturated for a specific product. Thus, additional income can be reaped from a particular technology system.[23]

Dependency Theory

The dependency theory assumes that the world is divided into two major segments: the industrialized and the nonindustrialized. This division results in the dependence of the latter on the former for growth. Dependency theory isolates technology as a key to development and consequently focuses on the MNC as the primary supplier of technology. This theory has taken various forms in the work of other economists.

As an extension of the dependency theory, some note that the concentration of R&D in the home country not only puts the developing nation in a position of "permanent import-dependence for technology," but also deprives the LDC of the multiplier effect. The multiplier effect can result from active domestic R&D programs in which local research organizations are in constant touch with local productive sectors.[24]

One of the most important conclusions of the dependency theory is that the presence of MNCs in the developing world inhibits development of the local infrastructure. The explanation for this conclusion is that the productive sector in developing nations tends to depend on foreign suppliers and fails to create local technical infrastructures to meet their needs.

Screening Approach

The screening approach argues for careful screening of technology and evaluating its contribution toward achieving national development goals. This perspective simply calls for the creation of national agencies to screen all potential technology projects and to determine the costs and benefits of each. The focus of this approach is geared more toward the project than the supplier. Therefore, the screening approach represents a more rational and practical method of development than the dependency theory.[25]

According to the screening approach, a developing country should carefully assess the net benefits of an investment.[26] By examining the positive and negative aspects of individual proposals, a more detailed evaluation of the technology imported may be made, which facilitates a more precise decision-making process. Supporters of the screening approach generally favor the presence of MNCs through joint ventures and licensing agreements instead of wholly owned subsidiary arrangements.[27]

Supplier Approach

The supplier approach attempts to describe the practical reasons behind a MNC's decision to transfer technology. The main focus of this approach is the cost to transfer to LDCs. Therefore, the major responsibility of MNCs involved in technology transfer is "to measure and explain the costs and benefits of their technology to development efforts."[19]

In a 1976 study, Teece found that there was an inverse relationship between the cost of technology transfer and the level of development of the environment of the receiving organization.[28] Transfer from a parent to a subsidiary is generally less expensive because of the familiarity with each other's operation. Marketing technology to inexperienced users who may not readily recognize its value can add considerable cost to a technology transfer.

Evaluation

After having reviewed the four theories of technology transfer, the next step is to evaluate them. Five weaknesses have been identified:

1. The four theories of transfer consider only the supply side of the equation by focusing on multinationals as the sole suppliers of technology. The transfer of technology is important to both developed and developing countries. Technology is successfully transferred only if it is

actually received, and it is, therefore, illogical to develop theories that address only one side of the equation.

2. A recent study concludes that "the large MNC is not necessarily the best institution for technology creation; however, it frequently brings ideas worldwide together, sometimes creating a most productive environment for technology creation."[24]

3. The four theories neglect some important alternative sources of technology, even though such suppliers are in many cases more experienced and better equipped to provide assistance. For example, all theories tend to disregard such important sources of technology as consulting firms, public training, universities, and foreign government programs, to name a few.

4. Some of the assumptions in these four theories are unrealistic. The screening approach, for example, assumes that strong managerial capabilities exist and, consequently, that national goals have been identified and agencies established that can screen and evaluate proposals.

5. The focus of the supplier consideration approach is the cost involved in technology transfer. It is the responsibility of a MNC to measure the cost against the benefit.

The assumptions made about technology transfer seem to contradict reality. In any given environment, individual firms will be at varying levels of development in terms of their internal capabilities. Some developing countries may have already developed a certain level of internal capability and established national goals. The majority of LDCs, however, do not have such high levels of managerial capability and, by implication, have neither identified national goals nor established capable screening agencies. A major obstacle to improving technology transfer activities in the majority of LDCs is the lack of managerial capability to set achievable goals or diagnose the need for technology.

AGRICULTURE AND INFRASTRUCTURE TECHNOLOGY

The areas of agriculture and infrastructure are prime targets for technology transfer to LDCs. In general, agriculture is the mainstay industry of most developing nations. When agricultural technology is modernized, fewer resources are needed to feed the population. This allows labor and capital to filter through the rest of the economy, which raises income and the demand for manufactured goods.

The technology can be as simple as a new hand tool or as complicated as the use of biotechnology in fish and insect farming. Improved fertilizers, insecticides, and animal feed are also needed.

In the past, LDCs have spent large amounts of money on expensive programs to update their infrastructures. One example is the construction of dams, which has produced both positive and negative results. On the positive side, dams have provided LDCs with new power sources, but on the negative side, they have increased the incidence of water-borne diseases, reduced soil fertility, and caused landslides. Today, LDCs are more apt to implement smaller scale technologies that encompass local maintenance and production.

A good example of technology transfer to LDCs is provided by Dow Chemical Company. Dow introduced a relatively inexpensive solar water purification system that transforms polluted water into safe, drinkable water. This type of technology would be ideal for LDCs.

In researching and developing other products, companies sometimes discover by-product technologies that would be appropriate for LDCs. For example, John Deere designed a small tractor but chose not to produce it for various reasons; instead, the tractor was licensed to a small company for sale in LDCs.

Many products have completed their life cycle and are no longer in use. An example of utilizing outdated technology is illustrated by a Chilean jam company that wanted to find an alternative to importing expensive glass jars. They found a solution to this problem by adopting a glass-making technology that dated back to ancient Egypt. The finished jars contained small bubbles and had a greenish tint.[29]

EFFECTS OF TECHNOLOGY TRANSFER ON THE FEMALE LABOR FORCE IN ASIA

MNCs have been a driving force in the export-led development strategy adopted by many Asian nations. However, the most important, as well as the most controversial, contribution of MNCs is the transfer of technology to LDCs.

Technology includes technoware and humanware. Project failure in developing countries is often attributed to insufficient attention to managing the human resource aspects. The main problem in managing human resources lies in the area of the female labor force. MNCs have transferred technology in the form of labor-intensive manufacturing in several Asian countries. Manufacturing operations in LDCs have been established in export processing zones, where a predominantly female work force is employed. The pursuit of lower manufacturing costs has led MNCs to use production processes that are hazardous to the health and safety of workers. Managerial techniques exploit female workers. Some believe that such technology will reduce labor input costs while simultaneously achieving high levels of output. However, transfer of these production and managerial technologies ultimately has a negative impact on the predominantly female labor force in export processing zones, and the counterproductive forces generated eventually increase labor costs and reduce productivity.

The supply of female labor is viewed by Asian governments as their principal resource for industrial developers.[31] Reports indicate that more than a million women work in MNC-related manufacturing operations in Asia. Two factors have been identified as reasons why MNCs prefer female workers:

1. MNCs are able to take advantage of gender-based wage differentials prevalent in Asian economies (women can be paid lower wages than men for the same task)

2. Women are considered more productive for gender-related reasons (it is assumed that they are naturally more adept at and dexterous in certain types work, such as garment manufacturing)

It is important to note that the combination of low wages and high productivity runs against traditional economic theory, which states that workers in a competitive society should be paid according to their productivity.

Negative Effects

MNCs that use a strategy focused on minimizing the per-unit labor cost accomplish two goals by paying the lowest possible wages to female workers. They are able to take advantage of lax regulations for health and safety in the workplace and they can employ such managerial techniques as high production quotas, assembly line speedups, and forced overtime in order to maximize output. However, some Asian countries are showing signs of the negative effects of this system. The physical and mental health of workers has been impaired, which diminishes productivity.

It is evident that alienating female workers is counterproductive. Both corporate and national interests make it vital to recognize the negative impact of past transfers of production and managerial technologies and how broader considerations would be affected if such practices are continued. Recognizing women workers as a human resource, rather than a disposable resource, can be to the distinct advantage of MNCs. On the supply side, it can reduce production costs in the long run. On the demand side, it can serve to cultivate new markets.[32]

Rather than adjusting to cultural traditions that subordinate and demean women, MNCs can and should demonstrate leadership in recognizing women as contributors and ensuring equal opportunity on a global scale.[32]

THE FRAMEWORK

A strategic theoretical framework is presented here. This framework (which is summarized in Table 13.3) is exploratory in nature; it is designed

TABLE 13.3   Strategic Framework for Acquiring New Technology

Stage	Requirements
1. **Preidentification**	Determine national goals (i.e., develop the agricultural or industrial sector or accommodate social needs)
2. **Identification**	Assess managerial capabilities and identify the necessary infrastructure
3. **Alternatives**	Look at other sources and determine a fair price
4. **Evaluation**	Evaluate the alternatives and determine the best form of investment (i.e., licensing, joint venture, or wholly owned subsidiary)
5. **Selection**	Select the most appropriate alternative
6. **Implementation**	Determine specific actions, programs, policies, timetables, resources, changes to the organizational structure, and reward and performance evaluation systems

to clarify the important stages of technology transfer and to serve as a tool for LDCs in acquiring new technology. The framework includes four major steps that must be followed before any decision to acquire new technology takes place, plus guidelines for selection and implementation.

Preidentification Stage

The first stage precedes identification of the technology needed. In this stage, a country needs to determine its national goals and priorities in light of its internal and external environments. For example, a LDC's national goals could be to (1) develop the agricultural sector, (2) develop certain parts of the industrial sector, or (3) fulfill social needs.

Identification Stage

The second stage is to determine what technology is needed for each goal identified in the first stage. Technology suitable in one environment is not necessarily suitable in another because of differences in the level of development or other internal conditions. This stage requires the following actions:

1. Identify available managerial capability and what must be done to raise it to a level that can absorb the technology needed. If managerial capability is lacking, the next step is to determine how it can be developed, either by intensive training of locals or bringing in experts.

2. Identify the infrastructure that must be available when the technology is used. The infrastructure includes roads, facilities, and information.

3. Identify the strengths and weaknesses of government regulations and policies and test whether they inhibit or encourage new technology. Regulations should be modified as necessary to make them more attractive to suppliers of new technology.

4. Identify the folkways, mores, or customs of a country that might oppose the introduction of new technology.

Search for Alternatives

The third stage is to search for alternatives to the technology identified in terms of sources and appropriateness. This stage requires identification of the criteria for selection of appropriate technology that satisfies a country's internal and external conditions. The first criterion is to determine a fair price, after a survey of all available sources of the technology. The second criterion is the degree of absorption. Does the capability exist to absorb the technology locally? The third criterion is appropriateness, which addresses the quality of the technology and its supplier. A LDC should establish criteria for the selection of the desired technology from either MNCs or from other sources that can provide similar technology.

Evaluation Stage

The fourth stage is to evaluate the alternatives available for acquiring the desired technology. In this stage, the best form of investment is determined, based on a LDC's internal and external environment. For example, MNCs are usually reluctant to license their technology, except under very profitable conditions. Even if these conditions are met, the technology might not be truly appropriate for a particular developing country. Therefore, a LDC needs to decide whether licensing, a joint venture, or wholly owned would be the appropriate form of investment.

Selection Stage

After the preceding evaluation, the next stage is to select the most appropriate technology, taking into consideration the cost/benefit to the entire nation.

Implementation Stage

After identifying the type of technology and its sources, the final consideration is how to implement it. The specific actions, programs, policies, timetables, and resources required need to be determined. Sometimes the organization receiving the technology needs to make structural changes. Reward and performance evaluation systems are important in adopting new technology. After adopting the technology and using it for two to three years, it is always important to revisit the entire process to determine whether any changes need to be made.

A firm that is committed to technology transfer, either by supplying technology or acquiring it internationally, encounters many new issues. For example, once a country gains a technological advantage, it wants to maintain that advantage. The technology market is very volatile. The need to maintain a competitive advantage in foreign markets is similar to the need to maintain an advantage in the domestic market. Maintaining advantage is also important in retaining bargaining power against government control policies. Trademarks and patents also serve to maintain advantage. An extensive research capability is one of the most important tools to develop new technologies and continue improvements.

Although technology is considered to be an asset, a firm's research and development (R&D) capability comprises its true technological advantage. It is not uncommon for host countries to pressure MNCs to establish R&D facilities in addition to production facilities. Foreign R&D facilities make a firm more competitive in both home and host country markets. R&D operations can be very helpful in the technology transfer process. Products can be made or adapted for local conditions, or new products can be developed specifically for foreign markets. According to one philosophy, "Scientists in one country are not good at answering the specific market needs of another country...We believe that the best way to overcome this problem is to have subsidiaries in important markets away from the parent company develop their own complete R&D organizations to take full and direct advantage of the opportunities peculiar to their environment."[33]

CONCLUSION

The final aspect of technology transfer is national control. Expectedly, the goals of buyers and sellers often differ from the interests of a country. Home countries expect higher return for their technology and usually are reluctant to share their advanced technology. "Home countries will continue to control technology transfers for national security reasons and to protect tax revenues."[1] Although it is unlikely that controls to protect international competitiveness will be developed, "host countries can be expected to become even more active in the national monitoring of international technology transfers."[1] The interests of the buyer, the seller, the home country, and the host country are affected by control. Managers must be informed, attempt to understand the motivation, and even forecast national control policies in managerial decision making. Managers should also keep in mind alternative strategies for technology transfer.

It is important to fully understanding international technology transfer. The topic has far-reaching implications and is very controversial. Technology transfer has been examined in detail in this chapter. A working definition was provided, followed by the various classifications of technology, the methods of transfer, the issues that face a firm entering into international technology transfer, the various strategies for a transfer, and pricing and control elements in the transfer of technology between nations. International management students must develop a good understanding of technology transfer and its importance in the international arena, as international technology transfer promises to take on increasing importance in the business environment of the future.

REFERENCES

1. H. Stefan Robock and Kenneth Simmonds, *International Business and Multinational Enterprises* (Homewood, Ill.: Irwin), 1983, pp. 461–479.
2. Abbass F. Alkhafaji, "Technology Transfer: An Overview as Related to LDCs," *Journal of Technology Transfer,* 11:55–66, 1986.
3. Earl Ingerson and Wayne C. Bragg (Eds.), *Science, Government and Industry for Development* (Austin: University of Texas Press), 1976.
4. Robert E. Driscoll and Harvey W. Wallender III, "Technology Transfer and Development," *Journal of Technology Transfer,* 11(1), 1986.
5. George Modelski (Ed.), *Transnational Corporations and World Order* (San Francisco: Freeman), 1979, pp. 270–384.
6. Yi-Kwan Fan, "Toward a Reconciliation of Conflicting Perspectives on North-South Technology Transfer," *Journal of Technology Transfer,* 9:1–7, February 1985.
7. Marcus B. Finnegan, "R&D for Developing Countries: LL—The Code of Conduct Issue," *Research Management,* p. 40, May 1979.
8. Susanna Watanabe, "Institutional Factor, Government Policies and Appropriate Technologies," *International Labor Review,* p. 171, March–April 1980.
9. Joseph Crastner and Charles S. Naiman, "Making Technology Transfer Happen," *Research Management,* p. 34, May 1987.
10. Harvey W Wallender III et al., *Technology Transfer and Management in the Developing Countries* (Cambridge, Mass.: Ballinger), 1979, p. 13.
11. Christopher M. Korth, *International Business Environment and Management,* (Englewood Cliffs, N.J.: Prentice-Hall), 1985, pp. 80–91.
12. Susan Moffat, "To Be a Leader in Technology You Must Share It," *Fortune,* 123:34–35, January 14, 1991.
13. P.W. Beamish and H.W. Lane, "Need, Commitment and the Performance of Joint Ventures in Developing Countries," Working Paper No. 330 (Canada: University of Western Ontario), 1983.
14. Robert Michel, "The Do's and Don'ts of Strategic Alliance," *Journal of Business Strategy,* 13:50–53, March–April 1992.
15. Gabriel Drilhon and Marie Florence Estime, "Technology Watch and the Small Firm," *The OECD Observer,* 182:31–34, June/July 1993.
16. Janice Forrest, "Strategic Alliances and the Small Technology Based Firm," *Journal of Small Business Management,* 28:37–45, July 1990.
17. Jules Arbose, "Making Appropriate Technology Work," *International Management,* p. 34, July 1979.
18. Yves L. Doz and C.K. Prahalad, "How MNCs Cope with Host Government Intervention," *Harvard Business Review,* p. 150, March–April 1980.

19. Arthur P. Lein, "Acquiring and Selling Technology: The Role of the Middlemen," *Research Management,* p. 29, May 1979.

20. Michael Jay Ginsberg, "A Process Approach to Management Science Implementation," doctoral dissertation (Cambridge, Mass.: MIT), 1975.

21. Dimitri Cienmidis, *Transfer of Technology by Multinational Corporations,* Vol. 2 (Purvis: OECD), 1977, p. 24.

22. Ingvar Svennilson, "Technology Assistance: The Transfer of Industrial Know-How to Non-Industrial Countries," in *Economic Development with Special Reference to East Asia,* K. Brill (Ed.) (New York: St. Martins), 1964.

23. Joseph Peno and Harvey W. Wallender III, "A Contingent Approach to Technology Policy Proposing a Cost/Benefit Analysis," in *Transfer of Technology: The Future of Regulation* (New York: Fund for Management Education), 1977.

24. Thomas N. Aladmin and Ingo Walter, *Multinationals in Conflict: Lessons in Conflict in Management* (New York: John Wiley & Sons), 1979.

25. Harvey W. Wallender III et al., *Technology Transfer and Management in the Developing Countries* (Cambridge, Mass.: Ballinger), 1979, p. 13.

26. Constantine V. Viatsos, *Intra-Country Income Distribution and Transnational Enterprises* (Oxford, England: Clarendon Press), 1973.

27. M.S. Wionezek, "A Latin American View," in *How Latin America Views the U.S. Investor,* R. Vernone (Ed.) (New York: Praeger), 1966.

28. David Teece, *The Multinational Corporation and the Resource Cost of International Technology Transfer* (Cambridge, Mass.: Ballinger), 1976.

29. Leslie M. Dawson, "Transferring Industrial Technologies to Less Developed Countries," *Industrial Marketing and Management,* 16:265–271, November 1987.

30. C. Jayachandran, "Role of Multiple Parties in the Choice of Technology Collaborations: Some Insights into Conflict Resolution," in Abbass F. Alkhafaji, *International Management Challenge* (Acton, Mass.: Copley), 1990, p. 204.

31. Jean Layson Pyle, "The Impact of Multinational Technological Transfer on Female Workforces in Asia," *The Columbia Journal of World Business,* 25:40–48, Winter 1990.

32. Paul A. Dawson, "Competition Breeds a Panoply of Policies," *Business Credit,* 92:38–39, July–August 1990.

33. Jafor Chowdhury, "The Evolving Contest of International Joint Ventures: Observations on Some Historical and Recent Trends," *Management Decision,* 29(6):75, 1991.

BIBLIOGRAPHY

Anderson, Bruce A., "Acquiring and Selling Technology—Marketing Techniques," *Research Management,* p. 26, May 1979.

Dawson, Leslie M. and Jean Larsonpyle, "The Impact of Multinational Technology Transfer on Female Workforces in Asia," *The Columbia Journal of World Business,* 25:40–48, Winter 1990.

Doctors, Samuel I., *The Role of Federal Agencies in Technology Transfer* (Cambridge, Mass.: MIT Press), 1969, p. 3.

Driscoll, Robert E. and Harvey W. Wallender III, "Technology Transfer and Development," *Journal of Technology Transfer,* 11, January 1986.

Findlay, Ronald, "Some Aspects of Technology Transfer and Direct Foreign Investment," *American Economic Association,* 68:275, May 1978.

Public Policy and Technology Transfer, Vol. I (New York: Fund for Multinational Management Education), 1964.

Sheridan, John, "Technology: Manage It as an Asset," *Industry Week,* 241:47–48, September 21, 1992.

Willard, Marcy, "Acquiring and Selling Technology—Licensing Do's and Don'ts," *Research Management,* p. 18, May 1979.

14 JOINT VENTURES

ABSTRACT

To stay competitive and enter new markets, companies need to internationalize their operations. It is crucial for all associated parties to recognize and pay close attention to the many factors involved in the process of internationalization. The different forms of internationalization are introduced in this chapter, and some of the processes are discussed briefly. Joint ventures are examined in detail.

CHAPTER OBJECTIVES

1 To examine the internationalization of companies

2 To analyze the different forms of internalization (licensing, franchising, foreign trade, etc.)

3 To study foreign trade in terms of importing and exporting

4 To examine the joint venture process in detail

5 To discuss the advantages and disadvantages of joint ventures

6 To address the selection of partner companies and managers in joint ventures

7 To study Japanese–American joint ventures

CASE STUDY
The Marriage of Two Companies

A joint venture is an economical but risky method of expanding into new markets, and that is exactly what Daimler-Benz's Mercedes unit is planning with Swatch. Mercedes hopes to build a low-cost automobile that would appeal to younger and more frugal buyers.

Although many such ventures have been executed successfully, some have failed and others never materialized. One joint venture that did not materialize was between Volvo, the Swedish automobile company, and Renault, the French automobile company. The merger would have created the world's third largest automobile manufacturing company and would have helped both manufacturers in some ways.

The marriage, so to speak, between Swatch and Mercedes is not the first that Swatch explored. Earlier, Swatch attempted ventures with Volkswagen, the German automobile manufacturer, and Opel, General Motors' subsidiary in Germany. Neither of these partnerships materialized. Despite such failures, joint ventures are an effective way to cut costs and expand into new markets.

For example, South Korea needs outside technology and increased market access for its products overseas, which would lend stability and financial assistance when North and South Korea unite eventually. For these reasons, South Korea and other countries are opening their doors to foreign companies. After trade sanctions against Vietnam were lifted, Vietnam also entered the market for joint ventures, which was already brimming with Southeast Asian countries. Developing countries seek joint ventures to access much needed technology, whereas developed countries seek joint ventures to keep their economies robust and to expand their markets.

Many companies have found joint ventures to be useful. Sony paired up with CBS to record and sell music (and eventually bought out the CBS recording division), with PepsiCo to sell Wilson sporting goods, and with Prudential to sell insurance. These ventures increase earnings, expand markets, share costs, and help diversify.

The details of the joint venture between Mercedes and Swatch were not revealed at the time of the announcement. The cost of the Swatchmobile (the name of the product), how much each would invest, and the level of quality control to which the product would be subjected were not specified. Mercedes, however, would probably produce the Swatchmobile through an independent subsidiary to minimize the risk to its reputation should the venture go aground. Manufacturing the automobile under the Swatch label would enable Mercedes to enter the subcompact car market, after years of manufacturing luxury cars, without losing its image.

Source: Audrey Choi and Margaret Studer, "Daimler-Benz's Mercedes Unit to Build a Car with Maker of Swatch Watches," *Wall Street Journal,* p. A15, February 23, 1994; Robert Keatley, "South Korea Loses Ground in Asia's Race," *Wall Street Journal,* p. A9, February 25, 1994.

INTRODUCTION

The process whereby one company establishes a relationship to deal with another company in a foreign country is called **internationalization**. This process can take place in the form of international trade, joint ventures, licensing, or wholly owned operations. There are several reasons why a company decides to internationalize: to expand into new markets, to make use of technological advantages, and because of local market saturation. Among large multinational corporations, there is clear evidence that there is a strong correlation between improved performance and the degree of internationalization.[1] The process of internationalization involves many tough decisions. The parties must decide how much they are willing to invest in the foreign company and what role each will play in manufacturing and marketing. Even after these initial decisions have been made, the parties need to decide who will control the investment.

LICENSING

A company can generate additional profits by licensing its proprietary advantages or technology. The licensor gains the opportunity to exploit its technology in small markets, which would otherwise not be profitable, and to enter markets that have restrictions on imports. The licensee benefits by acquiring technology at a low cost, circumventing the need for expensive research and development, and increases its ability to diversify. The licensor risks losing profits due to loss of technological advantage and reputation, while the licensee risks spending more than anticipated and not being able to exploit the technology.

FRANCHISING

Franchising is the fastest growing segment of international licensing. It involves granting permission to produce a product and to use its name, trademark, or copyright. In producing the product, the franchisee (the receiver of the rights) is usually required to follow a specific set of procedures, methods, and quality guidelines. In return, the franchiser (the supplier of the rights) receives a fee and/or royalties. In addition to the right to use its name, the franchiser generally sells the franchisee some array of products and services.

Franchise operations in retail and in the restaurant business are developing all over the world. For example, McDonald's and Kentucky Fried Chicken have restaurants in Japan, England, Canada, and Mexico, among other countries.

EXPORTING

Firms of any size face similar questions when considering expansion: which markets, how to enter those markets, and how to manage their foreign export operation.[1] While an ethnocentric company may not even consider importing goods or services, other types of companies need to decide whether it would be better to produce, purchase locally, or import goods.

Exporting is an important strategy for many companies. It is a way to gain access to a wider variety of goods for less than the cost of producing them at home. Exporting can include manufactured goods, services, information, and raw materials. It is favored by both large and small companies. The majority of international marketing is carried out by firms that sell domestically produced goods in foreign markets. Firms that are unable to acquire factories in foreign countries or fear the risks associated with production abroad may choose to export domestically produced goods to foreign markets. The reasons for exporting domestic production include the following:

1. To access new markets, new opportunities, new products, and new technology

2. To utilize near-full domestic production capacity

3. To overcome domestic market saturation

4. To explore new avenues of marketing and growth

5. To gain an understanding of international involvement

Indirect Exporting

Indirect exporting is a method whereby a company hires an agent or firm to export its products without the company being directly involved in the export of domestically produced products. There are at least six ways that a company can use indirect exporting:

1. A domestic company or entrepreneur buys foreign products to be resold in foreign markets

2. A large or entrepreneurial domestic company purchases foreign products to resell in the United States

3. An international company uses a foreign company's product in its production facilities abroad

4. An agent sells product overseas for a domestic manufacturer (manufacturer's export agent) or an agent buys from manufacturers for foreign markets (export commission agent)

5. A company resells its domestic products overseas

6. A company has trading offices in other countries (export management company) or has other companies manage its exports

Whether exporting directly or indirectly, it is essential that the exporter be informed and knowledgeable about export trade financial techniques and risk analysis procedures in order to minimize the risk. Although the increased growth of international trade makes it difficult to maintain a competitive edge, managers can gain some advantage by staying informed. International trade has grown consistently in recent years; it increased 19% in 1988, 15% in 1989, and 8.6% in 1989 to a total of $3.1 trillion.

Finance, Credit, and International Business (FCIB) was created to provide exporters with information about the complications of foreign sales and investments, including political risks, export documentation procedures, import regulations, methods of payment, foreign exchange controls, banking regulations, and how to obtain reliable customer information. This information can enhance exporting activities and make export managers more effective.[2]

Direct Exporting

In indirect exporting, a firm performs the export task rather than assigning the job to others. Some of the export tasks carried out by a direct exporter include analyzing the potential markets, selecting the foreign markets to enter, and choosing the distribution channels. Direct exporting is generally more involved, more expensive, and riskier than indirect exporting. However, many firms choose direct exporting over indirect exporting because it can result in higher sales.

Direct exporting evolves from indirect exporting in many cases. As its knowledge about overseas marketing grows, a firm may decide to do its own exporting. A first, a firm may choose to sell to wholesalers in its foreign markets, with support services provided by home office personnel or sales representatives in the foreign country. When sales reach a point that warrants a complete market affiliate, a company can move in that direction by establishing a sales company. Such companies can eventually become large establishments with extensive sales. This gradual evolution may end in full production facilities, which transforms a pure exporter into a foreign manufacturer.

Exporting is sometimes used in combination with other patterns of involvement in international trade. In addition, many multinational corporations export domestically produced products and components to their own foreign subsidiaries. The integration of domestic and foreign operations can assure supply, reduce costs, and improve coordination of production. Many domestic manufacturers prefer to do their own export marketing by entering foreign markets directly.

COUNTERTRADE

Countertrade is a process by which an importing nation imposes conditions that link imports to exports, which minimizes the net outflow of foreign exchange from the economy. Countertrade is usually practiced by those nations that have small reserves of foreign currencies or tightly controlled economies. Countertrade can take the following forms:

1. **Simple barter:**   Imported goods are traded for commodities of equal value produced domestically.

2. **Buy-back or compensation trading:**   This consists of the export of a technology package, the construction of an entire project, or the provision of services by a firm. The buyer in return pays back the supplier by delivering a share of the output of the project in the future.

3. **Counterpurchase or parallel barter:**   A seller is partially paid in terms of credits that must be used to purchase products from a specified list. Counterpurchase can also be viewed as a form of exchange control because it mandates making payments in terms of credits instead of hard currencies.

4. **Switch trading:**   At least three parties are involved in a countertrade transaction. A switch trade is used when the products received from the importer are not of any use to the exporter or cannot be converted to cash. It also refers to the credit in a clearing account when it is sold or transferred to another party.

5. **Offset trading:**   This is contingent on the procurement of a portion of the raw materials or components used in a product from local sources. Offset trading can be in the form of co-production, subcontracting, joint ventures, licensing, or turnkey arrangements.

6. **Evidence accounts:**   These are agreements between an exporter and one or more foreign trade organizations from the importing nation. Based on this agreement, the exporter sells a pre-arranged amount of goods or services to the foreign trade organization and in return buys local products from the same or other foreign trade organizations to balance the account.

Countertrade is increasing in popularity. It is usually a cost-saving arrangement and sometimes improves the efficiency of trade. Countertrade is generally a national response to environmental constraints and market imperfections.

TURNKEY OPERATIONS

In a turnkey operation, one company contracts another to do work. An example would be one company building a plant for another company and then "turning over the keys." Typical turnkey operations involve large-scale constructions projects, such as building dams, nuclear power plants, or airports. These projects often require expertise or knowledge that local firms do not have. For examples, telecommunications firms, such as Siemens of West Germany, NEC of Japan, and AT&T, construct telephone installations in foreign countries to be turned over to local operators.

Turnkey operations have helped many countries accelerate their rate of development. Countries such as the former Soviet Union, China, Iran, Turkey, and India have contracted firms to build plants that will be run by local people, who do not have the technical expertise to build these large projects. Turnkey operations can be to the benefit of both parties.

JOINT VENTURES

A joint venture is the participation of two or more companies in an enterprise in which each party contributes assets, owns the equity to some degree, and shares the risk.[3] Joint ventures are nothing new. In 1879, Thomas Edison teamed up with Corning Glass Works to make his experimental incandescent light bulb. Similarly, in the late 1880s, railroads in the United States formed partnerships for large-scale projects. The key to a joint venture is the sharing of a common business objective, which makes the arrangement more than a customer–vendor relationship but less than an outright acquisition.

Historical Observations

Joint ventures traditionally have occurred only between standalone operating companies. However, since 1984, when the United States passed the Joint Research and Development Act, which allows both domestic and foreign firms to participate in joint basic research efforts without fear of antitrust action, new forms of joint ventures have emerged. For example, an international consortium was founded in 1983 with the intention of spending $1 billion to develop a new jet engine. United Technologies' Pratt and Whitney division and Britain's Rolls-Royce each have a 30% share in the five-nation venture. The rest is divided among Mortoren-und-Turbinen Union of the Federal Republic of Germany, Fiat of Italy, and Japanese Aero-Engines (made up of Ishikawajima Heavy Industries and Kawasaki Heavy Industries).[4] According to the United Nations Economic Commission for Europe, joint venture registrations soared throughout Eastern Europe in the second half of 1989. The figure topped 3300 by year-end (including the Soviet Union) compared to 1375 at the end of June and just 165 in early 1988.[4]

Advantages of International Joint Ventures

A joint venture with a major foreign partner can be extremely advantageous. Participation in income and growth is a real plus to joint ventures.

The minority partner can share in the earnings and growth of the venture even if its own technology becomes obsolete or other similar joint ventures or substitute products are more profitable. It will share in the equity value of its know-how for an indefinite period, in addition to receiving royalty payments for a limited duration.

Joint ventures usually receive preferential treatment in developing countries of the Third World. These nations do not permit a subsidiary controlled by a foreign licensor to remit royalties or deduct them from taxable income. However, this policy does not affect a locally controlled joint venture. In fact, most developing countries usually favor this type of arrangement because it tends to offer the desired mix of foreign technological and capital involvement, guarantee local management, and effect the transfer of technology.[5]

Another advantage of a joint venture is the ready access to a new market and to market information. A close and continuing relationship between the managers of the venture and their foreign partners should help both parties anticipate supply requirements, determine pricing, exchange market and technological information, and avoid territorial restrictions. However, this is only true of friendly companies with shared interests that are reluctant to compete without regard for the other party.

Joint ventures are also less of a drain on a company's managerial resources. The minority partner's role in the development and growth of the venture and its market imposes a smaller burden on a company's management team than would a wholly owned and controlled subsidiary. In addition, the market and management experience of a minority partner in the host country is always a valuable asset. Joint ventures can also create equity value for the parent company. A U.S. company may decide to realize the value of its holding through disposal of its equity share.[5]

A joint venture may be the only way that a firm can participate in a certain market. For example, India restricts equity participation by foreigners in local operations to 40%. Many Western firms are using joint ventures to gain access to Eastern European markets. In the former Soviet Union, 49% foreign equity ownership in joint ventures is now possible as a result of economic reforms.[6]

Technology can be used more quickly and market penetration achieved more easily through a joint venture. One of the partners may have an established distribution system or may have better access to local suppliers, either of which can create a greater volume of sales in a shorter period of time.

The influence of government is a major rationale for joint ventures in less developed countries and is the main reason why joint ventures are used four times more frequently in less developed countries than in developed countries.[7] If the government is involved in a venture or the local partner is influential, the new venture may be eligible for tax incentives, grants, or other types of government support. Negotiations for certification or licenses may be easier if the authorities do not think that they are dealing with a foreign firm. The experience of a local firm can benefit the venture by providing insight into needs as the market changes.

A final commercial reason for participating in joint ventures is to minimize the risk of exposing long-term investment capital while at the same time maximizing leverage on the capital that is invested.[8] In minimizing the risk, the partners in a joint venture must understand that economic and political conditions in many countries are volatile. At the same time, corporations tend to shorten their investment planning time span more and more by expecting higher return in the early years of their investment. The financial rationale therefore takes on greater importance.

Drawbacks of International Joint Ventures

Joint ventures do have some drawbacks. One partner's business objectives may differ from the other's so radically that agreement on how to operate, fund, and benefit from the venture can be difficult or even impossible to reach. For example, the Japanese are traditionally more interested than Americans in market share, long-term competitive position, and employer–employee relationships; Americans are more concerned with annual or quarterly profits. Communication can also pose a major problem. The Japanese are much slower decision makers compared to the quick decisions that many American businesspeople tend to make. Differences between partners in business practices and culture can cause a breakdown in the relationship and can even lead to severing the arrangement.[8]

Inadequate or antiquated transportation systems and public utilities in various countries can present problems. Problems can also arise concerning confidentiality of technical information and the transfer of profits between countries. These problems are in addition to the typical logistical problems encountered by companies with more than one location. Probably the greatest problem is the difference in management style and the culture of the work force, through whose productivity the goals of the partnership must be reached.

Withdrawals by U.S. multinational corporations from overseas markets and investments are not uncommon. The large-scale database developed by the Harvard Multinational Enterprise Project reveals that out of a total of 13,795 subsidiaries entered by 190 U.S.-based multinational corporations between 1951 and 1975, almost 35% departed the parent systems through merger, liquidation, or expropriation. The manufacturing sector, which accounts for more than half of the total entries, experienced a failure rate close to one in every three.[9] The failure of a joint venture is often extremely costly for both partners. A failure can also cause political repercussions between the two countries, which may not be easily resolved. In a failed joint venture, one partner usually suffers a greater loss, whether financial or nonfinancial. It is not clear whether the multinational corporation or the local partner usually loses more. The corporation may suffer loss of reputation in the host country.[9] Another nonfinancial loss is the loss of goodwill, as well as a strained relationship between partners over settle-ment of claims, valuation of assets and liabilities, and division of assets. Adverse publicity in local and international papers can damage the image and reputation of a company as a potential joint venture partner in the future. This adverse effect can spill over onto the host country, with similar disastrous consequences. If the host country is perceived as a difficult marketplace, foreign investors may avoid doing business there.[9] The selection of a qualified partner is not an easy task. A poor choice can mean ineffective market penetration, lost time, and unrecoverable costs.

SELECTION OF A PARTNER

A number of institutions offer assistance in identifying potential candi-dates for joint ventures. These institutions include the International Trade Administration of the U.S. Department of Commerce, several large international banks, and chambers of commerce in various countries. Their services are often provided free of charge or at a small cost. Excellent information can also be provided by other industry-informed sources, such as major product users, suppliers, and experts or consultants in the field.

Once the priority partner has been identified, negotiations can begin. The most important part of the negotiation is to decide what the two parties are trying to accomplish. If this first step results in unresolved differences, negotiations should be terminated. In many countries, government regu-lation must be addressed before any joint venture takes effect.[5]

U.S. COMPANIES

A study conducted by the Conference Board,[10] in which large Fortune 500 companies were sampled, found that international joint venture activi-ties by U.S. companies are on the rise. The study was based on the responses of 145 U.S. companies to a mail survey and interviews at 23 companies. The observed growth trend in international joint ventures was summarized in the following terms: of those responding to the mail survey, just over half had participated in new international joint ventures in the past five years, and in well over half of these—one-third of the entire group of respondents—the rate of international joint venture formation also in-creased in the same five-year period.[4]

Hladik[11] conducted a study of 420 manufacturing joint ventures be-tween U.S. and foreign partners in the overseas market to identify the recent operating characteristics of these companies. By tracing the joint venture announcements in the business press, she was able to locate 599 references to international joint ventures undertaken by U.S.-based multi-

**TABLE 14.1 Yearly Announcements of
Manufacturing International Joint Ventures
Between U.S. and Foreign Firms in the Overseas Market (1974–82)**

Year	Announcements (no. of units)
1974	80
1975	34
1976	32
1977	32
1978	45
1979	85
1980	110
1981	112
1982	79

Source: K.J. Hladik, *International Joint Ventures: An Economic Analysis of U.S.–Foreign Business Partnerships* (Lexington, Mass.: Lexington Books), 1985, p. 47.

national corporations from 1974 to 1982. The yearly distribution of joint venture announcements is shown in Table 14.1. In general, it appears that the trend toward international joint ventures remained fairly strong and even increased in more recent years.

JAPANESE JOINT VENTURES IN THE UNITED STATES

It is difficult to determine to what extent joint ventures are pursued as a competitive strategy (to compensate for deficiencies in other areas, e.g., monopolistic advantage). The fact remains, however, that if multinational corporations based in some nations show a greater propensity to the joint venture mode, competition among multinational corporations as a whole increases, and the bargaining power of the host nation increases at least to that extent. Vernon[12] suggests, however, that since 1970 the attitude of Japanese multinational corporations toward joint ventures has changed somewhat. He maintains that Japanese-based multinational enterprises have been turning away from their earlier preference for joint ventures and have been setting up an increasing proportion of their manufacturing operations as wholly owned subsidiaries.[4]

According to Phillips,[13] mixing Japanese production methods and American work styles has been difficult in many joint ventures. Joint ventures were supposed to be a way for U.S. parts suppliers to gain access to the $6.6 billion Japanese auto industry. However, most of these joint ventures are losing money, and the number of new joint ventures is declining.

Underlying the failures are problems with different management styles, inflated expectations, and disputes over quality and labor practices. More important, the two sides often entered into such ventures with different agendas. American suppliers wanted access to the Japanese automakers. Japanese suppliers were looking further ahead, using their partners to gain footholds in the U.S. market. Now, as many of the ventures prove unworkable, the Japanese partners are beginning to strike out on their own. However, this is not to imply that all joint ventures between Americans and the Japanese have been unsuccessful. TRW, Inc. has three joint ventures with big Japanese auto suppliers to produce seat belts, engine valves, and steering gears. Chardon Rubber Company, a smaller supplier of weather stripping for doors and trunks, and its partner, Kenugawa Rubber Industry, do not compete in the same products.[13]

The number of joint ventures formed in the U.S. market is only a small fraction compared to the number of joint ventures set up overseas by U.S.-based multinational corporations. Recent evidence, however, suggests that international joint ventures in the United States are on the increase. At least two reasons appear to account for this interest. First, an increasing number of foreign companies are seeking to enter the U.S. market through cooperative arrangements, either to gain a foothold or to protect the market already developed through entry strategies without foreign direct investment. Existing trade barriers and/or perhaps anticipation of future trade barriers have played a part in the process. Second, in the domestic market, as it appears, more U.S. companies than ever before are now willing to enter into joint ventures with foreign partners.[14]

GROWTH TREND

Based on the tracking records of the Department of Commerce, Talaga[15] estimates that about 9% of all foreign entries in the United States from 1978 to 1983 were in the form of joint ventures. The Investment Analysis Division (IAD) of the International Trade Administration of the U.S. Department of Commerce identified 1627 acquisitions and mergers, 790 new plants and plant expansions, and 237 joint ventures undertaken by foreign firms during this period. The IAD identified another 50 joint ventures in 1984. However, based on clippings maintained by the IAD, Talaga[15] identified 93 cases of joint venture entries in the United States in 1984.[4] The yearly numbers for joint venture entries in the United States from 1978 to 1984 are listed in Table 14.1.

There has been a rising trend toward international joint ventures in most industries. *Chemical Week* reports that during the mid-1970s, U.S. companies were forming an average of about 130 joint ventures a year in the overseas market, but in 1981 that figure reached 210.[16]

CHANGING ATTITUDES

A number of companies that previously relied exclusively on wholly owned subsidiaries are changing their attitudes toward international joint ventures. One example is IBM. In the early and mid 1960s, faced with the Indian government's demand to share ownership in local interests, IBM chose to withdraw altogether from the Indian market. In the last few years, however, IBM has started to enter into joint venture arrangements. Levine and Byrne[17] indicate that at present IBM has at least twelve joint ventures with foreign firms. *Business Asia* reports the following change in attitude at IBM: "IBM Japan, Ltd., wholly owned subsidiary of the U.S. computer giant, has initiated a new strategy to regain market share in Japan. It centers around abandoning the long established lone-wolf policy and aggressively entering into production and marketing relationships with Japanese firms...[18]

IBM is not an isolated case. General Motors, for example, long opposed joint ventures and licensing arrangements, arguing that unambiguous control was essential to its worldwide strategy. By the mid-1970s, however, it had begun to form joint ventures outside the United States and stated its willingness to license technology without equity interest. Vernon and Wells[19] attribute this move by General Motors to such factors as the rise of competitors with a more flexible approach to ownership policy and a gradual decline in the barriers to entry into older industries, which resulted in increased options and bargaining power for host country governments. These factors, identified by Vernon and Wells as major undercurrents of the 1970s, appear to have become even more pronounced in the 1980s. When the steel industry in the United States lost market share to foreign exports, this decline encouraged the industry to change its attitude toward foreign competition. One example is Armco Steel Corporation's plant in Butler, Pennsylvania, which formed a joint venture with Kawasaki Company of Japan for specialty steel products.

THE JAPANESE FACTOR

One question that plagues many CEOs and top management is whether joint ventures with Japan are giving away America's future, as reflected in the following comments:

> They buy energy-intensive components here, like glass, tires, and steel. But when it comes to things that are labor-intensive, that stays in Japan.
>
> Terrence J. Miller
> Automotive Parts and Accessories Association

First you move the industrial part to the Far East. Then the development of the product goes there because each dollar you pay to the overseas supplier is ten cents you're giving them to develop new devices and new concepts to compete against you.

C.J. Van der Klugt
Vice Chairman, Philips N.V.

The overriding goal of Japanese managers is to keep complex production in Japan. Their intent is to develop national competitive strength in advanced production methods. Increasingly, American managers are aiding the Japanese in achieving their goals by channeling new inventions to Japan and providing a sales and distribution network for the products. The value of the sales and distribution provided by U.S. companies is replaceable. The U.S. companies are giving away a portion of their market franchises by relying on Japanese companies for manufactured products. They are encouraging the entry of a new competitor by providing the Japanese access to their customers and are selling themselves too cheaply by giving away valuable production experience.[20]

POSSIBLE SOLUTIONS

All joint ventures have either a positive or negative impact on a country, its people, and businesses. With increasing competition from abroad, it is imperative for U.S. companies to consider joint ventures if they want to enter the global market and be competitive. Government should create incentives for companies that do business in the United States, regardless of where a company is headquartered. By investing in production in the United States, American workers and engineers would reap the benefits of a stronger U.S. economy. Antitrust laws could be modified to permit American companies to invest jointly in complex production in the United States, thereby spreading the cost of the investment across several companies. The Federal Trade Commission allowed General Motors and Toyota to form a joint venture. Would it have approved a GM–Ford deal?[21]

The future of the United States depends upon the ability of Americans to learn, to improve production capabilities, and to be more competitive. American companies are shipping research overseas and seeing it returned as finished goods. This prospect should be the top concern of executives and government leaders alike.

FUTURE PREDICTIONS

More and more companies are recognizing the benefits of becoming active participants in foreign markets. The emergence of the unified European marketplace will facilitate more trade and foreign investment activity. Former U.S. Department of Commerce Secretary Robert A. Mosbacher has negotiated the opportunity of American companies in the new global business climate. The Department of Commerce issued a 92-page report which emphasizes the need for American businesses to take advantage of the commercial opportunities that exist.

Strategic alliances are not determined by the size of a multinational corporation. Many companies that hold a steady and unique position in the U.S. market see the international market through joint venturing as a means to expand and grow. Many large corporations see joint ventures with suppliers in foreign countries as a means to maintain market share or decrease their costs.

The European market is interested in buying American goods and services, and the American market purchases European goods and services. It seems inevitable that the only sensible answer is to join forces through international joint ventures. It is predicted that most future joint ventures will occur in Eastern Europe and China.

REFERENCES

1. P.W. Beamish, "Joint Venture Performance in Developing Countries," in Annual Conference, Academy of International Business, New York, December 1984, pp. 1–10.
2. Ray Schweitzer, "FCIB in the Service of International Trade," *Business Credit,* p. 5, November/December 1990.
3. Kathryn Rudie Harrigan, "Joint Ventures and Global Strategies," *Columbia Journal of World Business,* 19:7–16, Summer 1984.
4. Jafor Chowdhury, "The Evolving Context of International Joint Ventures: Observations on Some Historical and Recent Trends," in Abbass F. Alkhafaji, "Management Challenges: A Worldwide Perspective," *Management Decision,* 29(6):73, 75, 77–78, June 1991.
5. F. Kingston Berlew, "The Joint Venture—A Way into Foreign Markets," *Harvard Business Review,* pp. 49–54, July–August 1984.
6. Ikka A. Ronkainen and Anthony W. Schneider, "U.S.–U.S.S.R. Trade: Potential for New Trade Arrangements?" *NCEIS Trade Analyst,* p. 2, September–October 1986.
7. Paul W. Beamish, "The Characteristics of Joint Ventures in Developed and Developing Countries," *Columbia Journal of World Business,* 20:13–19, Fall 1985.
8. Charles Oman, *New Forms of International Investment in Developing Countries* (Paris: Organization for Economic Cooperation and Development), 1984.
9. Abbass F. Alkhafaji, "Management Challenges: A Worldwide Perspective," *Management Decision,* 29:36–37, June 1991.
10. Allen R. Janger, "Organization of International Joint Ventures," Report No. 787 (New York: The Conference Board), 1980.
11. Karen J. Hladik, *International Joint Ventures: An Economic Analysis of U.S. Foreign Business Partnerships* (Lexington, Mass.: Lexington Books), 1985.
12. R. Vernon, *Storm Over the Multinationals: The Real Issues* (Cambridge, Mass.: Harvard University Press), 1977, pp. 65–67.
13. Stephen Phillips, "When U.S. Joint Ventures with Japan Go Sour," *Business Week,* pp. 30–31, July 24, 1989.
14. C. Jayachandran, "Role of Multiple Parties in the Choice of Technology Collaborations: Some Insights into Conflict Resolution," in Abbass F. Alkhafaji, *International Management Challenge* (Acton, Mass.: Copley), 1990, p. 210.

15. James A. Talaga, "Foreign Firms that Enter in U.S.-Based Sole Ventures and Joint Ventures: An Empirical Test of a Modification of the Eclectic Theory of Foreign Direct Investment," Ph.D. thesis (Philadelphia: Temple University), 1987.

16. "Making Joint Ventures Work," *Chemical Week*, p. 31, August 17, 1983.

17. Jonathan B. Levine and John A. Byrne, "Corporate Odd Couples: Joint Ventures Are All the Rage—But the Matches Often Don't Work Out," *Business Week*, pp. 100–105, July 21, 1986.

18. Jean Layson Pyle, "The Impact of Multinational Technological Transfer on Female Workforces in Asia," *The Columbia Journal of World Business*, 25:40–48, Winter 1990; Susan Dentzer, "Meet the New Economic Bogeyman," *U.S. News & World Report*, p. 67, October 1993.

19. R. Vernon and L.T. Wells, *Economic Environment of International Business*, 3rd edition (Englewood Cliffs, N.J.: Prentice-Hall), 1981, p. 147.

20. J. Stewart Black and Mark Mendenhall, "Resolving Conflicts with Japanese: Mission Impossible?" *Sloan Management Review*, p. 83, Spring 1993.

21. Robert B. Reich and Eric D. Mankin, "Joint Ventures with Japan Give Away Our Future," *Harvard Business Review*, p. 86, March–April 1986.

SECTION VI

BUSINESS ETHICS AND CORPORATE RESPONSIBILITY

Business ethics and how it pertains to corporate social responsibility has become an issue of great concern to businessmen and scholars alike in recent times. The last decade has seen a heightened awareness of this and similar issues throughout society, but the most visible evidence of attention to ethical concerns is manifest in the many changes in corporate policy and decision making. This means that now, more than ever before, corporations are putting more time and effort into showing that they are ethical and socially responsible. An in-depth analysis of business ethics and corporate social responsibility is presented in this section.

15 SOCIAL RESPONSIBILITY: A REQUISITE FOR CORPORATE SURVIVAL

ABSTRACT

Corporate social responsibility is becoming a very important part of corporate decision making. The culture that surrounds management plays an important role in the productivity of an organization. No longer can an organization function just to maximize profit; it must also consider the environment and its inhabitants. Today's managers have to understand how their actions can be either helpful or harmful to the organization and its environment. Actions must be carried out in a way that is beneficial to the public as a whole. The concept of corporate social responsibility in both a domestic and international setting is discussed in this chapter. Examples of corporate social responsibility at a number of companies are provided.

CHAPTER OBJECTIVES

1   To explore the complexities of the business environment

2   To understand how social values change over time

3   To present corporate responsibility as a socioeconomic institution

4   To explore the argument for being socially responsible

5   To understand management's role in changing the expectations of society

6   To understand how companies should respond to the social issues in a global environment

7   To understand the international implications of corporate responsibility

CASE STUDY
Exxon Valdez Environmental Catastrophe

In March 1989, 260,000 barrels of crude oil spilled into Prince William Sound. Observers called it the worst oil spill in the history of the United States and said it was due to negligence. The oil was released in a region where marine life was abundant and people lived off the ocean. The effects were environmental, economical, and psychological. The clean-up work alone was estimated to cost $2 billion, while billion-dollar lawsuits were pending.

During the clean-up process, brown algae, known as rockweed, was virtually destroyed. Pink salmon and herring populations, among many other species of fish in the area, were affected by the spill itself and later by the clean-up process. Birds in the area of the spill were severely affected. They were immobilized by the oil that stuck to their feathers, and the oil that covered the surface of the water made fishing impossible. The detergent used to clean up the slick further destroyed the feathers of birds. There has been a decline in 11 bird species, which amounts to 86% of the population. The species most severely affected were loons, harlequin ducks, black oystercatchers, arctic terns, and mewgills.

Among the mammal population, harbor seals and otters were most affected. The seal population declined by about 34% in Prince William Sound. The solvents that were used to break down the oil particles were found to cause lesions to form in the brains of seals.

The restitution claims that Exxon sustained were phenomenal. Residents of the area were awarded $1 billion, although they sued for $2 billion. Exxon also incurred a major financial burden from the clean-up process, which cost $2.5 billion.

The disaster prompted Exxon, other oil companies, the government, and society to look closely at safety standards for oil tankers. The Oil Pollution Act was passed, which mandated better navigation equipment aboard ships, double hulls for oil tankers, and better clean-up methods. Because the captain of the Valdez was found to be under the influence of alcohol, Exxon implemented a policy to screen job applicants for drug and alcohol use.

Source: John Harold, "The Exxon Valdez and Assessment of Crises Prevention and Managerial Systems," *Interfaces,* 20:14–30, September–October 1992; David Seligman, "Exxon Loses Again," *Fortune,* 127:10–13, May 3, 1993.

INTRODUCTION

It is a fact that the activities of large corporations affect society. According to Leonard Silk, "corporations cannot avoid having a heavy and conspicuous effect on society, which the society, if sufficiently disturbed, will move to control or curtail."[1] As society has become increasingly upset by certain activities of corporations, the movement to control corporate activities has grown stronger, especially over the last three to four decades. Society increasingly expects corporations to curtail their actions that produce harmful effects and correct the problems that are the result of their previous actions. All of this has led to the creation of the concept known as corporate social responsibility.

It has become apparent that the quest for financial gain has to take place within the laws of society. Concern about social responsibility began to raise serious questions about corporations and their responsibility to society. Throughout the 1960s, social activist groups and others advocated a broader notion of corporate responsibility. The problems addressed by social responsibility advocates, such as pollution and unsafe workplaces, were in large part created by the drive for efficiency in the marketplace.[2] The clash between the economic performance of business and the changing social values of society brought questions of social responsibility to the forefront. The argument was that there was a divergence between the performance of business in the marketplace and the social aspects of business behavior. It was not until the 1970s that this message was made clear with the creation of the Environmental Protection Agency (EPA), the Equal Employment Opportunity Commission (EEOC), the Occupational Safety and Health Administration (OSHA), and the Consumer Product Safety Commission (CPSC).[3]

These new government bodies established that national public policy officially recognized the environment, employees, and consumers to be significant and legitimate stakeholders of business. From that point on, corporate executives have had to contend with how they will balance their commitments to the owners of corporations and their obligations to every group of stakeholders who claim both legal and ethical rights.[4] We are now at a stage where corporations have started to help solve some of society's problems.

There seem to be three compelling reasons why companies should help solve some of societies problems: (1) businesses exist as guests of society, as was evident during major war efforts from World War II to Desert Storm; (2) businesses are impacted by society, in that no business leader can escape the impact of governmental policies; and (3) businesses usually thrive or starve along with society, as monthly economic numbers usually reflect whether society is in a recession or a depression.[5]

DEFINITION

In general, corporate responsibility refers to corporate actions that protect and improve the welfare of society along with the corporation's own interests. More specifically, various definitions of social responsibility have been advocated, and there seem to be five key elements among most of these definitions:

1. Corporations have responsibilities that go beyond the production of goods and services at a profit.

2. These responsibilities involve helping to solve important social problems, especially those that businesses have helped to create.

3. Corporations have a broader constituency than just stockholders.

4. The impact of corporations goes beyond simple marketplace transactions.

5. Corporations serve a wider range of human values than can be captured by a sole focus on economic values.[2]

Most leading businesspeople and economists now agree that corporate social responsibility is a corporation's obligation to interact with society and to gain insight and judgment on public policy.[6]

Corporate social responsibility is a term that has emerged over the past 40 years to describe an increasing interaction between corporations and their stakeholders. Stakeholders include the shareholder owners, employees, customers or clients, and the community within which a corporation conducts its business. The relationship between a corporation and its stakeholders covers a wide variety of issues, but it mainly focuses on the effect, both positive and negative, that business has on the lives of all people. Individuals in corporations are being held responsible for policies that are socially unacceptable, and its becoming necessary for corporations to develop new ways to deal with and meet increasing social needs.

Originally, the owners or shareholders of corporations were entrepreneurs and managers who were close to their products, employees, and community. Corporations became public around the beginning of this century in the United States, and shares of corporations were sold. As time passed, public and corporate parties as shareholders grew in importance. The majority of American corporations are now owned by these parties through the purchase of common stock. Shareholders have evolved into passive rather than active owners of corporations and in most cases are no longer involved in the day-to-day management of their companies. The stock of a corporation can change hands several times a day. The owners of these companies are quite unimportant at annual meetings. Most shareholders view their ownership simply as an investment. Pride in involvement, accomplishment, or achievement in the community is a thing of the past. The fate of corporations has been left in the hands of managers,

DEFINITIONS OF CORPORATE SOCIAL RESPONSIBILITY

Responsibility refers to **1**: the quality or state of being responsible as **a**: moral, legal, or mental accountability **b**: RELIABILITY, TRUSTWORTHI-NESS **2** something for which one is responsible: BURDEN

Webster's Ninth New Collegiate Dictionary
(Springfield, Mass.: Pittman, 1987, p. 1005)

A private corporation has a responsibility to society that goes beyond the production of goods and services at a profit and that a corporation has a broader constituency to serve than that of stockholders alone.

Rogene A. Bucholz
Essentials of Public Policy for Management
(Englewood Cliffs, N.J.: Prentice-Hall, 1985, p. 5)

Corporate social responsibility refers to the obligations of businessmen to pursue those policies, to make those decisions, or to follow those lines of action which are desirable in terms of the objectives and values of our society.

Howard R. Bowen
Social Responsibilities of the Businessman
(New York: Harper & Row, 1953, p. 6)

The idea of social responsibilities supposes that the corporation has not only economic and legal obligations, but also certain responsibilities to society which extend beyond these obligations.

Joseph W. McGuire
Business and Society
(New York: McGraw-Hill, 1963, p. 144)

The social responsibility of business encompasses the economic, legal, ethical, and discretionary expectation placed on organizations by society at a given point in time.

Archie B. Carrol
"A Conceptual Model of Corporate Social Performance"
(Working Paper No. 79-055,
University of Georgia, 1979, p. 9)

Corporate social responsibility is, therefore, the obligation that corporations have toward their stakeholders and society at large, which goes beyond what is prescribed by law or union contracts.

many of whose expertise lies in areas such as return on equity rather than how to be a good corporate neighbor. This separation of management and ownership, combined with increased emphasis on return on equity, has led to the increased need for corporate social responsibility.

In general, corporate social responsibility encompasses those corporate activities that protect and improve the welfare of society. This means that corporations must do more than simply obey the law, because sometimes the law may lag behind society's values and expectations. Therefore, if corporations follows laws that are obsolete in terms of society's expectations and demands, which are the basis for defining socially responsible behavior, their attempts to be socially responsible will not be effective in reaching their goals.

According to some definitions of corporate social responsibility, the beliefs that are more prevalent in today's business world go beyond following the letter of the law and making a profit. These beliefs go so far as to say that corporations have a moral and ethical (if not intrinsic) duty to help society in alleviating its problems. Managers must take the initiative in such problems as cleaning up the environment and implementing community and employee programs. The latter will be focal to the discussion in this chapter, but Friedman's theory will be discussed to show the change in attitude about corporate social responsibility.

LEVELS OF SOCIAL COMMITMENT

According to Sethi, there are three levels of social commitment. The first level is **social obligation**. At this level, a corporation gets involved only because it thinks that it will benefit in some way and therefore does only what is required by law. The attitude here is that individuals, and not corporations, are responsible for contributing to society. The second level is **social responsibility**. At this level, a corporation is in tune with the needs of society and realizes that it must go beyond what is required by law. When a problem arises, a corporation takes full responsibility and quickly organizes corrective efforts without being told to do so by a regulatory agency. The highest level of social commitment, **social responsiveness**, is proactive. A corporation at this level is in constant communication with external groups, in an effort to anticipate problems and prevent them from becoming social issues.[7]

EVALUATION OF SOCIAL RESPONSIBILITY

The concept of social responsibility has broadened and changed over time as the values and norms of society have changed. During the Industrial Revolution, the corporation was seen solely as an economic entity whose primary objectives were to maximize profit, provide jobs, and protect the interests of its shareholders.[8] The **doctrine of self-interest** prevailed during the 1920s before the stock market crash. This doctrine reflected many people's interest in making as much money as they could and obtaining as much power and status as possible. Dunham and Pierce refer to this period as the profit-maximizing management stage of social responsibility.[9]

In the 1930s, the concept of corporate social responsibility moved into its second stage, **trusteeship management**, which lasted until the 1960s.[9] During this stage, the number of private companies declined due to the Great Depression, and the remaining organizations had to please groups both outside and within the company. Managers had to balance the interests of all stakeholders, some of whom pressured companies into using their wealth to meet the needs of society. This stage marks the first time that organizations had to become socially responsible in order to survive.

As the 1960s approached, once again society's values and expectations changed, and the concept of social responsibility moved into its third phase. This period was marked by **quality of life management**, in which managers were expected to manage the quality of life by helping to solve such problems as pollution and poverty at local and national levels and to become involved in activities that improved the quality of life in their communities.[10] Quality of life management is the stage at which social responsibility is today. According to Dunham and Pierce, two principles provide the basis for current views on social responsibility:[9]

1. **Principle of charity:** People who have should give to those who do not. This is the foundation for the belief that organizations should practice philanthropy.

2. **Principle of stewardship:** Corporations are obligated to meet the needs of society because they gained their power and wealth through operating within society. This principle developed dramatically during the 1970s and 1980s as people increasingly expected businesses to be held responsible for the ways in which they used resources.

Corporations do not really have a choice anymore in whether or not to be socially responsible, because social responsibility is just as important to their well-being as the manufacturing, marketing, and financial functions.[10] George Weissman, former CEO and chairman of Philip Morris, Inc., stated that corporate social responsibility is not just a fad, and organizations must realize that this concept deals with the "...fundamental existence and survival of the corporation."[11]

Large corporations are being asked not only to support social causes, but to solve society's problems as well. In addition to pursuing traditional economic goals, corporations are protecting and improving the welfare of the community and thus are being socially responsible. Although a manager's main responsibility is organizational effectiveness, managers must also keep in mind that they must behave ethically and in accordance with society's values when pursuing their goals. What makes all of this so difficult is that the demands of a corporation's stakeholders may conflict, which makes it hard to recognize what is the right thing to do.

According to Gorman, three factors have led to the latest concern for social responsibility:[12]

1. **Deregulation of industries:** The Reagan administration cut the budgets of the Federal Trade Commission and the Consumer Product Safety Commission.

2. **Hostile takeovers and buyouts:** While many bankers and CEOs became rich, thousands of employees lost their jobs, which eroded the credibility of businesses.

3. **Accidents:** The chemical spill in Bhopal, India reminded people of the destructive effects that the carelessness of companies can cause.

The public believes that corporations will not follow regulatory requirements if left to do so on their own and will try to get away with whatever they can, which is why government intervention is justified. A charter is permission granted to a corporation by a state to operate under its laws. It is a three-way contract, between the state, the corporation and the shareholders. This permission is established by the state, granted by the people, and can be withdrawn if the people conclude that a corporation is not acting in the public interest.[13] The government is supposed to represent what the people want and therefore can intervene in business activities if they affect society negatively. Small companies are usually left alone as long as they follow government regulations and rules, but large corporations have become political entities that operate on such a large scale that they cannot be left alone.

Government intervention reflects the belief that businesses have a responsibility to their constituencies other than shareholders. Passage of the Plant Closing Act, which requires companies to notify those groups affected by large layoffs and closings, clearly demonstrates this.[8] In this regard then, companies must identify their constituents and understand their demands and expectations in order to be socially responsible. In order to do so, Heath and Nelson suggest that "consistent application of short-term public opinion scanning and long-range monitoring should be sensitive to what groups believe, how intensely they believe it, and how willing they are to act on their beliefs."[11]

Even religious institutions can influence what business activities are considered legitimate. "Churches and civil rights groups have gone beyond condemnation of human-rights abuses under the apartheid system to a virtual declaration of war against that system and the regime that supports it."[14]

Consumers have also taken matters into their own hands. Today's consumers not only check the prices of items, but check for social responsibility as well. Many consumers use *Shopping for a Better World,* published by the Council on Economic Priorities, which "...ranks 1,300 products and their manufacturers according to ten criteria, including the promotion of women and minorities, testing on animals and environmental sensitivity."[12] In an effort to be heard, consumers are investing in corporations that they feel are socially responsible and are boycotting those that are not.

ARGUMENTS FOR CORPORATE SOCIAL RESPONSIBILITY

The arguments for social involvement revolve around the potential benefits to society and business (see summary in Table 15.1). Many of these arguments focus on the fact that social responsibility will benefit businesses in the long run. Favorable social actions that discourage government regulation or create a better community can be in the long-term self-interest of business. The arguments for social responsibility imply that social responsiveness and economic return are not necessarily mutually exclusive.

One of the strongest arguments for corporate social responsibility is that business exists only because it satisfies a valuable need(s) of society. Society grants business its charter to exist, and if business fails to live up to society's expectations, that charter may be revoked. In order for a business to be successful, it must respond to society's needs and expectations. This reasoning suggests that what society's wants is continually changing.

Expectations are moving in the direction of increased social output from business. The old economic outputs are no longer enough because the old needs have been met. According to Maslow's hierarchy of needs, as basic needs are met, more complex needs evolve. Production of goods and services is no longer the central focus of society. Society's needs are changing, as quality of life is becoming equally important to society as production of goods and services.

Another argument for corporate social responsibility has to do with potential results that can be achieved. If the results will be beneficial to both society and business, social responsiveness should be encouraged. Increased involvement by business should result in alleviating the social problems that would improve the quality of life. An improved social environment would also benefit business. A company that is most responsive to improving the quality of life will enjoy a more favorable environment in which to conduct its business in. For example, employee turnover will decrease, workers' quality of life will improve, and public support for the operation will increase.

It is also argued that by being socially responsive, business can avoid further government regulation. Regulation tends to reduce freedom for both business and society. Regulation of business tends to add economic cost and restrict flexibility in decision making. Freedom in decision making permits business to continue meeting the needs of the market and society. Both business and society can benefit by discouraging new government restrictions.

It can also be argued that a socially responsible business will have a better public image. The argument can be made that business should direct some of its resources toward solving social problems. Prevention is better than a cure. Because social problems must eventually be dealt with, it is more effective to address them before they become serious and costly. Finally, business has a moral obligation to help society and government solve the problems that it helped to create.

TABLE 15.1   Arguments For and Against Corporate Social Responsibility

For social responsibility	Against social responsibility
• Changed public needs and expectations	• Need for profit maximization
• Improves the social environment	• Threat to business's primary purpose; it sends mixed signals about organizational goals to the organization and the community
• Discourages further government regulation	
• Balances responsibility and power	
• Problems can become profits	• Business costs of social involvement may result in lower corporate efficiency
• Let business try	
• Prevention is better than a cure	• Cost to society
• Profit maximization should be realized through long-term goals because short-term profit goals do not take into account long-term consequences	• Costs are passed on to stockholders through lower dividends, to employees through lower wages, and to consumers through higher prices
• Promotes good will, public support, and corporate trust	• Business has enough power and would gain even more
• Enhances an organization's image and business	• Lack of social skills—businesspeople are not trained to deal with social problems
• Corporations have the resources to help solve society's problems	
• Corporations have a moral obligation to solve the problems they helped to create	• Lack of accountability—individuals in corporations cannot be held accountable for their actions
• As members of society, organizations have a moral obligation to help society with its problems and contribute to its welfare	• By defining their social responsibility too specifically, corporations may create problems in operations
• Advances technological and scientific knowledge through solving society's ills	• The corporation's main responsibility is to its shareholders
• Growing number of court awards against socially irresponsible companies	• Conflicts with the principles of the free enterprise system

ARGUMENTS AGAINST
CORPORATE SOCIAL RESPONSIBILITY

There are many arguments against corporate social responsibility (see Table 15.1). The classical economic doctrine of maximizing profit may be the most powerful argument against corporate social responsibility. This doctrine was presented by Adam Smith in 1776 and has contributed to economic thought ever since. It is to the benefit of the public when a business reduces costs and improves efficiency in order to maximize profit. Even though managers are motivated by the pursuit of profit, competition forces them to act in the public interest in the long run by reducing prices and costs. Therefore, when a business meets its economic interests, it is being most socially responsible.

Business must give top priority to economic efficiency when resources are limited. The function of business is economic rather than social, and economic values should be the only criteria used to measure success. Managerial decisions are controlled by the desire to maximize profits for the stockholders while still complying with laws and social customs. According to Milton Friedman, a major supporter of this argument, if companies followed a socially responsive course, their actions would raise the price for customers. Business would be spending their customers' money, because the cost of social responsiveness would result in higher priced goods and services and/or reduced wages for employees. Friedman indicates that the only responsibility of a business is to maximize profit, and, therefore, executives should only worry about the shareholders' demands and expectations.[15] He identified four basic obligations of an organization to society:[1,6,9,11]

1. Obey the law

2. Provide goods and services

3. Employ resources efficiently

4. Pay resource owners fairly in accordance with the market

According to this line of reasoning, when managers use resources for social purposes, they are spending other people's money without their input into the decision-making process. This line of reasoning relies on mechanisms other than the free market to allocate scarce resources for alternative uses, which inevitably leads to reduced economic efficiency. The result of social involvement, according to this point of view, is a net economic loss.

A related argument is that social involvement by business may so greatly reduce economic efficiency and divide the interests of the leaders that business will become weak and unable to function. These two distinctly different activities—social and economic—will create a house divided against itself. Collapse due to its own internal conflict and confusion of goals may be a direct result. In most societies, business is a principal producer of wealth. If business were to collapse, the result would be a poorer society with fewer resources to apply to social purposes. Even if business does not collapse, it will still experience problems. Placing too much emphasis on social response will cause the public to impose expectations on business that are impossible for it to accomplish. When these expectations are not satisfied, the public image of business will be damaged and people will turn against it, thus leaving business unable to function effectively.

Another argument is the excessive business costs of social involvement. Business has many resources available, but it must use them wisely because these resources will disappear quickly if they are not self-renewing. Business could invest small amounts of its resources in social obligations, as it has done in the past, but it cannot afford to commit major economic resources for social involvement unless the costs of these resources are paid by the government or other institutions.

As briefly stated earlier, society must ultimately pay the costs of social actions that are taken. Many social proposals do not economically benefit a company, which ultimately forces society to pay all the costs. If social programs add to business costs, then these costs must be recovered, and generally this cost is added to the price of a product. In cases where a product is sold in international markets, business could suffer a distinct disadvantage compared to competitors whose primary function is economic. Social costs could make products unfit for international competition.

An additional argument is that business already has enough power and that society should not allow it to gain more. Today, business is one of the most powerful institutions in society. The process of combining social activities with the established economic activities of business will give business a tremendous amount of power. Business already has all the power society can allow it to have. It can also be argued that many business leaders lack the perception and skills to deal effectively with social issues. Because many managers think primarily in economic terms, they may have difficulty grasping social concepts, which follow a different set of rules.

Another point of view is that business has no direct lines of accountability to its employees or society. It would be unwise to allow business to participate in activities for which it could not be held accountable. Until society can develop rules that establish direct lines of social accountability from business to public, business must remain uninvolved in social activities and pursue only the goal of profit.

A final point is that the social involvement of business lacks total support among all groups in society. If business should become involved in social matters, dissident parties may create friction, which would inhibit business in the pursuit of its economic objectives. Regardless of the reasons, the fact that there is divided support for social involvement means that business will operate in a somewhat hostile environment.

TREND TOWARD SOCIAL RESPONSIBILITY

The public's attitude toward business has changed. The public is insisting on greater social responsiveness by business and demanding higher business ethics and more responsible business behavior. The change in society's attitudes and expectations is reflected in the socioeconomic model of business. This model views business as a subsystem of society, with a need to satisfy both economic and social relationships. Business activities produce both social and economic outputs. These outputs must be greater than the inputs in order to achieve a net socioeconomic benefit to society. This model views society and business as part of a total system, which makes them dependent upon one another. This dependence requires cooperation by both parties. The model stresses that managers need to make decisions that protect and improve the welfare of society as well as their own interests. The net effect is to enhance the quality of life for society and business.

THE MANAGER'S ROLE IN SOCIAL RESPONSIVENESS

A manager is the main link between an organization and society. Management decisions must relate to the values and expectations of all members of the social system. Managers must interact with a multitude of clients, both inside and outside of the firm. Because each client or group approaches a situation with different values, perceptions, and expectations, managers need to be flexible in order to operate successfully. Managers must take into consideration the fact that value systems differ. They must also consider the political and other power structures in society and the different perceptions and expectations of those outside their organization. Management's role in both economic and social issues is complicated by all of these factors.

Traditionally, management's role has been the effective internal operation of an organization. However, this role has changed significantly with the appearance of social issues in business. Managers must ensure that the organization works in harmony with the environment and with society's expectations. Managers at all levels, as well as every employee in the organization, must become aware of the need to recognize both the social and economic aspects of the business.

The expectations of society and social issues have changed the role of management in two significant ways. The first change is that management has a continually increasing responsibility to treat employees with respect and to provide a better quality of work life. In the past, employees were simply considered an economic resource. Now, business must change its attitude and treat employees as individuals. Business is now seen as being responsible for helping people meet the highest level of their self-actualization needs (Maslow's needs hierarchy, as mentioned earlier). The role of management will become less autocratic and more participative in terms of employee needs. Modern managers are moving away from detailed task prescriptions and moving toward setting goals, which allows employees to operate more freely in the pursuit of their personal goals.

The second change is that management is expected to be effective in social system relationships that are external to the organization. Not only must managers understand micro- and macroeconomics, but they must also understand micro- and macrosocial systems. In a microsocial system, management deals with others from a leadership position of authority, while in a macrosocial system, management operates as an equal. Macrosocial system managers must rely on their problem-solving abilities. Managers will be accepted as leaders only if they can sense society's needs and offer solutions that help meet those needs. The macrosocial system provides a new challenge in terms of management's role. It requires new and different behaviors and presents both new problems and opportunities.

SOCIAL AUDIT

Social audits are voluntary in the United States, but they are required by law in Germany, Norway, France, and Spain. A social audit can identify social issues in which a company should be involved, examine what a company is actually doing in terms of those issues, and determine how well a company is performing. Some think that the social audit should only be used as an internal management tool, while others think that it should be disclosed to the public.

Although many companies are trying to be socially responsible, others still do not recognize the need for commitment to social issues. In explaining why infant mortality deserves attention, Thomas J. Watson, Jr., former CEO of IBM, said, "We've almost forgotten the philosophies of leaders like Roosevelt and other who felt that people at the bottom had to have some sort of net under them."[16] According to Charles Humphrey, instead of revolutionizing society and education, the PC industry has helped widen the gap between the haves and the have-nots. In order to compensate, he feels that the industry should give PCs to poor school districts and provide personnel to teach computer literacy.[17]

The simplest way for a corporation to be socially responsible is to avoid doing anything that it would not want printed in a newspaper. However, corporations should strive for higher levels of social responsibility if they want to do more than merely survive. A code of ethics should be developed and implemented. Corporations should work with the academic community by listening to academia's insights, and the academic community should freely provide information to business. Instead of turning to the government only during hard times, business and government should cooperate all of the time to deal with AIDS, health care, the environment, and other national issues. The key word here is *cooperate*. An adversarial relationship between government and business is worse than no solution at all.

The benefits of corporate social responsibility can be seen in events such as the Tylenol scare. When disaster struck, Johnson & Johnson survived not only because it immediately pulled all Tylenol bottles off the shelves and fully cooperated with authorities and the media, but also because it already had a strong reputation as being socially responsible and had earned the public's trust.

HIRING MANAGERS INTERNATIONALLY

The rationale for hiring international managers is simple. Through advances in travel and communication, the world of business is becoming smaller and smaller. National borders do not indicate what they did in the past. Leading firms that expect to be competitive in world markets must identify strategies to develop managers with an international perspective. **Global employees mobile and skilled** (GEMS) are workers who are multinational, multicultural, multilingual, and multidisciplinary. They are knowledgeable people who have no bias toward anything going on inside of an organization. Companies no longer have to limit themselves to experts within company borders and can now hire workers on an international level with no boundaries.

GEMS are not only used by businesses. Countries have also used these valuable resources. For example, "when the Berlin wall fell, South Africa, suffering a shortage of skilled workers and professionals, recruited tens of thousands of East Germans fleeing to the West," and "when the US realized its shortage of nurses, hospitals recruited qualified Filipino immigrants to fill the gaps."[18] GEMS are key to economic success, and the challenge is for human resource professionals to attract, retain, and invest in them.

DIFFICULTIES FACING MANAGERS WORKING INTERNATIONALLY

Difficulties can be encountered when hiring international managers. First of all, they must obtain passports and work permits. Enrique Ortega, human resource director at Digital Equipment Corporation, says that his primary concern will continue to be hiring the best person for the job, regardless of nationality. The only problem will be the time that it currently takes to get a work permit in Spain.[19]

Another difficulty is finding workers who will be mobile. In 1995 and beyond, professional mobility will fall mainly on university graduates just entering the labor pool. These people have the education and mental flexibility that go along with the desire to learn and gain experience.[19]

Apparently, to blue-collar workers, the social setting in one location is more attractive than career advancement in a different country.

Young graduates who have the desire to learn will also have to be open to differences in culture and language. A nation's culture includes shared knowledge, beliefs, and values, as well as the common modes of behavior and ways of thinking among members of the society. Schemas are categories that develop over time through repeated experiences, and they organize the way an individual views his or her environment. Culture influences individual schemas by determining their nature. Culture also determines the values associated with a schema, as well as the individual characteristics that determine whether a person or situation is placed in a particular category. People usually adopt certain schemas over the years, which makes it difficult for them to relocate to another country. This is especially true of older managers. Young graduates, however, tend to be more flexible.

International diversity is challenging. Culture creates significant differences in the cognitive structures of both managers and employees. These differences may make it difficult to categorize behavior and may thus encourage more controlled search and evaluation for both employees and employers. The typical expatriate manager is expected to perform efficiently immediately upon arrival at a foreign subsidiary. In doing so, the manager relies on automatic information processing prepared by the company or the subsidiary about the new location.

Communication is very important, in particular because misunderstandings often occur due to differences in the way that people express themselves from country to country. The Japanese, for example, distrust Americans who answer a question with a quick reply, which they view as lack of thought. Americans, on the other hand, who are often uncomfortable with silence, respond positively to a quick reply and view the person as being frank and open.

Managers in the international arena have to deal with employees from different cultures. What one culture sees as participative management another views as incompetence. Before undertaking an assignment in a foreign culture, a manager should know how to lead, make decisions, motivate, and control in ways that are appropriate to the cultural environment

In relationship-oriented societies, leaders should show a strong personal interest in employees in ways that are appropriate to a particular geographic area. Managers in Africa, Asia, the Arab world, and Latin America, for example, should use a more personal approach. This might include attending sporting events and birthday parties. In Latin America and China, managers should visit with workers and ask them about such things as morale and their health. Leaders should be especially careful about criticizing others. To many foreigners, loss of self-respect brings dishonor to the individual and his or her family.

In decision making, American employees may discuss a problem and give their recommendation to the boss. German employees, on the other hand, expect the boss to issue specific instructions. The Japanese prefer a bottom-up style of decision making, in which the manager's job is to guide and help employees.

Motivation also differs in each country and must fit within the culture. Employee motivation and the use of rewards depends on the perspective of the individual. It is up to the manager to understand what motivates his or her employees. For example, "an American executive in Japan offered a holiday trip to the top salesperson, but employees were not interested. After the manager realized that Japanese are motivated in groups, he changed the reward to a trip for everyone if together they achieved the sales target—which they did."[20,21]

When things go wrong, managers in foreign countries often find it difficult to terminate employees who do not work out well. The control a manager has over his or her workers in another country is affected by cultural influences. Therefore, managers must sometimes find creative ways of dealing with unproductive employees.

Unfortunately, there is no one solution to managerial success in foreign cultures. Success comes from understanding a culture and tailoring one's management style according to its values. Elvira Glauser, personnel director of Nokia Data, believes that professional mobility is likely to be from north to south.[22] England is given as an example of an area in which there are many professionals and the job market is competitive. Once there is free opportunity, individuals will look toward less developed countries, where there is still a lot to do.

The activities of many companies are global in nature and reflect some aspect of internationalism. These companies, therefore, better preparing their international managers. British Petroleum (BP) implemented Project 1990 to make the transformation from a British multinational to a European company. It located several headquarters in various European cities. The proportion of non-British expatriates to total expatriates increased. Luis Villa, director of human resources and external relations in Spain, said, "We are being urged in countries like Spain, where there hasn't been a tradition of sending people to other units, to prepare people for these assignments...Within two years, we will have achieved career planning which includes international destinations for about 80 percent of the positions within certain levels of the company." The changes in the company also meant changes in training. According to Villa, training in European languages other than English was scheduled to begin in 1991 and BP executives will be required to have an operational knowledge of a host country's language and culture before departure.[22]

Mars, Inc. has an English general manager, a French finance manager, and a Swiss personnel director. Overall, about 10% of the staff comes from foreign countries. In Europe, it is estimated that 20 to 30% of the company's staff members are from other countries. Cross-cultural realities result in cross-cultural training needs. Five times a year, Mars offers a two-day multicultural management course that is led by a Dutch expert. Not only does the course present a structural approach to intercultural and international management, but it also teaches the participants how to identify major differences in values that can lead to problems. After completing the course, participants must describe the stages of culture shock and indicate the actions they would take to minimize its negative effects on both themselves and others.

No criteria have been established to assess what makes a corporation a successful global competitor. An executive taking his or her company into the international realm of business has no guidelines or experience to fall back on. The reason for this may be attributed to the fact that no two global competitors are alike. The possible combinations of management styles, products, markets, strategies, countries, plants, and many other factors are virtually limitless. What works for one corporation may not work for another. "The magic of multinational management lies not so much in perfection of methods or excellence of men as in developing *respect* for other nationalities and cultures and for the *determination* to succeed in foreign markets." This idea, which was proposed more than a decade ago, is a valid today.

Entering the international business world and becoming a multinational corporation can be very complex and difficult. However, it is a move that more and more U.S. firms are going to have to make in the near future in order to remain competitive with foreign multinationals. Thus far, very few U.S. companies have entered the multinational business world; however, those that have, such as IBM, Dow Chemical, Caterpillar, Timex, and General Electric, have realized increases in productivity and profit. Understanding the basic criteria for becoming successful in the global market and studying those firms that have already reached global status will hopefully entice more U.S. companies to venture into the international arena. With increased global technology, especially in the area of communication, the world is becoming smaller every day, and the idea of a global market is very real. U.S. companies with enough initiative to accept the challenge of doing business abroad should have little difficulty becoming multinational corporations if they follow the lead of those firms that have successfully made the move.

INTERNATIONAL IMPLICATIONS

Many companies make huge profits abroad. In doing so, some multinationals ignore many of the health and safety standards set by their host nations. In response to today's environmental and health problems, many groups and host countries are pressuring multinationals to start giving back to society. Responsible multinationals must consider the effects of their actions on an international level.

Success in social responsibility starts with research. In order to be able to succeed overseas, a multinational must research its host nation's culture and beliefs. The ability to communicate in the host country is also a tremendous asset. When both sides can understand what the other wants to accomplish, social responsibility becomes an easier task.

Multinationals have many vague notions about their responsibility to their respective societies. There are three ways that a multinational can reduce the risk of failure in a foreign market: (1) research the culture of the country, (2) educate and properly train the employees, and (3) communicate with the public or government to clarify environmental issues. The friction that stems from issues of social responsibility can be minimized if a company follows these practices.

MORALE

Another important issue in business is morale. How the employees feel about a company affects the company, whether in terms of publicity or increased production. When business does not respond to society's needs, morale is affected, which affects every aspect of the business.

Morale is an important part of management, and it is determined in part by the way managers and administrators relate to the men and women who work for the company. When a corporation communicates a caring attitude, then the basic need for self-esteem is met, as individuals believe that management cares, which translates into positive feelings about the organization, employee loyalty, and increased productivity.[20,23]

Like corporate social responsibility, morale is also difficult to define. It is the feeling that exists within each individual employee in terms of how he or she is treated by the organization as reflected in the work environment. Positive morale grows out of an awareness that every individual in the company is important and that hard work is recognized and appreciated by the company. Unfortunately, however, positive morale is not the norm in most companies. The norm seems to be the feeling that nobody really cares and that individuals and their efforts are completely unappreciated.

The Foundations of Morale

Some of the principles that must form the foundation of any attempt to improve morale are discussed in this section. Managers must first realize that they cannot fool their employees; employees must be told the truth. If employees do not trust their managers, the organization suffers a loss of credibility. When morale is high, there is a high degree of reliability between what the managers say and what the company actually does. This is how trust is built between management and employees. When morale is low, employees feel that the company does not care about them. Morale is resistant to change. When trust has been established, high morale is often resistant to change. In the absence of trust, however, low morale is also resistant to change.

Perhaps the biggest mistake a manager can make is to assume that morale can be improved through material incentives. High morale does result in increased motivation and productivity, but it is not generated by offering more money or better fringe benefits. Managers—not just top managers, but all managers—must realize that they are responsible for morale. Although morale is resistant to change, it is also highly contagious. Employees interact with and influence other employees and thus constantly reinforce each others' views.

When morale is positive, employees tend to stay with a company, whereas when morale is negative, employees look for other jobs, and the best employees are usually the first to leave. High morale is built when employees know that they are valued for their skills and competence. Low morale is built when employees realize that their advancement and importance are based on how long they have been there instead of their skill levels.

Measuring Morale

How is morale measured? Today, a company can hire a consultant to formally evaluate morale, but good managers should be in tune with their employees and should constantly assess their employees' needs and feelings.

One way to measure morale is by listening to employee humor. Positive morale shows up as healthy, upbeat humor, whereas low morale shows up as negative humor. Managers should also be in touch with the informal lines of communication. Every organization has a grapevine, which can be a good indicator of morale.

Managers should also be aware of employee gripes and complaints. Morale can be affected by whether or not employees feel that managers and the company are responsive to their concerns. Valid issues should be addressed promptly.

Managers should examine attrition and absence rates. Low morale is reflected by high attrition rates, as good employees find other jobs, and high absenteeism, which can be caused by stress. When morale is low, sometimes employees just can't face going to work. High morale is reflected by low attrition rates and fewer absences from work.

Improving Morale

There appears to be a special company–employee relationship, because the factors that create high moral are the same factors that are present in every healthy family. Three factors can build morale within a company. The first is a sense of belonging. Employees must feel that they are a valued part of the company. The second is high self-esteem, which fosters high performance. The third is that employees should feel that they have the opportunity to mature and grow both personally and professionally.

Positive morale benefits everyone. When employees feel good about the company, they feel good about themselves, and the benefits can be immeasurable.

According to the modern concept of responsibility, a corporation must continue to broaden its focus and attend to the needs of its stakeholders groups. As stated by Cochran and Wartick, "the roar of the corporate governance issue area is not likely to subside in the near future. Senior management must first understand the issue area and then seek out interactive measures that promote not just their self interests or the interests of their shareholders, but also the interests of the business system and society in general."[24]

The concept of corporate social responsibility may from time to time be affected by various other focuses such as public policy, social responsiveness, or stakeholder management. However, a fundamental challenge for management and business is to define their responsibilities in terms of the constituency groups with which they interact and associate most often.

The companies mentioned in the next section are proof that being responsible makes everyone feel good and can even save a company money. Morale has a major impact on how employees and the community view a company in terms of accepting its responsibilities.

CORPORATE RESPONSIBILITY IN THE INTERNATIONAL MARKET

On December 3, 1984, a chemical leak from a tank at the Union Carbide plant in Bhopal, India killed 2500 people and injured between 30,000 to 40,000 more. Union Carbide formed a crisis management team to deal with the Bhopal incident. The team arranged relief for the victims, an investigation of the accident, and disposal of the remaining chemical at the plant. Union Carbide behaved in Sethi's stage of social obligation.[25] Union Carbide denied guilt by saying that its affiliate in India was responsible, since the Indian government had provided specifications for the building and design of the plant, and everything pertaining to the plant was, therefore, Indian. The Indian government said that Union Carbide was to blame because it had majority ownership in the plant and was responsible for its faulty design. Although Union Carbide claimed that it was not to blame, it tried to make a $350 million settlement with the victims.[26]

The Bhopal case came at a time when the rules for business and corporate international responsibility needed to be reevaluated. Union Carbide Chairman Warren Anderson stated that his firm had a "moral responsibility to provide aid," but denied that Union Carbide was criminally responsible for the accident.[23] The Indian government, on the other hand, stated that full responsibility rested with the multinational and not the local subsidiary. Thus, the Indian government sued only Union Carbide and not the Bhopal subsidiary. The suit argued that "multinationals engaged in hazardous activities are not entitled to the legal shields that usually protect parent companies."[27] Is this notion that a parent company is responsible for its foreign subsidiaries so farfetched? Not according to supporters of social responsibility.

In addition to social responsibility, health and safety standards of multinational corporations at their foreign subsidiaries have also been questioned. In a survey conducted by *Business Week,* 49% of respondents were convinced that multinationals maintain lower health and safety standards at overseas factories.[26] This kind of performance not only damages the image of multinational corporations, but also reinforces the perception that Americans are socially irresponsible on an international level. Such practices as lower safety standards do not represent social responsibility. A company that is truly socially responsible considers the effects of its actions both nationally and internationally.

The Bhopal disaster raised concerns about how multinationals operate around the world, particularly in Third World countries, and prompted inquiries into the health and safety standards of U.S. corporations at their foreign subsidiaries. In an effort to avoid U.S. laws and restrictions, many multinational corporations expand into foreign countries and use legal shields to insulate them from liability at these subsidiaries. These all-too-common actions of multinationals often appear as unethical and unjust. It is time to reevaluate the tendency of multinational corporations to overlook their international social responsibilities. A good way to do so is to take a look at how some companies have been able to show that they are socially responsible.

Socially Responsible Companies

Hyundai Motor.   Hydundai, the Korean automaker, set up a training center in South Central Los Angeles to train high school graduates to become auto mechanics. The training program runs for 18 weeks, after which the graduates are eligible for jobs at any of the seven Hyundai dealerships in the Los Angeles area. One reason why Hyundai started this program was in an effort to improve relations between the black and Korean communities.[28]

Liz Claiborne.   Liz Claiborne is the leading manufacturer of clothes for career women. The company sponsored a community-based project, called "Women's Work," to highlight issues of concern to women. The program involves commissioning works by leading visual artists in San Francisco and prompted Liz Claiborne to fund a 24-hour crisis line for battered women.[28]

Mattel.   Mattel, the second largest toy company, has shown its commitment to urban renewal through an effort to share some of its prosperity with its customers and the community. This commitment has grown even stronger since the riots in Los Angeles. One such project, "Mattel Learning

Centers," focuses on preschool and elementary school children, but provides services to everyone. The centers offer preschool classes for children and programs for their parents. All programs at the Mattel Learning Centers are available to members of the community free of charge.[29]

Pitney Bowes. Pitney Bowes has helped the community in many ways, including affordable housing, adequate health care, and other social services. During the last few years, however, "Pitney Bowes has placed the most emphasis on supporting education because the success of American business in the global marketplace is inextricably bound to the quality of the work force."[30] The company has come to realize that business does not operate in a vacuum. "Conditions in the community, such as large numbers of unskilled people, rising crime rates, substance abuse, and homelessness, challenge a business."[31]

Russell Corporation. Russell manufactures athletic wear and sweatshirts. Instead of laying off staff during a recent downturn, the company focused on cutting costs. One way that they were able to do so was by eliminating all solid waste headed for landfills. For example, Russell spent $100 million on new machinery over five years, which demonstrated their long-term commitment.[28]

Toyota. Toyota, Japan's leading automaker, is helping make dreams come true in run-down American neighborhoods through a program called "Christmas in April," which offers financial and volunteer support. The program is a nonprofit organization dedicated to renovating and repairing homes for the poor, elderly, and handicapped. It now operates in 150 communities. Toyota's support is more than just financial. The company gets many volunteers to participate in these neighborhood projects. For example, in Santa Ana, California, 87 Toyota volunteers renovated the Mercy House Transitional Living Center, a shelter for homeless men. They painted the entire house and installed new windows and floor coverings.[32]

Environmentally Concerned Companies

Many companies whose activities affect the environment are forming what are called "ecoefficient" corporate initiatives. As concern for the environment grows among the public, businesses must expand their efforts to recognize their environmental responsibilities. Consider the following examples.

3M. 3M developed a program called "Pollution Prevention Pays." The goal is to reduce all emissions to "as close to zero as possible." The company estimates that the program has saved $41 million over three years.[33]

Alcoa. Alcoa has developed innovative approaches to restore lands and forests affected by mining operations. The company focused on reestablishing jarrah forest communities in Australia.[32]

AT&T.   AT&T redesigned its circuit board cleaning process to eliminate the use of ozone-depleting chemicals. In addition to preventing environmentally destructive emissions, the company also achieved annual savings of $3 million.[33]

McDonald's.   In 1991, McDonald's launched a Waste Reduction Plan, which is a comprehensive environmental policy that concentrates the company's efforts on reducing the waste generated at its 8500 restaurants and its distribution centers. McDonald's studied ways to reduce, reuse, recycle, and compost materials. The company now uses recycled carryout bags and smaller paper napkins, has eliminated the use of styrofoam containers, recycles all corrugated cardboard, and continues to work on other ways to reduce waste.[33]

Northern Telecom.   Northern Telecom provided the technology to help Mexican industries cut their use of ozone-depleting solvents.[32]

Polaroid.   Polaroid stopped using mercury in its batteries, which were not recyclable. By doing so, the company eliminated environmentally dangerous chemical and created batteries that are recyclable.[33]

S.C. Johnson.   S.C. Johnson implemented an incentive program to encourage suppliers to reduce their packaging and manufacturing waste. The company promotes recycling and reducing waste. "Ignorance in the workplace costs. It reduces productivity and can lead to expensive errors that cost a loss in sales, customer loyalty, and the ability to attract new customers."[32]

CONCLUSION

As the public demands greater corporate social responsiveness, social issues such as equal employment, business ethics, environmental protection, and consumer relations are becoming an important part of corporate decision making. Economic concerns as the primary emphasis of business is a thing of the past. Business must address both social and economic concerns and work to improve the overall quality of life. The traditional approach of waiting for a problem to arise before taking action can only serve to increase society's negative perceptions of business Business must use a portion of its vast resources to meet the ever-increasing economic and social needs of society.

By being more socially responsive, business may also avoid further government regulation. Such regulation limits the freedom of business and in turn limits everyone's freedom. Business must work to avoid blanket government regulations brought on by social pressures. Managers must learn to perceive possible social problems before decisions are made and thereby reduce the risk of government regulation. The concerns of stockholders, as well as stakeholders, must be addressed by business in order to achieve overall efficiency.

Hiring international managers is becoming increasingly important. Good managers are valuable resources. Their technical knowledge and good interpersonal skills represent only the first step in the complex process of being an international manager. Culture also plays a major role when working internationally. Each country and organization has its own culture. Companies are beginning to realize the importance of educating their managers for international work, but true success in managing in foreign countries comes from understanding the cultures and tailoring management styles accordingly.

The future of business depends on its ability and willingness to respond to the changing expectations of society. Companies cannot wait until they are attacked by the public before becoming socially responsible. They must continuously present themselves as being committed to social causes. Those companies that do not get involved in solving social issues will not survive. There are many different views of the future for management. According to Harold M. Schroder, management needs to improve its ability to manage by improving competency in three areas: entry level, basic, and high performance.[15] Entry-level competencies are the individual characteristics, abilities, and skills that new personnel bring to organizations. Basic competencies are the more specialized technical skills. High-performance competencies are the skills related to building and motivating the work group. Schroder feels that if these three areas are improved, managers will be better able to handle the complexities of the future.[15]

As multinational organizations become more global in their operations, a growing trend toward global sensitivity is developing. Although management behaviors are starting to be based on cultural assumptions, there is a need to develop management theories that are effective and functional when applied in multiple settings. Although such theories will be difficult to develop, as people around the world come to know and understand each other better, the task might not be as difficult as expected. A major difficulty, however, is that even though all people have a common need for self-esteem, the behaviors that enhance and promote self-esteem vary significantly from culture to culture.[34]

In speaking about the future, Donna Wood raises some interesting points.[18] One is that management must be able to see opportunities where others see threats and problems. Another is what she calls the input–output view, which means that a company must take on what it needs to meet its objectives, but must also take on something of value to persons or groups external to itself. This helps a firm center its sights on how its actions affect its environment.

REFERENCES

1. Leonard Silk, "The New (Improved) Creed of Social Responsibility," *Business Month,* pp. 109–111, November 1988.
2. Rogene A. Buchholz, "Corporate Responsibility and the Good Society: From Economics to Ecology," *Business Horizons,* 34:19–31, July–August 1991.
3. Archie B. Carroll, "The Pyramid of Corporate Social Responsibility: Toward the Moral Management of Organizational Stakeholders," *Business Horizons,* 34:39–48, July–August 1991.
4. Adam Shell, "The Race to Manage Environmental Risk Is On," *Public Relations Journal,* pp. 6–7, August 1991.
5. Thomas L. Brown, "Doing Good or Doing Well?" *Industry Week,* 242:7, January 4, 1993.
6. Abbass F. Alkhafaji, *A Stakeholder Approach to Corporate Governance* (New York: Quorum Books), 1989.
7. Prakash Sethi, *Up Against the Corporate Wall,* 2nd edition (Englewood Cliffs, N.J.: Prentice-Hall), 1974.
8. Lloyd Dosier and Linda Hamilton, "Social Responsibility and Your Employer," *Personnel Administrator,* pp. 88–91, April 1989.
9. Randall B. Dunham and Jon L. Pierce, *Management* (Glenview, Ill.: Scott, Foresman), 1989.
10. Vernon E. Jordan, Jr., "Corporate Social Responsibility," *The Corporate Board,* pp. 1, 3, July/August 1989.
11. Robert L. Heath and Richard Alan Nelson, *Issues Management: Corporate Public Policymaking in an Information Society* (Beverly Hills, Calif.: Sage), 1986.
12. Christine Gorman, "Listen Here, Mr. Big," *Time,* pp. 40–41, July 3, 1989.
13. Neil W. Chamberlain, *The Union Challenge to Management Control* (New York: Archer Books), 1969.
14. Rafael D. Pagan, Jr., "A New Era of Activism," *The Futurist,* pp. 12–16, May/June 1989.
15. Diane McCue, "Managerial Competence: The Key to Excellence," *The Academy of Management Review,* 15:712–715, October 1990; Milton Friedman, "The Social Responsibility of Business Is to Increase Its Profits," in Tom L. Beauchamp and Norman E. Bowie, *Ethical Theory and Business,* 2nd edition (Englewood Cliffs, N.J.: Prentice-Hall), 1983, p. 81.
16. Edmund Faltermayer, "I Wish There Were a Little More Fear Around," *Fortune,* pp. 32–33, March 26, 1989.
17. Charles Humphrey, "The PC Industry Must Fulfill the Vision of Its Early Years," *PC Week,* p. 90, December 25, 1989.
18. Donna J. Wood, *Business and Society,* 2nd edition (New York: Harper Collins), 1994, pp. 5–37.
19. Phillip M. Rosenzweig and Jitendra V. Singh, "Organizational Environments and the Multinational Enterprise," *The Academy of Management Review,* 16:340–361, April 1991.
20. Rauf R. Khan, "Japanese Management: A Critical Appraisal," in Abbass F. Alkhafaji, *International Management Challenge* (Acton, Mass.: Copley), 1990, p. 27.
21. T.A. Chisholm and P. Krishnakumar, "The Changing Labor Force and the Status of Women in Japan," Association for Global Business Proceedings, Orlando, Fla., 1990, p. 138.
22. Abdalla F. Hayayjneh and Semer Haile, "The Challenge of Diverse Work Force: How to Manage? What Does It Imply for U.S. Global Competitiveness?" *IABD Proceedings,* pp. 344–348, 1993.

23. Ted Gest, Kenneth Sheets, and Ron Taylor, "As Lawyers Move in on India's Tragedy," *U.S. News & World Report,* p. 26, December 24, 1984.
24. T.A. Chisholm and P. Krishnakumar, "The Changing Labor Force and the Status of Women in Japan," Association for Global Business Proceedings, Orlando, Fla., 1990, p. 137.
25. S. Prakash Sethi, "A Conceptual Framework for Environmental Analysis of Social Issues and Evaluation of Business Response Patterns," *Academy of Management Review,* p. 63, January 1979.
26. Stuart Jackson, "Union Carbide's Good Name Takes a Beating," *Business Week,* p. 40, December 31, 1984.
27. William B. Glaberson and William Powell, "India's Bhopal Suit Could Change All the Rules," *Business Week,* p. 38, April 22, 1985.
28. Milton R. Moskowitz, "Company Performance Roundup," *Business and Society Review,* pp. 66–67, 70, 75–76, Fall 1992.
29. David R. Altany, "Urban Renewal: More than a Matter of Money," *Industry Week,* pp. 29–30, January 4, 1993.
30. George B. Harvey, "The Education of American Business," *Business and Society Review,* pp. 62, 63, Fall 1992.
31. Patrick McVeigh, "Ten Top Companies for the 1990s," *Business and Society Review,* pp. 33–34, Spring 1992.
32. Lani Sinclair, "Corporate Environmentalism Makes Good Cents," *Safety & Health,* pp. 76–77, July 1992.
33. J.A. Savage and J.M. Majot, "Industry Preaches Green, But Is Far from Clean," *Business and Society Review,* p. 41, Fall 1992.
34. Robert Doktor, Rosalie Tung, and Mary Von Glinow, "Future Directing for Management Theory Development," *The Academy of Management Review,* 16:362–365, April 1991.

BIBLIOGRAPHY

Carrol, B. Archie, "A Conceptual Model of Corporate Social Performance," Working Paper No. 79-055 (Athens: University of Georgia), 1979.
Davis, Keith, *Human Behavior at Work,* 5th edition (New York: McGraw-Hill), 1977.
Diebold, John, *Making the Future Work* (New York, Simon & Schuster), 1985.
"Music to Their Ears," *Inc.,* p. 112, August 1989.
Siwolop, Sana, "Ethical Investing?" *Financial World,* pp. 86–87, June 27, 1989.

16 BUSINESS ETHICS

ABSTRACT

Business ethics and how it pertains to corporate social responsibility has become an issue of great concern to businessmen and scholars alike in recent history. The last decade has seen a heightened awareness of this and similar issues across society, but the most visible evidence of attention to ethical concerns is manifest in the many changes in corporate policy and decision making. This would indicate that corporate managers are placing greater emphasis on ethical criteria in their strategic planning. This chapter is designed to show that ethics has become, and will continue to be, an important component in every business decision, whether domestic or international. Corporate codes of conduct and education in ethics are both important elements of a successful program aimed at increasing ethical behavior in the workplace. An even more important aspect, however, may be the values of a company's leaders.

CHAPTER OBJECTIVES

1 To show how business ethics has become an important issue in the business arena today

2 To discuss the concept of business ethics domestically and internationally

3 To review the arguments for and against being ethical in an international environment

4 To briefly discuss the theories of business ethics

5 To review the Foreign Corrupt Practices Act of 1977 and the amendments to it

6 To examine cross-cultural negotiation

CASE STUDY
The Issue of Ethics

Ethical issues have been brought to the forefront in Australia as the result of growing public concern. This concern is reflected in business management education at the advanced level in particular. It is also exhibited in the reports of illegal, scandalous, or other questionable behavior and practices across a wide spectrum of commercial and government activities. Economic times in Australia are poor. The vast number of personal, business, and corporate insolvencies in recent times has triggered public demand for an explanation. It has become apparent that illegal and other questionable business practices have contributed significantly to Australia's present economic troubles, and people are asking how such behavior can be prevented in the future. Some believe that the problem can be solved by maintaining higher ethical standards.

Codes of professional conduct or ethics both interact with and complement the law. The law reflects the standards, expectations, and values of a society as a whole and is enforced through the properly constituted courts of that society. It applies to all members of a society equally. Ethical codes of conduct are accepted by narrower common interest groups within a society. Members of these groups believe that they maintain higher expectations and values than those of society as a whole. If ethical codes are enforced at all, it is usually by each specific group. Possible exclusion from a particular association is an incentive to follow these standards.

Peregrine W.F. Whalley, of Northern Territory University, suggests, however, that it is naive to expect people to adhere to rules or principles that are not, and cannot be, clearly formulated. He believes that the business community is too diverse a group to follow standards above and beyond the law itself. The best way to ensure high ethical standards in business is to make legislators aware of and responsive to changing social values and conditions. Common interest groups must become active as lobbyists.

In Australia, certain large retail organizations are taking steps to develop international common interest groups while awaiting changes in legislation. They have had limited success in establishing clear standards for conduct and effective procedures for securing compliance.

Source: Peregrine W.F. Whalley, "Global Business Ethics: A Perspective from Australia," cited in G.R. Bassiry, Marc Jones, and A.F. Alkhafaji, *Business Ethics Around the Globe* (Santa Barbara: California State University), 1992.

INTRODUCTION

The word *ethics* comes from the Greek word *ethos,* which means character. Vincent Barry[1] explains business ethics as a code, where everyone conforms to a norm, which varies from business to business. Rogene A. Bucholz[2] refers to ethics as a conception of right and wrong in relation to human behavior. Ethics can be defined as the planned attempt to follow society's accepted norms, standards, and expectations that ought to govern human conduct and the values worth pursuing in life. Thus, the attempt is systematic and hence goes beyond what each reflective person tends to do in his daily life in making sense of his moral experience, organizing it, and attempting to make it coherent and unified. Ethics concerns itself with human conduct, which is taken here to mean human activity.

Morality is a term used to cover those practices and activities that are considered "right" or "wrong," the rules which govern those activities, and the values that are pursued or followed in operation and practice. The morality of a society is related to its mores (the customs accepted by a society or group as being the right and wrong ways to act) as well as its laws, which add legal prohibitions and sanctions to many activities considered to be immoral.

Business ethics first appeared in the 16th century. Before the 16th century, according to Christian theology, work was a curse and the pursuit of money was not moral. At the time, religion played an important role in society, with strong influence on both individuals and government. Because of the church's view, there was no need for business ethics, so businessmen did what they wanted. The Protestant Revolution paved the way for business ethics by making financial success moral.

A number of factors continue to contribute to the increasing role and importance of ethics in business. Glusman enumerates some of these factors as follows. Practices in the manufacture or representation of goods and services that jeopardize product safety are unethical and will not be tolerated. Companies conducting international business will be subject to different standards of ethical behavior in different countries. Certain practices that might be acceptable in one country might not be ethical in another. Therefore, multinational corporations need to fully understand the environment and expectations of their host countries. In today's global economy, domestic companies will be forced to compete with companies from abroad, and this increased competition will raise ethical issues and considerations.[3]

Economic exploitation of the environment by manufacturers, real estate developers, transportation companies, and a variety of other industries will not be tolerated. Such unethical and illegal activities will receive increasing attention and criticism, forcing companies to consider the environmental impact of business decisions.

In addition, the diversity of the work force will produce a number of ethical challenges for business in the future. These challenges range from equality in hiring, promotion, and compensation to the way businesses provide family benefits in such areas as child care and maternity and paternity leave.[3]

WHY BE ETHICAL?

Why are moral decisions made? In the 18th century, John Wesley said that wealth made a person indifferent to religion. In modern terms, it is social responsibilities that people are indifferent to because of wealth. Milton Friedman said that the individual, as opposed to businesses, should be accountable for social responsibilities. Businesses should make as much money as they can, while operating under their societies' laws. Fletcher Bryon, chairman of Koppers, says the opposite—that businesses have other purposes. For example, because James Burke, CEO of Johnson & Johnson, decided to remove all bottles of Tylenol from store shelves when three people died after using the product, Tylenol gained market share after it was returned to stores.

There are many arguments for and against business ethics. The main argument for is that if management followed good business ethics, there would be no need for government intervention. When the private sector does not maintain adequate ethical standards and/or when it does not respond to new ethical issues, government will continue to intervene by enacting legislation that can result in civil and criminal penalties for unethical practices. The outcome of this legislation will be regulations that have a widespread effect on all industries, from manufacturing, to service, to health care, to transportation.

An argument against business ethics is the free market theory, which states that if the market is left alone and everyone pursues his or her own self-interests, the good of society will follow as the end result. Another argument against is that business operates according to a special set of ethical principles which differ from society's.

THE CODE OF CONDUCT

Without proper communication and implementation, a corporate ethics policy or code of conduct isn't worth the paper it's written on. The code must be more than a document hanging on a wall—it must become ingrained in the corporate culture.[4] Of the five "lessons that can be learned," which were discussed in the February 1988 *Business Roundtable Report on Policy and Practice in Company Conduct,* the first lesson is "the role of top management—commitment, leadership, example." With regard to corporate ethics, no point emerges more clearly than the crucial role of top management. To achieve results, the CEO and those around him or her must be openly and strongly committed to ethical conduct and give constant leadership in tending and renewing the values of the organization.[5] This commitment is communicated in a variety of ways, including speeches, directives, company publications, policy statements, and, most importantly, actions.

The importance of understanding the values and traditions of host countries is essential for doing business overseas. This chapter is designed to help managers evaluate the significance of particular practices in their organizations and how they should be applied in different cultural settings. The importance of developing a code of conduct for all the organizations is discussed, along with certain measures that must be taken when unethical practices are prevalent. This code of conduct must be communicated by top management to all members of the organization, along with their commitment to enforce the code. It is important to make sure that expatriates are aware of the consequences of violating the code of conduct to the company as well as society at large.

REVIEW OF THE LITERATURE

No longer is profit the only justifiable motive for business activity. The notion that ethics is good business was emphasized by Henry Ford in the following comment to a stockholder:

> Business and industry are first and foremost a public service. We are organized to do as much good as we can everywhere for everybody concerned. I do not believe we should make such an awful profit on our cars. A reasonable profit is right, but not too much. It has been my policy to force the price of a car down as fast as production would permit and give the benefit to the users. The result has been surprisingly enormous profits to ourselves.[3]

This statement by Henry Ford represents the growing consensus that good ethics is good business. Although some organizations that appear to have successful operations function on the verge of questionable practices, they are usually based on a short-term focus. A long-term focus is both the best and the only way to go. Doing what is right is its own reward. Ethical behavior builds trust, trust builds confidence, and confidence builds profitable business relationships with customers, suppliers, investors, employees, creditors, and the general public.[6]

John Akers, former chairman of the board of IBM, argues that "business ethics are a key component of our competitiveness as a society."[7] In order to make sure that the atmosphere in which we work is characterized by confidence and mutual trust, an element of ethical instruction should exist. Mr. Akers contends that education in ethics should begin in childhood development and include practical devices as role models and codes of conduct, as well as a thorough study of literature and history. Furthermore, emphasis should be placed on the role of business within a greater hierarchy.

The fundamentals of instruction should begin in kindergarten and not in a school of business administration. A good beginning is to study the past, since our ethical standards are products of our religious, philosophical, and historical inheritance. Knowledge of the past will help to ingrain future ethical conduct. Perhaps the simplest and most powerful ethical support comes from role models such as parents and others who set us straight by example and precept on right and wrong as well as good and evil. Although this "grass roots" instruction is expanded throughout individual development, emphasis is placed on its importance in the early years as a basis for the development of good moral character.

Researcher John Pearce conducted a survey of 131 students majoring in business and discovered that, by a ratio of two to one, they "judged the climate in American business to be essentially unethical."[8] Half of the students believed that their ethical behavior would be compromised at some point in their careers.

For the most part, business ethics courses consist of the *study* of values as opposed to the *teaching* of values. This leaves the student to use his or her own standard of right and wrong when faced with a dilemma. It has been argued that it is too late to teach ethics in college, because values have already been set; however, such courses may still be beneficial in the sense that they create an awareness of the reasons that underlie moral principles. They may also be helpful in fostering the ability to reason when applying these principles to situations. A growing factor in the process of making ethics work is implementation. Emphasis on education and training in corporate ethics is considered by many organizations to be a vital part of ensuring compliance with company standards for conduct.

Some research on the effectiveness of teaching business ethics points to the contrary, however, and suggests that there is a decline in the ethical standards of students. Those students who are business majors are more accepting of questionable business practices than those who are nonbusiness majors. Also, students who have had courses in business ethics display the same or a greater tendency. These results are attributed to the sympathy directed toward those who face difficult ethical dilemmas. This theory is given further merit by Harvard professor Pat Burr, who, after teaching business ethics for years, concluded that his students were no more moral for it.[8]

Ethics workshops and training courses are just two forms of continuing education that may help employees find answers to difficult ethical issues. These forums can also serve to initiate ongoing processes for airing and resolving ethical issues as they arise. The overall result of these workshops and training sessions would be to enhance one's sense of pride in being part of an ethical organization.

Ethics codes are more than just rules and regulations; they embody basic values and epitomize corporate culture.[4] The most significant benefit of having an ethics code is its ability to set a highly responsible tone for the organization. In the long-term focus, higher ethical standards may translate into higher profits.

An important aspect of an organization communicating its commitment to its employees is the issuance of a corporate code of ethics. In a recent Conference Board survey, 80% of American and Canadian companies that responded (a total of 264 firms) indicated that they have such a code.[9]

There are, however, an alarming number of American managers who believe that almost anything written is a code. A number of the 238 codes in the Conference Board's Watson Library confirm this point. Some of these codes of conduct are merely conflict of interest statements. Although such statements are relevant to a company's ethical policy, they do not constitute a code of ethics as the term is understood, and when they are broadly stated, employees are able to dismiss them as cosmetic. Although no code will cover all situations, some form of written document that sets forth principles of conduct for the whole organization will serve to help and guide the judgments and consciences of employees as they make specific decisions. It is also important that these codes communicate clear expectations.

PHILOSOPHICAL BASIS FOR ETHICAL REASONING

Four groups of ethical theories are addressed in the literature: (1) consequential or teleological theory, (2) nonconsequential or deontological theory, (3) various hybrid theories, and (4) ethical relativism. The first two of these theories have been widely considered and have had a significant influence on world affairs.[10]

Utilitarianism is the name given to one approach to making decisions on ethical matters. This form of reasoning presupposes one overriding moral principle that serves as the criterion for ethical judgment: the greatest good for the greatest number. Utilitarianism is an ethical theory which holds that an action is right if it produces, or if it tends to produce, the greatest amount of good for the greatest number of people affected by the action. Utilitarianism adopts a teleological approach to ethics and claims that actions are to be judged by their consequences. According to this view, actions are not good or bad in themselves. Actions take on moral value only when considered in conjunction with the effects that follow from them. Actions by themselves have no intrinsic value. They are simply means to attain things which do have value.

The argument based on the utilitarian benefits that free markets provide to society was presented by Adam Smith in the 18th century. The idea is that the free market system with its private property will be able to generate greater benefits than any other of the tied market systems. Smith maintained that in a system with free markets and private property, buyers will seek to purchase what they want at the lowest price they can find. It will therefore behoove private businesses to produce and sell what consumers want and to do so at the lowest possible price. To keep the price down, private businesses will try to cut back on the costly resources they consume. Thus, the free market, coupled with private property, ensures that the economy is producing what consumers want, that prices are at the lowest levels possible, and that resources are efficiently used. The economic utility of society's members is thereby maximized.[10] Individuals using this approach compare the relative merits of various alternatives and select the one that promises the best results. However, in doing so, they think not merely of themselves, but act in a manner so as to maximize the amount of good done to all. In corporate/business situations, this approach would require a company to pursue not only its own benefits but the general welfare of anyone who may have an interest in, or be affected by, the company's decisions.[10]

While utilitarians measure the worth of an act or decision by its consequences, formalists measure ethical acceptability on the basis of the motives of the act. Supporters of this approach are not directly interested in the consequences or in comparing alternatives; instead, they inquire whether there is something about the action itself that could either recommend it or disallow it. Therefore, they decide on the ethical acceptability of a course of action by establishing whether such action can be consistently undertaken without disrupting the institutions upon which their own success depends. Applying this concept to ethics in an organizational context produces a system of principles or rules that "maps out" acceptable behaviors and leads to a collection of consistent and clear rules capable of resolving most disputes.[10]

The conclusion here is that while it is unlikely that a particular culture would choose one approach to ethical analysis over the other in all situations, it is possible that different cultures will exhibit varying degrees of predisposition toward one approach or the other. Consequently, countries would also differ in their use of the criteria applied for determining the ethical acceptability of an action or behavior.

ETHICAL ASPECTS OF FREE MARKET SYSTEMS

Although there is no free competition in the marketplace, the issue of competition is still the most important element that can be used to distinguish between the free market and the command market. Thus, the ethical aspects of competition could be used to explain the case of free market ethics for several reasons. Competition is supposed to be a mechanism for the free market production and distribution of goods and services that people want. Competition in the economic order has supported and furthered rivalry as an essential cultural characteristic of a free market society. Most activities of the free market can be viewed as a competitive contest in which people engage to provide products and services for a profit, as has been noted by many researchers.[11]

The Main Sources of Free Market Ethics

In addition to the economic nature of the free market system, there are some roots to ethics in such a market. Three widely accepted sources of ethics in a free market are market ethics, the Protestant ethic, and the liberty ethic. These three ethics set the stage for the Industrial Revolution and the accompanying growth in business. During this period, the industrial capitalist was allowed to run free—to build giant corporations, exploit workers, and engage in fiercely competitive practices for profit and economic expansion.

Market Ethics

The ethics of the free market system were set through the writings of Adam Smith. In *The Wealth of Nations,* Smith's message was in tune with a growing number of would-be entrepreneurs seeking academic rationalization for their views. England thus found in Smith's writings a market ethic—an economic sanction for the private initiative rather than mercantilism, competition rather than protection, innovation rather than economic stagnation, and self-interest rather than state interest—as a motivating force.[12]

The Protestant Ethic

In *The Protestant Ethic and the Spirit of Capitalism,* Max Weber set forth a connection between the Protestant ethic and capitalism. The Protestant ethic, sometimes called the work ethic, had its beginning in biblical times. Saint Paul stated, "If any one will not work, let him not eat." Martin Luther later provided additional religious sanction for work and achievement. There is, however, another widely held point of view of the Protestant work ethic, as stated by Rogene Buchholz:

> The Protestant ethic not only had behavioral implications, as Weber and others have pointed out; it also had ideological implications in providing a moral legitimacy for capitalism. As an ideology, the Protestant ethic served to legitimize the capitalism system by providing a moral justification for the pursuit of profit and distribution of income that are a part of the system.[13]

The Liberty Ethic

According to the writings of John Locke, "the liberty ethic placed man in a participatory role in government, encouraged private property, discouraged rule by dictatorial whims, and introduced more freedom and individualism in all spheres of life." The liberty ethic has encouraged the rise and applicability of the other two types of ethics. As Carroll stated: "The postulates of economic freedom (the market ethic) and the sanctions of individual rewards for worldly efforts (the Protestant ethic) can operate freely only in a political system that is conducive to individual liberty."[11]

Business Competition as a Game

According to Henderson, "Ethics in the broadcast sense provides the basic condition of acceptance for any activity. The ethics of a game or sport both implies its purpose and specifies rules of fair play."[14] In the same vein, Carr argued that the ethics of business is the ethics of a game, which is different from the ethics of religion or society, since business has its own characteristics as a game—a game that demands both a special strategy and an understanding of its special ethics.

Furthermore, Carr considered the business game as a poker game, in which certain rules govern the ethical behavior of managers within a company. The rules of the business game are the federal or state laws and the strategies within these laws that constitute the atmosphere of business behavior. Consequently, business should have the right to follow any approach to achieve its objectives within this atmosphere, regardless of the approach used, since no violation of the rules of the game occurs, as in the case of poker.[15]

However, according to LaCroix, there are three parallels between poker and business strategy: in the option to enter the game, in the demand to interpret, and in the resultant uncertainty in the mind of the opponent.[16] These similarities between business and poker might be clearly observed in bidding strategy which implies inverted signaling intended to create uncertainty in the mislead opponents. Hence, in poker, one correctly distrusts others, ignores claims of friendship, and knows that cunning, deception, and concealment of strengths, weaknesses, and intentions are vital.

Carr's concept attracted many business leaders. One executive, who cited several examples that support Carr's idea, concluded:

> What is universal about these examples is that these managers, each functioning on a different corporate level, are concerned with one thing—getting the job done. Most companies give numerous awards for achievement and accomplishment, for sales, for growth, for longevity and loyalty, but there are no medals in the business world for honesty, compassion or truthfulness.[17]

Carr's view has been questioned from various aspects.[1] Some argue that the comparison of business to poker is unfair and inaccurate in that business is too important an area of human endeavor to be regarded as a game. Others consider the idea to condone unethical business practices and say that a business executive cannot separate the ethics of his or her business from the ethics of his or her home life. With regard to the parallels which have been considered between business and poker, some argue that the argument, by analogy of course, does not demand complete parallels. All decisions may be decisions of strategy, but not all decisions need be in terms of a noncooperative zero-sum game. In business, one could participate as one of a group, or even as one of a society, and a cooperative solution, as defined, means that the individual player can gain more by cooperation than he or she could by going it alone. Finally, Carr's idea does not point out that if business fails to raise the moral level of its practices, it invites eventual reprisals from the public and government.[1]

The conclusion here is that the free market system has two major objectives: to produce the goods and services that consumers want and to distribute the outcome of the production process among those who participate in the process. Each of these objectives has at least one main criterion for evaluation. The main criterion for the production function should be efficiency, which means to produce goods of high quality at a low cost. The main criterion for the distribution function should be justice.

If each criterion is applied to its relevant function, one might say that, from the production point of view, the free market system is still the most efficient system in the world as compared to other systems, such as a command system or mixed economy system. However, no system can have a full degree of efficiency. However, from the disruption of outcome, the free market system fails to fit the criterion of justice among groups of society; rather, it creates a large job of the inequality situation compared to other market systems.

BUSINESS ETHICS IN AN INTERNATIONAL SETTING

Ethics is especially important for companies operating overseas. Very little has been written about business ethics in a cross-cultural environment. Although certain ethical values and traditions are the same in various countries, they are practiced differently. These differences in practicing certain ethical values create difficulties among managers of multinational corporations when dealing with other countries. As more corporations move into the global arena, dilemmas related to ethical values and traditions are becoming increasingly common. Scant attention has been given to understanding the differences in the processes used by people in different cultures to evaluate ethical situations. In 1987, Adler confirmed that differences in cognitive process and values are a good starting point for understanding intercultural differences. The issue of business ethics across cultures is difficult to address because it must deal with understanding how individuals from different cultures approach ethical issues and

CASE STUDY
Ethical Perceptions

Business ethics is a compelling issue in countries other than the United States. Studies on this topic over the past 30 years have focused mainly on Western countries. More recent studies have focused on other parts of the world. In an article entitled "Ethical Perceptions of Malaysian Managers," Md Zabid Abdul Rashid and Iskandar Abduallah discuss ethics in Malaysia. Some of the issues that arise in Malaysia deal with mismanagement, fraud, cheating, and criminal breach of trust. From 1973 to 1987, the number of such cases tripled, from 1160 to 4080. Because of these findings, a study was undertaken to research the ethical values of Malaysian managers.

The study was conducted by distributing surveys to 252 managers from different countries, but mainly Malaysia and China. Of the 252 surveys distributed, 63 managers completed and returned their questionnaires. Differences found in ethical decisions varied with job position, job specialization, ethnic group, age, and salary. The managers were presented with examples of unethical situations, such as favoritism in granting loans, falsifying reports, and calling in sick. One interesting aspect was the difference in attitude between US. and Hong Kong personnel; 77% of U.S. personnel said that they would report a defective or unsafe product, compared to 50% of Hong Kong respondents.

In short, the survey found that managers participated in or approved of four unethical situations: obtaining competitor information, false advertising, and giving out confidential information. Another finding was that ethical standards were lower at the time of the study than 15 years earlier. The most influential factor that affected the unethical behavior of Malaysian managers seemed to stem from the behavior of their superiors.

Source: Md Zabid Abdul Rashid and Iskandar Abduallah, "Ethical Perceptions of Malaysian Managers," cited in G.R. Bassiry, Marc Jones, and A.F. Alkhafaji, *Business Ethics Around the Globe* (Santa Barbara: California State University), 1992.

---

how differences in their approach affect the criteria by which they judge the ethical acceptability of a situation.

Many multinational corporations have developed codes of conduct to help their employees deal with different value settings. However, a 1988 study of 202 corporate codes of ethics indicated some discouraging news. The codes dealt with broad corporate relations with the U.S. government, in particular political contributions, foreign government bribes, and the integrity of financial records. They rarely covered specific ethical positions on a significant number of issues.[18] The above-mentioned study also revealed that about two-thirds of the companies surveyed did not discuss antitrust violations or product quality and safety.

THE FOREIGN CORRUPT PRACTICES ACT OF 1977*

The Foreign Corrupt Practices Act of 1977 (FCPA), established by the Securities Exchange Commission (SEC), made it illegal for American companies to make certain payments to foreign officials and other foreign persons when doing business overseas. The FCPA was aimed at eliminating questionable or unethical payments to foreign officials by American businesses in order to obtain or retain business in overseas markets. Since its inception, the FCPA has caused a furor throughout American-based multinational corporations. Its supporters feel that it is an essential step toward honest international trade. Its opponents believe that it severely hurts opportunities abroad. Almost everyone, however, agrees that the act contained numerous ambiguities and did not clearly define what constitutes an illegal payment. In the summer of 1988, after years of debate, modifications were made to the law by way of the Omnibus Trade Bill, which was signed by President Ronald Reagan on August 23.

Origin of the FCPA

Prior to 1977, the SEC developed a voluntary disclosure program that would enable discovery of how much liberty American corporations had taken in extending overseas payments. The voluntary disclosure enabled firms to report questionable domestic and foreign payments and accounting practices to the SEC. In addition to action by the SEC, the Justice Department could bring antitrust and fraud prosecution. The aim was to protect the shareholders and their right to full disclosure of "material" information. Materiality, in this context, is defined in three ways: (1) the payment itself is large; (2) the payment is not necessarily large but is related to a large transaction(s), or the deal is an important part of a firm's total operations; and (3) the payment reflects a lack of integrity by top management in setting up overseas slush funds.

The FCPA was passed by Congress after months of almost daily revelations that some of the biggest American corporations had been involved in bribery abroad for many years. In 1977, the SEC, through its voluntary disclosure plan, cited 527 U.S. companies for bribes and other dubious payments to win foreign contracts between 1960 and 1977. The following list[19] reveals the largest amounts uncovered by the SEC:

---

*Information in this section was taken from Richard David Ramsey and Abbass F. Alkhafaji, "Foreign Corrupt Practices Act," as quoted in Abbass F. Alkhafaji, *International Management* (Acton, Mass.: Copley), 1990.

Company	Total payment ($ million)
Exxon	59.4
Lockheed	55.0
Boeing	50.4
General Tire and Rubber	41.3
Northrop	34.3
Beatrice Foods	26.5
R.J. Reynolds	24.6

The Lockheed payments had a severe impact on the governments of Italy, Japan, and the Netherlands. President Jimmy Carter termed such actions "ethically repugnant." Congress considered the payments "bad business" and "unnecessary." Merely pointing out the problem, however, was ineffective. Congress heard extensive testimony that more legislative direction was needed on the subject of bribery and that accounting requirements in then-contemporary law were inadequate. More subjectively, post-Watergate morality, typical of the mid-1970s, led to the development of the FCPA.[20]

Contents of the FCPA

The FCPA is divided into three major sections (an introductory section [101] simply names the act). The first major section (102) is entitled "Accounting Standards." It mandates accounting standards for firms that report to the SEC. Section 102 of the FCPA amends Section 13 of the 1934 Securities Exchange Act to ensure that every publicly held company institutes internal accounting controls to prove that all transactions are made in accordance with management's specific authorization and are fairly represented in detail. Some consider this section of the FCPA to be the most important change in securities exchange legislation since 1934.[21]

The second major section (103) of the FCPA is entitled "Foreign Corrupt Practices by Issuers." It amends Section 30 of the Securities Exchange Act of 1934 and makes illegal any bribe or gift from an American company or any foreign official, political candidate, or party if the company is registered as an issuer with the SEC. All extensions of a company can be held criminally liable, including officers, directors, shareholders, and employees. Further, parent companies are responsible for the actions of their foreign subsidiaries. No actual payment is required to trigger the law; promises are substantial evidence to indict a firm.

The third section (104), "Foreign Corrupt Practices by Domestic Concerns," extends the restrictions in Section 104 to all domestic concerns, including those not registered with the SEC.

The law excludes from the definition of "foreign official" any foreign employee "whose duties are essentially ministerial or clerical." Thus, payments can be made in order to expedite nondiscretionary official actions. This type of facilitating expenditure is commonly referred to as a "grease" payment and is typically used for such matters as quick customs clearance. According to Michael V. Seitzinger, a legislative attorney for the American Law Division of the Congressional Research Service, the "legislative history" of the FCPA indicates that Congress did not intend for the law to cover grease payments.[22] Nonetheless, a common criticism is that the issue could have been more squarely addressed in the FCPA itself.

Arguments Pro and Con

Proponents of the bill share an obvious argument: bribery is unethical behavior, and thus the bill is essential for maintaining a code of ethics in the international market. This attitude is apparent in the following statement by Ray Garcia, vice president of the Emergency Committee for American Trade:

> The U.S. acting alone cannot end international bribery....[The FCPA] is a strong statement which shows our trading partners we are serious enough to take unilateral action;...it should help pave the way toward an internation treaty.[23]

Additionally, others find that the requirements of the bill sharpen the difference between right and wrong, so that there is less latitude for interpretation in decision making. Kieso and Weygandt, for example, authors of a highly respected accounting textbook, aver that the "legislation provides guidance to accountants who, prior to this legislation, often were forced to make their own moral judgments on these questions"[24] Big Eight accounting firms have consequently shown considerable interest in the legislation (Arthur Andersen,[25] Deloitte Haskins and Sells,[26] Coopers & Lybrand[27]). An additional argument is that as a superpower, the United States cannot harbor corporations that engage in distasteful practices without suffering adverse effects on American foreign policy and, therefore, on the best interests of free societies, which the United States epitomizes. Animating this argument is a feeling that foreign buyers need to be impressed with the overall integrity of things American. An additional benefit is that the FCPA makes all American corporations, whether scrupulous or not, play by the same rules.[28]

Others, however, disagree. The complaints of opponents of the FCPA are accurately summarized in the title of a 1982 article: "Confusion and Lost Sales Are the Payoffs from Foreign Bribery Act."[29] These complaints run the gamut from objections over simple ambiguities in the FCPA to feelings that the FCPA considerably limits opportunities for U.S. companies to compete abroad.

Most businesspeople agree that the FCPA, as originally signed into law, is too vague. There is no clear distinction between legal grease payments and illegal bribes. The FCPA excludes from the definition of foreign official "any department, agency, or instrument thereof whose duties are essentially ministerial or clerical," but fails to explain how, for example, a Minister of Commerce for a foreign government could avoid having essentially ministerial duties. Another common argument against the FCPA is that when an enterprise operates in a foreign country, proper procedure is to follow the customs and values of that country. Thus, if bribery is an accepted part of the culture of the host country, then a multinational enterprise is obliged to operate in this manner.[30] In other words, this argument posits that the FCPA projects U.S. sovereignty beyond the 12-mile limit; consequently, the FCPA seems to say that what is illegal in the United States becomes illegal for a U.S. corporation outside the United States, irrespective of the sovereignty of the government where the corporation operates. In the apt phraseology of Seitzinger, who has no ax to grind on the subject, a "frequent criticism of the 1977 Act was that the United States was more interested in exporting its cultural biases than its products."[22]

It is unclear whether or not the FCPA has substantially harmed U.S.-based multinational corporations. Several studies were completed by both sides, and the results generally support the views of the researchers or respondents involved in the study. Ball and McColloch[31] summarized several of these studies. For example, studies done by the SEC in 1976 and by a university professor in 1977–78 indicated that the FCPA would not hinder the ability of American businesses to compete abroad; however, a task force established by the Reagan White House to examine the FCPA estimated an annual cost of $1 billion in business lost abroad. In a 1983 Harris poll, nearly 70% of the executives questioned thought that the law was detrimental; 68% believed that detailed record-keeping should be reduced.[32] Similar results were reported by Kim[33] in a survey of *Fortune* 500 executives.

These results demonstrate the illusory nature of statistics. Gillespie also found such studies to be inconclusive and noted, among other things, the difficulty of drawing permanent conclusions in a time of "evolving social changes."[34] In an analysis perhaps both cynical and perceptive, Thomas found that the FCPA bolsters a sense of ethics but that "people with high ethical standards probably cannot be terribly successful in those kinds of environments."[35] Possibly no one will disagree that, at a minimum, the FCPA serves to keep honest people honest.

Specific Applications of the FCPA

Abbott Laboratories bid on a contract to supply baby formula to an African nation. The contract, however, went to a Dutch company, whose $2.5 million bid was higher than Abbott's. When asked about the incident, David W. Ortlieb, president of Abbott's international division, responded:

> Our representatives said we could have gotten the contract if we had paid a fee the United States now regards as an improper payment. We didn't—so there was no sale.[19]

A top executive of an international construction firm based in the United States adds the following remark:

> Our hands are tied...The lion's share of the construction jobs in the Persian Gulf, for instance, is now going to Korean and European companies, and payoffs have to be a major factor.[19]

In 1978, both Dow Chemical Company and Union Carbide Corporation withdrew from enormous deals after realizing that bribes would have to be paid.[19] These are only several examples of how the FCPA has influenced U.S.-based multinational corporations. Such incidents occur so regularly that Marvin Stone[36] writes:

> [Americans] see U.S. firms losing billions of dollars worth of sales abroad because they can't make payments that foreigners demand. The business they lose is going to foreign firms that are willing and able to make such payments. The American share of world markets is decreasing, and the U.S. trade balance is suffering as a result.

It is an unfortunate dilemma when one must choose between contributing to the disturbing U.S. trade deficit and doing something that is by U.S. standards both unethical and illegal.

A further complication brought on by the FCPA is that its requirements were a particular problem to small business in the international arena.[37] Large multinationals can do a variety of things: they can shuffle illegal practices so far off into the jungles and so far down in the accounting system that they will probably never be detected, they can accomplish the unethical through fly-by-night intermediary companies, and on and on. In the words of Jacoby et al., "the practice of making political payments has not been eliminated[;] ...it has merely been transferred to non-U.S. hands."[38]

Amendments to the FCPA

An attempt to reform the FCPA was made amid heated debate. The result was the Foreign Corrupt Practices Act Amendments of 1988 (FCPA 1988). This piece of legislation is Title V (Sections 5001, 5002, and 5003) in the Omnibus Trade and Competitiveness Act of 1988. It was signed into law by President Reagan on August 23, 1988, when he signed the overall bill, commonly known as the Omnibus Trade Bill. (An earlier version of the bill had been vetoed by the President, who objected to its inclusion of a requirement that management give 60 days' notice before invoking massive layoffs or closing a factory; this provision was then taken out of the vetoed bill and later passed as a separate bill, which the President allowed to became law without his signature.) For background on the Omnibus Trade Bill, see "After Three Years, Trade Bill Finally Clears."[39]

The 1988 Omnibus Trade Bill amended the FCPA as follows (see "Provisions of the Omnibus Trade Bill,"[40] p. 2221; for the full text of the Foreign Corrupt Practices Act Amendments, see Seitzinger,[22] pp. 10–14):

- The reason-to-know standard is modified so that criminal liability for circumventing the accounting requirements applies only to individuals who "knowingly" engaged in or tolerated such circumvention.

- The amount of detail required in record-keeping by a firm or its foreign subsidiary is defined as "such level of detail and degree of assurance as would satisfy prudent officials in the conduct of their own affairs." This change would seem to neutralize, at least in part, the complaint that the original FCPA favored large businesses, to which the accounting overhead was less of a burden than to small businesses.

- Criminal liability for illegal payments is limited to situations in which the payer knows or has reason to know that the payment would be used for illegal purposes.

- Grease payments are permitted.

- A payment is defined as illegal if it is intended to encourage a foreign official to act in a way incompatible with the official's legal duty (the official's "routine governmental action").

- The fact that a payment, although illegal in the United States, is legal in the country where it is made can be admitted as legal defense for the payment.

- Individuals can be prosecuted for violations even if the firm is not guilty.

- Penalties for violations are raised from $1 million to $2 million for firms and from $10,000 to $100,000 for individuals. Imprisonment is retained at five years. A new civil penalty of $10,000 is enacted.

Like many compromises, the 1988 modification to the FCPA has critics on both sides. The changes make the FCPA clearer and less onerous to U.S.-based multinational corporations, but do not accomplish what many want—to be disencumbered of the FCPA altogether.

The original designers of the FCPA had high hopes that it would lead the parade toward more pronounced ethics in multinational commerce. So far, however, the U.S. remains distinct in having such legislation, and no treaties are in sight. Although the 1988 Omnibus Trade Bill must, on balance, be viewed as a concession to business and as a general improvement in the specificity of language, the arguments pro and con remain virtually as they were in 1977. The FCPA promises to continue as a hotly debated topic in managerial and political circles for many years to come.

NEGOTIATING ACROSS CULTURES

International business negotiations face enormous cultural barriers, as illustrated by the difficulties that Westerners have had in negotiating business agreements with other cultures. When people from two different countries of origin try to negotiate on political or commercial issues, they have to understand and acknowledge any ethical dilemmas that might

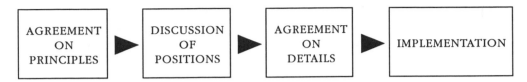

FIGURE 16.1 The Linear Model of Negotiation[16]

occur. These standards of conduct and moral judgment on any issue are the basis for deciding the outcome. One negotiator might misinterpret the message and views of another, which can cause an argument and create distrust. Basic concepts are fairness, dependability, friendship, and timeliness.

There are two models of negotiating, as presented by Solomon[41] and Bertrand:[42] the linear model, which relates to Chinese culture, and the encompassing model, which is said to be more descriptive.

The first stage of the linear model (Figure 16.1) is the discussion of **principles** or broad goals. In the culture of China, this stage is emphasized so that foreigners understand the commitments they make. The second stage deals with bargaining **positions**, or what each has to offer and wants to obtain. The third stage clarifies **details**. The fourth and final stage is **implementing** the process.

The encompassing model (Figure 16.2) includes the same stages but emphasizes the degree to which each stage is presented. The Chinese base their negotiations on enhancing their national goals, which include promoting national development, growth, and enhancement of life in China. The Chinese expect Western firms to sacrifice their goals if necessary in order that the Chinese may achieve their goals.

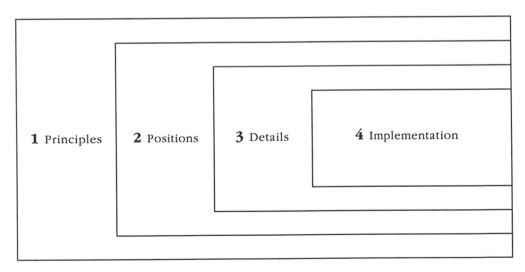

FIGURE 16.2 The Encompassing Model of Negotiation[16]

Western firms base their negotiations on such corporate goals as product quality, profit, and enhancing shareholder value. Sacrificing corporate goals would deny corporate responsibility, which is the main reason for negotiating.

Cultural barriers present ethical dilemmas in negotiating between cultures. Misinterpreted messages and views can create arguments and feelings of betrayal between participants. A particular problem may never be resolved, but it should at least be recognized during the process of negotiation.[43]

ETHICAL ISSUES

We would all like to believe that honesty is the best policy, that good triumphs over evil, that the man or woman with a reputation for fair dealings will prosper, and that those who maximize profit are perfectly honest. However, there are probably more examples where the opposite is true.

Moralists talk about how E.F. Hutton was brought down for check kiting or how Exxon promised that an oil spill was unlikely and that if one did occur, it could be controlled within hours. Then the Valdez spilled 260,000 barrels of oil, which Exxon could not clean up. These are two examples where punishment was imposed, but there are many instances where deceit is rewarded.

Suppose a vendor ships you 90 cases of widgets but bills you for 100. You would probably insist on credit. But what if 100 cases were shipped and you were billed for 90. Would you bring this error to the company's attention or would you rationalize that the company is so large that they'll never miss the money? What if a former co-worker goes to work for another company where he has access to proprietary or confidential information and offers this information to you? Providing insider information is illegal.

Ethical principles are derived from two major theories: the teleological and the deontological. They differ in their approach to determining the moral right or wrong of an action. Although they are not specific to business, they can be applied to business ethics. The **teleological theory** encompasses the idea of utility. Utility is defined as the capacity of an action to produce the greatest amount of good for the greatest number of people. Because happiness and pain cannot be measured, this theory is very difficult to apply. The theory seems to say the end justifies the means. The **deontological theory** embraces common elements. It focuses on right and wrong in terms of the act, regardless of outcome. The value of an act is in the motive. Right or wrong is determined on the basis of duty, honesty, and fairness.

A number of events have caused Americans to distrust big business. Watergate and political kickbacks in a number foreign countries added to the negative perceptions. Polls indicate that public confidence in heads of corporation is as low as 15% and that the general public and business executives see a decline in ethical behavior in the United States.[44] Recent scandals such as insider trading, Watergate, payments to foreign officials, and catastrophic industrial accidents have drawn public attention to business practices. Such shocking incidents have caused the public to distrust business, and stakeholders are demanding reform—no matter what the cost. Business in the United States has a somewhat different view of ethics. While business has attempted to address the issue of ethics, the overriding emphasis is still on profit and continued growth, and the cost of enforcing ethical practices is a matter of concern.

Gerald Cananary cites what he believes are the reasons for unethical behavior: immediate gratification, self-fulfillment, and short-term return.[1] Managers are caught between meeting corporate goals for growth and profit and how to do so ethically.

Individuals new to an organization are governed by corporate norms. By the time someone reaches the top, he or she is well entrenched in the norms of the organization. It seems to be a world where treachery pays, power is abused, and dishonesty is tolerated. According to Bhide and Stevenson, "The moral advantages are simple. Concepts of trust and more broadly of virtue would be empty if bad faith and wickedness were not financially rewarding. If wealth naturally followed straight dealings we would only need to speak about conflicts between the long term and the short, stupidity and wisdom, high discount rates and low. We would worry only about others' good sense, not about their integrity. It is the very absence of predictable financial reward that makes honesty a moral quality we hold dear."[45]

Power has the ability to do both great harm and tremendous good. People do business with someone they do not trust if it suits their purpose or accept a deal because it is too good to pass up. Sometimes the powerful leave others no choice but to play ball. Ethical questions fall into gray areas, and because competition has intensified, it seems plausible that more individuals will be pressured into seeing how far they can stretch the rules. Therefore, it is probably a good idea to ask the following questions when making any decision: Is it fair? Will I feel good about it?

To quote Ivan Boesky, "Greed is all right, by the way. I want you to know that. I think greed is healthy. You can be greedy and still feel good about yourself." Mr. Boesky was feeling very good about himself, and then he was indicted for insider trading. Insider trading is the use of confidential information, not available to the general public, to make capital gains in the market. Boesky cut a deal with the SEC. In exchange for allowing the SEC to tap his phone for two months, and testifying against any individuals or firms indicted as a result of the conversations, he agreed to put $50 million in escrow for the benefit of investors hurt by his illegal trading. He also agreed to pay the U.S. Treasury a $50 million fine. He was barred from the investment business in the United States for life and faced a five-year jail term. He was also permitted to dump $440 million of his portfolio onto the market before the SEC went public with his indictment.[45]

Insider trading can happen anywhere, as evidenced by FNB Corporation of western Pennsylvania. FNB of Hermitage went through a year-long probe by the SEC on charges of alleged insider trading tied to its acquisition of New Castle based Dollar Savings Association. Although a special panel of FNB's board found nothing wrong, the SEC charged Ernest W. Swanson, then a FNB director, with tipping off two friends on October 10, 1989 to ongoing merger negotiations between FNB and Dollar Savings.

In the next eight days, W.J. Johnston and D. Stoudt proceeded to buy 1400 and 600 shares, respectively. When the merger agreement was announced on October 26, Dollar's stock went up $3.00, resulting in profits of $3250 and $1000. Then, on August 14, 1990, Swanson learned that FNB planned to sue Dollar to call off the merger. He passed this information on to Johnston, who sold his shares the next morning. At noon, FNB announced its lawsuit and the stock fell $6.00. Mr. Johnston avoided losses of $8400. The merger was completed after Dollar agreed to lower the purchase price.

Without admitting wrongdoing, the three men consented to a federal court injunction prohibiting them from violating securities laws in the future. Swanson paid a fine of $12,650. Johnston agreed to pay $11,650 in disgorged profits and to make up losses avoided plus a penalty in the same amount. Stoudt gave up $1000 in profits and paid a $1000 penalty. Swanson voluntarily resigned as director of FNB of Mercer. FNB Corporation stated that it did not know if his resignation was tied directly to the investigation.

Will businesses assume a larger social role in the future? Keith Davis feels that the public will ultimately make the decision, depending on how long and how loudly they make their demands known.[46] Social responsibility is an issue that will require much time and thought to solve—because there really is no easy answer.

REFERENCES

1. Rogene Buchholz, *Business Environment and Public Policy: Implications for Management and Strategy,* 3rd edition (Englewood Cliffs, N.J.: Prentice-Hall), 1989, pp. 43, 83, 84.
2. Rogene A. Buchholz, "Essentials of Public Policy for Management" (book review), *Public Relations Quarterly,* 30:4–5, Spring 1985.
3. David H. Glusman, "The Increasing Burden of Ethics," *Pennsylvania CPA Journal,* pp. 9, 10, Summer 1990.
4. Edward L. Hennessy, Jr., "Business Ethics: Is It a Priority for Corporate America?" *Magazine For Financial Executives,* p. 17, October 1986.
5. "Corporate Ethics: A Prime Business Asset," *The Business Roundtable Report on Policy and Practice in Company Conduct,* p. 4, February 1988.
6. Thomas J. Von der Embse, "The Ethical Dimension at Work," *Manage,* p. 29, March 1990.
7. John F. Akers, "Ethics and Competitiveness—Putting First Things First," *Sloan Management Review,* p. 69, Winter 1989.
8. Daniel E. Maltby, "The One-Minute Ethicist: Can Business School Ethics Courses Really Make Us Better?" *Christianity Today,* pp. 26, 27, February 1988.
9. Ronald E. Berenbeim, "An Outbreak of Ethics," *Across the Board,* p. 16, May 1988.

10. Kamalesh Kumar, Sarath A. Nonis, and Charles Yauger, "Cross-Cultural Differences in Negotiation: How Differences in Negotiating Style Affect the Negotiation Process," *IABD Proceedings,* 1991.

11. Archie B. Carroll, *Business and Society: Managing Corporate Social Performance* (Boston: Little, Brown), 1981, pp. 14–16.

12. Daniel A. Wren, *The Evaluation of Management Thought* (New York: John Wiley), 1979, p. 27.

13. Rogene A. Buchholz, "The Protestant Ethic as an Ideological Justification of Capitalism," *Journal of Business Ethics,* 2:51, 1989.

14. Verne E. Henderson, "The Ethical Side of Enterprise," *Sloan Management Review,* 23(3):37–47, Spring 1982.

15. Albert Z. Carr, "Is Business Bluffing Ethical?" in *Ethical Theory and Business,* Tom L. Beauchamp and Norman E. Bowie (Eds.) (Englewood Cliffs, N.J.: Prentice-Hall), 1983, p. 318.

16. Joanna M. Banthin and Leigh Stelzer, "Ethical Dilemmas in Negotiating Across Cultures: The Absence of Universal Norms," in Abbass F. Alkhafaji, "Management Challenges: A Worldwide Perspective," *Management Decision,* 29(6):52–56, 1991.

17. Timothy B. Blodgett, "Showdown on Business Bluffing," *Harvard Business Review,* 46(3):163.

18. Mathews M. Cash, *Strategic Intervention in Organizations: Resolving Ethical Dilemmas in Corporations* (Newbury Park, Calif.: Sage), 1988.

19. D. Pauly, J. Lowell, P.S. Simons, J. Moreau, and J. Walcott, "Business Without Bribes," *Newsweek,* pp. 63–64, February 19, 1979.

20. J.S. Estey and D.W. Marston, "Pitfalls (and Loopholes) in the Foreign Bribery Act," *Fortune,* pp. 182–184, 188, October 9, 1978..

21. M.A. Tipgos, "Compliance with the Foreign Corrupt Practices Act," *Financial Executive,* pp. 38–48, August 1981.

22. M.V. Seitzinger, *Foreign Corrupt Practices Act Amendments of 1988,* Report No. CRS 88-589 A (Washington, D.C.: Congressional Research Service, Library of Congress), August 30, 1988.

23. "The Antibribery Bill Backfires," *Business Week,* p. 143, April 17, 1978.

24. D.E. Kieso and J.J. Weygandt, *Intermediate Accounting,* 6th edition (New York: John Wiley), 1989.

25. Arthur Andersen & Co., *Subject File Rider—President Carter Signs Foreign Corrupt Practices Act of 1977* (Chicago: Arthur Andersen), December 21, 1977.

26. Deloitte Haskins and Sells, *Internal Accounting Control—An Overview of the DH&S Study and Evaluation Techniques* (New York: Deloitte Haskins and Sells), 1982.

27. Coopers & Lybrand, *Audit Committee Guide,* 3rd edition (New York: Coopers & Lybrand), 1982.

28. W. Proxmire, "The Foreign Payoff Law Is a Necessity," *New York Times,* p. 16F, February 5, 1978.

29. E. Bowers, "Confusion and Lost Sales Are the Payoffs from Foreign Bribery Act," *Iron Age,* 225(2):33, March 1, 1982; Richard D. Ramsey and Abbass F. Alkhafaji, "The 1977 Foreign Corrupt Practices Act and the 1988 Omnibus Trade Bill," in Abbass F. Alkhafaji, "Management Challenges: A Worldwide Perspective," *Management Decision,* 29(6):61–65, 1991.

30. John R. Schemerhorn, *Management for Productivity* (New York: John Wiley), 1984.

31. D.A. Ball and W.H. McColloch, Jr., *International Business* (Plano, Tex.: Business Publications), 1985.

32. "Antibribery Act Splits Executives," *Business Week,* p. 16, September 19, 1983.

33. S.H. Kim, "On Repealing the Foreign Corrupt Practices Act: Survey and Assessment," *Columbia Journal of World Business,* pp. 16–21, Fall 1991.

34. K. Gillespie, "Middle East Response to the U.S. Foreign Corrupt Practices Act," *California Management Review,* pp. 9–30, Summer 1987.

35. J.B. Thomas, Jr., "Ethics in Government," *Internal Auditor,* pp. 18–21, April 1989.

36. M. Stone, "Doing Business Abroad," *U.S. News & World Report,* p. 88, June 22, 1981.

37. R.D. Ramsey, A.R. Parsinia, J. Kinard, and P. Wright, "The Foreign Corrupt Practices Act and Its Impact on U.S. Small Business Engaged in International Trade," in *Proceedings of the Southwestern Small Business Institute Association 1983 Annual Conference: Contemporary Issues and Technologies in Small Business,* R. Peterson (Ed.) (Las Cruces, New Mex.: College of Business Administration and Economics, New Mexico State University), 1983, pp. 155–162.

38. N.H. Jacoby, P. Nehemkis, and R. Eells, "Naivete: Foreign Payoffs Law," *California Management Review,* pp. 84–87, Fall 1979.

39. "After Three Years, Trade Bill Finally Clears," *Congressional Quarterly Almanac* (100th Congress, 2nd Session), 44:209–222, 1988.

40. "Provisions of the Omnibus Trade Bill (HR 4848)," *Congressional Quarterly Weekly Report,* pp. 2217–2222, August 6, 1988.

41. Richard H. Solomon, *Chinese Political Negotiating Behavior* (Palo Alto, Calif.: The Rand Corporation), 1983.

42. Kate Bertrand, "Learning a Different Ballgame," *Business Marketing,* 136(3):8, 76, 1986.

43. Joanna M. Banthin and Leigh Stelzer, quoted Abbass F. Alkhafaji (Ed.) *International Management Challenge* (Acton, Mass.: Copley), 1990.

44. Abbass F. Alkhafaji, *A Stakeholder Approach to Corporate Governance* (Westport, Conn.: Greenwood), 1989.

45. Amar Bhide and Howard H. Stevenson, "Why Be Honest if Honesty Doesn't Pay?" *Harvard Business Review,* pp. 121–129, September–October 1990.

46. Keith Davis and Robert L. Blomstrom, *Business and Society: Environment and Responsibility,* 3rd edition (New York: McGraw-Hill), 1975.

BIBLIOGRAPHY

Adams, Jane, "A Job You Can Believe In," *New Woman,* pp. 90–94, March 1991.

Andrews, Kenneth R., "Ethics in Practice," *Harvard Business Review,* p. 102, September–October 1989.

"Assuring America's Competitive Preeminence," *Business America,* pp. 3–12, March 2, 1987.

Berney, Karen, "That Ethical Edge," *Reader's Digest,* pp. 177–180, April 1988.

Bowers, E., "Confusion and Lost Sales Are the Payoffs from Foreign Bribery Act," *Iron Age,* p. 33, March 1, 1982.

Cook, J.M. and T.P. Kelley, "The Foreign Corrupt Practices Act Has Made the Internal Accounting Controls of Public Companies a Matter of Law," *Journal of Accountancy,* pp. 56–64, January 1979.

"Foreign Corrupt Practices Act of 1977," *United States Code Congressional and Administrative News* (95th Congress First Session 1977, Vol. 1, 91 Stat., Public Law 95-213 [S. 305]), pp. 1494–1500, 1977.

Lieber, J., "Bribery is Back," *New Republic,* pp. 7–9, September 30, 1981.

Lissakors, K., "Don't Help Bribery Make a Comeback," *Washington Post,* p. C7, July 3, 1988.

"Misinterpreting the Antibribery Law," *Business Week,* p. 150, September 3, 1979.

Odiorne, George S., "Ethics for the Nineties," *Manage,* pp. 8–14, 33, April 1988.

Sandroff, Ronni, "How Ethical Is American Business?" *Working Women,* pp. 113–116, September 1990.

SECTION VII

STRATEGIC ISSUES IN INTERNATIONAL MANAGEMENT

The global company is becoming the most viable force in world trade and international relations. The strategic aspects of managing multinational corporations is the focus of this section. Developing a strategy and a structure to operate in the global market is explored. How such companies can deal with the restrictions and guidelines put forth by host nations is also examined.

17

INTERNATIONAL STRATEGIC MANAGEMENT

ABSTRACT

The world is changing so fast that many companies find it difficult to keep up. Global competition is the name of the game. Firms must formulate, successfully implement, and control global strategies in order to survive and prosper in the future. How companies operating in the international market formulate their global strategies is the focus of this chapter. The importance of designing a strategy, the factors that need to be considered in the planning process, and the benefit of the process are discussed. The difference between domestic and international planning is also explored.

CHAPTER OBJECTIVES

1 To understand the strategic management process

2 To present an overview of multinational firms and their environments

3 To examine variables in the domestic and foreign environments

4 To analyze the effects of large corporations on host countries

5 To understand the process of strategic planning and introduce the basic steps

6 To discuss the types of strategies used in strategic planning

7 To provide examples of the different uses of strategic planning

CASE STUDY
GM Discovers Asia

General Motors has finally discovered Asia. The Detroit giant has shifted its strategy there 180 degrees. Instead of viewing Asia mainly as a cheap source of labor for cars, GM now recognizes the region as one of the world's fastest-growing consumer markets. The company is on the move from China to Indonesia. GM owns a 30% stake in a $100 million plant in China that will produce up to 60,000 light trucks annually by 1998. It has boosted distribution and marketing of Opels in Hong Kong and Singapore. GM exports 14,000 U.S.-made cars to Taiwan annually and plans to assemble 20,000 Opels a year there. GM is also planning to set up auto assembly operations in Indonesia, Malaysia, and Thailand.

For decades, Japanese automakers have dominated the Asian markets in their backyard by setting up a network of local assembly plants. GM is planning to do the same with a truck plant in China and other investment moves in Taiwan and Southeast Asia. GM has found that the cost disadvantage of its cars can be overcome. Taiwan and China are eager to import more from the United States and less from Japan in order to deflect political pressures. In 1991, most of the 14,000 cars GM sold there were large prestige cars, but in June 1992 it started selling Saturns through two dealerships in Taiwan. The cars are proving as hot there as they are in the United States. In two months, the Taiwanese purchased 500 Saturns at $22,800 each.

GM's prospects also seem bright in China. With economic growth surging at 10%, joint ventures by Chrysler, Volkswagen, and Peugot cannot meet demand. Although most of the imported cars are Japanese, Chinese officials say that they prefer working with Westerners in manufacturing joint ventures. GM's strategy is to bypass cars and focus on trucks, for which there is strong domestic demand and negligible foreign competition. GM's stake in the multi-million dollar joint venture in Shenyang will produce 60,000 pickup trucks to meet the new demand.

Source: Peter Engardio, Karen Lowry Miller, and James B. Treece, "GM Finally Discovers Asia," *Business Week*, pp. 42–43, August 24, 1992.

INTRODUCTION

The traditional measurement is not the right measurement; if it were, there would be no need for decisions.

Peter Drucker

A well-developed international decision-making system is a continuing source of international strategic management. The quality of the decisions that management makes will influence the successes of strategic management. The international strategic management process and some concepts that are used in decision making are considered in this chapter.

U.S. companies must take their products abroad. They must recognize that global considerations have to be a part of their future plans. They must create new markets and new products if they want to be competitive in the international market. This can be done through joint ventures, mergers, and acquisitions. Companies have to learn to think globally without sacrificing local markets.

Many firms outside the United States are gaining power globally. Nine of the ten largest banks in the world in 1990 were Japanese, as opposed to only one 10 years earlier. The U.S. foreign deficit of about $200 billion a year over the last 10 to 15 years was the result of trade with Japan and other Pacific Rim countries. This deficit is what gave Japan its power. The position of the United States has changed from the world's largest lending nation to the world's largest debtor nation. Undoubtedly, U.S. companies are being challenged in the global business arena.

Michael Porter[1] identifies four factors, called Porter's dynamic diamond, that determine whether or not a firm will be competitive globally: factor conditions, demand conditions, related and supporting industries, and company strategy, structure, and rivalry. Factor conditions determine a nation's ability to turn the basics, such as natural resources and education, into a specialized advantage. Demand conditions depend on the number and sophistication of domestic customers for a particular industry's product. Related and supporting industries are the different people a company deals with, such as suppliers and competitors. Company strategy, structure, and rivalry complete the dynamic diamond. In order for American companies to compete globally, they must be able to compete in such key markets as Europe, Southeast Asia, and North America.

The Japanese market is especially important. In Chapter 8, the business environment in Japan was examined, and some important variables to be considered when doing business in Japan were presented, such as a highly educated work force, technology, constructive business–government relationships, and a high savings rate. U.S. corporations must try to establish competitive strategies in this market.

DEFINITION

Strategic management can be defined as the process of assessing a corporation and its environment in terms of meeting the long-term objectives of the firm, so that it can conform to its environment and take advantage of the opportunities in the market to the best of its ability. Next, the term *international* must be defined in order to fully understand the phenomenon of international strategic management. International may be defined as activities that involve two or more countries. Thus, the concept *international strategic management* can be defined as the effect and interaction of strategic management between two or more nations.

THE STRATEGIC MANAGEMENT PROCESS

Strategic management is the function of top management in running an organization successfully. The process involves three basic components:

1. Strategy formulation and planning

2. Strategy implementation

3. Evaluation and control

When business activities are extended to be international in scope, new challenges and opportunities are presented to management. Management must first understand the decision to pursue business activities on an international level. Management must also carefully examine the interaction of variables that constitute international strategic management.

Two objectives motivate an organization to extend its operations to other countries:

1. **Profit:** To take advantage of increasing demand for goods and services in foreign countries.

2. **Stability:** New sources of demand which become evident in other countries may have a positive effect on an organization's production process.

The following variables are attributed to international strategic management and the various interactions that it encompasses: culture, environment, and government. Each of these variables interacts with the others to create complex situations that must be considered if an organization's activities are to be managed effectively. Some of the issues that must be addressed before executing strategic management in an international sense are as follow:[2]

- **Tariffs:** Tariffs are government-imposed taxes that are charged on either imported or exported goods. They are imposed as a means of raising revenue or protecting a country's producers from the competition of imported goods.

- **Payment for international transactions:** International business activity requires the exchange of currencies between countries. Problems may arise relative to foreign exchange rates, as they tend to fluctuate in value.

- **Government control over profits:** Businesses that own facilities in foreign countries would naturally expect to receive profits from their operations. Problems may arise when host country governments regulate foreign access to local currencies, thus, in effect, controlling the amount of profit that parent companies actually receive.

- **Taxation:** Businesses conducting operations in foreign countries are subject to the laws and regulations of those countries. Local taxes may be very high due to the lack of other sources of revenue, thus shifting the tax burden to multinational corporations.

- **Culture:** Different cultures are brought together through international business activity. Complex problems may arise as the result of language barriers and differences in cultural values, tastes, and attitudes.

Each of these issues and their associated variables must be carefully considered in order to ensure effective international strategic management.

STRATEGIC PLANNING VERSUS LONG-RANG PLANNING

People often have a difficult time distinguishing between long-range planning and strategic planning. In a sense, all strategic planning involves long-range planning, but not all long-range planning involves strategic thinking. In defining strategic planning, it is important to recognize that there is a difference between strategic planning and long-range planning. Long-range planning fails to recognize the changing environment and simply extends present trends into the future. Strategic planning, on the other hand, addresses the wants and needs of an organization; in other words, it considers a firm's mission. (A mission statement defines a firm's reason for being.) This approach enables a firm to identify its strengths and weaknesses and helps determine what to do in order to get the job done.

Strategic planning provides direction and clarity and identifies where a firm should be three to five years down the road. Strategic planning is not about mechanical data analysis, predictions, and economic forecasts; it is a way of thinking and structuring business ideas—like a game of chess.

The problem with long-range planning is that it is not a way of thinking, but rather a way of formulating a plan to organize, realize, or achieve something, without considering the changing environment. The typical socialist five-year plan is a good example of long-range planning, and it proves the dangers of ignoring economic and political changes.

Strategic planning is often viewed as a team effort in which management responds to complex environmental changes and makes preeminent decisions in times of swift change. In strategic planning, management should answer three strategic questions: (1) What business do we want to be in? (2) What future direction will we take for development and growth? (3) What is the overall relationship between the external environment in terms of geographic boundaries, target markets, competition, and product offerings and the financial results we seek to achieve?[3]

MULTINATIONAL FIRMS AND THE ENVIRONMENT

The importance of strategic management in a multinational firm cannot be overemphasized. The fall of the Berlin Wall (which was followed by reduced tariffs for developing, nonindustrial nations) and improvements in transportation technology are two examples of recent developments that have caused decision makers in multinational corporations to review their procedures for identifying optimal investment sites abroad. Companies looking to expand into these economic areas face several issues.

One consideration is which market to penetrate. For example, a company needs to understand the restrictions to trade in various regions (i.e., tariffs, quotas, etc.). A community is larger than just one country; it may consist of a group of countries that have aligned themselves for efficiency. These communities are constantly changing, and companies must stay well informed to ensure the competitive advantage of international expansion. Multinational prospects must also consider the long-range implications of international business, one of which is the relationship between Free Trade Associates and the members of the Common Market.[4] History has shown that although these two groups will likely move closer together, real differences in taxes, social policies, and location incentives will persist for at least another decade.

The foreign exchange rate can present problems in international markets. Fluctuations in the exchange rate affect the foreign cost structure of products within three to six months. Although this may present gains as well as losses, a company must ask itself if its competencies lie in manipulating different currency positions or are based on certain skills and transferable assets.[4] The foreign exchange rate can have a significant impact on where an organization will expand.

Multinational expansion provides companies with a back door to Europe. Certain regions of the world provide a distinct advantage in terms of tax and wage differentials which the prospective investor cannot afford to overlook. Management must exercise careful judgment in evaluating the different types and amounts of incentives. Incentives to companies locating in specific areas take a variety of forms, such as programs for training and housing.

Companies that seek new markets in foreign countries must do an environmental analysis, both internal and external. The most common environments that organizations evaluate are the economic, technological, societal, political, and ecological. The economic environment is the most critical and also the most difficult to analyze because it deals with the national economic scene. A number of economic trends are of particular interest to businesses, including the stability of the U.S. dollar, the projected growth in the gross national product, the expected growth in the consumer price index, and changes in the federal income tax structure.[4]

In many cases, the technological environment may be the deciding factor in expansion. The success of a business can depend on its ability to stay on the cutting edge of technology. Several technological trends that may interest a firm are microcircuits, solar heating and other alternative energy sources, and metal alloys.[5]

The political environment, which includes regulations, is an extremely critical variable in the long-term efficiency and success of a firm. Firms in regulated industries need to pay special attention to environmental trends in order to be able to predict future courses of action. Significant issues in the political environment include corporate income taxes, retirement age, public interest groups, and government permits.

Finally, the ecological environment must be recognized. This area has come under severe scrutiny as people seek to make the earth a safer place. Today, firms must carefully plan projects so as not to have an adverse impact on the environment. Issues in the ecological environment that are of broad interest include clean water requirements, emission standards, bans on certain types of businesses, and noise and air pollution requirements.

Firms interested in expanding into international markets must consider many factors. They must weigh the advantages and disadvantages of expansion and then analyze the following environments to determine if the advantages will produce a significant profit.

The Foreign Environment

Working in another country or with an organization from another country demands knowledge and consideration of their environmental forces in order to create a good strategic plan. To be successful in international business, managers must be students of the cultures with which they deal. In the strategic management process, the attitudes and beliefs of business partners and employees must be taken into consideration. It is also important to overcome language barriers.[5] Other important interfering forces include aesthetics and religion. Recognizing their importance and considering them in plans eases relationships and increases effective utilization of human resources.

International operating companies must have a strategic management plan that takes into consideration the real and potential forces in a foreign environment, as well as the forces at work in the domestic environment. A manager has to understand the new environment, which means understanding the people and their culture.

Physical forces and geographic factors determine transportation and production costs. Mountains and deserts are barriers to the movement of people, ideas, goods, and services.[6] Proximity to an urbanized area can be an advantage if the infrastructure is good. However, it can also be a disadvantage, because real estate and labor are more expensive.

Another important area is legal considerations, both domestic and international. Where a company decides to register its headquarters affects jurisdiction. Knowledge of the laws in both host and home countries, as well as international law, is essential. Specific legal considerations include tax laws and their relative enforcement, liability laws, employee–employer relations, and, most importantly, quotas and other restrictions on imports and exports. In dealing with foreign countries, agreeing on the legal basis for international relations and enforcing such laws are equally problematic.

Political forces can have an impact on organizations operating in foreign countries. Political instability should be reason enough for a company to carefully weigh potential gains and losses. Two volatile political forces are nationalism and expropriation. The political environment is a critical variable in the long-term efficiency of a firm. Government involvement is of particular concern in terms of regulation, and firms in regulated industries should pay special attention to environmental trends to predict future courses of action. Strategic management should be based on careful observation and analysis of the political environment.

An organization that plans to establish a branch in a foreign country should examine the labor pool; skills, social status, religion, gender, and age are major factors that can influence the success of a business. Unknown competitive and distributive forces can interfere as well. A strategist must explore the strengths, weaknesses, and competitive forces in a host country as part of the strategic management process. Distribution channels (international or within a country) for goods and services must also be considered. A more highly developed country also has a higher concentration of wholesalers and retailers. Finally, measuring the economy in terms of gross national product (GNP), per capita GNP, and income structure can indicate whether a country would provide an appropriate environment.

Examining all of these variables is mandatory for successful strategic management in the international arena. Strategic management in a company that operates exclusively in a domestic environment, where management is familiar with most of the influencing factors and has ready access to reliable information, might be nothing more than determining cost, revenue, and profit; the same cannot, however, be said for a company that goes international.

Larger corporations are more likely to affect developing countries, as opposed to smaller corporations with fewer international operations. This is due to several factors:

1. **Size:** According to Ball and McCulloch, the total sales of General Motors in 1985 was less than the GNP of only 21 nations.[7] All other

nations of the world had GNPs that were less than the total sales of General Motors.[7]

2. **Diversity:** Because these large corporations are geographically diversified in their operations, they are minimally dependent on any location. This increases their bargaining power in dealing with their host countries. Influence in a relationship is the result of the power differential between the two parties.[8] Therefore, the greater the balance of power in favor of a multinational corporation, the more likely that it can affect the environment of its host country.

3. **Flexibility:** This refers to the ability of multinational corporations to adapt to changing environments. They diversify in numerous ways (products, processes, locations, etc.), which enables them to respond to any threats or opportunities in their environments.

4. **Magnetism:** This refers to the ability of multinational corporations to integrate and coordinate a global system, which gives them the power to affect the social, political, and economic development of the nations with which they do business.

The Domestic Environment

The domestic environment is composed of internal (controllable) forces, such as personnel, production, finance, and marketing, and external (uncontrollable) forces, such as the social-cultural, political-legal, business-economic, and technological forces that operate within a country. These forces are the basis of any organization and are extremely important in the international environment. Social-cultural forces include education, religion, values, tradition, language, population trends, and other factors that provide the basis for the social behavior of individuals in a society. Political-legal forces include the government, the legal and judicial system, politics, and other factors that affect how a society governs itself and the stability of the process. Business-economic forces includes GNP, income distribution, structure of the economic sector, taxes, labor, marketing and distribution, the financial sector, infrastructure, foreign trade, and management style. Technological forces include computerization, automation, telecommunications, research and development, and other factors that relate to the overall level of technological development in a country.

Changes in the political factors may mean that a government suddenly restricts exports and imports, which would have a definite impact on doing business overseas. Therefore, a thorough strategic management effort in a multinational company should include research into all domestic laws that regulate international trade or transfers.

The International Environment

The international environment of a multinational enterprise consists of independent multinational organizations, such as the United Nations, the World Bank, the International Monetary Fund, and the International Organization for Standardization, as well as international treaties and exchange rates. The main purpose of these organizations is to facilitate, promote, and provide security for the international exchange of products, services, and money. Therefore, these valuable resources should be integrated into the strategic planning process of a multinational operation.

The World Bank consists of the International Bank for Reconstruction and Development, the International Finance Corporation, and the International Development Association. It mainly serves to provides less developed countries (LDCs) with loans and credit. The borrowers (LDCs) spend millions of dollars provided by the World Bank to buy the products they need for a variety of projects. Therefore, an international company should improve its understanding of these new potential markets. Information about the activities of the World Bank can be a valuable asset in identifying potential buyers in LDCs. The World Bank also facilitates business relations by addressing the money needs of future business partner in LDCs. In addition, the bank's center for arbitration works to resolve difficulties encountered by businesses in foreign countries. Awareness of the existence of the center for arbitration can radically change the basis of international strategic management, because it creates an atmosphere of fair play. This is particularly critical when dealing with cultures where business philosophies and missions vary. Foreign partners, whether governments or companies, supported by such organizations as the World Bank tend to have better infrastructures, which facilitates business relations in terms of transporting products and communicating.

The World Bank is an example of a multinational organization that facilitates large projects between nations and multinational enterprises. The International Organization for Standardization (ISO) is an example of an organization that facilitates business relations of all sizes by standardizing measurements. Both are representative examples of multinational organizations in the international environment that facilitate relations, supply information, and provide security. International organizations are catalysts of international business and should be integrated into the strategic planning process right from the start. They can offer a variety of reasonable alternatives and provide information to help evaluate those alternatives. Even more important is their impact on implementation and control. The World Bank has a major interest in the success of any project it funds. Therefore, integrating the services of this organization adds the support of one of the most powerful forces in the world.

STRATEGIC PLANNING

Management sets the course for an organization through the formulation of organizational plans. Organizations are attempting to respond to the growing need to anticipate changes in the environment—both internal and external—through organizational planning. Although this type of effective planning has dominated outstanding organizational performance, the complexity of change has increased so dramatically that additional planning has become fundamentally important.

A strategy is the "big picture" in terms of what a firm is capable of doing. A strategic plan is made up of a strategy and the time-related details for carrying out that strategy. It should include:

1. Marketing mix (the target market)

2. Drain on company resources

3. Anticipated sales and profits

4. Control procedures to ensure that the plan is following its intended course

Strategic planning does not take place in a vacuum. The plan is used by marketing, accounting, production, human resources, and all the other specialists. "A strategic plan lets everybody in the firm know what they are trying to accomplish and it gives direction to the whole business effort."[9] Effective strategic planning requires that all aspects of the plan are carried out efficiently at all levels of operation. Every departmental decision is capable of casting a shadow on the final outcome of the strategic plan; therefore, all levels of operation must carry out their assignments completely.

Planning has been defined as "drawing from the past to decide in the present what to do in the future."[10] When a company implements strategic planning, it must first analyze its present situation and then formulate and implement those strategies that will be most beneficial in the long run. Extreme care and precision are required to match resources with market opportunities over the long term. Strategic planning differs from day-to-day operational planning in that it is very long term in purpose and direction. Because a company's very existence may rest on the outcome of the strategic plan, it is considered to be an extremely intense and important aspect of company development.

Solid commitment to the strategic plan and its anticipated outcome must be built from the top level of management all the way down through the operational levels. Unlike operational day-to-day planning, where one change after another may be implemented to facilitate an outcome, the final outcome of a strategic plan may take years to realize. Without proper guidelines (policies), a strategic plan may not have the flexibility to achieve its final outcome, which is why it is critical to select a plan that has been well thought out and focuses on the very best interest of the company. Everyone in a company will feel the consequences of a poorly constructed strategic plan. An operational plan ensures the smooth flow of work on a day-to-day basis; in contrast, a strategic plan indicates a company's present position as well as what its position is destined to be in the future.

The Basic Stages of Strategic Planning

Step 1: Assess Corporate Strategy

This process requires a firm to asses its own position relative to its environment. In doing so, an organization must include a SWOT (strengths, weaknesses, opportunities, or threats) analysis to determine its strengths and weaknesses. After analyzing its strengths and weaknesses, an organization must evaluate its potential and identify where the opportunities and threats lie in the external environment. Strategic analysis allows an organization to define its range of strategic alternatives and choose the one most appropriate for its present external environment.

Step 2: Strategy Formulation

In the process of strategy formulation, an organization first creates a set of realistic and comprehensive goals and objectives. An appropriate strategy is then selected based on the results that the organization wants to accomplish. Strategy formulation allows an organization to identify the strategy that can best meet its realistic goals.

Step 3: Strategy Implementation

This is the most important step in strategic planning. A plan that is formulated perfectly but implemented incorrectly will not produce the desired result. The implementation strategy must have an operational plan that can organize and move resources when they are needed. To do this effectively, such variables as culture, personnel, and the structure and design of the organization must be assessed.

Many companies find the consequences of not planning adequately and then not implementing correctly extremely hazardous. With the arrival of the computer age, the external and internal environments at most companies are constantly changing. Technology is constantly improving, government regulations are constantly changing, and management policies and personnel are constantly being replaced. This view is even more apparent in the world market. Those who cannot plan in a multicultural mode will lose market share in the global economy. Those who cannot adapt to new technology, changes in foreign policy, and cultural differences will be dropped from the world market as others who plan and implement better strategies take their place. Lack of planning in the global market can mean loss of profits or even failure to survive.

Types of Strategies Used in Strategic Planning

The types of strategies used in strategic planning are discussed in this section. It is important to note that planning problems often originate due to lack of support data for a subsidiary. They can also be caused by inexperienced local planners.

CASE STUDY
The Impact of Faulty Strategy

In the early 1980s, General Signal Corporation was a successful manufacturer of industrial and electrical control systems for firms that produce capital goods. Because of the maturity of that business and an accompanying desire to diversify its operations, General Signal decided to enter the relatively new, high-tech business of semiconductor equipment manufacturing. By 1985, the diversification was well under way. GSA chose to acquire semiconductor equipment manufacturers, among them GSA, an industry leader, rather than start its own operations. During the mid-1980s, General Signal spent $240 million to acquire high-tech companies in its effort to diversify.

Unfortunately, General Signal's move into semiconductor equipment manufacturing happened just as several large Japanese corporations, including Nikkon and Canon, also entered the field. With their huge cash reserves, technical capabilities, and distribution systems, these Japanese competitors were able to establish a dominant 80% market share by 1990, which reduced General Signal's GSA division to the position of a bit player with a 4% share. Coupled with a recessionary decline in its core industrial and electrical control business, General Signal suffered substantial losses and was forced to withdraw from much of its high-tech diversification through the sale of over $200 million in assets and a 20% reduction in its work force. In addition, a new CEO was hired, the sale of additional assets was expected, the company was bound by $395 million in debt created by a 1988 stock buyback, and some operations had to be discontinued and written off.

The new CEO chose to emphasize the process control business, which he expected to contribute 80% of total sales in 1992 compared with 59% in 1987. Furthermore, he initiated programs to force division presidents to improve profits and efficiency, required companywide training in inventory control, ordered cuts in administrative costs, and indicated that subsidiary businesses that failed to earn a 20% return on assets would be sold off. Unfortunately, GSA is highly unlikely to meet that goal and is even less likely to find a buyer. Therefore, the centerpiece of General Signal's diversification into high-tech operations may very well have to be shut down and written off.

Source: Aubrey R. Fowler (Youngstown State University), based on "Can General Signal Escape Its High-Tech Hell?" *Business Week,* pp. 94–96, March 18, 1991.

CASE STUDY
Going Global Fujitsu Style

The largest seller of computers in the world is IBM. Surprised? Probably not. However, the number two seller of computers may be a surprise. Fujitsu Ltd., which is number one in Japan by a small margin, is second to IBM in worldwide computer sales. Fujitsu, which is only about one-third the size of IBM, posted revenues of $21 billion in 1992, but it makes several products that are industry leaders: the world's fastest conventional supercomputers, the world's lightest cellular phones, and the world's largest memory chips. Fujitsu's lack of recognition results primarily from its failure to become a major player in the PC market.

Fujitsu has captured the number two position through investments in companies like Amdahl Corporation (44%) and International Computers Ltd. (recently purchased 80%). Amdahl, which is located in the Silicon Valley, makes IBM-compatible mainframes and has annual revenues of $2.2 billion. ICL, with sales of $2.7 billion a year, is Britain's largest computer company. Of Fujitsu's $5.2 billion in overseas revenue last year, almost half came from Amdahl and ICL.

Why doesn't Fujitsu either stand on its own or completely take over these companies? First of all, these companies provide Fujitsu with needed technology. Amdahl was founded by IBM's former chief mainframe designer. Fujitsu supplied venture capital in exchange for technology to be used in building mainframes in Japan. Also, Fujitsu recognized the world's suspicion of Japan's industrial might. Fujitsu is becoming international by becoming

In order to be successful in the international market, a firm must be astute, because the environment changes rather quickly. The real key to being astute in this global situation is to have good strategic planning tools and the ability to use them. This means that a firm must know when to use certain types of strategies in order to maximize production and sales. In order for a firm to be successful in an international market, it must know when to use certain strategies and when to make adjustments to them to gain an advantage over the competition.[11]

There are two basic strategy typologies used by organizations. The first is tied to the scope of an organization (either global or national) and its market share objectives (high or low). The second typology is seen as a continuum and is made up of the home market mode, the multidomestic mode, and the global mode. In order to be successful, a firm must choose the appropriate strategy in terms of its objectives and implement it effectively.

The first typology of strategy includes four basic strategic orientations. The first is the **global high share strategy**. In this strategy, firms that local, almost neighborly. Amdahl and ICL operate autonomously, maintaining their Western management, developing their own strategy, and even competing against each other. Fujitsu views business as taking place in a borderless economy, but with an awareness of increasing nationalism.

Fujitsu has found a way to balance integration and autonomy. Within Fujitsu's basic structure, each division—telecommunications, computer, semiconductor—is managed independently. Cooperation takes place only on special projects.

Fujitsu has not always been successful in buying Western companies. In the mid-1980s, it attempted to buy Fairchild Semiconductor Corporation. The Fujitsu proposal came at the time when the United States was accusing Japanese chip-makers of dumping their products on the U.S. market below cost. The Department of Commerce succeeded in pressuring Fujitsu to drop its offer, citing national security concerns. (Ironically, Fairchild was already foreign owned.)

Fujitsu has continued to pursue partnerships. The major strategy change has been to focus on smaller companies. Fujitsu is finding ripe fields among small, creative companies—in many cases, companies in the United States that were formed by engineers with an abundance of know-how and a shortage of capital.

Fujitsu is pushing for the lead held by IBM, but it is attempting to avoid the appearance of being another Japanese company out to dominate yet another critical world industry.

Source: J. Michael Jenkins (Southeastern Louisiana University), based on Brenton R. Schlender, "How Fujitsu Will Tackle the Giants," *Fortune,* pp. 78–82, July 1, 1991.

operate in world markets and want high market shares use pricing, promotions, and products that are popular in world markets. Very large corporations that compete in international markets usually use this type of strategy. IBM is a good example; it expands into new areas, keeps prices competitive, and advertises aggressively. The second type of strategy is the **global niche strategy**, which is used by organizations that operate in world markets but wants to achieve only a low market share. Small firms competing in global markets use this strategy to gain a small market share by trying to pursue a specialty.[11] The third strategy is the **national high share strategy**, which is used by companies that want high volume and low cost in a competitive national market. Firms that use this strategy do not have to pay the tariffs and quotas that global firms do. Therefore, they can also take advantage of government subsidies and tax breaks. The fourth strategy is the **national niche strategy**. Firms that use this type of strategy specialize in national markets where there are few competitors. They survive on the hope that large international corporations will find these markets unattractive and choose not to pursue them.[12]

The second typology is made up of three modes: the home market oriented mode, the multidomestic mode, and the global mode. Firms that are just entering the global marketplace use the **home market oriented mode**. Basically, they produce goods overseas for export to their original environment. They do so in order to lower production costs and still produce goods geared toward the home market. Firms in the **multidomestic mode** choose to compete in several different foreign markets.[12] They develop specific strategies to fit markets in specific countries. They do not try to take products or services that fit the market in one country to another country. Firms that use this type of strategy usually compete globally. Firms in the **global market mode** pursue an integrated strategy in major world markets. There are no national boundaries to determine where their products can be sold. They compete in the world market.

PLANNING: THE KEY TO STRATEGIC MANAGEMENT IN BOTH DOMESTIC AND INTERNATIONAL MARKETS

Planning is a necessary task at any level of management, but when a company tries to compete in another country, the variables for operating an organization change. For example, when the Japanese began to buy and locate strategic business units (SBUs) in the United States, their management teams were faced with differences in culture, work ethic, and business practices. What did the Japanese management teams do? Some of the techniques and strategies that they employed in dealing with the business/manufacturing sector in the United States are highlighted in this section.

In an article in the *Harvard Business Review,* Steven C. Wheelwright praised the Japanese for their discipline and dedication in the manufacturing sector and the value that their management teams place on strategic operational planning and policy. As an example, he cited Matsushita Corporation's purchase of a Motorola television plant in Franklin Park, Illinois. The plant suffered from very low productivity and quality (more than 150 defects per 100 sets). The Japanese increased productivity by 30% and reduced the number of defects to fewer than 4 per 100. Although this performance did not equal that of comparable factories in Japan, where defect rates average 0.5% or less, the improvements do suggest that much of their expertise may indeed be transferable.[13]

The basic strategy credited for the above success was simply planning. Japanese management teams tend to plan day-to-day production schemes in a deliberate, thorough, and painstaking way. When a group of American managers visited three Japanese companies (Tokyo Sanyo Electric, Toshiba Tsurumi Works, and Yokagawa Electric Works), one reported, "we have known all along how to do these things the Japanese are doing, but we have lacked the discipline, both managers and workers, to follow through and do what we know how to best. They just work more consistently, and they work together."[14] In Japanese companies and their SBUs located in the

United States, Japanese management teams treat virtually all operational issues as strategic, whereas U.S. managers usually separate the decision-making tasks. The Japanese have taken their strategic operational decision-making techniques and implemented them at their SBUs located in the United States. As a result, Japanese-owned automobile, television, and picture tube manufacturing plants located in the United States have become more cost effective and efficient.

Some companies in the United States do implement plans similar to those of the Japanese. Hewlett-Packard, IBM, and McDonald's tend to look to the long term and were consistently making strategic operational decisions years before the Japanese expansion into the United States. The point is that corporate strategies can be transferred to SBUs located in foreign countries as long as the cultural aspects of a country are considered before implementation. In *Global Companies,* George W. Ball addresses the key issues that a company will face as it ventures into the global arena, and the issues are similar to those faced by the Japanese when they located their SBUs in the United States.[15]

Global companies are becoming one of the most potent forces in world trade and international relations. These companies must deal with the restrictions and guidelines put forth by their host nations in terms of expansion. For example, Japanese automobile manufacturers were faced with quotas imposed by the American government when it became apparent that their exports were taking market share from American automobile manufacturers. The Japanese countered with their strategic planning expertise and located SBUs in the United States. With the approval of the U.S. government, these Japanese-owned manufacturing plants pumped out automobiles with the same Japanese nameplate—and put many unemployed Americans back to work in the process. A foreign company (Japanese companies in this case) must always employ environmental scanning techniques to stay in tune with its host country (the United States in this case).

A foreign company that wants to do business with or locate a SBU in another country has to employ strategic planning. Careful examination and consideration of the local culture, government regulations, competition, and the work force can ensure a good fit for both the host country and the future member of its business community.

A UNIFIED MODEL FOR INTERNATIONAL PURPOSES

Definition

Countries differ socially, economically, technically, and politically. In order to be successful in the international business environment, it is essential that these differences be recognized and taken into consideration in managing international activities.

Several basic questions should be asked when considering opportuni-

CASE STUDY
Sarah Lee Going Global

The Sarah Lee Corporation is as American as apple pie, but its recipe for success has international appeal. Sarah Lee ranks among the top five U.S.-based consumer products companies in Europe and has a rapidly growing market share in Asia and South America—all thanks to a management team that knows how to adapt the product mix to satisfy diverse local tastes.

Sarah Lee is best known in the United States as the maker of desserts that "nobody doesn't like." However, a major part of its revenue, both at home and abroad, comes from its collection of panty hose and underwear companies. The Chicago-based conglomerate owns such U.S. powerhouses as Hanes, L'eggs, Champion, Bali, and Playtex. In recent years, Sarah Lee has expanded globally by buying a multitude of foreign companies in related industries. Acquisitions completed since 1989 include Europe's leading hosiery maker, Dim; Spain's top underwear manufacturer, the Sans Group; Hungary's largest coffee roaster, Compack Trading and Packing Company; and Australia's biggest apparel producer, the Linter textiles group—just to name a few.

In every case, the strategy is the same. Sarah Lee makes a quick entry into a market by acquiring a product leader with a well-known brand name. It then builds on existing market share by expanding into a line of related products, creating what it calls a "megabrand." For example, after taking over the French hosiery maker Dim, Sarah Lee sewed the popular label into a new line of underwear, socks, and T-shirts. It then built common packaging and advertising to build brand loyalty.

There is another key ingredient to Sarah Lee's international strategy. It keeps foreign nationals in its top posts abroad, reasoning that local managers better understand the culture and market. Take the 1992 acquisition of the Sans Group in Spain. Pedro Sans Llopart founded the company and built it into the leading underwear and knit manufacturer in the country. Even after Sarah Lee's acquisition, Sans stayed at the helm to continue building on the success of the past 40 years.

In the former Eastern bloc, it was even more important for Sarah Lee to keep local managers in place, not only to overcome language barriers but to help ease the transition of acquired companies from government-owned bureaucracies to private corporations. "The most important thing is the industrial relations—motivating the people. Without an understanding of the feelings of the workers and a knowledge of the language, it would be difficult to manage the business," says Bogo Laszlo, general manager of both an acquired company and a new Sarah Lee division.

Sarah Lee's appetite for global expansion is far from satisfied. Even though a recent buying spree added $1 billion in sales to its income statement, it is always looking for new opportunities. As chairman John Bryn puts it, "The world has literally opened up to do business."

Source: Arthur G. Bedian, *Management,* 3rd edition (Orlando: Dryden Press), 1993 (original article by Carol Cerulli).

ties in foreign markets: Should we go international? In what parts of the world should we look for such opportunities? How soon should we begin our venture in the international market? What are the best means to exploit these opportunities? In deciding whether to enter foreign markets, management should:

1. Evaluate the opportunities for the firm's products and services in foreign markets, as well as the potential threats, problems, and risks associated with such opportunities

2. Evaluate the strengths and weaknesses of the firm's managerial, material, technical, and operational (finance, marketing, etc.) capabilities to determine whether the necessary resources are available to successfully exploit potential opportunities in foreign markets

Two basic steps are used in developing a model for international strategy: an environmental analysis and an internal resources audit. The general focus of the **environmental analysis** is on the discovery and evaluation of business opportunities and threats and the associated problems and risks. In an international sense, three different levels of environmental analysis should be considered: (1) multinational, (2) regional, and (3) country. **Multinational** environmental analysis consists of broadly identifying, forecasting, and monitoring critical factors in the world environment. It involves the study of global technological developments, various trends in government intervention, and changes in overall values and lifestyles. These items are evaluated in terms of their degree of impact, both now and in the future. **Regional** environmental analysis focuses on a more detailed study of the critical factors within a definite geographic area (e.g., Western Europe, the Middle East). This level is directed toward identifying marketing opportunities for a company's products, services, and/or technology in a specific region. The third level, **country** environmental analysis, involves an even more refined examination of the critical environmental factors. This level continues to focus on the economic, legal, political, and cultural factors in an even smaller number or refined group of countries. This analysis, however, must be oriented toward the specific strategy to enter each individual market in order ensure successful planning.

The second step which aids in the development of an international strategy is the **internal resources audit**. The primary purpose of this audit is to appropriately match a company's managerial, technical, material, and financial resources with those required for successful operation. This audit is related to the business rather than the environment. It focuses on key business success factors, which are simply defined as the key factors essential for success in a particular business. This audit is also considered to be country related in that the amount of resources required will vary relative to the country involved.

In summary, formulating a unified model for international purposes must include the following:

1. Evaluating international opportunities, threats, problems, and risks

2. Evaluating a firm's strengths and weaknesses in order to exploit opportunities in foreign markets

3. Defining a firm's scope relative to international business involvement

4. Formulating a firm's international corporate objectives

5. Developing specific corporate strategies for a firm as a whole—an international corporate strategy

Examples

As discussed, various differences (social, economic, technical, political, etc.) exist from one country to another. Although it is difficult to formulate a unified model for international strategic management, the steps previously mentioned would certainly assist a firm in achieving its international objectives. The implications of failing to consider such differences are illustrated in the following examples:

- A U.S. firm in Spain tried to import its policy of holding a company-sponsored picnic for workers hosted by management. The picnic turned into a fiasco rather than a morale booster. Lower level staff stayed together and felt awkward being served by their superiors. The Spanish attitude toward class distinction kept workers and executives from socializing.

- A U.S. firm built a pineapple cannery at the delta of a river in Mexico. The plan was to barge the ripe fruit downstream from the plantation to the cannery and load it directly onto ocean liners for shipment. However, at the time the pineapples were ripe, the river was in its flood stage, which made it impossible to backhaul the barges upstream. Since there was no other feasible method of transportation, the firm was forced to close down. It sold its new equipment to a group of Mexicans at 5% of the original cost. (The natives subsequently relocated the cannery and the operation was successful.)

- To market its "3T" tire cord in Germany, Goodyear used its American ad, which demonstrated the strength of the cord by showing that it could break a steel chain. The German government intervened, stating that the use of superlatives was not permitted in advertising copy. In Germany, it is illegal to imply that another product is inferior.

These examples illustrate exactly how important it is to carefully assess and evaluate the various factors relative to international strategic management. If all of these relative factors are carefully considered, such failures can ultimately be avoided.

REFERENCES

1. Michael E. Porter, "From Competitive Advantage to Corporate Strategy," *Harvard Business Review,* pp. 43–58, May–June 1987.
2. Leslie W. Rue and Lloyd L. Byers, *Management: Theory and Application* (Homewood, Ill: Irwin), 1983, pp. 617–637.
3. Peter Drucker, *Technology, Management, Society* (New York: Harper & Row), 1970, p. 25.
4. Bernard Leontiades (Taylor), and John R. Sparkes, *Corporate Strategy and Planning* (New York: John Wiley), 1977, pp. 274, 276, 281.
5. James B. Whittaker, *Strategic Planning in a Rapidly Changing Environment* (Washington, D.C.: Lexington Books), 1978, pp. 21, 22.
6. Bobbye D. Sorrels, *Business Communication Fundamentals* (Columbus, Ohio: Charles E. Merrill), 1984, p. 22.
7. Donald A. Ball and Wendell H. McCulloch, Jr., *International Business* (Plano, Tex.: Business Publications), 1985, pp. 89–389.
8. *The World Bank Atlas* (Washington, D.C: The World Bank), 1987.
9. R.M. Emerson, "Power Dependence Relations," *American Sociological Review,* 27:31–40, 1962.
10. William J. Stanton, *Fundamentals of Marketing,* 7th edition (New York: McGraw-Hill), 1984, p. 51.
11. E. Jerome McCarthy, *Basic Marketing,* 7th edition (Homewood, Ill.: Irwin), 1981.
12. Arthur A. Thompson, Jr. and A.J. Strickland III, *Strategic Management: Concepts and Cases,* 5th edition (Homewood, Ill.: BPI Irwin), 1990.
13. Steven C. Wheelwright, "Japan, Where Operations Are Really Strategic," *The Harvard Business Review,* pp. 65–68, July–August 1981.
14. George W. Ball, *Global Companies* (Englewood Cliffs, N.J.: Prentice-Hall), 1982.
15. *Gabler's Wirtschaftslexikon* (Weisbaden, W. Germany: Dr. Theo Gabler, GMBH), 1983, pp. 2193–2220.

BIBLIOGRAPHY

Alkhafaji, Abbass, "Technology Transfer: An Overview as Related to LDC," *Journal of Technology Transfer,* pp. 55–65, 1986.

Babatunde, Thomas, "Foreign Investment and Technological Flow," in *Importing Technology into Africa* (New York: Praeger), 1976, pp. 9–32.

Blank, Stephen, "We Can Live Without You: Rivalry and Dialogue in Russo–Japanese Relations," *Comparative Strategy,* 12:173–198, 1993.

Chinta, Ravi R. and Linda F. Lange, "Strategic Planning in Commercial Banks: A Review and Critique," *IABD Proceedings,* pp. 231–236, Spring 1992.

Cohen, Warren, "Exporting Know-How," *U.S. News & World Report,* pp. 53–57, August–September 1993.

Davidson, William, "International Investment and Technology Transfer," *Experience Effects in International Investment and Technology Transfer,* University of Michigan Research Paper, 1980, pp. 3–7.

Dentzer, Susan, "Meet the New Economic Bogeymen," *U.S. News & World Report,* p. 67, October 1993.

Higgins, James M. and Julian W. Vincze, *Strategic Management and Organizational Policy* (New York: CBS College Publishing), 1993, p. 57.

Huynh, Buu Son, "Strategy in the Open Door Era," *Columbia Journal of Business,* pp. 6–8, Fall 1993.

Impoco, Jim, "Smashing Trade Barriers," *U.S. News & World Report,* p. 71, October 1993.

Kemp, Evan J. Jr., *U.S. Equal Employment Opportunity Commission Public Administration Review,* 35:129–134, March/April 1993.

Korth, Christopher, "Barriers to International Business," in *International Business* (Englewood Cliffs, N.J.: Prentice-Hall), 1985, pp. 80–91.

Rue, Leslie W. and Phyllis G. Holland, *Strategic Management: Concepts and Experiences* (New York: McGraw-Hill), 1986, p. 5.

18 MULTINATIONAL COMPANIES: AN INTEGRATED STRATEGY

ABSTRACT

Integrated strategies and logistics and the complex factors that affect the outcome of strategy formulation, such as international cultures, international law, and environment, are the focus of this chapter. The importance of the leaders of a corporation, who are responsible for making the strategic decisions and motivating the subsidiaries to comply with those decisions, is also examined. These topics are related to specific corporations where appropriate.

CHAPTER OBJECTIVES

1 To identify the steps required to enter the international environment

2 To understand integrated strategy

3 To describe the critical tasks required to manage a network efficiently

4 To identify restrictions that host countries place on multinational corporations

5 To understand competitive advantage

6 To identify communication channels used by multinational corporations

7 To explain the effect of legal systems on multinational corporations

8 To explore due process

9 To identify the types of industries that subsidiaries of multinationals can operate

CASE STUDY
Global Enterprise

The Global Enterprise is awaiting a new day, anticipating the encounter with its international competitors. The Global Enterprise is visualized as being capable of outmaneuvering its predecessor, the international corporation, by reacting to market demands more efficiently and effectively. Multinational corporations identify themselves in terms of such barriers as national borders and sociocultural differences; their customers are domestic markets, and they allocate products according to the preferred tastes of each country. The reward and control structures of multinational corporations are oriented more toward the growth of domestic markets than the growth of the world as a market.

Unlike the multinational corporation, the Global Enterprise does not limit itself to the boundaries imposed by national markets and views the whole world as its market. Instead of running subsidiaries under the control of a centralized management structure, the Global Enterprise is a decentralized system, composed of various management, manufacturing, marketing, resource, and financial nodes. The nodes are structured to operate with full efficiency and effectiveness. The manager of each node is given the latitude and authority to adapt the operation to local conditions and, occasionally, to contact counterpart nodes to resolve problems directly. As the name implies, a multinational corporation should be well positioned to become a Global Enterprise. A small but growing number of companies that are not multinationals may, however, be better positioned to become a Global Enterprise because they already have the flexible, efficient structure that many multinationals lack.

For a company that would aspire to become a Global Enterprise, the time to make the transition is now. Those that wait will not be prepared to face new forms of competition on a truly global scale.

Source: Daniel F. Hefler, Jr. ,"The Dawn of the Global Enterprise," *Journal of Business Strategy,* pp. 86–87, Winter 1984.

INTRODUCTION

In recent years, it has become necessary for many corporations to expand their business activities beyond their domestic borders in order to achieve growth. American markets for many goods and services have become saturated. As demand for their products decreases, corporations move abroad to find new markets. The region of international expansion can be divided into three main areas (see also Figure 18.1):

1. **OPEC countries:** Somewhat underdeveloped, yet very wealthy (e.g., Kuwait)

2. **Third World countries:** Underdeveloped and poor (e.g., Nicaragua, Kenya, Yemen)

3. **Fourth World countries:** Desperately poor countries characterized by starvation and annual per capita income less than $100 (e.g., Somalia, Ethiopia)

The multinational corporation (MNC) is the first institution in human history to plan on a global scale. Its purpose is to organize and integrate economic activity around the world in order to maximize profit. Its failures and successes are measured through growth in global profit and market share. International trade usually benefits all parties involved. The basic assumption in such trade is that the growth of the whole strengthens the welfare of all. The overall focus is increased efficiency. International

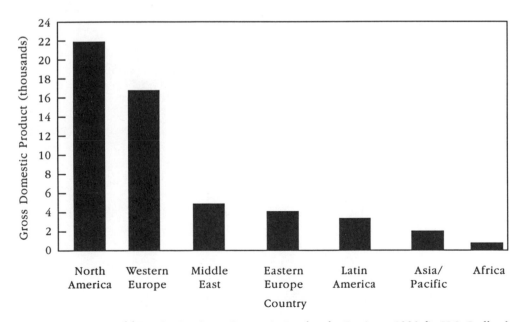

FIGURE 18.1 World Per Capita Gross Domestic Product by Region—1990 (in U.S. Dollars) (Source: The World Market Atlas (New York: Business Edition), 1992)

TABLE 18.1   Ten Leading World Trading Countries (in $U.S. million)

Country	Total exports and imports	Total imports	Total exports
United States	781,378	459,565	321,813
Germany	637,055	281,572	355,483
Japan	452,263	187,348	264,915
France	345,818	178,026	167,792
United Kingdom	335,222	189,753	145,469
Italy	265,779	138,665	127,114
Canada	220,599	107,736	112,863
USSR	217,788	107,229	110,599
Netherlands	203,361	99,800	103,561
Belgium	185,366	92,579	92,787

Source: 1986 International Trade Statistics Year Book (New York: United Nations), 1988.

companies now have significant influence on world productivity and technological advancement. Their influence has grown so vast that it affects all aspects of society.[1] Furthermore, the average rate of growth of the most successful MNCs is two to three times higher than that of most advanced countries. MNCs have grown considerably over the past 20 years. Their growth and power are best illustrated by the fact that 49 of the world's 100 largest economic entities are multinational corporations and not, as expected, countries. Companies such as General Motors, Standard Oil (New Jersey), and Ford have larger annual products than countries such as Austria, Saudi Arabia, or Norway.[2]

In the United States alone, the percentage of the gross national product contributed by MNCs has risen dramatically from 12% in 1960 to 34% in 1984. Consequently, U.S.-based corporations have become increasingly dependent on foreign profits since 1964. A study of the top 298 U.S.-based global corporations showed that they earn 40% of their net profits outside the United States.[1] This growth of MNCs in the United States is reflected in the balance of U.S. trade with the rest of the world. As shown in Table 18.1, the United States is indeed the single largest participant in international trade (measured by the sum of imports and exports) and is a major trading partner for many other countries.

MANUFACTURING FIRMS

Manufacturing firms usually follow a four-step process to enter the international environment:

TABLE 18.2 Company Sales Figures for 1990

Company	Foreign earning as percent of total	Foreign assets as percent of total
NCR	61.9	44.5
Coca-Cola	61.2	40.0
IBM	60.7	52.2
Digital Equipment	55.0	43.6
Johnson & Johnson	51.7	45.9
Eastman Kodak	43.6	29.5
Goodyear Tire & Rubber	42.7	38.3
McDonald's	41.7	43.2
Procter & Gamble	39.9	35.2
Ford Motor	36.7	31.8
General Motors	30.3	29.2
Philip Morris	23.6	26.9

Source: "The 100 Largest U.S. Multinationals," *Forbes,* pp. 286–288, July 22, 1991.

1. A corporation exports goods requested by foreign customers.
2. A firm initiates marketing activities abroad.
3. A firm establishes other functional activities overseas, such as manufacturing. Firms in this stage are called **multinationals**.
4. A firm is characterized by widespread operations and is no longer identified with just one particular country. Firms in this stage are called **transnationals**.

The revenues of these transnational corporations exceed the gross national product of many of the countries in which they operate. For example, IBM (one of the best-known transnationals) earned 60.7% of its total gain from foreign revenue, as indicated in Table 18.2.[3]

GOING INTERNATIONAL

Modern corporations are trying to gain an advantage over their competitors. Most are finding that a good way to do so is through the complex process of going international. By going international, corporations can extend their product lines to other cultures. They can also save money on labor costs by taking advantage of the lower standard of living in some countries. One big advantage of doing business in foreign countries, particularly developing countries, is that high unemployment rates provide inexpensive and vast labor pools. This helps companies to generate more capital and, therefore, bring in more revenue. These countries are ideal for industrial companies in labor-intensive industries.[4] Many U.S. manufacturing firms have found that they incur lower input costs by locating their manufacturing facilities outside the United States and thus can export their products at lower prices than if those same products were manufactured at home. The *maquiladora* in Mexico is a case in point; by sending parts to Mexican plants for assembly, manufacturers can save on labor costs.[5] By going international, a company can make and save money simultaneously, depending on the geographic area.

Several factors both influence the decision to go international and make the move feasible. The ever-pressing need to get ahead of the competition may be a good reason to go abroad. In underdeveloped nations, labor is inexpensive, which means that a company pays less to get the same job done. Another reason for going abroad is rapid expansion, in an effort to keep up with product demand. A home-based company may be expanding rapidly, but not rapidly enough to keep up with market demand. An overseas facility can satisfy such demand. A final reason for going international is the absence of trade barriers and/or lower transportation costs. International trade has become vital to many economies throughout the world. This trend is reflected in the increased efforts of many countries to promote international trade. For example, at the Uruguay round of GATT (the most ambitious trade agreement ever attempted) talks, some 108 nations agreed to lower tariffs and other barriers on textiles and agricultural goods, protect intellectual property, and open their borders to banks, insurance companies, and other services in an effort to attract international trade.[6]

STRATEGY FORMULATION

Objectives and strategies are formulated by considering mission, strategic policy, and information. When a firm operates outside its home country, its strategic objectives and overall strategy change. To adjust its strategy to its various environments, a firm can implement a number of options. Depending on the type of change required, it can choose either expansion or expansion and diversification. However, a firm that chooses expansion as its strategy to achieve corporate development and efficient use of existing resources for higher profits will soon find that it needs to diversify to maintain systematic growth. In the diversification strategy, a firm has two alternatives for expansion:

1. **Geography** (the international route):   A strategy is prepared to weigh the pros and cons of developing foreign markets and the implications of the decision.

2. **Product**:   A firm can choose a move into a new business as an alternative to going international or as a way to enter foreign markets.

A company can also purchase another business that operates in a foreign environment.[7]

The stages of strategy formulation can be categorized as follows: (1) decision preparation stage (also called long-term planning), (2) matching stage (also called intermediate-term planning), and (3) implementation stage (also called short-term planning). In the preparation stage, strategists gather questions and ideas and develop ways to measure and determine feasibility. Other activities include establishing a more objective view of the company's future and setting policies to aid in achieving corporate objectives. It also involves the preparation of a timetable for supplementary decisions. The strategists at this stage plan for the efficient use of corporate resources to the greatest possible advantage and design a system to manage the constant flow of information. When the basic decisions about strategy have been made, a corporation is ready to undertake the next step. The matching stage involves the development of systematic guidelines to forecast opportunities and threats, along with setting deadlines to measure progress and establishing mechanisms to cope with possible problems. The strategists develop a structure for international logistics to purchase raw materials and distribute products. Then the strategists select methods to integrate and compromise between the company's resources and the design of the decision system. In the third stage, tasks and available machinery are assigned to each operating unit for implementation. Other activities in this stage include developing efficient inventory procedures, financial practices, and the flexibility to accommodate delays when a part of the program runs late.[7]

MNCs are highly dependent on a strategic advantage, as are most organizations. Many multinational firms key in on the superiority of some resource, such as capital, labor, or technology. Capitalizing on an advantage can compensate for a weakness. Strategy formulation gives a company a competitive advantage in that it improves quality and reduces costs. It also facilitates innovation through open lines of communication among team members.

A key factor for success in going multinational is a strong integrated strategy. An integrated strategy should always include costs and margins. A corporation that wants to be strong in the international arena must consider competitive advantage. In a long-range strategic plan, it would be senseless to operate an international subsidiary whose costs exceed its profits. The same is true in integrated strategy. For example, to gain a competitive advantage in its internal business process, John Deere implemented strategic integration, which provided the means to contain cost, improve quality, and maintain consistency in product design. It was applied across their entire product line. In some cases, strategic integration is in reaction to a move made by a leading competitor that has changed its strategy to position itself for a competitive advantage. In order to be competitive, John Deere needed to implement a new business process. The first phase was collocation and integration, which involved moving both designers and manufacturing engineers to a design center where they would work collectively—as a team, instead of as individuals—on new

CASE STUDY
Electrolux Goes International

Electrolux experienced several integration problems when it attempted to enter the international market. The company's experience is highlighted here. In 1983, the dream of a single European market started taking shape. Based on studies that showed a convergence of European lifestyles, Electrolux, the Swedish appliance maker, bought Italy's Zanussi Group and became Europe's largest appliance maker.

Southern Europeans, who shop daily, want small refrigerators; northern Europeans, who only shop once a week, want large refrigerators. Southerners like the freezer on the top, and northerners like it on the bottom. The British prefer more freezer space because they consume more frozen foods.

Electrolux is still making money, but its profits have fallen. Although the company had $14 billion in sales, it earned only $32.6 million. As a result, Electrolux cut its dividend in half, the first reduction in nearly a century. A little less than two-thirds of its sales are generated from household appliances; the rest is from auto parts, mining, and forestry and garden equipment. Electrolux officials acknowledged that the flagship appliance business was hit the hardest.

Electrolux's experience offers a clear warning to companies thinking about selling their products in Europe. The American model does not apply there. For example, four firms control about 80% of the U.S. appliance market, whereas 100 appliance makers are battling it out in Europe. Most American refrigerators have the freezer on top, come in only a few sizes, and are sold under a few national brand names. In Europe, Electrolux produces as many as 120 basic designs with 1500 variations.

In response to the hard times, Electrolux decided to scale back some of its initial goals. Lief Johansson, president of Electrolux, said, "My strategy is to go global only when I can stay local when I must," although he thinks that Electrolux must implement a global strategy if it is going to be successful in the long run.

In the mid-1980s, Electrolux was selling throughout Europe. In 1986, the company crossed the Atlantic by purchasing White Consolidated in the United States. Electrolux has numerous brands in Europe, ranging from Arthur Martin in France to Zoppas in Italy, and it kept them all. In addition, two general European brands were created: Zanussi, primarily for younger customers, and Electrolux, for well-to-do older buyers.

Electrolux is looking to the former Soviet Union, Asia, and the United States for expansion. It sells merchandise under the Frigidaire brand name in the United States and is currently a distant number three in sales. The company's modest aim is to fill some market niches in the United States. In summary, Lief Johansson said, "I want to be a good Frenchman in France and a good Italian in Italy."

Source: "Europe and Beyond," Appliance Manufacturer, 41:33–36, April 1993; Norman C. Remich, Jr., "The New Europe," Appliance Manufacturer, 41:5, February 1993.

designs. Under this setup, the lines of communication were opened up and everyone was involved in the development of new product.[8]

Two assumptions are connected with a successful multinational integration strategy: (1) integration provides a MNC with an advantage over its competitors and (2) an organization can trade off some proceeds of its competitive advantage with host governments. Once these assumptions have been implemented, a company must pay close attention to economies of scale and the economic situation in the countries to which it expands.

Another function of integration is supplier partnership, which facilitates better communication with suppliers and can prove to be valuable in product design. For example, the final stage of integration at John Deere was the focused factory. The factory floor was divided into manufacturing cells, which were positioned near each other to reduce handling and just-in-time inventory from aisles. The greatest advantage of the focused factory is that it involves the people on the floor in improved design and communication.[8] Management needs to monitor the manufacturing network efficiently, which requires three critical tasks: (1) creating and maintaining an efficient manufacturing system in both location and types of process technologies used (this also includes suppliers and subcontractors, (2) programming production efficiently to exploit economies of throughput, and (3) managing logistics effectively to minimize transportation and inventory costs.[9]

Implementing an integrated strategy usually requires several compromises with the host country. These usually involve sharing the economic benefits of the new subsidiary or branch of the MNC. Laws and regulations, whether domestic or international, also need to be considered, because they differ from country to country.

An integrated strategy should also consider customer needs and tastes, which vary from culture to culture. For example, McDonald's uses spicier ingredients in Spain than in the United States. An integrated strategy allows a company that is going international to adjust its product line to suit a variety of customers and cultures. It also allows room for improvements, such as new distribution channels, for optimal international commercial practices.

A strong integrated strategy includes logistics management, which is the central operational task. Logistic strategy analysis must start with economic factors, because the production–marketing system exists to implement the resource transmission capabilities rooted in these factors. The major factors are economic differentials and the efficiencies available through a unified global system. However, analysis based on economic factors must be modified by other influences, including government actions and corporate characteristics.[10] Logistics strategy for a MNC has three main goals:

1. To efficiently transmit resources so as to maximize their flow in a natural direction as determined by economic differentials and government actions

TABLE 18.3   When GM Charges More Than $10,000 for a Pontiac Lemans

$3000	To South Korea for labor and assembly
4000	To employees and shareholders of GM
1850	To Japan for engines and electronics
700	To Germany for design
400	To Taiwan and Singapore for small components
250	To Britain for advertising and marketing
50	To Ireland for data processing

Source: "The Myth of 'Made in the U.S.A.,'" *Wall Street Journal,* p. A6, July 5, 1991.

2. To utilize the potential and make maximum use of the special advantages of a MNC as a global organization

3. To effectively implement resource transmission, with special regard to communication as a critical factor[10]

MNCs use logistics systems to keep production balanced and to check inconsistencies in the schedules of integrated plants. At monthly meetings, key managers and company experts schedule production lines and corporate goals for the upcoming month. A key topic is generally inventory control. For example, a MNC with several subsidiaries that build components for a final product that is assembled in the United States needs to control inventories to keep costs down. Most of the large automakers in the United States use this type of system, which needs to be controlled in order to be effective. An example is given in Table 18.3.[11]

Unfortunately, many companies fail due to inconsistencies. Decisions in the expansion of an integrated system are more complicated than the daily operations of a domestic corporation. Efficiency of operation and flexibility of supply must be carefully monitored on a daily basis. The number of integrated plants should be kept at a limited or optimal level in order to avoid unnecessary complexities. For example, when Volkswagen invested in the United States, it did not realize the magnitude of the risk involved. First, the cost of labor was extremely high. Then, when the dollar rose dramatically, the cost of operation was affected by the exchange rate, which made the integration obsolete. Integration strategies and logistics play an important role in the expansion process, not only for U.S.-based companies but for growing companies throughout the world.

HOST COUNTRY CONTROLS AND REGULATIONS

Companies must adhere to different rules in international marketing, and, therefore, strategies must also be altered. Indeed, the governments of different countries impose different regulations on MNCs, in varying degrees. Hal Mason[12] reports that host countries often restrict the following:

- **Ownership**: Host countries typically require that a local firm own a majority or controlling interest.

- **Employment**: Almost all host countries demand that certain managerial and technological positions be held by host country nationals.

- **Profits and fees**: Profits and fees are typically set at some maximum level.

- **Internal debt capital**: Internal debt capital is often set according to a preestablished formula.

- **Training and development**: Insistence on training and development for host country nationals is common.

- **Host country markets**: Most host countries demand development of their exports.

- **Technological bases**: Most host countries seek technology-based industries rather than extractive industries.

Setting objectives is also significantly affected by a multinational environment because:

- Growth may be legislatively limited.

- Efficiency may be held to an undesirably low level by extra costs as dictated by governments.

- Use of resources may be set at specified levels; contribution to owners (profits) is usually set at arbitrary levels.

- Contribution to customers may be modified to meet government-established levels.

- Contribution to employees focuses on technical training and often includes guaranteed employment as opposed to true development.

- Contribution to society is stressed by the government's involvement in all areas. Social concern, however, does not take the form to which we are accustomed in the United States and Canada, such as emphasis on pollution control, despite the fact that in many Eastern bloc countries, such as Poland, the pollution is devastating.

A basic strategy of Japanese companies is to diversify early in their history. U.S. firms do not diversify quite as early, and European firms tend to diversify later still. Japanese companies pay closer attention than any other country to quality in production. Japanese management philosophy is oriented toward the group or team. In virtually all countries, negotiation with the government is becoming increasingly more critical than it has in the United States and Canada. While objectives and strategies will vary, *the basics of strategy are the same.* The differences in the basic strategies of MNCs can be traced to cultural/historical factors.

STRATEGIES AT STRATEGIC BUSINESS UNITS

The factors that affect strategy at the strategic business unit (SBU) level are significantly modified in multinational operations. All of the factors involved in the marketing mix are affected in some way by the international situation. Majaro[13] emphasizes the impact of the environment, competition, institutions, and the legal system on the factors in the marketing mix.

Obviously, the product itself is very important. Design, packaging, and special needs to accommodate certain sizes and dimensions for consumers in different countries are very important. Promotion is also governed by local practices. Price is frequently determined by cultural customs that influence the amount of money that should be spent on a product. Distribution is affected by, among other things, availability of roads and other transportation channels. A firm must consider all of these factors in order to be successful. The following are examples of ventures that failed because these factors were not taken into consideration:

• Many companies fail because they simply do not research the market sufficiently. American corn flakes flopped in Japan because the Japanese did not like the general idea of breakfast cereal. Catsup also did not do well because the Japanese overwhelmingly prefer soy sauce. Kentucky Fried Chicken (KFC), which had hoped to open 100 stores in Brazil, had low sales when it began operations in São Paulo because it did not sufficiently research the competition, which was low-priced, charcoal-broiled chicken that was sold on virtually every street corner. KFC developed a new plan (to sell hamburgers, enchiladas, and tacos) only to find that customers were not interested in products they had never heard of.

• Campbell Soup Company's research suggested a potential market in Great Britain. At first, however, sales were lower than expected. The problem was that the company did not realize that the British were unaccustomed to canned soup in condensed form. To the British, the can contained only half the soup for the same price. The company boosted its sales by adding water to its product.

• McDonnell Douglas put together a brochure for potential aircraft customers in India with photographs that depicted men in turbans. The catalog did not promote their product well because the pictures were taken from an old issue of *National Geographic* in which Pakistani men, and not Indians, wore turbans.

• One company printed an entire catalog with "OK" stamped on each page. OK is offensive in some parts of South America, and the company had to incur a costly six-month delay to reprint the catalog.[14]

Financial strategies should address currency exchange rates. Fluctuations in exchange rates can cause many problems in terms of profits. Production strategies must cope with the logistical problems that accompany inadequate transportation systems, a dearth of suppliers, and a largely unskilled work force. Personnel strategies should consider laws and customs in regulating work and authority.

The specifics of management functions vary among countries. Managers have different expectations in terms of motivation and leadership style. Different countries have different management hierarchies, motivational techniques, and long-range planning priorities. Control strategies are very important to multinational firms, as are functional strategies, such as communication habits and decision-making skills. If a multinational organization is to survive and prosper, it must be able to adapt.

One of the most important factors that affects MNCs is the host country's culture. People in different parts of the world have different beliefs. Language is also an important consideration. The same word can take on a different meaning in a different culture. Before a company plans to integrate into another country, extensive research must be done on the area's culture. An important cultural factor that affects management is how competition is viewed. This can influence motivation, leadership style, the compensation system, and the type of people hired.[9]

An additional factor in the success of MNCs is the use of comparative management, which is defined as the analysis of cross-cultural management practices and techniques.[15] Many international managers fail because they are unfamiliar with patterns in the local culture. The American way of doing things is not always the proper way in other cultures. Combining cultures in managerial decisions promotes understanding. To work effectively in a foreign country, a manager must understand the culture of the host country. For example, AT&T representatives at the company's first privately held exhibit in Tokyo were well prepared. In addition to language skills, they had also acquired information about the shared knowledge, beliefs, and values of potential Japanese customers, as well as their ways of interacting and conducting business.[16]

A corporation should also consider local attitudes and beliefs in terms of time value, punctuality or promptness, achievement, work, and change. These factors have a major influence on the business functions of a MNC and may require adaptation.[17]

Sociocultural components include religion, folklore, music, and art. Advertising a product in a commercial with music in the background may not be appropriate in certain cultures. Americans may enjoy the music , but other cultures may find it distasteful or even sacrilegious.

Material culture involves technology and how a product will interact in a specific culture. For example, what if all Ford automobiles sold in Europe had the steering wheel on the left side? They would be unsuccessful because most Europeans drive on the right side of the vehicle. This would be both a cultural and a technological error.

Education plays a major role in the success of a MNC. A company can both improve product quality and achieve its goals by sharing technology and information. Implementing this idea in a multicultural research and development program can improve a company's product line. When a product that is successful in the United States needs to be adjusted to suit a new region, both cultures can work together to create a suitable product. Participants in a multinational venture need to sit down and communicate their differences. For example, exchanging gifts is customary in some countries, whereas in the United States it is seen as bribery. Differences in language must also be addressed. These differences should be discussed before a program begins.

There are so many differences between cultures that it is impossible to cover them all at once. The point is that in order to be successful, a manager of a MNC should be sensitive to and aware of these differences. A manager will gain the respect of his or her employees by trying to understand what they stand for and what their beliefs are, and the same is true for the employees. By understanding the differences in other cultures, a MNC fosters better employee relations, which in turn affects output and the operation in general in a foreign region. Many companies have failed in the past due to a lack of knowledge about other cultures. It is important for a MNC to gain an advantage over its competitors, and one way to do so is by understanding the culture of its host country.

While learning about a host country's culture, it is also important to build excellent communication channels. In the international market, a complex pattern of communication is often created by the combination of diversity of activities, spread of operations, pressures of environment and competition, and individual characteristics of the parties involved.[10]

All top-level managers in an integrated multinational business need channels for communication and information. These channels are important in keeping subsidiary managers from developing self-serving arguments against integration. All the branches of a MNC should be focused on the same goals. Communication channels have a strong influence on the overall integrated strategy. A functional channel provides feedback on market performance of existing products, requests for new products and review of development projects. Functional channels are limited when communication on a key competitive issue is misinterpreted, which is usually due to a lack of knowledge about the host country.

Global strategic decisions affect the entire company. Managers value input from subsidiaries and work back and forth with top executives in decision making. This type of dialogue requires open lines of communication, even at lower levels. It also means that a company must learn to trust and respect the decisions of lower level managers.

Two-way communication can sometimes result in heated debates. As people split into factions, they begin to distrust one another. According to Kim and Mauborgne, "Moreover, when subsidiary managers participate in global strategic decision making, they come to view the decisions as their own." This leads to debate over who is right, as people defend their decisions. When information and ideas are exchanged freely, global strategic decision making can be both informative and productive. It allows managers at all levels to express their opinions and hear the opinions of others. When managers feel that their views are taken into consideration, they are likely to be satisfied with the strategic decisions made.[18]

The communication channel that involves interface with senior management can be formal or informal. It includes program plans and possible environmental strategies. These plans involve a specific purpose and are aimed at a specific area in need of improvement. The program is discussed well in advance and involves a specific purpose. An environmental strategy is a response to important conditions or issues in the natural environment, such as worker codetermination in Germany.[9] Here, a subsidiary manager brings the problem to the attention of corporate management at headquarters, although sometimes it is better for a subsidiary to act autonomously and depart from corporate patterns.

When top management cannot resolve or deal directly with an issue that affects an operation in the integrated network, the corporate managing committee has the final decision in the issue resolution process. For example, a subsidiary that feels that its budget is insufficient can approach the corporate managing committee with a request to have it increased. Some integrated companies assign key senior executives as local advocates. They represent key subsidiary or regional interests at corporate headquarters in order to facilitate communication. A strong global market requires strong localism. The integrated strategies for communication must be brought to the attention of the performance of the strategic business units. Thus, a balance must be struck between decision making and communication. The following excerpt illustrates the importance of well-integrated communication channels at a bank in Japan:

> With branches in every Japanese prefecture, DKB, the Dai-Ici-Kangyo-Bank, has the resources to effectively service foreign companies doing business almost everywhere in Japan. With a corporate culture oriented to customer service, it seeks to create financial services products suited to customer requirement. Some two hundred foreign companies already rely on DKB not only for regular banking services, but also for advice on business expansion in Japan including M&A and assistance in arranging loans from government financial institutions. Moreover, given DKB's strength throughout Asia, many use the bank to help expand their business in the wider regional market. In North America, much of DKB's business focuses on helping Japanese—as well as U.S. and Canadian—clients operate more effectively. The bank has operations based in New York, Chicago, Los Angeles, San Francisco, Atlanta, Houston, Toronto and Vancouver.[19]

LAWS AND REGULATIONS

One of the most difficult and complicated areas that affects a MNC is the different laws and regulations involved in international trade. Special attention should be given to researching the legal systems of the countries in which a MNC operates. In the world of business, the legal environment is based on the following laws:

- **Islamic law:** Derived from interpretation of the *Qur'an* and the teachings of the Prophet Mohammed; found in most of the Islamic countries.

- **Socialist law:** Derived from the Marxist socialist system and found in countries such as the former Soviet Union and China.

- **Common law:** Derived from English law and found in countries such as England and Canada.

- **Civil or code law:** Derived from Roman law and found in the remaining non-Islamic and nonsocialist countries.[20]

Procedural justice is defined as the extent to which the dynamics of a multinational's strategic decision-making process for its subsidiary units is judged to be fair by subsidiary top management. This term can be broken down into five parts:

1. There is a need for two-way communication in every interaction.

2. Lower level managers and workers have the right and responsibility to challenge their managers.

3. The head office must acknowledge and be aware of the local situation at subsidiaries.

4. When a final strategic decision is made by top management, it is relayed down through the chain of command.

5. The head office is consistent in its decision making as it affects subsidiaries. This allows management to judge strategic decision making across subsidiary units to be just.[21]

The more subsidiaries a corporation has in different countries, the more regulated that company will become. Domestic laws, host country laws, and international laws all must be considered. A MNC based in the United States can suffer extreme levels of taxation. The higher the income, the higher the income tax. Double taxation takes place by taxing the stockholders and investors. In addition, a subsidiary can be taxed by its host country, which puts it in the position of triple taxation. There is also capital gains tax, which is paid on the sale of an asset at a greater amount of cost. Many countries that host MNCs have a tax treaty. The countries involved sign a treaty in which each country outlines its tax laws and programs.

Tariffs and quotas are another national legal force. Tariffs raise federal funds and at the same time protect the well-being of a country's free enterprise system. Quotas are enacted to protect domestic producers.

Another important factor that a company should consider before going multinational is the right to keep property in the event of a crisis. A legal option that is open to certain countries is the right to seize foreign-owned property within national borders. This is known as expropriation or confiscation, and it is legal as long as a country has defined it by law.[9]

There are three classifications of international legal forces: (1) contract enforcement; (2) solutions to jurisdiction, interpretation, and enforcement problems; and (3) patents, trademarks, and trade secrets. It is usually difficult to solve a multinational problem that involves a contract, because contracts are usually handled through goodwill. Sometimes, however, arbitration can be effective. Trademarks protect against counterfeiting. They are usually good for 10 to 20 years, but the specifics vary from county to country and can affect a company's profits. Copyrights protect the rights of authors, while trade secrets protect information that companies want to keep confidential. Patents protect the rights of inventors of new products and are usually good for 15 to 20 years, although, again, they vary from country to country. MNCs should look into the laws and regulations that govern contracts in order to prevent espionage. One law of major importance to MNCs is the Foreign Corrupt Practices Act. It outlaws certain types of bribes, but does not specify any in particular. It holds management responsible for maintaining records of the company's behavior to ensure that no violations occur.[9]

INTERNATIONAL MARKETING

A final topic in multinational business is marketing formalities. When marketing internationally, a corporation needs to consider the differences in the marketing mix. International marketing involves relationships with distribution channels and advertising media, which vary among different cultures. A key consideration is to develop good relationships with host country distributors and to allow people familiar with the area to market the product. The development and efficient management of an integrated network in a multinational operation involves a series of focused trade-offs:

1. Integrating R&D management (avoiding duplication but possibly stifling creativity) versus letting various R&D centers freely develop competing designs and ideas (but forgoing the benefits of integration)

2. Improving the productivity of the manufacturing network versus enhancing its acceptability to host governments (when to optimize versus when to compromise)

3. Developing uniform marketing approaches for "world products" versus adapting approaches to multiple national conditions

The danger in an integrated MNC is that managers can feel so strongly about global competitive strategies that they fail to recognize these trade-offs,[9] which is why marketing is an important element of international business. Therefore, it can be said that the strategic management process is the same for domestic and international management; however, the environment is often different. MNCs that have multinational markets and sources of capital, labor, manufacturing, and supplies are confronted with four major problems:

1. The international marketplace is highly competitive. Many countries have forged substantial international competitive units. The strategic advantages enjoyed by many of these firms, from low labor cost to high technology, make competing with them very difficult.

2. Operations are conducted in widely varying economic, social, political, and cultural environments. Economics varies from developing to mature, and marketing segments to which a company sells in the parent country may not exist in the host country.

3. The relative values of currencies vary rapidly. This has a major impact on a firm's financial position. One major U.S.-based company recently lost one-third of its profit when the value of the dollar declined. Some firms lose all their profits.

4. Relations among the home government, the host government, and the MNC have significant bearing on results.

PROBLEMS MULTINATIONAL CORPORATIONS FACE IN IMPLEMENTING GLOBAL STRATEGIES

In discussing the problems that MNCs face in implementing global strategies, the issues that affect managers of subsidiaries in implementing the strategies formulated by top management are specifically addressed in this section. The traditional view of subsidiary managers in implementing global strategies is that they are motivated by compensation, monitoring systems, and the magnitude of specific rewards and punishments. This view is no longer feasible in modern management practice. Top managers of subsidiaries feel that the issue of **due process** is one of the most important factors, which means that they want an open policy that is fair and consistent.

Kim and Mauborgne have done extensive research over the past four years on how to effectively implement global strategies.[18] In practical terms, they state that due process means that (1) the head office is familiar with the local situation at subsidiaries, (2) the global strategy development process includes two-way communication, (3) the head office is relatively consistent in decision making across subsidiary units, (4) subsidiary units can legitimately challenge the strategic views and decisions of the head office, and (5) subsidiary units are given an explanation of final strategic decisions. The following example illustrates how the concept of two-way communication may serve as an important element of a global decision and its success:

> Toshiya Kohama, Kawasaki Heavy Industries' (KHI) executive managing director, remarks that modern day economic activities are taking on global dimensions. And they are entering an era of a borderless economy. This can create as many problems as opportunities. KHI's product line-up includes aircraft, ships, railroad rolling stock, motorcycles, plant engineering and a broad range of machinery. Organizationally, KHI has made some changes. Due to rapid technological innovations and changes of market structure, there are occasions when the established divisional management cannot quickly or effectively respond to market needs and customer requirements. This led KHI to set up an "Inter-Divisional Activities" unit as a corporate headquarters staff organization. Its mission is to develop marketing strategies and promote activities for the penetration of new markets. This unit is responsible not only for sales, but for imports into Japan, expanding overseas production, strategic planning and promoting joint R&D projects. This should have a significant impact on KHI's already substantial presence in the U.S. as the company has a number of U.S. plants.[22]

These authors have held extensive interviews with 63 subsidiary presidents to gather information about how multinationals can make global strategies work. The main concern of the top executives was the concept of due process. They want the head office to understand the local economy and consider this factor in its decision making. They feel that a corporation will make a wiser decision if it understands the local economy. They feel that two-way communication is the second most important factor. They want to be able to voice their opinions and know that their concerns will be considered. Third, they want consistent decision-making practices across subsidiary units. Each subsidiary should be given the same respect and consideration. Subsidiary managers realize that each subsidiary is unique in its own way, but they feel that a consistent policy toward global decision making should be followed across all subsidiaries. Fourth, they want to be able to refute decisions made by top management. They want the power to challenge the head office without fear of being penalized. Managers say that this will make them more willing to follow final decisions because their opinions were given serious consideration. Finally, managers want an explanation of the final decision. They want to know why the top executives chose a particular strategy. This will make them more content with the decision and make it easier to follow.

In another study, Kim and Mauborgne examined the attitudes generated by procedural justice and analyzed the theoretical bases. They concluded that procedural justice will directly affect compliance, commitment, trust, and outcome satisfaction.[18]

CASE STUDY
Due Process

When an employee has a grievance, it is usually handled in a certain manner. David Ewing, author of *Justice on the Job*, conducted a study of due process in several corporations. He alleged, "In companies lacking due process, thousands of employees silently endure shame and humiliation because they are afraid to challenge an unfair or neurotic supervisor for fear of losing their livelihood."

Polaroid Corporation has developed an effective due process program that consists of a five-step grievance process. The fifth and final stage of the process is binding arbitration, by which both the employee and the employer must abide. This is a rare situation for nonunionized employees.

The process works as follows. First, the employee takes the problem to his or her department manager. Second, if the problem is not resolved, the case proceeds to the division manager. If the case is still not resolved, the third step involves a Personnel Policy Committee to review the matter. The committee is composed of three officers and five peers. If the problem still exists, the fourth step is for the employee to take the problem to the company president or his or her designee. The fifth and final step is arbitration. An employee can choose to either represent himself or herself or can designate someone else to act as his or her representative during arbitration. A typical dispute may arise over job selection or similar issues. This procedure is time consuming, but such a policy is needed to ensure strong employee loyalty.

Most companies have mechanisms to prevent a manager from retaliating against an employee. A typical company may require cases to be evaluated by a peer review board or a human resource strategy group, depending on the situation. This ensures objectivity and confidentiality. After the peer review board or human resource strategy group hears the case, they vote on the outcome. Their decision is reviewed by the senior vice president of human resources. This system promotes positive employee relations. The simple fact that the system exists is comforting to many employees, even if they have no need to use it.

There are a number of benefits to having a due process program. Due process ensures justice for employees, helps hold unions at large, reduces the number of lawsuits filed by former employees, boosts morale, and fosters employee loyalty.

Source: Robert S. Seeley, "Corporate Due Process," *HR Magazine,* 37:46–49, July 1992.

In their study, they distinguished between two different types of industries that subsidiaries of multinationals can operate: multidomestic and global. Because these industries are extremely different, they require different strategies for success. **Multidomestic industries** lack cost efficiencies and must, therefore, they try to optimize global market performance by maximizing local efficiency. The strategic mission of **multinational industries** is to exploit homogenous markets and to strive for global cost efficiencies. The differences between these industries also affect subsidiary compliance. While subsidiaries operating in multidomestic industries exercise relatively high levels of compliance, those in multinational industries exercise low levels of compliance. In either case, the use of procedural justice is an important element in implementing corporate strategic decisions.

According to Kim and Mauborgne, there were no objective and quantitative measures of subsidiary top management compliance. Consequently, they measured the following control variables in their studies: decision outcome fairness, decision outcome favorableness, reward system, and procedural justice. Although the study did not offer any specific recommendations on the issue of how to motivate subsidiary compliance with corporate strategic decisions, it would seem appropriate to measure the control variables mentioned by the authors when implementing a corporate strategic decision.

In conclusion, the effective implementation of global decisions is a challenge that top-level managers face. Unfortunately, they are losing the battle, although there is hope. Top management must understand the concept of due process and make a serious attempt to implement it in the decision-making process. There are additional problems to contend with. The collapse of appraisal and control capability, the eroding power of the head office, and the decline in common values and expectations are among the serious issues confronting managers. Managers also have to go beyond their normal duties and be creative in their decision making.

Managers of multinational concerns must have a broad understanding of the cultural and political environments in which they are doing business. Careful business management is critical in international markets, where the possibility of both loss and gain is high and many complex factors can affect the outcome. All management functions should be followed along with an integrated strategy. Despite the complexities, the promise for multinationals is high, not only in monetary terms, but also in the accumulation of knowledge and new business ideas.

REFERENCES

1. R.J. Barnett and R.E. Muller, *Global Reach* (New York: Simon & Schuster), 1974, pp. 14, 20.
2. Abdul A. Said and Luiz R. Simmons, "The Politics of Transition," in *The New Sovereigns: Multinational Corporations as World Powers,* Abdul A. Said and Luiz R. Simmons (Eds.) (Englewood Cliffs, N.J.: Prentice-Hall), 1975, p.18.

3. "U.S. Corporations with the Biggest Foreign Investment: The 100 Largest U.S. Multinationals," *Forbes,* 22:286–288, July 1991.

4. Stephen Herbert Hymer, *The International Operations of National Firms* (Cambridge, Mass.: MIT Press), 1976.

5. Philip R. Cateora, *International Marketing,* 5th edition (Homewood, Ill.: Irwin, 1993), p. 334.

6. William Echkison, "Dangerous Times for Trade Treaties," *Fortune,* p. 14, September 20, 1993.

7. Ingo Walter and Tracy Murray, *Handbook of International Management: International Corporate Planning* (New York: John Wiley), 1988.

8. Richard E. Anderson, "Strategic Integration: How John Deere Did It," *Journal Business Strategy,* pp. 21–26, August 1992.

9. Abbass F. Alkhafaji, *A Stakeholder Approach to Corporate Governance: Managing in a Dynamic Environment* (New York: Quorum Books), 1989.

10. John Fayerweather, *International Business Strategy and Administration* (Cambridge, Mass.: Ballinger), 1978, pp. 286, 534–543.

11. Robert Reich, "The Myth of 'Made in the U.S.A.,'" *Wall Street Journal,* p. A6, July 1991.

12. Hal Mason, "Some Observations on the Choice of Technology by Multinational Firms in Developing Countries," *Review of Economics and Statistics,* 55(3): 349–355, 1973.

13. Simon Majaro, *Marketing: A Strategic Approach to World Markets* (London: George Allen and Unwin), 1977.

14. D.A. Ricks, *Big Business Blunders* (Homewood, Ill.: Dow Jones-Irwin), 1983.

15. Wolfgang Scholl, "Codetermination and the Ability of Firms to Act in the Federal Republic of Germany," *International Studies of Management and Organizations,* Volume XVII, Summer 1987.

16. George B. Northcraft and Margaret A. Neale, *Organizational Behavior: A Management Challenge* (New York: Dryden Press), 1990, p. 770.

17. Fred D. Baldwin, *Conflicting Interests: Corporate-Governance Controversies* (Toronto: Heath), 1984.

18. W. Chan Kim and Renee A. Mauborgne, *Sloan Management Review,* 34:11–27, 1993.

19. "DKB: The Dai-Ici-Kangyo-Bank," *Business Week,* p. 85, July 13, 1992.

20. Don Alan Evans and Thomas Buwers, "The Legal Environment of International Business (book review): A Guide for United States Firms," *American Business Law Journal,* 28:517–523, Fall 1990.

21. W. Chan Kim and Renee A. Mauborgne, "Effectively Conceiving and Executing Multinationals' Worldwide Strategies," *Journal of International Business Studies,* 24(3):419, Third Quarter 1993.

22. "Kawasaki Heavy Industries: Improving International Coordination," *Business Week,* p. 92, July 13, 1992.

BIBLIOGRAPHY

Bedeian, Arthur G., *Management* (New York: Dryden), 1986, pp. 639–643.

Kold, Endel-Jakob, *Environment of International Business* 2nd edition (Boston: Kent), 1985, p. 1.

Negandhi, Anant R., *International Management* (Boston: Allyn and Bacon), 1989.

U.S. Department of Commerce, "U.S. Trade with Leading Partners in 1988," *Business America,* p. 6, September 11, 1989.

19 THE STRUCTURE OF GLOBAL ORGANIZATIONS

ABSTRACT

The structural design of global organizations in a complex environment is discussed in this chapter. Firms operating in international business find themselves faced with greater environmental complexities and uncertainties due to diversities in language, government, and culture and the communication and transportation problems that are inherent in the greater distances involved.

CHAPTER OBJECTIVES

1 To understand structural design in a complex environment

2 To review recent investigations of international strategy–structure relationships

3 To examine how structure can be implemented

4 To discuss the screening process for new people entering an organization

5 To understand the difference between formal and informal organizations

CASE STUDY
The Walt Disney Corporation

Walt Disney, the amusement business titan, went through a restructuring process to open up new market opportunities in Europe. Euro Disney, the company's newest addition to its amusement parks, is a transfer of traditional American entertainment, but accented with European traditions. Disney realized the need to compete globally and enter new markets. Many other amusement parks have followed suit and expanded globally, with new parks opening in Germany, China, and Brazil. Disney has also gone through restructuring in the United States and has plans to add a new theme park dedicated to U.S. history by 1998.

Source: Warren Cohen, "Fun Boom," *U.S. News & World Report*, p. 14, November 22, 1993.

INTRODUCTION

Empirical research on structure has consistently failed to find successful formal structures for global companies whose strategies require both efficiency and sensitivity to local needs or demands. However, research has uncovered the importance of the informal organizational structure in the success of global operations. Such a structure helps an organization reach the higher levels of information processing capacity and responsiveness that are necessary to compete in this complicated business environment. It recognizes the realm of international business by quantifying environmental complexity in terms of the degree of foreign product diversity, the percentage of foreign sales and the degree of foreign manufacturing employed.[1,2]

Researchers have been able to find strategy–structure correlations for firms operating in the lower regions of environmental complexity, but have failed to find support for any correlations in regions of high environmental complexity. A matrix structure, in which activities are grouped by functional logic on the vertical axis and activities are organized by product or project, is often suggested as appropriate for complex environments. However, these studies have found only weak support for such an argument, if any at all. Bartlett and Ghoshal studied the adaptation of several multinational companies to evolving worldwide technology and market conditions. They concluded that to be successful in this arena, organizations must be able to "simultaneously optimize efficiency, responsiveness, and learning..."[3] A major contribution of this work is their analysis of the methods that several successful companies used to achieve this goal. This and other research on international strategy–structure relationships concludes that:

1. Conventional formal organizational structures (e.g., the international division; organizations segmented by function, product, market, or geography; or matrix structures) inherently lack the information processing capacity and responsiveness that are required to be successful in a complex business environment.

2. Successful companies purposely developed their informal organization to enhance their information processing capacity and responsiveness.[4] Of the traditionally defined formal organizational structures, the matrix structure provides a well-defined basis for decisions on a broad range of influences.

RESTRUCTURING FOR GLOBAL COMPETITION

Americans can be more successful if they recognize that foreign managers see them differently.

Arthur Whitehall

Modern-day American managers view themselves as the best businesspeople in the world. Their perception of business is the only true perception compared to other managers of the world. American business managers believe that their way of managing is the best way. This misconception by American managers is costing American businesses large sums of money in lost market share. This attitude has contributed to the decline of American productivity and creativity. Foreign companies have recognized the need to be culturally diverse. Countries such as Japan and Germany have used negative American attitudes to their advantage. These two countries recognize the importance of being culturally diverse and aware.

Foreign revenue as a percent of total revenue already exceeds 50% in hundreds of American firms, including Exxon, Gillette, Dow Chemical, Citicorp, Colgate-Palmolive and Texaco.[5] If American companies are to be successful in the international market, then U.S. companies must restructure typical management thought. Fully 95% of the world's population lives outside the United States, and this group is growing 70% faster in number than the American population.[5] American companies need to prepare themselves for the new world market. To better compete in world markets, American managers must gain an understanding of the historical, cultural, and religious forces that motivate and drive people in other countries. Most Americans have only one perception of the world. Managers need to start thinking about other ways of conducting business. U.S. managers must learn the customs and codes of conduct of other societies in order to gain their trust and friendship. The Japanese have quickly learned the traditions and customs of the United States. The large number of U.S. businesses that are Japanese controlled is evidence that Americans welcome Japanese companies.

Americans must overcome the weakness of being culturally illiterate. American firms lack an understanding of Far Eastern cultures, including how Asians think and behave. This is only one example out of a long list of problems that U.S. firms face. If American firms are to survive in the global market, then the attitudes of American managers must be restructured and reprogrammed to handle diverse cultures.

The Matrix Structure

The matrix structure in a domestic company is a relationship between function and project, or projects when the employee has a dual responsibility. The matrix structure is often suggested for firms operating under a complex environment. The design of multinational corporations is found to resemble some of the characteristics of the matrix structure. The majority of the focus or dual focus and information is found in the informal structure of the organization.[2] Liaison structures and other mechanisms are typically employed in these organizations. These mechanisms can be identified as follows:

1. Hiring managers with a strategic perspective

2. Developing informal channels of communication

3. Using committees and task forces staffed with people from different areas

4. Improved articulation of corporate objectives

5. A reward system that enforces the desired adaptation behaviors

6. Role models among corporate executives who emphasize cooperation

These mechanisms are examples of how an emphasis on responsiveness and information processing can be achieved in the informal structure of an organization. Successful firms in a highly complex environment optimize their performance by consciously and purposely using both the formal and informal structures, which are characterized by the following:

1. A hierarchical structure based on legitimate power

2. Subunits are independent in some dimensions but are linked to the central organization

3. Actions among the various units of the organization are coordinated through adaptation

The International Work Group

An international work group is an informal group that sets its own goals based on the cultural values or beliefs of its members. The group is familiar with and has studied the values of the host country culture in the context of production-oriented tasks. This because it is a unit of organization for any but the simplest of tasks.

These groups form naturally when people work together, and there is no way to prevent them short of prohibiting the same people from working together on a day-to-day basis in the same place at the same time. Therefore, managers have little choice but to accept these groups and manage them to work to their benefit.

These group tasks of management have three main functions: (1) to influence the behavior of the group so as to be consistent with the goals of the organization, (2) to influence the formation and composition of groups, and (3) to coordinate interaction and interdependencies in the group. The best way to control group membership is through a screening process for all new members of the organization. It is, therefore, important to find people who will commit to the goals and mission and be part of organizational team.

CULTURE INTERVENTION AND INTEGRATION

Most successful organizations have a clear statement of their mission and purpose. This statement must be thoroughly understood throughout the organization, and it must be credible. It makes changing the culture of an organization a less difficult task. Direct doctrine is frequently used to disseminate the message of an organization's purpose and mission. If managers stress this doctrine, a company will be full of believers and ringleaders who can help form the culture of the organization. The target of integration is the members. Therefore, it is important for a global company to have a clear statement of its mission and goals, so that the employees will be on the same track as the company. New members who fail to socialize and acculturate tend to be rejected by group members. Therefore, it is important to screen new members in an effort to ensure that their values and beliefs will be compatible with those that exist in the group.

MOTIVATION

Individuals may be thought of as wanting to maximize their own personal value in terms of fulfilling their personal needs. Secondary motivation comes from the desire to maximize the value of a group. Managers can influence members of a group, and thus the group itself, by establishing reward systems for both individuals and groups that are consistent with the goals of the firm.

Motivation can essentially mean the difference between success and failure of an organization's activities. If the work force is content in their work, eager to please, and motivated by incentives, it is highly likely that productivity will be high and staff turnover low. When productivity is high, economies of scale will follow, resulting in reduced costs, which will be reduced further by the low turnover rate. Less money will have to be spent recruiting, selecting, and training new staff.

Finding one set of incentives or one motivational method for an international company is almost impossible. Each individual culture would have to be examined to find any common features, which simply may not exist. This can be illustrated by comparing the United States and South America. In the United States, money is the preeminent incentive, whereas in South America, respect and social acceptance rank high as incentives.

Motivation can also be affected by the structure that an organization uses in a host country. For example, the Japanese are used to a very structured organization, where decisions are centralized at the top and orders are passed through the ranks. Americans, however, use a web structure which is much less formal. Although a central figure still makes major decisions, other decisions are decentralized and made by department heads. There is also much more interaction between employees at all levels.

If an American company were to implement this strategy in Japan, Japanese employees would probably feel disorientated and insecure, because they are used to a different structure. To avoid this, a company should research the host country's culture and be willing to adapt in order to reap the full benefits. This could be facilitated by educating people about cultural differences so that they are aware of how culturally diverse the world really is. Unfortunately, the majority of Americans have never ventured out of the United States.

GLOBAL STRATEGY

This section deals with establishing appropriate interdependencies, creating opportunities for group formation, human networks, and organizational power and politics. A new reality is confronting the American business: global competition and global competitors. Global expansion enables a company to add value by transferring core skills overseas, using global volume to cover product development costs, realizing economies of scale from global volume, and configuring value-creation functions in locations where value-added is maximized. Companies pursuing a global strategy can gain cost economies by integrating manufacturing, marketing, and competitive strategies across national boundaries, but they must give up a certain degree of responsiveness to national conditions. A purely global strategy is appropriate when the pressures for global integration are high and the pressures for local responsiveness are low, as is the case in the electronic components industry.

Establishing appropriate interdependencies is important because they play a large role in determining the shape of the informal organization.

CASE STUDY
McDonald's International Division

In 1969, McDonald's Corporation, one of the largest fast-food restaurant chains in America, formed its international division to meet the needs of its world customers. McDonald's is restructuring its international division in order to gain more market share. The company accomplished this expansion by restructuring its operations. Expansion outside the United States was accomplished by (1) wholly owned subsidiaries, (2) granting franchises to individuals, and (3) affiliate companies in which McDonald's generally holds 50% or less equity and the remaining equity is owned by a resident national.

The international division accounts for nearly 50% of all new restaurants. McDonald's restaurants can be found in the former Soviet Union, Italy, South Korea, Israel, the Gulf states and former Yugoslavia. The company saw the need to restructure and enter the global market. This restructuring process has helped McDonald's grab the largest market share of any global fast-food restaurant.

Source: John B. Clark, *Marketing Today* (Englewood Cliffs, N.J.: Prentice-Hall), 1990.

They are also a major contributor in motivating members of the organization. If these interdependencies are mismanaged, friction will result. Reciprocal interdependence refers to establishing relationships between both individuals and groups in which goal accomplishment for one is dependent on goal accomplishment of the other.

Creating Opportunities for Group Formation

The informal organization has a greater ability to detect and respond to change than the formal organization. The informal organization usually takes the action of forming an ad hoc committee, which is a group formed from affected parties for the purpose of dealing with a problem. Companies offer seminars, training programs, and purely social activities that provide members with an opportunity to become acquainted with each other. These committees can be formed any time a member becomes aware of a need and meets someone who can help fulfill it.

An informal work group is an example of a human network, which is a system of individuals connected by some common interest. These networks offer the opportunity to expand influence and information across a larger area. They also help to form communication channels with the formal organization.

Power Politics

Power is the ability to influence others. Politics is the use of power toward some goal. According to French and Raven,[6] there are five sources of power: reward power, coercive power, legitimate power, referent power (based on respect), and expert power. The first three can be bestowed by a group. Balancing power in a group usually serves to increase the power of the group and discourages such dysfunctional behavior such as domination and groupthink.

Enhancing the ability of an organization through the development of its informal structure can add to the ability of the organization to process information and respond to the rapidly changing demands of the international business environment. It can also add to the ability of the informal organization to engage in dysfunctional behavior if the goals of its members are not consistent with the goals of the formal organization.

CONCLUSION

Peter Drucker predicts that the organization of the future will be "…knowledge-based, an organization composed largely of specialists who direct and discipline their own performance through organized feedback from colleagues, customers and headquarters."[7] Such an organization is what Drucker calls information-based, and much of the work will be done by specialists in task-focused teams.

These organizations of the future are evolving through a painful trial-and-error process. Strategy–structure research indicates that numerous firms have failed by clinging to the old ways, looking to their formal structures to provide the necessary organizational capacity to compete in a complex global business environment. This same research is beginning to provide hints of the practices that organizations are finding successful in this environment. These practices emphasize the information processing capability necessary for the knowledge transfer that permits optimization of responsiveness and efficiency. They also look to self-direction and self-control by task-oriented individuals and teams.

It is in the context of informal work groups that we can best understand the motivation and behavior of both individuals and teams. Behavior is shaped by the norms of a group which, in turn, are shaped by the values and beliefs of its members. It is obvious that if the behavior of these informal work groups is to be consistent with the strategies and goals of a firm, the values and beliefs of its members must also reflect that congruity.

Managers can directly control the shape of the formal organization and can do many things to influence both the shape of the informal organization and its culture. A few of these things have been outlined here, and the subject is abundantly covered in the literature on motivation and group behavior. The difficult task for managers is to forfeit direct control of parts of the organization in order to achieve enhanced organizational capability. Through the use of authority, managers can substitute for direct control the indirect control that can be derived only from managing the culture.

REFERENCES

1. J.M. Stopford and L.T. Wells, Jr., *Managing the Multinational Enterprise* (New York: Basic Books), 1972.
2. W.G. Egelhoff, "Strategy and Structure in Multinational Corporations: A Revision of the Stopford and Wells Model," *Strategic Management Journal,* 9:1–14, 1988.
3. Christopher A. Bartlett and Ghoshal Sumantra, "Managing Across Borders: New Organizational Response," *Sloan Management Review,* pp. 43–53, Fall 1987.
4. Ron M Sardessai and D.J. Melton, "Strategy and Structure in Multinational Business," Proceedings, Southwest Division of the Institute of Decision Sciences, New Orleans, March 1989.
5. Fred R. David, *Strategic Management* (New York: Macmillan), 1991.
6. R.P. French and Bertram Raven, "The Bases of Social Power," in *Studies in Social Power,* D. Cartwright (Ed.) (Ann Arbor: University of Michigan Press), 1959, pp. 150–167.
7. Peter F. Drucker, "The Coming of the New Organization," *Harvard Business Review,* pp. 45–53, January–February 1988.

BIBLIOGRAPHY

Bartlett, Christopher A., "MNCs: Get Off the Reorganization Merry-Go-Round," *Harvard Business Review,* pp. 47–56, Spring 1983.

Bartlett, Christopher A. and Ghoshal Sumantra, "Managing Across Borders: New Strategic Requirements," *Sloan Management Review,* pp. 7–17, Summer 1987.

Branch, Shelly, "A Good Plan Is Key to Business Success," *Black Enterprise,* November 1991.

Chandler, A.D., *Strategy and Structure: Chapters in the History of Industrial Enterprise* (New York: American Elsevier), 1970.

Chandler, Alfred D. Jr., "Corporate Strategy and Structure: Some Current Considerations," *Society,* March/April 1991.

Clark, John B., *Marketing Today* (Englewood Cliffs, N.J.: Prentice-Hall), 1990.

Cohen, Warren, "Fun Boom," *U.S. News & World Report,* p. 14, November 22, 1993.

Daniels, John D., Robert A. Pitts, and Marietta J. Tretter, "Organizing for Dual Strategies of Product Diversity and International Expansion," *Strategic Management Journal,* 6:223–237, 1985.

Galagan, Patricia A., "Beyond Hierarchy: The Search for High Performance," *Training and Development,* August 1992.

Hampton, David R., Charles E. Summer, and Ross A. Weber, *Organizational Behavior and the Practice of Management* (Glenview, Ill.: Scott, Foresman), 1987.

Kefalas, A.G., *Global Business Strategy* (Cincinnati, Ohio: South-Western), 1990.

Mechanic, David, "Sources of Power of Lower Participants in Complex Organizations," *Administrative Science Quarterly,* December 1962.

Schilit, Warren K. and Edwin A. Locke, "A Study of Upward Influence in Organizations," *Administrative Science Quarterly,* June 1982.

Tallman, Stephen, "A Strategic Management Perspective on Host Country Structure of Multinational Enterprises," *Journal of Management,* September 1992.

Thompson, J.D., *Organizations in Action* (New York: McGraw-Hill), 1967.

BIBLIOGRAPHY

JOURNALS

Adler, N.J. and M. Jelinek, "Is 'Organization Culture' Culture Bound?" *Human Resource Management,* 25:73–90, January 1986.

Adler, N.J., R. Doktor, and G.S. Reading, "From the Atlantic to the Pacific Century: Cross Cultural Management Reviewed," *Journal of Management,* 12:295–318, February 1986.

Bolling, L.R., "Religion and Politics in the Middle East Conflict," *Middle East Journal,* 45:125–130, Winter 1991.

Caudron, Dhari, "Training Ensures Success Overseas," *Personnel Journal,* 70:30, December 1991.

Cava A., "Evaluating the Professional: New Perils for Management," *Business & Economic Review,* 35:27–29, April 1989.

Cole, W.E. and J.W. Mogab, "The Transfer of Soft Technologies to Less-Developed Countries: Some Implications for the Technology/Ceremony Dichotomy," *Journal of Economic Issues,* 21:309–319, January 1987.

"Companies in Europe Seeking Executives Who Can Cross Borders in a Single Bound," *Wall Stret Journal,* January 25, 1991.

Coon, C.S., "Pique Performance," *The Economist,* 32:144–145, 1991.

Dalton, D.R. and I.F. Kesner, "Composition and CEO Quality in Boards of Directors: An International Perspective," *Journal of International Business Studies,* pp. 15–32, Fall 1987.

Dickey, C., "Why We Can't Seem to Understand the Arabs," *Newsweek,* pp. 26–27, January 7, 1991.

Dumane, Brian, "How to Manage in a Recession," *Fortune,* 122:58–60, November 5, 1990.

Eaton, Leslie, "Strategic Management: In Trouble with the SEC," *Barron's,* p. 68, December 19, 1988.

Edström, A. and J.R. Galbraith, "Transfer of Managers as a Coordination and Control Strategy in Multinational Organizations," *Administrative Science Quarterly,* pp. 248–263, 1977.

Friberg, Eric G., "1991: Moves Europeans Are Making," *Harvard Business Review,* pp. 85–89, May–June 1989.

Godiwalla, Yezdi H., "Multinational Planning—A Global Approach," *Long Range Planning,* 19:110–116, April 1986.

"Going Global: The Chief Executives in Year 2000 Will Be Experienced Abroad," *Wall Street Journal,* February 27, 1989.

Harris, James E., "Moving Managers Internationally: The Care and Feeding of Expatriates," *Human Resources Planning,* 12:49–53, January 1989.

Hays, R.D., "Expatriate Selection: Insuring Success and Avoiding Failure," *Journal of International Business Studies,* 5:25–37, 1974.

Heenan, David A., "A Different Outlook For Multinational Companies," *The Journal of Business Strategy,* 9:51–54, July/August 1988.

Hoffman, Richard C., "The General Management of Foreign Subsidiaries in the USA: An Exploratory Study," *Management International Review,* 28:41–55, 1988.

Howard, Cecil G., "How Best to Integrate Expatriate Managers in the Domestic Organization," *Personnel Administrator,* pp. 27–33, July 1982.

Howard, Cecil G., "Expatriate Managers," *Proceedings of the International Academy of Management and Marketing,* 1991.

Johnson, H.G., "One Vacant Chair," *The Economist,* 320:30–32, 1991.

Johnson, Michael, "Change or Die," *International Management* (Europe edition), 43:46–48, April 1988.

Kim, W.C., P. Hwang, and W.P. Burgers, "Global Diversification Strategy and Corporate Profit Performance," *Strategic Management Journal,* 10:45–47, 1989.

Kumar, Kamelesh, "American Multinational Enterprises in Islamic Countries," *Proceedings of the International Academy of Management and Marketing,* 1990.

Labich, K., "Making Over Middle Managers," *Fortune,* pp. 58–64, May 8, 1989.

Leap, T. and T.A. Oliva, "General Systems Precursor Theory as a Supplement to Wren's Framework for Studying Management History: The Case of Human Resource/Personnel Management," *Human Relations,* 36:627–640, 1983.

Maruca, Regina Fazio, "The Right Way to Go Global: An Interview with Whirlpool CEO David Whitman," *Harvard Business Review,* pp. 134–145, March–April 1994.

McInnes, J. Morris, "Corporate Management of Productivity—An Empirical Study," *Strategic Management Journal,* 5:351–365, October–December 1984.

McLenahen, John S., "Can You Manage in the New Economy?" *Industry Week,* 242:24–26, April 5, 1993.

Mendenhall, M. and G. Oddou, "The Dimensions of Expatriate Acculturation: A Review," *Academy of Management Review,* 10:39–47, 1985.

Mendenhall, Mark E., Edward Dunbar, and Gary Oddou, "Expatriate Selection, Training, and Career-Pathing: A Review and Critique," *Human Resource Management,* 26:331–345, 1987.

Negandi, A.R. and P.A. Donhowe, "It's Time to Explore New Global Trade Options," *The Journal of Business Strategy,* 9:27–31, January/February 1989.

Nussbaum, Bruce and Judith H. Dobryzynski, "The Battle for Corporate Control: Management Is Being Assailed from All Sides—Who's in Charge Here?" *Business Week,* 102:6, May 18, 1987.

Paul, Karen and Robert Barbato, "The MNC in the LDC: The Economic Development Model vs. the North–South Model," *Academy of Management Review,* 10:8–14, 1985.

Peretz, D.T., "The Middle East," *Pension World,* 10:70–74, 1991.

Pinney, D.L., "Structuring an Expatriate Tax Reimbursement Program," *Personnel Administrator,* 27:19–25, 1982.

Rau, Pradeep A. and John F. Preble, "Standardization of Marketing Strategy by Multinationals," *International Marketing Review,* pp. 18–28, Autumn 1987.

Razi, G.H., "Legitimacy, Religion and Nationalism in the Middle East," *American Political Science Review,* 84:70–85, March 1990.

Ruchsberg, Gilbert, "As Costs of Overseas Assignment Climb, Firms Select Expatiates More Carefully," *Wall Street Journal,* pp. B1, B4, January 9, 1992.

Tung, R.L., "Selection and Training of Personnel for Overseas Assignments," *Columbia Journal of World Business,* 16:68–78, 1981.

Tung, Rosalie L., "Strategic Management of Human Resources in the Multinational Enterprise," *Human Resource Management,* 23:129–143, 1984.

Turnbull, Peter W., "Interaction and International Marketing: An Investment Process," *International Marketing Review,* pp. 7–19, Winter 1987.

Wittenbert-Cox, Avivah, "Delivering Global Leaders," *International Management,* 46:52–55, February 1991.

Wolniansky, Natalia, "International Training for Global Leadership," *Management Review,* 75:27–28, May 5, 1990.

Wood, Van R. and Jerry R. Goolsby, "Foreign Market Information Preferences of Established U.S. Exporters," *International Marketing Review,* pp. 43–52, 1987.

Wright, Peter, David Townsend, Jerry Kincaid, and Joe Iverstine, "The Developing World to 1990: Trends and Implications for Multinational Business," *Long Range Planning,* 15:116–125, 1982.

BOOKS

Acuff, F., *International and Domestic Human Resources Functions. Innovations in International Compensation* (New York: Organization Resources Counselors), 1984, pp. 3–5.

Aldag, R.J. and T.M. Stearns, *Management* (Cincinnati, Ohio: South-Western), 1991.

Ali, A. and Mohammed Al-Shakhis, *The Meaning of Work in Saudi Arabia* (Hays, Kans.: Fort Hays State University), 1987.

Alkhafaji, A.F., *Toward a Better Understanding of Islam* (Slippery Rock, Pa.: Slippery Rock University), Spring 1990.

Asheghain, Parviz and Bahman Ebrahimi, *International Business* (New York: Harper & Row), 1990.

Bahr, Lauren S. and Bernard Johnston, *Collier's Encyclopedia* (New York: Maxwell-Macmillan), 1992, pp. 150–177.

Carroll, S.J. and C.E. Schneier, *Performance Appraisal and Review Systems* (Glenview, Ill.: Scott-Foresman), 1982.

Cohen R.B., "The New International Division of Labor and Multinational Corporations," in *The Transformation of Industrial Organization: Management, Labor and Society in the United States,* Frank Hearn (Ed.) (Belmont, Calif.: Wadsworth), 1988.

Copeland, L. and Lewis Griggs, *Going International: How to Make Friends and Deal Effectively in the Global Marketplace* (New York: Random House), 1985.

Davis, S., *Managing and Organizing Multinational Corporations* (New York: Pergamon Press), 1977.

Desatnick, R.L. and M.L. Bennett, *Human Resource Management in the Multinational Company* (New York: Nichols), 1978.

Ellsworth, P.T., *The International Economy* (New York: Harper & Row), 1990.

Helfgott, R.B., *Computerized Manufacturing and Human Resources* (Lexington, Mass.: Lexington), 1988.

Jackri, Ernest, *Background of the Middle East* (Ithaca, N.Y.: Cornell University Press), 1952, pp. 145–157.

Kefalas, A.G., *Global Business Strategy* (Cincinnati: South-Western), 1990.

Latham, G.P. and K.N. Wexley, *Increasing Productivity Through Performance Appraisal* (Reading, Mass.: Addison-Wesley), 1981.

Murray, F. and Ann Murray, "SMR Forum: Global Managers for Global Businesses," in *Selected Readings in Business,* Mrya Schulman (Ed.) (Ann Arbor: The University of Michigan Press), 1986, pp. 247–252.

Nolte, Richard H., *The Modern Middle East* (New York: Atherton), 1963.

Peters, T., *Thriving on Chaos* (New York: Alfred A. Knopf), 1988.

Peters, T. and R.H. Waterman, *In Search of Excellence* (New York: Harper & Row), 1982.

Robinson, R., *Internationalization of Business: An Introduction* (Chicago: Dryden), 1984.

Robock, Stefan and Kenneth Simmonds, *International Business and Multinational Enterprises* (Homewood, Ill.: Irwin), 1983.

Rostyn, J.D., *The Cambridge Encyclopedia of the Middle East and North Africa* (Tennessee: Thomas Nelson), 1990.

Scarpello, V. and James Ledvinka, *Personnel/Human Resource Management: Environments and Functions* (Boston: Kent), 1987.

Schonberger, R.J., *Japanese Manufacturing Techniques: Nine Hidden Lessons in Simplicity* (New York: Free Press), 1982.

Sonbol, Amira El-Azghany, "Egypt," in *The Politics of Islamic Revivalism*, Shireen T. Hunter (Ed.), 1988.

Sonfield, M.C., *Exporting from the U.S.* (California: Prima), 1989.

Stevens, Georgiana G., *The United States and the Middle East* (Englewood Cliffs, N.J.: Prentice-Hall), 1964, pp. 49–69.

Stoddard, Philip H., *Change and the Muslim World* (Syracuse, N.Y.: Syracuse University Press), 1988.

Striner, H., *Regaining the Lead* (New York: Praeger), 1984.

Thompson, Arthur A. and A.J. Strickland, *Strategic Management: Concepts and Cases* (Homewood, Ill.: Irwin), 1990.

Tomasko, R.M., *Downsizing: Reshaping the Corporation for the Future* (New York: American Management Association), 1987.

Torbiorn, J., *Living Abroad* (New York: John Wiley), 1982.

World Executive Compensation and Human Resources Planning (New York: Business International Corporation), 1982.

GLOSSARY

Aesthetics: Sense of beauty and good taste in a particular culture.

Affiliated company: A subsidiary to a parent company. Usually the parent company owns less than 100% of the subsidiary.

Appropriate technology: The technology that best suits the country in which it is being utilized.

Attitude: Evaluative statement concerning objects, people, events, or other issues.

Authoritarianism: An individual's belief regarding the status and power hierarchy in organizations.

Authority: The right of a supervisor to issue commands and to expect those working under him or her to follow them through.

Brain drain: When the intellect of one country emigrates to other countries.

Capitalism: National resources are allocated by private holders.

Centralization: A procedure in which critical decisions are made by the few in upper-level management.

Code of ethics: A list of ethical values and rules by which employees of a company are expected to abide.

Codetermination: A West European system in which the board of directors includes workers as well as shareholders in making important decisions.

Collective bargaining: A process utilized to negotiate labor contracts. It is conducted between an employer and union represen-tatives and addresses such issues as wages, hours, administration of labor contracts, and employment conditions.

Communism: National resources are allocated by the government. Also refers to the structure of classless society conceived by Marx. Lenin, Stalin, and others developed it differently.

Comparative advantage: When a country is efficient in producing particular goods or services and exports them, meanwhile importing those in which it does not have an absolute advantage.

Competitive analysis: A procedure which differentiates between companies by rating their goals, strengths, weaknesses, and products.

Culture: The values, attitudes, behaviors, interests, customs, routines, language, religion, and artifacts that are characteristic of a certain population; evolves as a result of previous experiences.

Decentralization: When the decision-making power is transferred from upper-level management to lower-level personnel.

Developed countries (DCs): Countries that have become industrialized.

Developing countries: The countries of the world that have smaller incomes and are less industrialized than developed countries.

Direct exporting: A form of transferring a product or service between a company and a foreign country.

Effectiveness: The ability of a company to achieve its objectives and goals as set forth.

Efficiency: An attempt to maximize output from the same input in order to minimize resource costs.

Entrepreneurship: Those who are willing to take risk in starting new businesses, pursuing opportunities, and being innovative.

Environment: Internal and external forces which have an effect on a company's operation and success.

Environmental complexity: The number of elements in a company's surroundings and how much is known about each.

Environmental scanning: The process of reviewing large amounts of information from around the world and becoming educated about trends that may affect the corporation.

Environmental uncertainty: The amount of possible change in the surroundings of an organization.

Ethics: The values and rules that determine what is acceptable and unacceptable performance.

Ethnocentric MNC: A MNC that emphasizes nationalism and usually selects home office people to hold key international management positions.

Ethnocentrism: A belief that one's own ethnic group is superior to others.

European Community (EC): About 320 million people who live in 12 countries: Belgium, Denmark, France, Greece, Ireland, Italy, Luxembourg, the Netherlands, Portugal, Spain, the United Kingdom, and West Germany.

Expatriate: An employee of a MNC who is sent by the company to live and work away from his or her home country but is still a citizen of the home country.

Export incentives: Subsidies, financial aid, and tax rebates paid to companies or individuals by governments to encourage them to export.

Export license: An authorization from a government permitting the exporter to export designated goods to certain destinations.

Extended family: A person's relatives other than the nuclear family consisting of mother, father, brothers, and sisters.

Factor endowment: Whether or not a country is equipped with the elements of production, capital, labor, and natural resources.

Flexible manufacturing system: A system using computer technology that enables a product to be mass produced.

Foreign Corrupt Practices Act (FCPA): A U.S. law passed in 1977 that made influencing foreign officials through payment illegal.

Geocentric MNC: A MNC that utilizes employees from various countries, nationalities, or races in the decision-making process.

Globalization: Marketing of a standardized product or service to many different countries throughout the world.

Global strategies: Methods used in gaining a competitive advantage over other companies in foreign countries.

Gross domestic product (GDP): The estimated value of a country's output attributable to factors of production located in the country's territory.

Gross national product (GNP): The estimated market value of all the final goods and services produced by a national economy over a particular period of time, usually a year.

Home country: The country in which the headquarters of a MNC is located.

Home country national: Expatriate manager who is a citizen of the country in which a MNC is based.

Host country national: Native manager employed by a MNC.

Implementation: Following through with decisions and strategies that have been designed and agreed upon by management.

Indirect exporting: When a company or individual decides to sell certain goods and services through various types of home-based exporters.

Individualism: The tendency of members of a culture to only look after themselves and their immediate family.

Industrial democracy: The right that is given to employees to help make important executive decisions.

Information: Important data intended to help managers in their decision-making process.

Infrastructure: The basic elements of an economy such as modes of transportation, communication, water and energy supply, etc.

Innovation: The process of creating new or improving current ideas, products, services, techniques, or operations.

Integrative technique: Procedure that assists an overseas operation in becoming a component of the host country's infrastructure.

International environment: Interaction between domestic and foreign environmental forces.

International joint venture (IJV): Companies agree to have access to each other's market. Usually these companies are located in different countries.

International law: General principles that are accepted and respected by all countries in their relations with each other.

International product life cycle: A theory that helps explain both trade flow and foreign direct investment on the basis of a product's position in one of four stages: (1) exports of an industrialized nation, (2) beginning of foreign production, (3) foreign competition in export markets, and (4) import competition in the country where the product was introduced originally.

Islam: A religion of more than a billion people around the world. Moslems believe in the oneness of God. They believe that the future is ordained by Allah (God). The *Qur'an,* a collection of Allah's revelations to the Prophet Mohammed, the founder of Islam, is accepted as God's eternal word.

Job analysis: An evaluation that describes all of the jobs in an organization and what skills are necessary for each.

Job context factors: Elements of employment that are controlled by the corporation, such as hours, earnings, benefits, promotions, etc., which are primarily used for employee motivation.

Job description: A written statement characterizing the nature of a particular position, how it is done, and why it is done.

Job design: All of the duties required for a job that relate it to others in the company.

Job satisfaction: An employee's general attitude toward his or her fulfillment in doing the job.

Job specification: A written statement describing the minimum acceptable qualifications that an incumbent must possess to perform a given job successfully.

Joint venture: A situation in which two or more organizations own, have access to, or manage a business in a foreign land.

Just-in-time: A system that helps to minimize inventory cost and eliminates delay.

Inventory items are delivered when they are needed, eliminating the need for storage.

Key factor for success: Element necessary in order for a business to be competent in the marketplace.

Labor–management relations: The standard interactions between the union members and management representatives of an organization.

Labor union: The group of representatives chosen by the employees of an organization to stand up for the rights and interests of the workers.

License: A consensus between two parties that allows one to use an industrial property right in exchange for compensation.

Licensing: The act of granting a license.

Management by objectives (MBO): A participative system in which employees are included with the various levels of management in designing and implementing company strategies. Progress toward targets is periodically reviewed, corrective measures are taken if necessary, and rewards are given on the basis of the progress of participants.

Management information system (MIS): A computerized system that provides quick access to information about all the company's units necessary for corporate decision making.

Maquiladora industry: An arrangement between the United States and Mexico to provide U.S manufacturers with the opportunity to ship raw materials to their Mexican-based factories, construct products, and ship them back out of Mexico while only being taxed on the value added.

Masculinity: A measure of a culture's emphasis on being aggressive and obtaining money and material items.

Mission: What sets a company apart from other companies in the market. It is a company's reason for being, prepared in a written statement that describes the business, its customers, and its markets.

Motivation: When an individual is willing to put forth extra effort to meet performance standards set by the organization, along with satisfying one's inner needs.

Multinational corporation (MNC): An organization originated in one country and operating in another. The more countries it operates in, the more multinational it is.

National culture: A unique behavior pattern of an individual or a group in a particular country.

National economic plans: A government strategy for achieving economic goals of the nation in a particular period of time, e.g., five years.

Need: Individual necessities that make certain outcomes appear more attractive to certain organizations.

Need for achievement: The desire to be successful and achieve goals set forth.

Need for power The desire to have control over others.

Network: A connection of computers that enables people at different terminals to exchange information and access common pools of data.

Parent company: The original company that owns or controls subsidiaries in a different market, i.e., various geographical locations.

Participative leadership: The art of convincing subordinates to work together toward accomplishing corporate objectives.

Political risk: The possible endangerment that a MNC might face when conducting business overseas due to political instability in the host country.

Polycentric: A management philosophy in which important decisions are made based on the host country's cultural characteristics.

Portfolio investment: The diversification of ownership in order to reduce financial risk.

Power distance: The extent to which members of a larger organization understand and accept the inequality of power distribution.

Privatization: Transfer of ownership and power of a company from the government or publicly held companies to a private holder.

Protestant work ethic: The duty of Christians to glorify God by hard work and the practice of thrift.

Quality control circle (QCC): Groups of employees and supervisors who get together periodically to discuss ways of improving quality of products and services.

Regiocentric: A management philosophy in which important decisions are made with the requirements of the subsidiaries in mind.

Repatriation: The return of an expatriate or a company's assets to the home country.

Ringi: The Japanese way of making executive decisions through compromise.

Self-actualization needs: The inner drive that prompts people to strive to be all that they can possibly be according to Maslow's hierarchy of needs.

Self-managing teams: A group of employees who manage themselves; some members take responsibility for learning how to perform the function of each position so that they may rotate jobs periodically.

Sensitivity training: A means of changing the behavior of others by providing unstructured group interaction.

Sexual harassment: Uninvited and unaccepted behavior from another party that might be physical or verbal and considered sexual in nature.

Skilled labor: Employees qualified to perform task-specific jobs.

Socialism: A system in which the national resources are jointly allocated between the government and private holders.

Social issues management: Identifying, measuring, and evaluating the effect corporations have on society.

Social obligation: The responsibility of an organization to meet economic and legal guidelines or doing the bare minimum required by law.

Social responsibility: Business activities that have a positive effect on the society and go beyond what is required by law.

Social responsiveness: An organization's ability to predict social tensions and take proactive measures to solve the problem.

Span of control: The number of employees a manager can competently and efficiently manage at one time.

Stakeholders: Those groups who have a direct interest in the organization. Without their interest, the company might have difficulty existing. Examples of groups are stockholders, employees, managers, major suppliers, major creditors, and major consumers.

Stereotyping: The act of holding preconceived ideas and attitudes about someone based on a group that he or she may be a member of.

Strategic alliance: Cooperation between two or more companies to gain an advantage in the market; usually an exchange of information.

Strategic business unit (SBU): A division or separate entity of a large company with a clearly defined business strategy that determines how this unit will compete with another unit in the same market.

Strategic management process: The continual evaluation of a business and its environment. It involves formulating a strategy, implementing the strategy, and evaluation and control.

Strategic plans: How a particular company tries to achieve its future objectives, given the company's environment.

Strategy implementation: The steps a company follows to put its strategic plan into practice; how the company chooses to match its tasks, equipment, and human resources.

Strong culture: An organization whose values are strictly followed and shared by a large majority.

Structural changes: A strategic management approach that deals with redesigning the organization of a company as a whole. It may also involve relocation of its resources and employees.

Subsidiary: A company that is bought, controlled, affiliated with, or a branch of another company.

Subsidiary board of directors: A group of people in a company who manage the affairs of an overseas operation.

Team building: Activities designed to get members of work crews to cooperate with each other and learn more about each other's jobs and responsibilities.

Technological forecasting: The prediction of changes in methods or equipment and their availability in the market.

Technology: The methods or the tools an organization utilizes in converting inputs into outputs.

Third country national: A manager working in a company's foreign division who is not a citizen of that country or of the country the where the corporation's headquarters is located.

Third World: Countries with relatively low literacy rates and low GNP. This includes all countries other than the Eastern bloc countries ruled by the former Soviet Union and the countries of the West, primarily the OECD countries.

Total quality control system: A process that utilizes all areas of a business in order to improve a service or product.

Total quality management (TQM): A management technique that provides the highest quality goods and services possible to ensure customer satisfaction.

Traditional economy: An area that has not become industrialized and whose people use more primitive forms of survival.

Uncertainty avoidance: The level of tolerance toward risk and unconventional behavior by members of a particular culture.

Uncontrollable environmental forces: Outside factors that influence corporate strategy and over which management has no direct control.

Unspoken language: Nonverbal communication such as body language.

Utilitarian view of ethics: Making a decision based on the consequences of the act.

INDEX